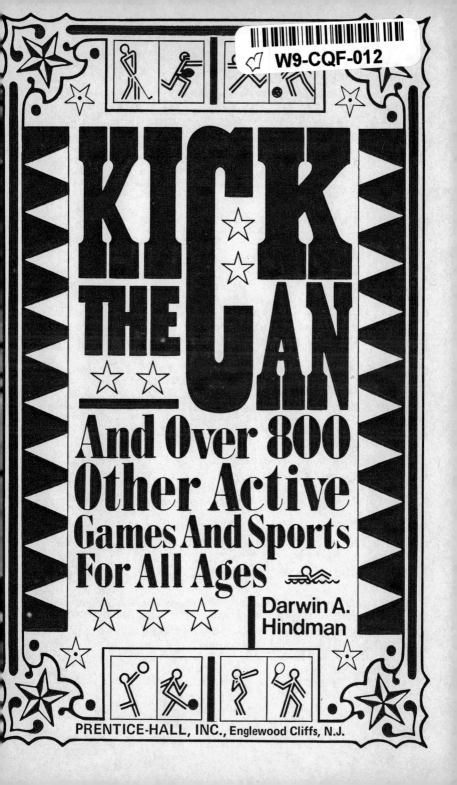

KICK THE CAN

And Over 800 Other Active Games And Sports For All Ages

Darwin A. Hindman

PRENTICE-HALL, INC., Englewood Cliffs, N.J.

To "The Judge": Francis Samuel Philbrick

*Kick-the-Can and Over 800 Other Active
Games and Sports for All Ages* by Darwin A. Hindman, Ph.D.
Published in original form under the titles
*The Complete Book of Games and Stunts, Hand-
book of Indoor Games and Stunts* and *Handbook
of Active Games,* copyright © 1956, 1955 and
1951, respectively, by Prentice-Hall, Inc.
Printed in the United States of America
Prentice-Hall International, Inc., London
Prentice-Hall of Australia, Pty. Ltd., Sydney
Prentice-Hall of Canada, Ltd., Toronto
Prentice-Hall of India Private Ltd., New Delhi
Prentice-Hall of Japan, Inc., Tokyo
Prentice-Hall of Southeast Asia Pte. Ltd., Singapore
Whitehall Books Limited, Wellington, New Zealand
10 9 8 7 6 5 4

Library of Congress Cataloging in Publication Data

Hindman, Darwin Alexander.
   Kick the can, and over 800 other active games and
sports for all ages.

   Originally published under title: Handbook of active games.

   SUMMARY: Directions for play activities, grouped under
such headings as tag games, dodgeball games, combat games,
target games, bombardment games, and goal games.

   1. Games.   [1. Games.   2. Sports]   I. Title.
[GV1201.H63 1978]   790   77-14156
ISBN 0-13-515163-5 pbk.

May '80

TABLE OF CONTENTS

		PAGE
	The Definition and Classification of Active Games	1
I-A	Continuous Tag Games	8
I-B	Noncontinuous Tag Games	38
II	Running Games With No Tagging	89
III	Dodgeball Games	112
IV	Combat Games	137
V	Stunt and Alertness Games	157
VI	Target Games	184
VII	Propel-and-Catch Games	231
VIII	Bandy Games	249
IX	Baseball Games	297
X	Bombardment Games	338
XI	Goal Games	350
	Index	416

PREFACE

THIS BOOK IS INTENDED FOR PLAYERS OF GAMES AND FOR THEIR leaders, especially active and prospective teachers of physical education. It describes and explains a large number of play activities—classed as active games.

The games are arranged in a logical classification and are treated so as to show their interrelationships and to indicate the ideas and principles upon which they are based. It is hoped that this plan will aid greatly in understanding the games and in remembering them.

It is not unusual for several different names to be used for a single game, and conversely for a single name to be used for several different games. For example, the popular game called *Circle Touchball* has been found in responsible sources under ten different names, and the word *kickball* has been found as the name of three different games. In this book all such names are retained and are included, with appropriate cross-references, in both text and index.

DARWIN A. HINDMAN

THE DEFINITION AND CLASSIFICATION OF ACTIVE GAMES

ARE THE OLYMPIC GAMES REALLY GAMES? IS A RELAY RACE A GAME? Just what is a game? What is an *active* game? These are questions to which there are no official or generally accepted answers but which every person may, with considerable latitude, answer to suit himself. Accordingly, the first part of this introductory chapter will consist of a definition of the term *active games,* as it is to be understood in the following pages. The remainder of the chapter will discuss the classification, names, and descriptions of the games.

· Definition of Active Games

Games are one kind of play activities. It will suffice here to say that play activities are those that are carried on for the pleasure or satisfaction of practicing them—because they seem to the participants to be inherently worthwhile—as contrasted with those that are carried on in the hope of an extrinsic reward in the way of money, health, prestige, or the like. It is obvious that whether a given activity can be called *play* depends not on the nature of the activity but only on the spirit in which it is practiced, and that almost any conceivable activity can, under certain circumstances, be play. It seems proper, nevertheless, to speak of certain activities as play, meaning that they were developed or devised for use as play, that they are in fact usually practiced as play, or that they are recommended for use as play.

It is possible, and sometimes useful, to distinguish between play which, like reading or card playing, involves little activity, and that which, like tennis or swimming, requires comparatively strenuous activity. The former may be called *quiet play* and the latter, *active play.* It is unfortunate that there is no satisfactory name for active play. If the word *gymnastics* could be freed from the connotations that it has acquired and used in its original sense, it would probably be satisfactory; the term *athletics* might be interpreted so as to serve; and the term *sport* is used to some extent as applying to all forms of active play. However, none of these terms is generally accepted. Active play is, in general, the subject matter of physical education.

Consideration must be given to the distinction between active games and other forms of active play. To facilitate this distinction, brief definitions will first be given of certain forms of active play, specifically *stunts, contests* and *combats.*

A *stunt* is an activity in which the performance is not measured in degree, but which is entirely a matter of success or failure. In executing a stunt, each performer is free to do his best without hindrance or opposition from an opponent. A boy may try the common stunt known as the handspring, and he either succeeds or fails, without any question of time or distance. Of course there is often a qualitative standard of some sort, and this standard may be highly subjective. For example, there may be some doubt that the boy has actually accomplished a handspring.

In a *contest,* each participant works without opposition or hindrance, as he does in a stunt, but his performance is always measured either directly or by comparison with that of others. He not only does something, but he does it as far, or as fast, or as many times, as he can. The participants in a contest usually act as individual or independent men, but often as members of groups or teams. When each of the groups performs as a unit the result is a team contest, usually a team race. An example is the three-legged race. When the members of a group perform in turn, the contest is a relay. Relays and team contests are in every sense genuine contests.

A *combat* is a fight or struggle, in which each participant tries to secure direct personal mastery or control over an opponent. In wrestling, a typical combat, each wrestler tries to secure control over his opponent in order to pin his shoulders to the mat. It has already been said that in a stunt or a contest each participant is free to do his best without hindrance or opposition; obviously the exact opposite is true of a combat.

Active games are not so sharply defined as stunts, contests, and combats, but they may have much in common with one or more of these. The chief characteristic of a game is its relative complexity, and this complexity may be in the variety of activity, in the organi zation, or even in the scoring system. Obviously here is a situation that allows room for personal opinion and choice. Golf, for example, seems to satisfy all the requirements for a contest, and possibly should be so classed. But Golf is here classed as a game because its variety and complexity seem to set it apart from contests. A contest is a valid comparison of performances in a single and simple activity. When a contest develops the variety of activities and situations found in Golf, and when the scoring ceases to be a comparison of simple and direct measurements, the contest has become a game. Combats, likewise, easily develop into games. If each of two men hops on one foot and tries to overbalance the other, the two men are engaged in a simple combat. But if ten men participate and each tries to be the last to lose his balance, the activity has lost much of its simplicity and directness, and has become a game. Again, when boys engage in a variety of stunts in the form of Follow-the-Leader, the whole process has become a game. Bowling is probably one of the best examples of a case on the border line between contests and games. If the score were determined simply by counting the number of pins upset, Bowling would unquestionably be a contest. But Bowling has a complicated and fascinating scoring system that prevents a simple and direct comparison of performances. For this reason, Bowling is considered to be a game.

Games, then, are relatively complex and are, in part, defined negatively as not being stunts, contests, or combats. In addition, games always involve competition and are always played according to definite rules, although the rules are often only traditions. Thus, the collection of games that follows does not include Farmer in the Dell or any other singing or dramatic "game," and it does not include any relay races.

The Classification of Games

When the descriptions of several hundred games are collected in a book, they must be arranged in one way or another. An alphabetical arrangement is possible, but it would satisfy few people. The uncertainty and variation in the names of the games alone are probably sufficient grounds for rejecting this method. There is little doubt that the best arrangement is one in which the games are grouped on the basis of common elements, in one of many possible ways. Games have been grouped, for example, according to the number of players, the age and sex of the players, the organization or formation, the place or season for which they are suitable, or the equipment used. These and many other methods have merit and considerable advantage over a random or alphabetical one, but none of them is used in this book. Here the games are classified according to their basic principles or central ideas, or in other words, according to the real objectives of the players. In nearly every case this objective is the method by which a player can score, and must be clearly distinguished from any secondary objective that is of value because of its contribution to the real one. For example, in Basketball there is a great deal of throwing and catching, and at any given instant the objective of two teammates may be to throw and catch the ball. But no amount of successful throwing and catching will win a basketball game, for only throwing the ball into the goal scores a point. Accordingly, the central idea of Basketball, and the basis of its classification, is here taken to be that of throwing a ball into a goal. Field-hockey and Golf could be placed together on the basis of the fact that in each game players hit a ball with clubs. But the reason for hitting the ball with the clubs is different in the two games, and it is this reason that determines the classification of each game. On such a basis the games in this collection have been arranged first in eleven large classes, and the first and largest class—Tag Games—is divided into two subclasses. Each of the eleven classes is broken down into sections, and in most cases the sections are divided into groups.

All classifications are subjective and personal; they do not exist in objective fact, but only in the minds of the classifiers. Many different classifications are possible even when the basis is the same, and a classification is not right or wrong, but only logical and useful, or illogical and not so useful. Accordingly, no unique virtues are claimed for the classification presented here, but it is hoped that it will be found logical and helpful. The reader who uses this book in a serious effort to learn about games is strongly urged to study the principles and ideas upon which the classification is based, and to learn the games by groups, not individually.

Rules for Games

For most games, the only rules are traditions and customs. There is no such thing as *the rules* for Three Deep, or Prisoner's Base, or One Old Cat, and there is no basis for argument as to the correct way to play any of these games. On the other hand, there are, . a small minority of games, including many of the best known ones, sets of rules that have been carefully formulated. These rules are widely distributed in printed form and are accepted to a greater or lesser degree as "official." The word *official* used in this connection is of doubtful validity and probably misleading. No rules are official in the sense that players are obliged to follow them or that those who do not follow them are playing incorrectly. Rules do not have any legal status or any authority, only prestige. The essence of any game is that the players have an advance agreement or understanding about the rules that will govern the game. If a satisfactory set of rules is available, it is only natural that players should adopt them in preference to making up some of their own. For example, a voluntary private organization called the United States Lawn Tennis Association formulates and publishes rules for the game of Tennis. These rules are the product of careful thought and much experience, and to most people seem good and satisfactory. The rules and the association responsible for them have acquired so much prestige that when two people prepare to play Tennis they assume as a matter of course that they will play according to these rules. In fact the players do not know of any other rules, and to them the USLTA rules are simply "the rules of Tennis." In few games is the rules situation so simple as it is in Tennis. In a great many cases there is more than one set of "official" rules, the different sets either applying to different classes of players and teams or in some cases competing for recognition.

Of course the agreement to follow a certain set of rules is not necessarily made for each game separately, but can be made on a wholesale basis. This is especially true of interschool athletics, in which each school is likely to be bound to follow certain rules that are made or chosen by an organization or conference of which the school is a member.

In the case of a game with rules that are accepted as official, these rules are the ones adopted for this book, and if there is more than one such set, all are given. The great majority of games, however, do not have rules that are in any sense official. On the contrary, they show considerable variety and some confusion in the rules under which they are played. In such cases the policy has been to describe each game in the form that, in the opinion of the author, is the best, giving as variations or possibly as different games other forms that seem common or that merit inclusion for some other reason.

Names of Games

The question often arises as to the correct or real name of a game. Is it Soccer, or Soccer Football, or Association Football, or just Football? Is it true that real Tennis, and the only game to which the word can be applied with strict correctness, is the old game now commonly called Court Tennis, and that the modern game must be called Lawn Tennis?

The name of a game is determined in the same way as the name of anything else—by usage—and there is always some personal choice as to which usage one shall follow. Names are not once chosen and forever fixed, but are subject to change with changes in usage, so that a name that is correct today may become obsolete and incorrect tomorrow. A word that starts as a nickname or a slang term may become accepted as respectable and, in fact, as the strictly correct name of a game.

It might be thought that the question of the correct name for a game could be answered by referring to the official rules, but this can hardly be true. In the first place, it is an interesting fact that formal rules of games are likely not to give names. One searches in vain through the rules of the American Bowling Congress for the name of its game. One reason for the common belief that Tennis is properly called Lawn Tennis is that the rules come from the United States Lawn Tennis Association. Actually, this association does not say in its rules that the name of the game is Lawn Tennis, but, in fact, appears to believe that the name is *tennis*. In the second place, rules cannot make names. No matter who says that the name of the game is Lawn Tennis, the name is really *not* Lawn Tennis unless the game is so designated by the people who play it, write about it, and teach it.

The simple fact is that there is no such thing as an official, or real, or strictly correct name for a game; there is only a name that is in conformity with the usage of well-informed people and one that serves the purposes of a name with the greatest efficiency and least confusion. It follows from this that frequently one must recognize more than one name for a single game, the selection depending on the circumstances or on personal taste. For example, the usual

name for the football game played in American colleges is Footba.
and a newspaper man writing about the Army-Navy game certainly
is strictly correct in referring to the game as Football. On the other
hand, there are other games that are also called Football, and in a
situation where confusion might develop it is wise and useful, and
completely correct, to call the same game by a different name,
American Football. Another example is the game, which, in the
United States, is usually called Soccer Football, at least in careful
or formal speech and writing. This is probably the best, hence the
most correct, name for the game, but at the same time it must be
recognized that the game is very often called simply Soccer, and
this word must also be accepted as a correct name. One who, in the
United States, insists on calling the game Association Football, is
confused, not learned. It should be recognized that the best name
for a game is not always the same in all countries.

In this book, one name is selected for each game as the best one
according to the principles discussed above, and this name is given
first. Other names that seem appropriate or that are used to any
extent are given on a line below. Generally speaking, the first-
mentioned name is considered superior to any of the others. However, there are cases where this is not true and where a name on
the second line is considered just as good as (but never better than)
the one given first.

Where possible and appropriate, an attempt has been made to
interpret names, and students are urged to take an interest in the
significance of the names. In some cases, something is said about the
history of the games, but the history is not treated exhaustively.

CONTINUOUS TAG GAMES

OF ALL ACTIVE GAMES THE MOST NUMEROUS ARE RUNNING GAMES: those in which one man pursues another in an effort to tag or capture him, or in which several men race in order to see which one will be first—occasionally last—to reach a designated place or object. Running is prominent in many additional games, but only because of its contribution to the real objectives of the players. For example, running is important in Basketball and Tennis but only because of its contribution to success in throwing the basketball into the goal or in striking the tennis ball with the racket in such a way that the opponent cannot return it. In a running game a successful run is the *only* objective of the players.

Some running games involve racing or chasing without the element of tagging, but most of them include both chasing and tagging. These chase-and-tag games, named simply *Tag Games*, constitute the first of the eleven classes into which all active games are grouped. This first class, unlike the others, is divided into two subclasses corresponding to the two rather distinct types of Tag Games: those in which play is uninterrupted and continues indefinitely, and those in which play is halted and a fresh start made after each pursuit. The "Continuous Tag Games," therefore, constitute subclass A of Class I, or Class I-A, and they are the ones to be described first. They are arranged in three parts, each part being called a *division*.

Division One: Ordinary Tag

In any game of this division the chaser [1] pursues any or all of the other players, all being equally vulnerable to tagging. The chaser must continue until he succeeds in tagging a runner, and when he

---

[1] With considerable regret the decision has been made not to use the traditional word *It* in this book. *It* is a player who is singled out from the rest and has some special duty assigned to him. This duty is not always that of chasing other players and sometimes there is a question as to which player should be

does, the one tagged immediately becomes the chaser and the game continues without interruption, ending only when the players decide to quit. In most of these games the chaser is one man and the runners are independent, each individual playing only for himself. In some games, however, the chaser is two or more men, and in others the runners are in pairs or groups. For convenience, the games in which all players are single and independent will be described first, and those with dual or multiple chasers, or with runners in pairs or groups, will be described separately.

Section I: All players are independent

GROUP A: SIMPLE TAG

1. SIMPLE TAG
Ordinary Tag. Tag.

One man is selected to be chaser. He pursues the others, trying to tag any one of them, all being free to run wherever they wish. When a runner is tagged he immediately becomes chaser and takes up his new duty without pause.

2. BOUNDARY TAG
French Tag

Boundary Tag is merely Simple Tag played with boundary lines, with the provision that any runner who touches the ground out of bounds is considered to be tagged. Out of bounds is interpreted as in Basketball, a man who touches the line being out. The playing court should be fairly small, a volleyball court or half of a basketball court being about right in most cases.

GROUP B: METHOD OR PLACE OF TRAVELING IS SPECIFIED

These games are all played in exactly the same way as Simple Tag (or Boundary Tag) except for various restrictions on the locomotion of the players, the nature of the restriction being the distinguishing characteristic of each game. The restriction may be on the

---

called *It*. Because of this ambiguity it has been decided to use the words *chaser* and *runner*, the latter always referring to a player who is the object of pursuit by the chaser.

method, the place, or both. The games are all described as variations
of Simple Tag, with the understanding that they can also be played
as variations of Boundary Tag.

1. SKIPPING TAG

Same as Simple Tag, except that all players must travel only by
skipping.

2. STIFF-KNEE TAG

Same as Simple Tag, except that all players must travel with knees
stiff.

3. IMITATION TAG

Same as Skipping Tag or Stiff-knee Tag, except that the chaser
specifies any method of locomotion that he chooses, and this method
must be used by all players until the chaser changes the method.
Possible methods, in addition to skipping and stiff-knee travel, are
gallop, frog jump, hop, and backward run.

4. SORE-SPOT TAG
Hit-the-Spot Tag. Japanese Tag.

A man who is tagged and thus becomes the chaser must hold one
hand on the spot touched by the tagger and keep it there as long
as he remains the chaser. Otherwise the game is the same as Simple
Tag.

5. DRAG TAG
Tail Tag

The chaser drags a rope, 10 to 15 feet long, along the ground, and
may tag a runner only while holding the rope. The runners may at
will tantalize the chaser and interfere with him by grasping the rope
or stepping on it. When a runner is tagged he takes the rope and the
game continues.

6. DIZZY TAG
Dizzy-Izzy

When a man is tagged he must bend forward with his hands on
his knees and turn around three times before beginning to chase
the runners. Otherwise, the game is the same as Simple Tag.

7. LINE TAG

This game must be played where lines are marked on the ground or floor, as in a gymnasium with lines for various games. The lines need not form any particular pattern, and the more numerous and complicated they are, the better. The game is the same as Simple Tag, except that all players must run only on the lines, and one who does not do so is considered tagged.

Figure 1. Fox-and-Geese Tag. Diagram to be trampled in the snow.

7. FOX-AND-GEESE TAG

Fox Trail. Single-rim Fox and Geese.

This game, a special form of Line Tag, is played on lines trampled in the snow; it could, of course, be played elsewhere if the paths could be distinctly marked. The paths are in the form of a wheel with a diameter of 15 to 30 feet, with a hub and spokes, the usual number

of spokes being eight. All players must run only on the lines, and a
runner who leaves the rim and starts down one of the spokes must
continue across the wheel without returning to the spot that he has
just left. This last requirement does not apply to the chaser. When
a runner is tagged or leaves the lines he becomes chaser, and the
game continues in the same way as Simple Tag.

The game is similar to Fox and Geese. (page 16).

9. WATER TAG
Simple Water-Tag

This game is Simple Tag played by swimmers. It is likely not to be
successful unless played in an enclosure or with boundary lines and
for this reason is usually played in a pool. Players may stand or walk
in the shallow end of the pool, if any, but may not leave the pool.

10. STROKE TAG (Aquatic)

From time to time the leader calls out the name of a particular
swimming stroke and all players must immediately begin using this
stroke. Thus, this game is practically the aquatic form of Imitation
Tag (page 10).

11. MOUNTED TAG

The game is Simple Tag played on horseback. To tag a runner, the
chaser must touch him, not his horse. It must be played in an
enclosure or with boundary lines.

GROUP C: METHOD OF TAGGING IS SPECIFIED

These games are characterized by the fact that the chaser tags
a runner, not simply by touching him, but by some other specified
method. The particular method is the distinguishing feature of each
game.

1. SWAT TAG
Whip Tag

The chaser carries a swatter, strap, or switch, and tags a runner
by hitting him with it. Otherwise the game is the same as Simple
Tag.

2. ROPE TAG
Lariat Tag

The chaser carries a rope, about ten feet long, with a soft weight at each end. The rope sometimes used on high-jump standards is very good, but a clothesline with a softball tied to each end will serve as well. To tag a runner the chaser must hit him with one of the weights without releasing his hold on the rope.

3. SHADOW TAG

To tag a runner, the chaser must step on some part of the runner's shadow and call his name as he does so. The game can, of course, be played only outdoors and only while the sun is shining.

4. TOUCH-THE-SPOT TAG
Sore-spot Tag

While tagging a runner, the chaser must hold one hand on the spot at which he himself was tagged by the last chaser. He is not required to hold a hand on the spot while running, but only while tagging. Compare Sore-spot Tag (page 10).

5. WATER FOOT-TAG

Same as Water Tag, except that the chaser must tag a man on the foot.

GROUP D: RUNNER CAN OBTAIN IMMUNITY FROM TAGGING

These games are like Simple Tag with the very important exception that a runner can obtain immunity to tagging. He obtains immunity in some games by touching material of a designated kind or by touching a particular object or area, and in others by performing a specified act or assuming a specified position. It is obvious that such a game would be ruined and pointless if the runners should try too hard to be safe, and if no restriction were placed on their right to obtain immunity. The best way of avoiding this possibility is for all players to have the spirit of venturesomeness, always choosing to take chances and to tantalize the chaser to the limit. In cases where this spirit is not so well developed as it might be—and it may be lacking in a few players although present in the others—various devices may be used to prevent abuse of the immunity privilege. Among such devices are the following:

1. When immunity is obtained by being in a certain place or touching a certain object, it may be ruled that any new arrival can claim the place or object and force the old possessor out.

2. A runner may be limited in the number of times that he can claim immunity while one man is chaser. The limit is usually two or three.

3. A runner may be prohibited from obtaining immunity in the same place twice in succession, and may be required to run a certain distance, say 30 feet, from one place of immunity to another.

4. It may be ruled that when the chaser approaches close to a runner who has immunity and then retreats for five steps, the runner loses immunity and must leave the spot. A modification of this rule permits the chaser to stand five paces from a runner and count to ten, after which the runner loses immunity.

(a) Immunity is obtained by touching object, area, or material

1. WOOD TAG

Same as Simple Tag, except that a runner is immune to tagging while he is touching any piece of wood. The rule is sometimes made that growing plants are not considered wood.

2. IRON TAG

Same as Wood Tag, except that the safety material is iron.

3. STONE TAG

Same as Wood Tag, except that the safety material is stone.

4. WOOD TAG VARIATIONS

Any other material or type of object may be used instead of wood, iron, or stone, and the game named accordingly. Suggestions are: Tree Tag, Grass Tag, Paint Tag, Wall Tag.

5. SAFETY-ZONE TAG

Several zones or areas are selected or marked out, and a runner is immune to tagging while he is touching any one of them.

6. STRADDLE TAG
Straddle-the-Pole

A line 10 to 20 feet long is drawn on the ground and a runner is immune while he stands straddling this line. A crack in the pavement, or some other line already existing, serves very well, and a pole laid on the ground is especially good.

Variation. Runners are free to run at will, but the chaser is restricted in that he may not cross the line but must always run around it.

Figure 2. Fox and Geese. Diagram to be trampled in the snow.

7. FOX AND GEESE

Double Fox-and-Geese. Double-rim Fox and Geese.
Fox Trail. Wolf and Rabbit.

This game is traditionally played in the snow and is the best known snow game. Paths are marked by trampling the snow, forming a large wheel with a hub, spokes, and a double rim. The size of the wheel varies with the number and age of the players but should seldom have a diameter of less than 30 feet, with the inner rim about six feet from the outer one. All players run at will, but they may not leave the paths. The intersections of the spokes and the outer rim are safety spots and a runner who stands on one of these is immune to tagging. It is best for the number of safety spots to be less, preferably just one less, than the number of runners. Sometimes the rule is made that a runner may be forced from a safety spot by a new arrival. With the exceptions noted, the game is the same as Simple Tag. Another game, Fox-and-Geese Tag (page 11) uses a similar diagram.

8. WATER IMMUNITY-OBJECT TAG

Various Immunity-object Tag Games can be adapted to the use of swimmers, the safety object or zone depending on availability.

9. MOUNTED IMMUNITY-OBJECT TAG

Various Immunity-object Tag Games can be adapted to the use of players on horseback. For example, the immunity object could be the rail at the side of the paddock.

(b) Immunity is obtained by designated position or action

1. SQUAT TAG

Stoop Tag

Same as Simple Tag, except that a runner is immune to tagging while he is in the squatting position. He is required to have his knees fully bent and to be reasonably upright.

2. STORK TAG

Same as Squat Tag, except that a runner is immune while he is standing on one foot.

3. FLOOR TAG

Same as Squat Tag, except that the immunity position is with one hand on the floor.

4. TURTLE TAG

Same as Squat Tag, except that to be immune a runner must be flat on his back with both hands and both feet off the floor.

5. STATUE TAG

The chaser demonstrates some posture, preferably a ludicrous one, and any runner in this posture is immune to tagging.

6. HANG TAG

Tree Toad

A runner is immune while he is hanging from any support, with both feet off the ground or floor.

7. TREE-TOAD TAG

This game is a special form of Hang Tag and must be played among trees. A runner obtains immunity to tagging by wrapping his arms about the trunk of a tree and lifting both feet from the ground.

8. HINDU TAG

Hindoo Tag. Mohammedan Tag. Turkish Tag.

A runner is immune to tagging while he has both hands and his forehead on the floor, with or without knees on the floor.

9. NOSE-AND-TOE TAG

Nose-and-Ankle Tag. Skunk Tag.

A runner is immune to tagging while he holds one foot in either hand and his nose in the other. Instead of the foot, he may be required to hold an ankle in one hand.

10. OSTRICH TAG

Skunk Tag

A runner is immune to tagging while he is standing on one foot with the opposite arm under the free leg and with the opposite hand grasping the nose. For example, standing on right foot, left arm under left knee, left hand grasping nose.

11. SITTING TAG
Old-Man Tag

A runner is immune to tagging while he is in the sitting position. He may sit on the floor, or, where the situation permits, on a chair or other seat.

12. WOOD-AND-WHISTLE TAG
Touch Wood and Whistle

A runner is immune to tagging while he is touching wood and, at the same time, continuing to whistle. Other material may, of course, be substituted for wood. This game is usually quite comical, as the chaser tries to force the runners to laugh and hence to be unable to whistle.

13. ROLL TAG
Somersault Tag

A runner may secure immunity to tagging by turning a forward roll and remaining in a sitting position. He is immune as long as he retains the sitting position.

14. FENCE TAG
Same-side Tag

This game requires a length of solid fence, a row of gymnasium apparatus, a row of school seats, or other obstacle over which players can vault. The game begins with the chaser on one side of the fence and all runners on the other. Both chaser and runners may vault, or jump if possible, over the fence, at will. The chaser may tag a runner only when they are both on the same side of the fence. He may not reach over the fence to tag a man, nor tag him while he is on his way over the fence. Thus the game is immunity tag, a runner having immunity whenever he is not on the same side of the fence as the chaser.

Variation 1. The obstacle is one over which one can jump but cannot vault. A ditch is suggested, but a small stream, a rope, a low hedge, or similar obstacle may be used.

Variation 2. Two parallel obstacles are used, either fences, as in the basic form, or ditches, as in variation 1. The chaser may tag a man only when both are between the obstacles or in the same outer space.

15. FEET-OUT TAG (Aquatic)

A swimmer is immune to tagging while on his back with both feet out of the water.

16. OTHER WATER SAFETY-POSITION TAGS

Other safety positions and actions may be used in aquatic immunity tags; for example, head under water, foot in hand, hand on the bottom of the pool, treading water.

17. CLIMB-A-MAN TAG

Horse Tag. Mount Tag.

When one man is mounted on the back of another, so that both feet are off the floor, both men are immune. A runner may not mount the same man twice in succession. Only one runner may mount one man.

Variation. More than one runner may mount, or at least try to mount, the same man.

18. BACK-TO-BACK TAG

When two runners stand back to back, both are immune.

19. FOOT-TO-FOOT TAG

Affinity Tag. Sole-mate Tag.

When two runners sit on the floor with the soles of the feet of one man against those of the other, both are immune.

Variation. For mixed groups it may be required that the immune pair be a boy and a girl.

20. ANKLE TAG

A runner is immune while he holds another runner by the ankle or ankles. The one held is not immune unless he also holds a runner by the ankle, either the one holding him or another. The one held may try to break away.

Section II: Some or all players are in pairs or teams

In the games thus far described there is only one chaser, and each runner is strictly independent. In those now to be described there is an element of cooperation or teamwork, or at least division of labor. In most cases, the games are basically the same as the former ones, but they are segregated as a matter of convenience in describing them. They are divided into two groups: those in which the runners are independent, and those in which the runners are in pairs or teams.

GROUP A: RUNNERS ARE INDEPENDENT

1. TWO-CHASER TAG

Same as Simple Tag, except that two men act as chasers at the same time. Cooperation is not prescribed, but the two chasers may, of course, pursue the same man.

Variation 1. Three or more men act as chasers, instead of two. This variation is not recommended, except in unusual situations.

Variation 2. The double chaser or multiple chaser may be used in many of the other games already described, as well as in Simple Tag.

2. POSSE TAG

This game carries the multiple-chaser idea to the limit, for in it only one man is runner and all the rest are chasers. One man flees and all the others pursue him. A man who tags the runner becomes the new runner.

3. CATCH-THE-SNAKE
Snake Catch

This game is the same as Posse Tag except for the method of tagging. The runner drags a rope five to ten feet long. The others pursue him and try to grasp the rope. One who grasps the rope securely becomes the new runner.

4. DOUBLE-CHASER TAG

Two men are chasers; they keep elbows hooked and act as a unit. Without releasing elbows the two chasers pursue the other players, who run independently and at will. When either chaser tags a runner he trades places with him.

5. ISLAND TAG
Helper Tag

Several mats on the floor serve as safety zones. Only one man is chaser, but he has a helper. The chaser pursues the other players, as in Simple Tag, and the runners may obtain immunity to tagging by standing with both feet on one of the safety zones. However, the helper of the chaser runs at will and pushes runners off the mats so that they lose immunity; he may not take hold of the runners, but only push and charge them. When a man is tagged he becomes a helper, the old helper becomes chaser, and the old chaser joins the runners.

GROUP B: RUNNERS ARE IN PAIRS OR TEAMS

1. BRONCHO TAG
Catch-the-Caboose

One man is chaser, all the others are runners. The runners are in groups of three, in tandem formation, each man with his arms wrapped about the waist of the man in front of him. The chaser pursues the groups of runners, trying to catch on to the rear man of any of the groups. When the chaser succeeds, he becomes the rear man, and the front man of the group becomes the new chaser.

Variation 1. The game can be played with two men, or with four or more, in a group, instead of three.

Variation 2. Each man holds his hands on the shoulders of the man in front of him, instead of wrapping arms about his waist.

2. CATCH-THE-CABOOSE
Fox and Chickens. Fox and Gander. Fox and Geese. Fox's Tail. Shepherdess and Wolf. Snake Tag.

This game is a special form of Broncho Tag, in which the number of men in a group of runners is increased until it includes them all. That is, one man is chaser, the others are runners. The runners all form in a single column, each man with his hands on the shoulders, or his arms about the waist, of the man in front of him. The line of runners may flee, turn, and twist at will, and the one at the head of the line may use his arms to ward off the chaser. When the chaser succeeds in grasping the rear man in the prescribed way he remains

as rear man, and the man in front of the column becomes the new
chaser.

Variation 1. If it appears undesirably difficult for the chaser to
grasp the rear man in the prescribed way, he may be required only
to touch him.

Variation 2. The rear man has a handkerchief or other piece of
cloth hanging from his belt. He is tagged when the chaser succeeds
in removing the handkerchief.

3. COUPLE TAG

All players, chasers and runners, are in couples, each couple
with arms locked or hands joined, as prescribed. One couple is
chaser, the others runners, and the game proceeds like Simple Tag.
When either member of a couple of runners is tagged by either of the
chaser couple, the tagged couple becomes chaser and the old
chasers join the runners.

4. TANDEM TAG
Broncho Tag

All players are in pairs, one man behind the other and with hands
on his shoulders. One pair is chaser, the others runners. Only the
front man of the chaser pair may tag, but he may tag either member
of the runner pair. When either man of a runner pair is tagged, he
and his partner trade places with the chaser pair. The two men in
each pair should exchange places from time to time.

Variation. The front man of each pair is a horse, the rear man a
cowboy. Only a cowboy can tag or be tagged. In order to tag a
runner, the cowboy takes one hand from the shoulder of his partner
but must keep the other in place.

5. PICKABACK TAG
Cowboy Tag. Horse-and-Rider Tag.

All players are in horse-and-rider pairs, that is, one man rides on
the back of the other with his legs around the body of the latter, just
above the hips. One pair is chaser, the others runners. Only the rider
may tag or be tagged. Any horse and his rider may exchange places
at any time, and should do so frequently.

6. BODYGUARD TAG
Bodyguard. King's Bodyguard.

All the players are chasers except three. Of these three only one, the king, can be tagged, but he is helped by the other two men, his bodyguards. The chasers pursue the king, trying to tag him. The bodyguards protect the king by blocking, holding, or tackling the chasers. When the king is tagged, he joins the chasers, the tagger becomes the first guard, the first guard becomes second guard, and the second guard becomes king.

Variation. The two guards must hold hands. They do not block or hold the chasers, but need only tag them. Thus, the chasers try to tag the king, while the bodyguards try to tag the chasers. Any man who is tagged trades places with his tagger.

Division Two: Single-Runner Tag

In each of the games described in Division One, every player is always either a chaser, or a runner subject to pursuit by the chaser. The games of Division Two are basically different because in each of them there is at any one time only one runner being pursued, although this single runner is in certain games a pair or group of men acting as a unit. Thus, in these games most of the players are inactive, being neither chaser nor runner. But inactive players must be alert, for each game includes a device by which the job of runner may be transferred from one to another. The method by which this transfer is made is the distinguishing characteristic of each game. In some games the inactive players stand or run at random, and in others they are in a circle or other definite formation; in either case, they may be single and independent or they may be in pairs or groups.

Section I: Inactive players are independent

GROUP A: VULNERABILITY IS TRANSFERRED BY PASSING AN OBJECT

1. GIVEAWAY TAG
Cap Tag. Flag Tag. Dumbbell Tag. Kidnaper's Tag.

Players are scattered at random and run without restriction; one is the runner, another the chaser, the rest inactive. The runner carries an object of some sort and he may at will hand, not throw, this object to any of the inactive players. The inactive player is not allowed to refuse it. As soon as the object has been transferred, the new possessor of it is runner and the old one inactive. If the object is a rag doll, the game is called *Kidnaper's Tag;* a flag, cap, dumb·bell, or the like, may be used and the game named accordingly.

Variation 1. The object need not be handed to the next man, but may be handed or thrown. This variation should be used only with a heavy and bulky object, such as a medicine ball.

Variation 2. The game may be played with more than one runner, each carrying an object.

2. POSTURE TAG

One man is the chaser, one is the runner, and the others stand at random. The chaser has a book, beanbag, or other object balanced on his head without the use of hands, and the same is true of the runner. The runner may become immune and make an inactive player the runner by transferring the book to the head of the latter, who may not refuse it.

GROUP B: VULNERABILITY IS TRANSFERRED BY POSITION OR ACTION

1. SPOT TAG

One man is the chaser, another is the runner; all others stand at random, each in a small circle marked on the ground. The runner may step into any circle with either or both feet; then the occupant of the circle becomes the runner and the old runner takes his place.

Variation. The game may be played without using circles, each inactive man merely remaining in place. When the runner touches a man, the latter becomes runner and the old runner takes his place.

2. CROSS TAG

One man is the chaser, one is the runner, and the others stand or move about at will. When any third player crosses the imaginary line between the chaser and the runner, the job of runner is immediately transferred to him. Usually a man crosses the line intentionally in order to make himself runner, but he may do so unintentionally, either by accident or because the runners run around him.

3. KICK-THE-BLOCK

Strideball Tag

One man is chosen chaser. He stands astride a block or tin can which is on the ground. The other players gather around him, and, at a favorable opportunity, one of them kicks the block and thus makes himself runner. He remains runner until he is caught or until some other player chooses to kick the block, which he may do at any time. When a man kicks the block he immediately becomes runner.

4. HOUND AND RABBIT

Dog and Rabbit. Fox and Squirrel. Rabbit's Nest.

A chaser pursues a runner. The other players stand in groups of four; of each four, three form a circle by standing with hands on each other's shoulders, and the fourth stands erect within the circle thus formed. The runner may at any time enter one of the circles. When he does so he is immune to tagging, and the old occupant of the circle immediately becomes runner. At frequent intervals the center man of each group should trade places with one of the men of his circle.

Variation. Instead of three, a circle may include two men, or four or more.

5. CHASE-THE-CHASER TAG

A chaser pursues a runner, the other players all standing at random. The runner may at will touch any other player and thus make himself immune to tagging. In this game, however, the man touched does not become the new runner, as in the games of this group thus far described. Instead, the man touched by the runner becomes chaser, the old chaser becomes runner, and the game continues as before.

6. TWO DEEP

All but two players form a circle facing the center, with intervals of about three feet between men. One of the odd men is the chaser, the other is the runner. The chaser pursues the runner around the outside of the circle and the runner may at will step or jump in front of any man in the circle. The old runner thus becomes immune and the circle man becomes the new runner, the old runner replacing the new one in the circle.

7. SITTING TWO-DEEP

A chaser pursues a runner. All other players form a circle by sitting on the floor facing the center, at intervals of about three feet. The runner may at will sit in front of any circle player, thus forcing the latter to become the runner and making himself immune. The old runner replaces the new one in the circle.

8. LEAPFROG TWO-DEEP

Leapfrog Tag. Two-Deep Leapfrog.

A chaser pursues a runner. The other players stand in a circle facing the center, each making a "back" by leaning forward and grasping his ankles. The runner may at will make a straddle-vault over any circle man and thus make the latter the new runner. The old runner replaces the new one in the circle.

9. STRADDLE-JUMP TWO-DEEP

Sitting-circle Tag

A chaser pursues a runner. The other players form a circle by sitting on the floor facing the center, at intervals of about three feet. The runner may at will do a straddle-jump over any circle player. When he has done so he replaces the circle player and the latter becomes the new runner.

10. UNDERNEATH TWO-DEEP

Leg-dive Tag

A chaser pursues a runner. The other players stand in a circle at intervals of about three feet, facing the center, with feet wide apart. The runner may at will crawl or dive in either direction between the legs of any circle man. When he does so he replaces the circle man and the latter becomes runner.

Variation 1. The runner may go only forward between the legs of a circle man.

Variation 2. When the old runner replaces a circle man he stands with his feet together. The game continues until all circle men have feet together. Thus, this game is really a form of Elimination Tag (see Division Three) and does not logically belong here in the classification. It is placed here because it is a variation of the basic game that does belong here.

11. TWO BROAD

A chaser pursues a runner. The other players stand in a circle facing the center at intervals of about three feet. The runner may at will step or jump to a position at the right of any circle player. When he does so he replaces the circle player and the latter becomes runner.

12. CHAIR TAG
Partner Tag

A chaser pursues a runner. The other players form a circle, each sitting in a chair facing the center. The runner may at will sit on the chair with any circle player. When he does so he replaces the circle player and the latter becomes runner.

Section II: The inactive players are in groups of two or more

These games are all very much alike. In each of them a chaser pursues a runner and the inactive men are in pairs, or in a few cases, larger groups. The runner joins one of the groups, thus making himself immune and "freezing out" one man of the group, forcing him to become the new runner.

1. THREE DEEP
Fox and Goose. Three-deep Tag. Twos and Threes.

A chaser pursues a runner. The other players stand in two concentric circles, all facing the center at intervals of three feet or more. The rear man of each pair must stand directly behind the front man. The runner may at will step or jump in front of the front man of any pair in the circle. When he does so the rear man of the pair becomes the runner and the old front man becomes the rear man. Both chaser and runner are free to run through or around the circle, but must not leave the immediate vicinity of the circle.

Variation 1. The game is sometimes played with running through the circle prohibited.

Variation 2. There are two runners and two chasers at the same time.

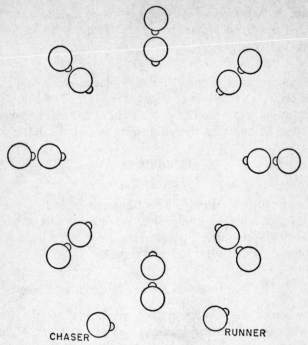

CHASER   RUNNER

Figure 3. Three-Deep.

2. THREE HIGH

This game is the same as Three Deep, except that the runner steps behind the rear man of a circle pair, and the front man of the pair becomes the new runner.

3. THREE BROAD

A chaser pursues a runner. The other players stand in a single circle facing the center. They stand in pairs, the two of each pair close together, side by side, and with intervals of three feet or more between pairs. The runner may at will step or jump to a position at either side of any circle pair. When he does so the partner of the man beside whom he stands becomes the new runner.

4. HANDGRASP TAG
Three Broad

A chaser pursues a runner. The other players stand in a single circle, facing the center. The circle players hold hands in pairs, with intervals of three feet or more between pairs. The runner may at will grasp the hand of any circle player, thus making the latter's partner the new runner. Thus the game is the same as Three Broad except for the addition of the handgrasp.

Variation. The circle players are in a double circle facing counter-clockwise.

5. HOOK-ARM TAG

Circle Lock-Tag. Lock-arm Tag. Lock Tag.
Partner Tag. Three Broad. Three Wide.

A chaser pursues a runner. The other players stand in a single circle, facing the center. They form pairs by hooking elbows or joining hands, with intervals of at least three feet between pairs. Each circle man stands with his free hand on his hip and his elbow extended from his body, forming a loop through which the runner can thrust his arm. The runner may at will hook arms with any circle player and thus make the latter's partner the new runner.

Variation 1. Same as above except that the inactive pairs are scat-tered at random, instead of being in a circle.

Variation 2. In the description given, it is assumed that the in-active players will remain still and not interfere with the runner's attempt to hook arms with them. It may be varied, however, to allow the couples to twist and squirm, without moving the feet, so as to make it more difficult for the runner to hold arms with any of them.

6. UNDERNEATH THREE-DEEP

A chaser pursues a runner. The other players stand in a double circle facing the center, with intervals of about three feet between pairs. Each man stands with his feet wide apart. The rear man of each pair must stand directly behind his partner and close to him. The runner may at will crawl or dive, either forward or backward, between the legs of both men of any circle pair. When he does so the rear man of the pair becomes the new runner.

Variation. The runner must travel forward between the legs of the circle pair.

7. THIRD MAN

Freeze-Out

A chaser pursues a runner. The other players stand in a double circle. The outer circle faces inward and the inner circle outward, thus forming pairs in which each man faces his partner; the partners should be about three feet from each other. The runner may at will step or jump between the two men of a pair, facing either one of them. The man to whom the runner's back is turned is the new runner.

Variation. The couples are scattered at random instead of being in a circle.

8. ANIMAL CAGE
Basket Three-Deep. Nest Tag.

A chaser pursues a runner. The other players stand in two concentric circles, the inner circle facing outward and the outer circle facing inward, thus forming pairs standing face to face. Each circle man joins hands with his partner, or it may be prescribed that he place his hands on his partner's shoulders. The runner may at will step or jump between two partners, facing one or the other. The man to whom his back is turned is the new runner.

9. THREE-DEEP CHASE-THE-CHASER
Dog and Rabbit. Last-Man-It.

A chaser pursues a runner. The other players stand in two concentric circles, all facing the center. The runner may at will step or jump in front of the front man of any pair, as in Three Deep. When he does so, the rear man of the pair, instead of becoming runner as in Three Deep, becomes the chaser. The old chaser becomes the new runner. Thus the game is a combination of Chase-the-Chaser (page 25) and Three Deep.

10. BRONCHO THREE-DEEP
Broncho. Broncho Tag. Circle Broncho-Tag.

A chaser pursues a runner. The other players stand in two concentric circles, all facing the center. Each rear man wraps his arms about the waist of the man in front of him. The runner may at will wrap his arms about the waist of a rear man, thus becoming immune and making the front man the new runner. The circle men twist and squirm to interfere with the runner's attempt to hook on, but they must stay in place, and may not use their hands.

Variation. The couples are scattered at random, instead of being in a circle.

11. BRONCHO THREE-DEEP ON SKATES

This game is Broncho Three-Deep played by skaters. It is an excellent game but is probably better if played as Broncho Four-Deep or with even more men in each group.

12. BRONCHO FOUR-DEEP

The same as Broncho Three-Deep except that each circle group consists of three men, one behind another, instead of two.

Division Three: Elimination Tag

This division is the last of the three into which the continuous games of tag are divided. In a game of Division Three, play is continuous, but it does come to an end when all players have been eliminated. In most of the games elimination means actually leaving the game; in a few of them it means that a player is eliminated as a runner but remains in the game as an additional chaser, the game ending when all have become chasers. It must not be inferred from the small number of games in this group that there are few elimination tag games. In fact, although there are only a few such games among the continuous ones that constitute class I-A, there are very many in the noncontinuous games that constitute Class I-B.

Most of these elimination games are similar to contests, as they are defined in the opening chapter—so similar that one could not be blamed for classing them as contests and not as games at all.

Section I: Runner who is tagged leaves the game

1. CIRCLE PURSUIT-RACE
Circle Race

Some kind of circular or other closed running course is needed; a course is usually improvised by marking it with posts, chairs, or other obstacles, or even with inactive players. The runners are stationed at equal distances around the course, each with his own starting line; there is no finish line. At a starting signal all begin running at once, and each runner tries to overtake and tag the runner next in front of him, and also to avoid being tagged by the runner next behind him. When a runner has been tagged, he immediately leaves the course and the game, but the tagger continues to run, trying to tag the man who now has become the one next in front of him. This game continues until only one man survives; he, of course, is the winner.

2. SACK PURSUIT-RACE

Sack Chase

Same as Circle Pursuit-Race, except that each runner is in a sack, as in the ordinary Sack Race. In this game the course should be short.

3. REVERSE PURSUIT-RACE

Circle Race. Reverse Chase.

The game is exactly the same as Circle Pursuit-Race except for this important addition: while the players are running, the leader gives an occasional signal, such as the blowing of a whistle. When this signal is given all players reverse their direction and run the other way.

4. CENTIPEDE PURSUIT-RACE

Centipede Overtake-Race. Link Pursuit-Race. Link Tag.

Same as Circle Pursuit-Race, except that the runners are in several equal-sized teams. Teams may be of any size, from two to twenty men each. Each team forms in single file behind its starting line, each man with his arms about the waist of the teammate just ahead of him. At the starting signal all run at once, each team trying to enable its front man to tag the rear man of the team just ahead. When a rear man of any team is tagged the entire team leaves the course and the game. A team that breaks apart or leaves the course is considered tagged.

5. SNAKE CHASE

Crocodile Chase

This game is for two teams only, and does not use a track or race course. Each team, consisting preferably of ten men or more, has a length of rope, and each man grasps the rope with his left hand. At a starting signal each team tries to enable its head man to tag the tail man of the other team. The first to do so is the winner. If any man releases his hold on the rope his team loses the game.

6. WHEEL PURSUIT-RACE
Cat Tail

This game is for two teams only and does not require a track or race course. A team should consist of at least ten men, and preferably more. An additional man, neutral and not on either team, is needed. To start, all form in a single straight line with hands joined. The neutral man is in the middle with one team on each side of him. The teams face in opposite directions; the neutral man may face in either direction. At the starting signal, all run forward in a circle, pivoting about the neutral man, who turns in place. The object of each team is to enable its outermost man to tag the outermost man of the other team. The team that does so is the winner.

7. PURSUIT RELAY
Overtake Relay

Two or more teams are stationed at equal intervals around an improvised running course. At a starting signal one man from each team runs exactly as in the Circle Pursuit-Race, except that a man does not run more than one lap. A man who is tagged by the one behind him drops out, and his whole team is out of the game. However, if a runner completes the lap without being tagged, he touches the second man of his team and the team continues as in any ordinary relay race. Whenever any man is tagged, his whole team is out. The game continues until only one team survives. If more than one team survives when all have run, they begin again with the first man without pause.

8. CAGEBALL PURSUIT-RELAY

Same as Pursuit Relay except that each runner carries a cageball or large sport ball, which he must hand, not throw, to the next man.

9. LEAPFROG PURSUIT-RELAY
Pursuit Vault-Race

This game is for two teams only. All players form a single large circle, with at least six feet between men, facing counterclockwise. Each half of the circle is a team. Each man bends forward and makes a "back" by placing his hands on his knees. At the starting signal the rear man of each team travels completely around the circle by doing a straddle-vault over each of the men in the circle, teammate and opponent. When he has returned to his original position in the circle he touches the teammate just in front of him and forms a "back" for the other vaulters. When the second man is touched he repeats the process just completed by the first man, and the game continues until one man overtakes his opponent.

10. PURSUIT ELIMINATION
Pursuit Race

All players stand in a single circle, facing the center, and count off by fours. There are no teams, the game being played each man for himself. All men with number one step outside the circle and, at a starting signal, run a pursuit race as in the Circle Pursuit-Race. When only one of these runners survives, a similar race is run by those with number two, then three, and then four. After these four races are completed and four winners determined, the four winners run a pursuit race around the circle of players; the last survivor of these four is winner of the game.

11. CIRCLE PURSUIT-ELIMINATION
Circle Chase. Four-man Circle-Chase.

Players form a single circle and count off by fours, exactly as in Pursuit Elimination. All with number one step back and run a pursuit race, but instead of completing the race as usual, they run only once around the circle. Men who are tagged drop out and all survivors resume their places in the circle. The same process is repeated with the men of the other three numbers. Then all survivors form a new circle, count off by fours again, and repeat this procedure, continuing until there is only one survivor. The circle must be kept larger than usual in order to provide sufficient opportunity for tagging. Also, when the number of survivors has become rather small, two or more turns around the circle may be prescribed instead of only one.

12. PURSUIT ELIMINATION (Team Form)
Circle Touch-Race

All players stand in a single circle facing the center, and are divided into equal teams. Teammates stand side by side; for example, the first five men may be a team, the next five another team, and so on. All with number one step outside the circle and, at a signal, run a pursuit race until only one survives. He scores one point for his team. The process is repeated for the other numbers until all numbers have run. The team with the largest score is the winner.

Variation. The game may be played on the negative-score basis. Each pursuit race is continued only until one man is tagged. This man scores one point against his team.

13. RANDOM PURSUIT-RACE

Four men, *A, B, C,* and *D,* are in an area with boundary lines. At a starting signal, *A* chases *B, B* chases *C, C* chases *D,* and *D* chases *A,* all running at will as long as they stay within bounds. The first runner to tag his man is the winner. With larger numbers, the game can be repeated any number of times, with a different group of four each time. The winners, of course, can run a play-off. Three runners may be used instead of four, but a larger number than four is not likely to be successful.

14. ELIMINATION SWAT-TAG
Swat Down

This game is played by two equal teams, each within its own area in the form of a circle or square, except that one man from each team, armed with a swatter, is within the area of the opponents. At a starting signal each of the latter two men begins to chase and swat his opponents. As soon as a man has been swatted, or goes out of bounds, he leaves the game, and the men with the swatters continue until one of them has eliminated the entire opposing team and has thus scored a point for his own team. The teams are formed again, with new swatter men, and the process is repeated until each man has had his chance with the swatter. The team wins that has the larger score at the end.

Section II: Runner who is tagged joins the chasers

In these games, a man who is tagged is eliminated as a runner but does not leave the game. Instead, he becomes an additional chaser. Thus the number of runners decreases and that of chasers increases until only one runner remains. He is, of course, the winner of the game.

1. CHAIN TAG

Line Tag. Link Chase. Team Tag.

This game is identical with Simple Tag until the first runner has been tagged. Then the man tagged joins hands with the original chaser and the two together are chaser. They run, keeping inner hands joined, until another man is tagged. The latter joins hands with either one of the chasers so that there are now three chasers with hands joined. They chase as before and the game continues in the same way until only one runner survives; he is the winner. Only men at the ends of the line may tag. Runners may crawl under the line but not break through.

Variation. Runners may break through the line of chasers.

2. PARTNER TAG

This game is identical with Simple Tag until the first runner is tagged. The first man tagged joins hands with the original chaser and the two together continue as chaser.When the next man is tagged he becomes a third chaser, but runs alone until still another is tagged, when the two join hands and continue as a second pair of chasers. The game continues thus until only one runner survives, this one being the winner.

3. HIP

Help Tag

This game is the same as Simple Tag until the first runner is tagged, except that the chaser carries a swatter and tags by hitting a runner with it. The original chaser continues throughout the game as the only one to tag runners, always by hitting them with the swatter. However, any man who is tagged by the chaser ceases to be a runner and, instead, becomes a helper to the chaser. He helps by catching the runners and holding them until the chaser can swat them. Thus the number of runners decreases and that of the helpers increases until only one runner is left, the winner.

4. DOG AND DEER

This game is played on a diagram trampled in the snow, the diagram being a single endless path with various convolutions that frequently come within two feet of each other. The exact pattern is not important. The game starts with two men as chasers (dogs) and the others as runners (deer). All must remain on the paths but may jump across the narrow spaces. When a deer is caught he becomes an additional dog and the game continues until only one deer remains; he is the winner.

Class I-B

NONCONTINUOUS TAG GAMES

In all the games thus far described—those that constitute Class I-A—play is continuous and, except in one small division called Elimination Tag, goes on indefinitely. In the games of Class I-B, just the opposite is true, for play is conspicuously noncontinuous. Each of these games consists of a series of chases, each chase being of short duration and ending when a runner has been tagged or when all runners have reached a place of safety. After each such chase, play is halted and the players make ready for the next one.

The games are in six divisions: Goal-change Tag, Straightaway Tag, Circle or Maze Tag, Tantalize Tag, Home Tag, and No-flight Tag.

Division One: Goal-Change Tag

In Goal-Change Tag games, runners may be tagged only while they are running from one line, area, or object to another and are immune to tagging at other times. In the great majority of such games, they run from one to the other of two parallel lines, but in a few cases they run between goals of a different kind. In most cases the runners change goals at a specific signal, which is usually given by the chaser or chasers, but which in a few games is given by the runners themselves or by a neutral person.

Section I: Goals are parallel lines

GROUP A: MAN WHO IS TAGGED JOINS CHASERS

In any game of Group A, a chaser stands in the middle of the field and tries to tag one of the runners as they all run between two parallel goal lines. A man who is tagged on the first chase becomes an additional chaser for the next one. The second chase is just like the first one except that now there are two chasers instead of one. Other chases follow, each man tagged on any chase being added to the chasers for all subsequent ones, until all are chasers and there are no runners left. The last runner to be tagged is the winner.

(a) Running and tagging are unrestricted

In all these games the runners rush from one line to the other when they hear a call or signal, usually a defiant one, given by one or all of the chasers. All the games are identical except for the nature of this call. It might be considered, therefore, that they are really the same game, but they are not so classed because the call is believed to be so important a part of such a game that a distinctly different call makes a different game. Pom-Pom-Pullaway, the best known of the games, will be described in detail, but for the others only the distinctive call or signal will be given.

1. POM-POM-PULLAWAY [2]
Pullaway

Two parallel lines are marked about 60 feet apart, with side lines about 50 feet apart. One man is chosen as first chaser and he takes his position in the middle of the field. All other players are runners, and they stand behind one of the two parallel goal lines. The chaser issues this challenge in a loud voice, "Pom-pom-pullaway, come away or I'll pull you away." In some localities the word *fetch* is used instead of *pull,* and other variations of the call are also sometimes used. At the completion of the call all runners must dash for the opposite goal line and as they do, the chaser tries to catch one of them and to tag him three times. If the chaser succeeds in tagging a man three times, this man becomes a second chaser. Then the two of them stand in the middle, issue the call, and try to tag runners as they run back to the original goal line.

Other chases follow; each time, only the surviving runners change goals, and all who have been tagged act as chasers. This continues until the last runner has been tagged. He is, of course, the winner of

---

[2] Also spelled Pom Pom Pull Away, Pom-Pom-Pull-Away, Pom Pom Pullaway, Pom-Pom Pullaway. In the spelling recommended here, *pull* and *away* are made one word because it is believed that they are so pronounced, and probably so considered, by most players.

the game. Any number of runners may be tagged on one chase. When a new game is started, the usual custom is that the first player to have been tagged in the preceding game is first chaser in the new game. Sometimes, however, the right to be the first chaser is considered an honor, and is given to the man who was last tagged. The call is usually given only by the original chaser.

Variation 1. Instead of all being behind one goal line, the runners are divided equally between the two lines, each man running from his line to the other.

Variation 2. Chasers are required to tag only once.

2. HILL-DILL

Hill-Dill is identical with Pom-Pom-Pullaway except for the signal, which is "Hill dill, come over the hill." Sometimes it is "Hill dill, come over the hill or else I'll catch you standing still"; or "Hill dill, come over the hill or I'll come over after you."

3. ALL ACROSS

Identical with Pom-Pom-Pullaway except for the signal, which is simply "All across!"

4. COME, BLACKEY

Identical with Pom-Pom-Pullaway except for the signal, which is "Come, Blackey."

5. RUN, GEESE, RUN

Fox and Geese. Kentucky Fox and Geese.

Identical with Pom-Pom-Pullaway except for the signal, which is "Run, geese, run."

6. HAM, HAM, CHICKEN, HAM, BACON (Variation)

Ham, Chicken, Bacon

Identical with Pom-Pom-Pullaway except for the signal, which is "Ham, ham, chicken, ham, bacon." The better known game, of which this is a variation, includes the principle of the misleading call; it is listed under (c) in this same group (page 44).

7. ONE STEP OFF

Identical with Pom-Pom-Pullaway except for the signal, which is "One step off and all the way across."

8. OVER-THE-BRIDGE

Identical with Pom-Pom-Pullaway except for the signal, which is "All over."

9. RED ROVER

Identical with Pom-Pom-Pullaway except for the signal, which is "Red rover, come over, or I'll pull you over."

10. CROSSING NO-MAN'S-LAND

Identical with Pom-Pom-Pullaway except for the signal. In this case the signal is given by a nonplaying leader and is merely a whistle blast.

11. BLACK MAN

Who's Afraid of the Black Man?

Identical with Pom-Pom-Pullaway except for the signal. In this case, as also in the case of the following game (Bogey Man), the runners reply to the challenge of the chaser before starting to run. The chaser calls "Who's afraid of the black man?" The runners in unison reply "No one," and then start to run.

12. BOGEY MAN

Identical with Pom-Pom-Pullaway except for the signal. The chaser calls "Are you afraid of the bogey man?" The runners reply "No," and run for the opposite goal line.

(b) Running or tagging is restricted

In each of these games there is a restriction either on the method by which the players travel or else in the method of tagging. Except for this restriction and, of course, for the starting signal, they are all identical with Pom-Pom-Pullaway.

1. COUPLE HILL-DILL

All players, chasers and runners, form groups of two, holding hands. The call is "Hill dill, come over the hill." The game may be varied by having three or four in each group, instead of two.

2. CHINESE WALL

A tagging zone, 10 to 15 feet wide, is marked across the middle of the field, parallel with the goal lines, and a runner may be tagged only within this zone. Any signal may be used. Otherwise, the game is the same as Pom-Pom-Pullaway.

3. TACKLING POM-POM-PULLAWAY
Catch-and-Throw

Identical with Pom-Pom-Pullaway, including the call, except that the runner must be tackled and thrown to the ground, not merely touched. One is considered tagged if he touches the ground with any part of the body other than the feet.

4. HOPPING POM-POM-PULLAWAY

Identical with Pom-Pom-Pullaway, including the call, except that all players, chasers and runners, travel only by hopping. A runner who touches the ground with his raised foot is considered tagged.

Variation. A runner is considered tagged *only* when he touches the ground with his raised foot. Accordingly, to tag a runner the chaser must push or charge him so as to force him to put his foot down. The chaser may push with his hands but may not hold.

5. CHAIN POM-POM-PULLAWAY
Bears and Cattle. Bound Hands.

Identical with Pom-Pom-Pullaway, except that all chasers join hands in line. No tag is valid if made while the line is broken. Only the two men on the ends of the line may tag.

6. TWO-COURT POM-POM-PULLAWAY
Court Tag

The playing field is divided into two equal parts by a center line and the game begins with two chasers, one in each half of the field. The game is the same as Pom-Pom-Pullaway, including the call, except that each chaser is confined to his own half of the field. A runner who is tagged by either chaser joins him in his half of the field.

7. DARE BASE

A line is drawn across the middle of the field parallel with the goal lines. The runner is safe while he is touching this line with either foot, but when he leaves it he must continue in his original direction and may not return to the line that he last left. Otherwise, the game is the same as Pom-Pom-Pullaway. Any call may be used.

8. CROSS-THE-POOL (Aquatic)

The runners stand on one side or end of a swimming pool and the chaser stands or swims in the middle. The chaser calls "Cross the pool," and all must swim to the other side. The game is continued in the same way as Pom-Pom-Pullaway.

9. UNDER-THE-WATER (Aquatic)

The chaser is stationed in the middle of a swimming pool while the others are on one side or one end. The chaser calls "Under the water." Then the others must all dive in and swim under water to the opposite side. The chaser, of course, must duck under the water in order to tag a runner. The game is continued in the same way as Pom-Pom-Pullaway.

10. WATER FISH-NET
Fisherman

The original chaser is in the middle of the pool and all the other players are on one side or end. The chaser gives a signal and all others swim across, the chaser trying to tag one. The game proceeds like Pom-Pom-Pullaway until two men have been tagged, making a total of three chasers. These three men must join hands and only the end men can tag. Runners tagged after this are added to the ends of the line. Tagging can be done only by the two end men.

11. MOUNTED POM-POM-PULLAWAY

The game is identical with Pom-Pom-Pullaway except that it is played by men on horseback and that a runner must be tagged only once, not three times.

(c) Chasers use a misleading signal

These games are basically the same as Pom-Pom-Pullaway or the variations described above, but they all have the interesting feature of a misleading signal. A runner is to leave his goal only when a specified signal is given in complete and exactly correct form, and if he leaves the goal on an incomplete or incorrect signal he is con-

sidered caught. The chasers try to induce the runners to leave at the
wrong time, by giving misleading signals or making false motions.

1. BLACK TOM

This game is identical with Pom-Pom-Pullaway except for the
misleading signals. The correct signal is, "Black Tom, black Tom,
black Tom." After this signal is given in correct and complete form,
the game is no different from Pom-Pom-Pullaway, but the chaser
may vary the signal by substituting the word *blue* for *black,* by giving all the words of the signal but one, or in any other way. Any
player who leaves the goal line before a correct and complete signal
has been given, in considered caught.

2. WHEEL AWAY

Identical with Black Tom except for the signal. The correct signal
is, "Wheel away, wheel away, wheel away."

3. COME ACROSS

Identical with Black Tom except for the signal. The correct signal
is, "Come across, come across, come across."

4. HAM, HAM, CHICKEN, HAM, BACON

Identical with Black Tom except for the signal. The correct signal
is, "Ham, ham, chicken, ham, bacon."

5. ONE-FOOT-OFF

This game adds a new element, that of command following, to
the games just described. Otherwise, it is the same as Black Tom.
The correct signal for running is "Both feet off." When this signal is
given all must run as in the other games, and one who runs at the
wrong time is considered caught. In the meantime, the chaser may
give various other commands, the distinctive feature of this game
being that these commands must be obeyed. He may call "Right
foot off," "Both feet on," and so on. A player is considered caught
not only if he starts to run on an incorrect or incomplete signal, but
also if he fails to make a correct response to any of the other commands.

GROUP B: MAN WHO IS TAGGED DOES NOT JOIN CHASERS

1. ANIMAL CHASE

The Hunt

The chaser stands in the center of the playing field with all runners on one goal line. Animal names are given to the runners, each name to several different runners. When the chaser calls out any animal name, the runners with this name must rush to the opposite goal, the chaser of course trying to tag one as he passes. When the chaser tags a runner he trades places with him and assumes his animal name. Thus, there is always only one chaser.

Variation. After the first runner has been tagged, the game is played with two chasers. Each time that a runner is tagged he becomes a chaser and the first of the two old chasers replaces him.

2. TWO-MAN CHANGE-TAG

The chaser stands in the center of the field with the runners equally divided between the two parallel goal lines. The chaser calls the name of one player in either line. This player calls the name of any player in the other line. The two runners then rush to exchange places, the chaser trying to tag either of them. A runner tagged by the chaser trades places with him and the game continues as before.

3. HINDER TAG

The game begins with two men in the center of the field and the runners on one of the two goal lines. Of the two men in the center, only one is chaser. The other is called the "helper," but he is a helper of the runners and an opponent of the chaser. He does what he can to interfere with the chaser's attempts to tag the runners. He is not permitted to take hold of the chaser but may do anything else to hinder him. When a runner is tagged he becomes helper, the helper becomes chaser, and the chaser joins the runners.

4. ONE-MAN TAG

In this game only two men are active at any one time, one chaser and one runner. The players are divided into two equal teams and each team forms in line behind one of the two parallel goal lines. At a signal from the leader the first man in Team *A* leaves his goal line and runs to the opposite one; the first man from Team *B* runs at the same time, leaving his goal line and attempting to tag the runner from Team A before the latter succeeds in reaching the opposite goal line. For the next chase, a man from Team B tries to run to the opposite goal line and a man from Team A tries to tag him. Thus each team furnishes alternately the runner and the chaser, and the game continues until each man has run twice, once as runner and once as chaser. For each separate chase a point is scored for the team of which the winner is a member. In this game, and in other games of this sort, the best way to keep score is not with pencil and paper, but by using the players themselves as counters. There are several satisfactory ways of doing this, the most common one being for each winner to take his defeated opponent as prisoner and place him in a certain location reserved for this purpose. At the end of the game the team with the larger number of prisoners is the winner.

5. NO-MAN'S-LAND
Crossing No-Man's-Land

The players are divided into two equal teams. Team A lines up on one of two parallel goal lines and Team B forms a line across the middle of the field. At a starting signal all of the men on Team A start at the same time, each one trying to reach the opposite goal line without being captured by Team B. After Team A has started the rush, members of Team B may run at will anywhere on the field. They may work independently or in cooperation. To capture a man of Team A, a member of Team B must tap him on the back three times. After Team A has run and all its members have been captured or have reached the opposite goal line, the game is repeated, this time with Team B as runners and Team A as chasers. The team that captures the larger number of opponents is the winner of the game.

Variation. A man is captured only when he is tackled, that is, when he touches the ground with some part of his body other than the feet.

6. FISH NET
Catch-a-Fish.   Catch-of-Fish.   Fish and Net.
Fishing.   Snake and Bird.

Players are divided into two equal teams and each team stands on one of two parallel goal lines. The men of Team A join hands to form a "net," or a "snake." At a starting signal the men of Team *B*, each man independently, run for the opposite goal line. At the same time Team *A* moves toward the center of the field and captures as many of the runners as possible. To capture a runner Team *A* must, without breaking its line, completely encircle him. A runner may not break through, or crawl under, the line of chasers. After the first chase is completed the process is repeated, this time with the members of Team *A* as runners and those of Team *B* as chasers. The team that captures the larger number of opponents is, of course, the winner.

7. KICKOFF TAG
Kickoff Ball

The teams line up and prepare for a kickoff exactly as in a regular football game, except that the field need not be a standard one. One team makes a kickoff and the other returns it, again as in a football game. The runner is only touched, not tackled, and as soon as he is touched by an opponent he is down and the players prepare for the next chase. The teams now trade places and a kickoff is made by the team that received the first one. The teams continue alternate kicking and receiving for any agreed number of times.

Each team scores according to the distance that the ball is returned, and the team with the larger score at the end of the game is the winner. For determining the score the field must be divided into five-yard zones and the zones numbered from the goal line. The score on each run-back is the number of the zone to which the ball is returned. For example, if the man with the ball is touched between the 15- and 20-yard lines, he scores four points because he is tagged in the fourth zone.

Section II: Goals are not parallel lines

This small section includes all the goal-change games in which the goals are other than the parallel lines used in the ones already described. Most or all of the games are very similar to some others that will be described later in Class II. In these latter games, the odd man or chaser does not tag the runners as they change goals, but, instead, he tries to secure one of the goals.

1. EXCHANGE TAG
Exchange. Goal Tag. Numbers Change.

A chaser stands in the center of a circle formed by the other
players, who stand facing the center. Each circle man has a number.
The chaser, or perhaps better the leader or other neutral person,
calls out two of the numbers, whereupon the two runners with these
numbers must exchange places. As the runners are in the process
of exchanging places the chaser tries to tag either one of them; if he
fails he tries again, but if he succeeds, he trades places with the one
tagged.

Variation. Instead of two numbers, three or even more are called.

2. WATER EXCHANGE-TAG
Water Numbers-Change

This game is Exchange Tag played by swimmers. Usually it is
played in water chest deep, but it can be played by good swimmers
in deeper water.

3. PARTNER-CHANGE TAG

One man is chaser, all others are runners. The runners stand,
either in circle formation or at random, in couples holding hands,
and one of each couple is numbered one, the other two. The chaser,
or the leader, calls out either "Ones change!" or "twos change!"
When such a call is made, each number one or number two, according to the call, must leave his partner and find a new one. During
the exchange the chaser tries to tag one of the runners, and if he
succeeds he trades places with the one tagged.

4. PUSS-IN-CORNER TAG

One man is chaser, the others are runners. Each runner has a spot
or goal; this may be a circle marked on the ground, but a post, tree,
or other object is better. At will, one runner beckons to another and
the two run to exchange places, the chaser trying to tag one of them
while they are doing so. A runner who is tagged trades places with
the chaser.

This game is not the well known Puss-in-a-Corner, which is not
a tag game but a running game with no tagging. It is included in
Class II.

Division Two: Straightaway Tag

In any game of this division the players all gather close together, and, usually after some preliminary play or dialog, the chaser pursues the others as they flee. In nearly all the games, the runners flee to a line or goal, where they are immune. In any case, play is halted after a short flight, the players form again, and the process is repeated.

Section I: Chaser pursues all other players

These games are all very much alike. In each case the game begins with one man as chaser and all others as runners. After the prescribed preliminary procedure, the chaser pursues the others until they reach a safety line or goal, where they are immune. A man who is tagged on one chase replaces the chaser for the next one. There are two variations, either or both of which can be applied to any of the games in this section:

(*a*) The safety line or zone can be eliminated, each chase continuing until a man has been tagged.

(*b*) The game can be played with cumulative chasers, that is, a man who is tagged on the first chase becomes an added chaser for the second, so that he and the original chaser are both chasers for the second round. Each time that a man is tagged he becomes an added chaser, so that the number of runners is gradually reduced and that of chasers increased until the last runner is tagged; he is the winner.

These variations will not be included in the descriptions of the various games, since it is understood that they apply to all of them with a very few exceptions that are indicated in the descriptions. The games are divided into three groups on the basis of the nature of the signal at which the chase begins.

Group A: Chase Begins at Will of Chaser

(a) Chase begins without signal

1. WHO'S AFRAID OF THE BLACK MAN?
Black Man

One man is chosen to be chaser; he is the black man. All others gather around him saying: "Who's afraid of the black man?" Without any reply black man gives chase, the others fleeing to a safety line some distance away. Any runner tagged by the black man before reaching the safety line is black man for the next chase, the old black man becoming one of the runners.

2. SPIDER AND FLIES
Spider and Fly

The spider sits on the ground within a small circle which is midway between two parallel safety lines. The runners tantalize the spider by skipping and dancing around him and into his circle. Suddenly the spider jumps to his feet and gives chase, the others fleeing to either of the two safety lines. A runner who is caught trades places with the spider for the next chase.

3. CAT AND MICE

The cat stands behind a post. Others come up to the post and scratch on it. At will the cat gives chase, the mice running for safety behind a goal line. The one tagged trades places with the cat for the next chase.

4. CIRCLE SQUAT-TAG

The chaser takes a squatting position inside a two-foot circle which is in the center of a much larger circle. The runners come close to the chaser and tantalize him with remarks and motions. At will, the chaser jumps up and chases the runners, who flee to safety outside the large circle. Thus, this game is the same as Spider and Flies, except that the chaser squats instead of sitting, and that the safety area is marked by a circle instead of by two straight lines.

5. LAME FOX AND CHICKENS
Dog and Rabbit. Fox. Fox-in-the-Hole.
Hop Tag. Lame Goose.

The fox stands in the center of a ten-foot circle, the others being scattered about at random. The runners tantalize the fox by coming up to and into the circle, and taunt him with such expressions as "Lame fox, lame fox, can't catch anybody." At will the fox pursues the others; while he is in the circle he may run, but while he is outside the circle he must hop. There is no safety line and the fox continues the pursuit until he tags a runner, but he may at any time return to his circle and make a fresh start.

Variation. There is no large center circle, but only a two-foot one. The fox, in leaving the circle, may take three running steps and thereafter must hop.

6. LOG (Aquatic)

This game is the aquatic form of Spider and Flies. One swimmer floats on his back in the center of a pool, and the others swim around him as near as they dare to come. At will and without warning, the Log turns over and swims in pursuit of the others, who rush for either end of the pool where they are immune to tagging.

(b) Chase begins with signal by chaser

1. SCAT

The runners stand in line, with the safety line some distance behind them. The chaser stands facing the line of runners. The chaser leads the runners in calisthenic exercises. Suddenly he calls, "Scat," and pursues the runners, who flee to the safety line.

2. RUN, RABBIT, RUN

The hunter stands facing the runners, who are in line a short distance from him. The hunter points out any object some distance away—a tree, post, mat, wall, or the like, and then calls "Run, rabbit, run." All the runners flee toward the designated object and are safe when they reach it. The hunter pursues them and tries to tag one before he reaches the place of safety.

3. MIDNIGHT

Twelve O'clock at Night. Twelve O'clock Midnight.

The chaser stands within a small circle. The others approach as close to him as they dare to come and ask him, "What time is it?" The chaser may give any answer at all, but nothing happens except repetition of the question, unless the answer is "Midnight." When this answer is given it is the starting signal for the runners to flee to a safety line some distance away, with the chaser in pursuit.

4. THE BOILER BURST

The runners all gather around the chaser, who starts to tell a story to them. The chaser develops the story in any desired way and then, at some point he includes in the story the phrase "and the boiler burst." This phrase is the starting signal for the chaser to pursue the runners to the safety line.

GROUP B: CHASE BEGINS AT END OF RHYME OR COUNT

1. MARCHING CHASE

The chaser stands, or sits, within a small circle. He announces any number in advance. The other players march around the chaser in single file and as close to him as they dare to come. As they march they count aloud and in unison, from one up to the announced number. When they reach this number, their calling it constitutes the signal for the chaser to pursue them to a safety line.

2. RED LION

The chaser, red lion, stands within a small circle. The others advance toward him, with no definite formation, calling in unison as they advance "Red lion, red lion, come out of your den; whoever you catch will be one of your men." The last word of this rhyme is the starting signal for red lion to chase the others to a safety line.

3. KING'S LAND

This game is the same as Red Lion except for the rhyme. The chaser, king, stands inside a small circle and the others approach him, calling in unison as they advance "I'm on the king's land, the king's not at home; the king cannot catch me 'til I say 'Come'." At the last word the king pursues the others as they flee to the safety line.

Variation. The runners advance with hands joined.

GROUP C: CHASE BEGINS WHEN A CERTAIN EVENT OCCURS

1. POISON TAG

Poison

In this game there is no predetermined chaser, the chaser being determined as the game develops. Furthermore, the game cannot be played with the cumulative-chaser principle.

All players join hands in a circle, facing the center. In the center of the circle is a group of Indian clubs. The circle of players starts moving around the clubs and each player tries to make some other player knock down one of the clubs. When this happens, the one at fault becomes the chaser and he immediately pursues the others as they flee to the safety line.

Instead of a group of clubs an inner circle may be used, any person becoming chaser when he touches the floor inside this circle. The size of the inner circle or the number of clubs must be such that a circle man can be forced to knock down a club or to enter the forbidden circle without too much difficulty or delay.

2. PINCH-O

A chaser stands about four paces from and facing the runners, who are in line holding hands. The line of runners walks forward and the chaser walks backward at the same rate. As the line of runners starts forward, the man on the left squeezes the hand of the man next to him, calling "Pinch!" The second man squeezes the hand of the third, the third man the hand of the fourth, and so on to the right end of the line. When the man on the right receives the hand squeeze he calls out "O!" His call is the signal for the chase, and the line turns around and runs for a safety line in the rear, the chaser in pursuit. None of the runners calls except the first and the last, and the squeezing should be passed down the line without letting the chaser follow its progress.

3. SHEPHERD AND WOLF
Big Black Bear. Hide-and-Find. Wolf.

This is the only hide-and-seek game included among Tag Games. The other hide-and-seek games involve racing, but not tagging, and are therefore included in Class II. One man, chosen to be the original chaser, runs and hides as the other players gather around a goal with eyes closed and count to one hundred. When the count is completed, the runners go in search of the chaser. When any runner sees the chaser he calls, "Wolf!" and this word is the signal for the chase. The chaser pursues the others, who flee to the goal and safety. A man tagged by the chaser is the chaser for the next time. When the game is played with cumulative chasers, the various chasers may hide in the same place or in different places.

Variation. When a runner is tagged on his way to the goal he has the right to tag another runner, and this one still a third runner, and so on, the last one tagged being the chaser to start the next game.

4. FLOWER AND THE WIND (Variation)

The basic game of Flowers and the Wind is a team game (see Section III following), and this variation is its nonteam form. The chaser is the wind; he stands still as the others—flowers—approach him. The flowers, having agreed upon the name of a particular flower, ask the wind to guess which one it is. The wind makes his guesses until he guesses correctly. His calling of the correct name constitutes a signal for the chase, the wind pursuing the flowers to a safety line.

Section II: Chaser pursues only one or two players

In the games just described under Section I, each chase involves all the players, each man being either a chaser or a runner. In the games of Section II, this is not true, since each chase involves only some of the players, usually only two, and the other players remain inactive while they wait for their turns. These games correspond more or less to Division Two of the "Continuous Tag Games."

GROUP A: CHASER IS PREDETERMINED

In these games, as in most games, a man knows when he starts to run that he is runner, or he knows that he is chaser. This is in contrast to the games under Group B, in which a player must await developments of the chase before he knows whether to pursue or to flee.

1. SLAP-AND-RUN

Oyster Shell. Oyster Supper. Spat 'Em.
Strike-and-Chase. Tag-a-Third. Third Slap.
Touch-and-Run.

Two parallel lines are marked on the ground, 40 or 50 feet apart. All men but one stand side by side on one of these lines, each man with one hand extended forward, palm up. The odd man approaches and, after various feints, slaps one of the upturned palms. The man slapped then chases his slapper, the latter fleeing for safety behind the other of the two lines. The winner of the chase is slapper for the next chase. This game is not well adapted to the cumulative-chaser idea.

Variation 1. The odd man slaps the hands of three men in turn. The third one slapped is the chaser.

Variation 2. Two equal teams line up, one on each of the two parallel lines. One man from Team *A* slaps as above, and on the next chase a man from Team *B* is the slapper. Then a second man from Team *A* slaps, a second from Team *B*, and so on until each man has acted as slapper. The winner of each separate chase scores a point for his team, and the team with the higher score is the winner. Thus this variation is a series of games for individuals with a team method of scoring.

Variation 3. Starting with the same formation as in Variation 2, one whole team crosses over to the other team. Each man of the advancing team picks out one of the opponents and slaps him, the game continuing as in the basic form. Then the teams form again and the other team advances and slaps. The team with the larger number of wins in the individual chases is the winner. It should be noted that a chaser may tag only the man who slapped him.

2. STEEPLECHASE

Two parallel goal lines are marked 50 or 60 feet apart and between them, but nearer one than the other, is placed an upright, such as a low jump standard, with a piece of cloth placed on top of it. The players are divided into two equal teams and each team forms on one of the goal lines. This is not a true team game, but a series of individual tag games with team scoring.

At a signal, two men run, one man from each team, from their respective goal lines. The man nearer the upright runs in an attempt to obtain the cloth and return with it to his own goal line without being tagged by the other man. One point is scored for the winner of this chase and the same thing is repeated with two other men until all have run.

3. GATEBALL

All players but one stand in a circle facing the center, at intervals of three feet, the odd player standing in the center. The center man has a basketball. He tosses the ball to any one of the circle players, and the latter throws it back to the center man. Upon receiving the return throw the center man runs in an attempt to escape from the circle by going between two of the players, pursued by the circle man who threw the ball to him. The runner wins if he escapes from the circle before he is tagged. The loser of the chase is center man next time.

4. LAST-COUPLE-OUT

All players but one form a column of twos, with the odd man standing a few feet in front of the column and facing in the same direction. The odd man, the chaser, calls out "Last couple out!" whereupon the couple in the rear of the column runs forward, one player on each side of the column, trying to come together and join hands in front of the chaser. If the chaser tags either member of the couple before they join hands, he trades places with him.

GROUP B: CHASER IS NOT PREDETERMINED

These games are all essentially the same. They are for only two men at a time, with the team method of scoring. The distinctive feature of the games is that when a man starts to run he does not know whether he will turn out to be the chaser or the chased.

1. PIN SNATCH [3]
Club Snatch

An Indian club or similar object stands midway between two parallel goal lines, and two men prepare to run, one from each of the lines. At a starting signal both men run to the club, where each of them has a choice: he can win by picking up the club and returning with it to his own goal line without being tagged by the other man; or he can win by allowing the other man to pick up the club and then tagging this man before he returns to his goal line.

---

[3] Frequently the name given to a game includes the term *pin, tenpin, club,* or *Indian club,* in reference to the fact that the game is played with an Indian club or a bowling pin. Since these two items of equipment are interchangeable and any game can be played with one as well as with the other, it seems desirable that the four terms mentioned be reduced to one. For this reason, the word *pin* is used in this book. This word is chosen because it seems to be more widely used, and especially because in a few games it is so well established that to change it would violate tradition. In spite of the fact that the word *pin* is used in their names, it is recognized that the games will usually be played with Indian clubs, and the descriptions are all based on the use of Indian clubs.

The game is nearly always played with two equal teams, the men of each team running in succession until all have run, and the winner scoring a point for his team.

Variation. The captain of Team *A* sends his first runner to the start, and the captain of Team *B* selects a man to run against him. For the second round, Team *B* sends out a man and Team *A* selects an opponent for him, and so on. This method permits a certain amount of strategy.

2. SNATCH-THE-HAT

Same as Pin Snatch, except that instead of an Indian club a hat is used. It is best for the hat to be placed on an upright stick, or a chair.

3. SNATCH-THE-BEANBAG

Same as Pin Snatch, except that a beanbag, placed on a chair or other elevated place, is used.

4. SNATCH-THE-HANDKERCHIEF

Same as Pin Snatch, except that the game uses a handkerchief or other piece of cloth, placed on top of an upright stick, a pail, or a chair, or hung on the branch of a tree.

5. STEAL-THE-FLAG

Same as Pin Snatch, except that a flag stuck into the ground is used instead of an Indian club.

6. BALL SNATCH

Snatchball. Touchball.

Same as Pin Snatch, except that a ball placed on the ground is used instead of an Indian club.

7. SOCCER BALL-SNATCH

Same as Pin Snatch, except that a soccer ball is placed in the center of the field, and a man wins by kicking the ball back to his own goal line, or tagging the opponent who tries to do so. Instead of being placed in the center of the field, the ball may be rolled across the field by the leader.

8. HOCKEY BALL-SNATCH

Same as Soccer Ball-Snatch except that each runner carries a field-hockey stick and one of them tries to dribble a field-hockey ball from the center of the field to his own goal.

Variation. The same, except that the players do not have sticks when they start to run. Instead, two sticks are placed on the ground near the ball in the center of the field.

9. SWATTER SNATCH

This game starts like Pin Snatch, but includes an interesting variation. A swatter is placed in the center of the field. The two opponents run toward the swatter and either man can win by (*a*) picking up the swatter and hitting the opponent with it before the latter reaches his own base line, or (*b*) waiting for the opponent to pick up the swatter and then returning to his goal line without being hit by the opponent with the swatter.

10. PLUS-AND-MINUS PIN SNATCH
Plus-and-Minus Club Snatch

This game is the same as Pin Snatch, except for the little bit of mental arithmetic involved in determining which men shall run. Two teams line up, one on each of the goal lines, and the men of each team are numbered consecutively starting with number one. One team is designated the plus team, and the other the minus team. A neutral leader calls out two suitable numbers. The plus team adds these two numbers and the sum of them is the number of their runner. The minus team subtracts the smaller of the two numbers from the larger and the difference is the number of their runner. For example if the leader calls out "Six and two," player number eight of the plus team runs against player number four of the minus team.

11. GRAB-THE-BONE
Snatch-the-Bone

Midway between the two goal lines are two or three benches placed end to end so as to form an obstacle at least 12 feet long; on one of the benches is a softball or beanbag. Players form and the game starts as in Pin Snatch, but the ball can be snatched by one of the players only when he has one or both feet over the bench in enemy territory, either by straddling the bench or by jumping over it. The man who snatches the ball must return to his own goal line and in doing so must go over the bench, never around it.

Section III: One whole team chases another

In these games the players are divided into two equal teams. At the specified signal, all members of one team pursue and try to tag the members of the other, tagging as many of them as possible in each pursuit. The chasing team scores according to the number of opponents that they tag.

GROUP A: CHASING TEAM IS PREDETERMINED

Here all players know in advance which team will chase and which will be chased. This is in contrast to the games of Group B in which they do not know which is which until the starting signal is given.

1. TRADES

Austin Boston. New Orleans. New York.
Old Woman from the Woods.

Two equal teams face each other, each team on one of two parallel goal lines. Team *B*, selected as chaser, remains on its line and Team *A* marches up close to it. After a short dialog, Team *A* proceeds to act out the motions suggestive of a trade, occupation, or activity which they have selected in advance. The members of Team *B* make as many guesses as necessary as to the nature of the trade or activity. A correct guess is the signal for the chase; the acting Team *A* rushes back to its goal with Team *B* pursuing it and tagging as many of its members as possible. The game is repeated with the roles of the two teams reversed and the numbers tagged are compared.

Naturally the words of the dialog that precedes the acting out of the trade vary considerably, but the following example is typical and commonly used. Team *A* is the acting and Team *B* the chasing team.

TEAM A: "Here we come."
TEAM B: "Where from?"

TEAM A: "New York." (Or "New Orleans.")

TEAM B: "What's your trade?"

TEAM A: "Lemonade."

TEAM B: "How's it made?" (Or "Show us some if you're not afraid.")

At this point the acting and guessing begin. If necessary, Team A gives the initials of the trade, or other hints.

In this game, as in many others, it is sometimes specified that a man tagged in one chase becomes a member of the enemy team for the next chase. This procedure is considered unsound and is not recommended.

2. FLOWERS AND THE WIND

Two teams face each other, each team on one of two parallel lines. One team, having agreed upon the name of a flower, remains on its line, and the other marches up to it, as in Trades. The team that has marched up to the other proceeds to guess the name of the flower that has been selected. When a correct guess is made, the guessing team must flee from the other team, running back to its original line, where it is safe. The game is repeated with the roles of the teams reversed and the numbers tagged are compared.

3. MARCHING SIGNAL-CHASE

Marching Attack. Marching Tag. Signal Chase.

Two equal teams stand, each team toeing one of two parallel goal lines and all men facing in the same direction. The team in the rear marches forward at command of a neutral leader; it must keep step and keep its line straight. When the leader blows a whistle, or gives some other signal, the marching team turns and flees to its goal with the other team in pursuit. The game is repeated with the roles of the teams reversed and the numbers of men tagged are compared.

GROUP B: CHASING TEAM IS NOT PREDETERMINED

In each of these games there are two equal teams, and one chases the other, but neither team knows until it hears or sees the starting signal whether it is to be the runner or the chaser. Thus, these games resemble Pin Snatch, except that in the latter each runner has some choice in the matter, whereas in the following games he has none.

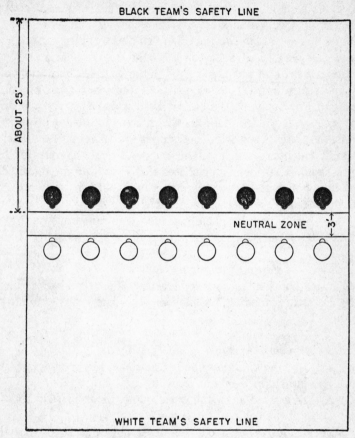

Figure 4. Black and White.

1. BLACK AND WHITE

Black and Red. Blue and White. Crows and Cranes.
Day and Night. Day or Night. Heads and Tails.
Heads or Tails. Oyster Shell. Riding-the-Snail.

The playing field is marked with two parallel goal lines about 50 feet apart. Two other lines parallel to the goal lines make a zone three feet wide across the middle. Two equal teams line up facing each other three feet apart, one team on each of the two lines across the center. In other words, the teams face each other across the three-foot center zone, and each team has a goal line 25 feet to the rear. One team is designated black, the other white. A neutral leader has a wooden disk about ten inches in diameter, painted white on one side, black on the other. The leader stands at one end of the center zone and tosses or spins the disk so that all players can see it. If the disk comes to rest with the white side up the white team must turn and flee to its goal line, the black team pursuing and tagging as many as possible. If the disk comes to rest with the black side up the black team flees with the white team in pursuit. That is, the team whose color comes up is the team that flees. Scores are kept and compared, each man tagged counting one for the tagging team. The number of chases that constitute a game is decided in advance and must, of course, be equal for the two teams in order to make the scores comparable.

This extremely popular game is played with numerous variations. The most important of these variations are as follows:

Variations in starting formation

(*a*) Instead of standing face to face, the teams stand back to back.

(*b*) Instead of standing, the players sit, or kneel, or lie supine on the ground.

Variations in starting signal

(*a*) A disk of the kind described is suspended by a cord, spun by the leader, and stopped by him at will.

(*b*) A disk is used as in the basic game, or as in (a), but the leader calls out the name of the color.

(*c*) The leader tosses a coin or other object so small that the players cannot very well see which side comes up, and calls out the side that does come up. This variation is naturally accompanied by a variation in the name of the game and of the teams. The object most commonly used is a coin and in this case the game and the teams are naturally called Heads and Tails.

(*d*) The leader rolls a large cube, which is painted white on three faces and black on the other three.

(*e*) The leader does not use a disk or other object at all, but merely calls one of the colors arbitrarily.

Variations in interpretation of signal

The rule is often used that the team whose color comes up is the chasing team, instead of being the fleeing team.

Variations in scoring methods

(*a*) A man who is tagged on one chase becomes a member of the enemy team for the next chase. The game is intended to continue until all men are on one team, but usually must be terminated earlier. This is probably the most common form of the game, but is not recommended.

(*b*) A man who is tagged drops out of the game, and the game is continued until one team is completely eliminated.

Other variations

(*a*) A man is considered tagged only when he is touched three times, or even when he is tackled so as to touch the ground with some part of the body other than the feet.

(*b*) A man who is tagged must give his tagger a ride back to the latter's goal line.

2. HEADS AND TAILS
Crows and Cranes

This game is essentially the same as Black and White, except that there is no center zone and the players do not form in line but mingle at random. Two goal lines are marked about 50 feet apart. The players are divided into two equal teams, and the teams must be distinguishable. A neutral leader tosses a coin and calls the side that comes up. If he calls "heads," all men on the heads team flee for their goal with the tails team in pursuit; if he calls "tails," the tails team flees with the heads team in pursuit. Scoring is the same as in Black and White.

3. BEARS AND BULLS

This game is the same as Black and White except for the following added feature: One member of each team, his identity unknown to the other team, carries a ring, a coin, or some other small object. If the man with this small object is among those tagged, each member of the tagging team gets a free ride to his goal line on the back of a member of the other team. If he is not among those tagged, each member of his team gets the free ride.

4. WATER BLACK-AND-WHITE
Water Crows-and-Cranes

Same as Black and White, except that it is played by swimmers
in the water. The players may line up standing in water chest deep
or swimming in deeper water.

5. STORY OF THE CROWS AND CRANES
Tale of the Crows and Cranes

This game is identical with Black and White except for the starting signal. One of the two teams is known as crows, the other as
cranes. The leader tells a story, which he makes up as he goes along.
From time to time he uses a word beginning with the sound of *cr*;
when he does so he always prolongs the sound *crrr* ... and then
completes the word. If the completed word is *crows*, then the crows
team flees with the cranes in pursuit, and vice versa. However, if
the completed word is neither *crows* nor *cranes*, nothing happens.
Sometimes the game is played with the rule that the player who
makes a false start is considered tagged, but it is more usual, and
probably better, to have no such rule, merely using the words to
keep the players alert.

6. BLACK AND BLUE
Crows and Cranes. Crows, Cranes, and Crabs.
Marching Rush.

The players are divided into two equal teams and each team lines
up on one of two parallel goal lines. One team is called black, the
other blue. The leader gives the command "Forward ... march,"
and both teams march forward in a straight line toward the middle
of the field. As the teams approach the middle of the field the leader
begins a word starting with the sound *blll* ..., prolonging it for
some time. He finally completes, perhaps after one or more false
words, either the word *black* or the word *blue*. The game continues
exactly as Black and White.

Variation. The teams are known as crows and cranes and run on
these words. The leader may, however, say "crabs", and at this
signal no one must run and one who does so is considered tagged.

Division Three: Circle or Maze Tag

The games included in Class I-B, "Noncontinuous Tag Games," are in six divisions, and much the greater part of the total is included in the two divisions that have already been described. The first of the remaining four divisions, all quite small, will now be described. In any of these games there is a runner and a chaser, as in Division Two of Class I-A, and the runner flees, not from one goal to another as in Division One, and not straightaway as in Division Two, but always in and out among the inactive players, or around a circle formed by them.

Section I: Pursuit is to a gap in a circle of players

1. CIRCLE-CHASE TAG
Slap Jack

All players but one stand in a circle facing the center and are required to look straight ahead. The odd man runs around outside the circle and, when he chooses, slaps any circle man on the back. Then he reverses direction and runs entirely around the circle, pursued by the man whom he has just slapped. If the runner reaches the vacant space in the circle without being tagged he remains there and the chaser proceeds to run around the circle and slap a man as in the beginning. If the runner is tagged, he must again proceed as in the beginning, the chaser resuming his original place in the circle.

Variation. Same, except that all players are in pairs, holding hands, each pair working as a unit exactly as the individual men do in the basic game.

2. SKIPPING CIRCLE-CHASE
Skip Tag

Same as Circle-Chase Tag, except that runner and chaser must travel only by skipping.

3. TWICE AROUND
Two Times Around

Same as Circle-Chase Tag, except that the chase continues twice around the circle.

4. HIGH WINDOWS

This game is essentially the same as Twice Around. All players but one stand in a circle, facing the center, and join hands. The odd man runs around outside the circle, slaps a circle man, and then reverses and runs with the slapped man in pursuit, as in Twice Around. The chase continues twice around the circle, and while it is in progress the circle players beside the gap hold hands and close the gap. If the runner, having gone twice around the circle, reaches the gap without being tagged, the two who were at the sides of the gap raise arms high, calling "High Windows," allowing the runner to enter the circle and be safe.

5. HAVE YOU SEEN MY SHEEP?

This is a circle-chase game in which the starting signal is a correct guess. All men but one stand in a circle facing the center. The odd man walks or runs around the outside of the circle, stops behind one of the circle men, taps him on the shoulder, and says to him, "Have you seen my sheep?" The odd man describes the clothing of one of the other players and the tapped one guesses the identity of the one described until he guesses correctly. When the correct guess is made, the odd man says "Yes" and flees around the circle, in either direction, with the guesser in pursuit. The chaser tries to tag the runner before the latter reaches the vacant space in the circle.

6. DROP-THE-HANDKERCHIEF

All players but one stand in a circle facing the center. The odd man runs around outside the circle and drops a handkerchief on the floor behind any circle player. The latter chases the one who has dropped the handkerchief, trying to tag him before he returns to the vacant space. Both may run around or through the circle.

Section II: Pursuit is in and out among inactive players

1. CIRCLE WEAVE-TAG

Follow Chase. Fox and Farmer. Fox and Gardner.
Garden Scamp. In-and-Out-the-Window.

All players but two stand in a circle facing the center, each man with both arms held horizontally sideward and with hands on the shoulders of the men next to him. Of the odd men, one is chaser and one is runner. The game starts with the chaser outside the circle and the runner inside. At a signal the runner flees and the chaser pursues. The runner weaves in and out at will, running under the outstretched arms of the circle men, and wherever he goes the chaser must follow his exact path. Since the chase must continue until the runner is tagged, it is up to the circle players, possibly with a hint from the leader, to see that it is not prolonged too much. To do this they help the chaser by raising their arms, thus facilitating his passage through the circle, but lowering them for the runner. When the runner is tagged, he becomes chaser, the old chaser joins the circle, and a new runner is appointed by the leader.

2. LINE WEAVE-TAG

Fox Chase. Hunt-the-Fox. Rabbit and Hound.

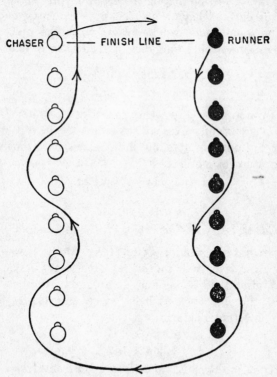

Figure 5. Line Weave-Tag.

All players stand in two parallel and equal single columns, with about five feet between the columns and three feet between the

players of each column. At a signal the front man of one column
chases the front man of the other, and must follow his exact path,
as in Circle Weave-Tag. The runner travels to the rear of his own
column and to the head of the other, weaving in and out as he goes.
He runs through each column at will, except that he must go at
least three times through each of the two columns. The chaser,
following the path of the runner, tries to tag him before he reaches
the head of the second column. The winner of this chase scores
one point for his team, the old runner and chaser fall in at the rear
of their respective columns, and the chase is repeated with the men
now at the heads of their columns. This time the chaser is from the
team represented by the first runner, and vice versa. The game
continues, the teams alternating in furnishing the chaser, until all
have run, or until all have run twice, once as chaser and once as
runner. The same game can be played with the players in two
parallel lines, one behind the other, instead of in columns.

3. GARDEN SCAMP
Knave-in-the-Garden

Same as Circle Weave-Tag, with this added feature: The runner
does various stunts and makes various motions as he runs in and out;
the chaser not only must follow the runner's path, but also must
imitate his stunts or motions.

Figure 5. Line Weave-Tag.

4. CAT AND RAT
Cat and Mouse. Sheepfold. Wolf and Sheepfold.

All players but two stand in a circle facing the center and holding
hands. The cat is outside the circle and the rat inside. The cat
chases the rat and either one may go around or through the circle
at will, but the circle players help the cat and hinder the rat by
raising and lowering their arms.

5. MAZE TAG
Fence and Bars. Fox and Hound. Hare and Hound.
Streets and Alleys.

A chaser and a runner are selected and the other players stand in a
columns of sixes or eights, each column at double-arm distance

from the next. The width of the column should be such that the group approximates a square. The players in the columns extend arms horizontally sideward and the chaser pursues the runner up and down the passages thus formed; neither may break through the arms. The leader from time to time blows a whistle or gives some other selected signal, whereupon the column players make a right face, so that the passages are now perpendicular to their former direction. This change is confusing and frustrating to both chaser and runner, but the leader should time the changes so as to favor the chaser. The chase continues until the runner is tagged; then he becomes chaser, the old chaser joins the group, and a new runner is appointed.

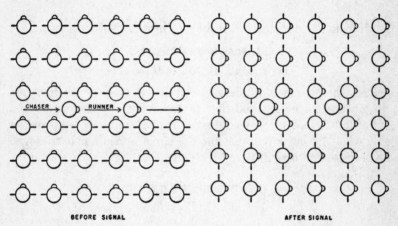

BEFORE SIGNAL   AFTER SIGNAL

Figure 6. Maze Tag.

6. LINE INTERFERENCE

A runner and a chaser are appointed. The other players form in two lines of equal numbers, each line with arms locked. These lines are not stationary, but run about at will. The chaser pursues the runner; the men in the two lines try to help the chaser. When the runner is tagged he becomes chaser, the old chaser joins one of the lines, and a new runner is appointed.

Division Four: Tantalize Tag

Tantalizing of the chaser by the runners is necessary for the success of many tag games of all kinds. That is, the runners must not do everything possible to avoid tagging, but, on the contrary, must deliberately place themselves in positions of danger and defy the tagger to catch them. In most of the games, however, the chaser does not need to wait for the runners to come to him, but is free to go out after them. The present group of tag games is unique in that the tantalizing is the basis of the whole game, for the chaser cannot go out in pursuit of the runners, but is able to tag them only when they choose to place themselves in positions of danger.

Section I: Runner has no objective in enemy territory

1. PUSS-IN-THE-CIRCLE
King's Land. Rabbit-in-the-Circle.

Puss, the chaser, is inside a circle 30 feet or more in diameter. All others are runners, and they tantalize Puss by running in and out of his circle. Puss may not leave the circle but may tag a runner only when the latter ventures into the circle. When a man is tagged he becomes the new Puss and the game continues.

2. TOMMY TIDDLER'S GROUND
Tommy Tiddler's Land

Tommy Tiddler is inside a large circle and all other players, who are runners, are outside, exactly as in Puss-in-the-Circle. The runners run into and out of the circle, coming as close as they dare to Tommy, and tantalize him by calling out, "I'm on Tommy Tiddler's ground, picking up gold and silver." A runner who is tagged by Tommy Tiddler while both are in the circle becomes the new Tommy. This game is really the same as Puss-in-the-Circle, but there is a difference as the two games are usually played. In Puss-in-the-Circle, the runners usually run in and out one at a time and continuously, the chase going on constantly. In Tommy Tiddler's Ground, there is usually a tendency for Tommy to stand still while the others come up in groups and defy him with their challenge, and then for Tommy to make a sudden start in pursuit of them.

Variation. Same, except that the field is a rectangle divided into two equal parts by a middle line. Tommy's ground is one of the halves of the field.

3. THRONE TAG

Kingdom Tag

The formation is the same as for Puss-in-the-Circle, except that the chaser, called the king, stands in the center of his circle on top of a box or other elevated platform. The runners tantalize the king by running into the circle and by slapping him whenever possible. Suddenly the king leaves his throne and goes in pursuit of the runners. The runners may be armed with swatters with which to hit the King while they are tantalizing him. A runner who is tagged becomes the new king.

4. BARLEY BREAK

A long narrow field is divided by cross lines into three equal parts; in other words, the field consists of three equal spaces in line. The center space is the barley field and in it are two chasers, who must always keep arms linked. All other players are runners and they are divided between the two end spaces. The runners are in pairs, that is, each one has a partner, but the two run independently and they do not link arms.

The runners tantalize the chasers by entering the center space and trampling down the barley. At will the chasers, with elbows linked, chase and try to tag the runners. When one runner is tagged he stands inactive in the barley field until his partner is also tagged. Then the two of them link arms and become the new chasers, the old ones joining the runners. A runner may not cross the barley field from one end space to the other, but must always return to his original space.

5. DOG TAG

Monkey Tag

One end of a rope about 15 feet long is tied to a post or other fixed object. One man, the chaser, holds the free end of this rope and must not release his grasp. All others are runners. They tantalize the chaser by running near him, and he tries to tag one without releasing the rope. One who is tagged is new chaser.

6. SIMPLIFIED PRISONER'S BASE
Prisoner's Base

This game is not true Prisoner's Base because it does not include the rule that a man may tag only an opponent who left his line before the tagger left his own. A rectangular field is divided into two equal parts by a middle line, and the game begins with one team in each half of the field. Any man may, at any time, enter the enemy's half of the field, at the risk of being tagged by one of them. When a man is tagged he is put into the enemy's prison, which is a small rectangle in one of the rear corners of the field. A runner may release a teammate from prison if he can get to him and touch him without being tagged, both the runner and the freed prisoner being permitted to return to their field without being tagged. Only one prisoner can be freed by one runner at a time. The game continues until all of one team are in prison, or, better, a time limit is set in advance and the team with the larger number of prisoners at the end of this time is the winner.

Variation. A man may win the game for his team by entering the enemy prison without being tagged and while there are no prisoners there.

Section II: Runner has objective in enemy territory

In the games of Section I, the runners enter enemy territory and run wherever they choose or dare, their only purpose being to come close to and thereby tantalize the chaser. In the games of Section II, the runners have some definite objective to accomplish, such as knocking down a pin or running around a certain object.

1. BASTE-THE-BEAR
Bear and Keeper

All players but two are runners; of the odd two, one is the bear and the other his keeper (the chaser). The keeper is the only one who tags. A rope is tied about the waist of the bear and the free end of this rope is held in one hand by the keeper. Both bear and keeper are restricted to a 20-foot square or circle. The runners venture close and, when possible without being touched by the keeper, they swat the bear, either with bare hands or with regular swatters. When a runner is tagged by the keeper he becomes bear, the bear becomes keeper, and the old keeper joins the runners.

2. GRAB-A-PIN

One man is chaser; all others are runners. The chaser is within a 20-foot circle, and standing on the floor within the circle are ten or more Indian clubs, placed at random. Runners enter the circle at will and try to carry away the Indian clubs without being tagged by the chaser. When the chaser tags one of the runners, the latter becomes chaser, the clubs are set up again, and a new game begins. If the runners succeed in stealing all the clubs before any runner is tagged, the old chaser must remain as chaser.

3. STEALING STICKS

Chips. Flag Raid. Stealing Ammunition.

The players are in two equal teams, one team in each half of a rectangular field, which has a middle line. In the middle of each end line is a square with six or eight Indian clubs standing in it. Any player may at any time run into the opponents' half of the field at the risk of being tagged. If he can succeed in reaching the square with the enemy's clubs in it, he takes one club back to his own square, being permitted to return without liability to tagging. If, however, he is tagged before reaching the square, he becomes a prisoner and must stand in the square with the enemy's clubs. If a runner reaches the enemy square while one of his teammates is prisoner there, he releases the prisoner instead of taking a club, but may release only one prisoner at a time. The game continues until all of one team's clubs are gone or until all members of one team have been taken prisoner.

4. PRISONER'S BASE

The players are in two equal teams, each behind one of two parallel goal lines about 50 feet apart. The field should also have side lines, so that it approximates a 50-foot square. Any man may, at any time, venture from the area behind his goal line and run out into the neutral area between the goal lines. When he does so, the distinctive feature of the game comes into operation: Of two opponents, only the one who last left his goal line may tag the other. That is, any man may tag an opponent who left his goal line before he himself did, and conversely may be tagged by any opponent who left after he himself did.

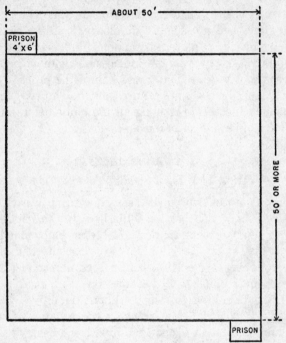

Figure 7. Prisoner's Base.

Suppose that *A, B,* and *C* are three players of one team, and that *X, Y,* and *Z* are three players of the opposing team, and assume that all players are behind their respective goal lines, with action not yet started. Now, *A* makes a preliminary dash into the field to see how far he can go and still return in safety. *X* leaves his line in pursuit of *A* and *A* retreats. Then *B* goes out after *X, Y* goes after *B,* and *C* goes after *Y.* At this point, *C* can tag *X* or *Y, B* can tag only *X, Y* can tag either *A* or *B, X* can tag *A,* but *A* can not tag anyone. *A* now withdraws from the field and *X* soon does likewise. *C* takes after *Y,* pursues him almost to the latter's goal line and is about to tag him when *Z* dashes out and tags *C.* At this point *Z* as the captor, is immune to tagging, as explained in the next paragraph. It can readily be seen that this is a most important factor in the game. In the example just given, C hoped to tag Y before he himself should be tagged by Z or by another of Y's teammates, and if he had succeeded in doing so he could not have been tagged by Z. Thus, this little portion of the game was not just a pursuit of Y by C, but it was at the same time a contest between C and Z to see which one could make a tag first.

When a man tags an opponent, both are temporarily immune to tagging and the tagger proceeds to take his victim to the tagger's prison, the prison being a rectangle marked on the ground behind, and at one end of, the goal line. The prisoner remains in the prison and his captor returns to the game. Any prisoner may be freed by a teammate who succeeds in reaching and touching him, and both are immune to tagging while they return to their base line. Only one prisoner can be released at one time by a teammate. If two or more men are in the same prison, only one of them is required actually to stay in the prison, the others stretching out in line holding hands, reaching as far as possible into the field. Thus, as the number of prisoners becomes greater, it becomes easier for one of them to be released.

Variation. A rectangular goal is marked behind the center of each goal line. Any man can win the game for his team by running into this goal while he is still free.

5. EVERY MAN IN HIS OWN DEN

Den. Den-Tag Elimination.

Each player has a well marked den, that is, a post, circle on the ground, or the like. Any man may leave his den at any time and venture near some other den, or any place on the field, at the risk of being tagged. The right to tag and vulnerability to tagging are determined as in Prisoner's Base; that is, of two opponents only the one who last left his den may tag the other. When a man is tagged he is a prisoner of the tagger; he remains inactive in the vicinity of the tagger's den while the tagger continues with the game. When a man with prisoners is tagged, he and all his prisoners become prisoners of the new tagger. The game continues until one man has all the others as prisoners.

Variation. When a man is tagged he becomes a teammate of his tagger, he and the tagger working independently from the tagger's den. The game continues until all players are on one team.

Division Five: Home Tag

The games of Division Five are similar to those of Division Two in that in each chase the pursued runner seeks safety at a certain line or goal. The distinctive feature of the games in Division Five is that the safety goal is at or near the starting position, so that instead of fleeing to a distant place of safety, the runner must go out from the starting line or home and find his way back home without being tagged in the process.

1. DUCK-ON-THE-ROCK
Duck-on-a-Rock

A throwing line is marked 25 to 40 feet from a large rock called the duck rock. One man, the chaser, takes a position near the duck rock, and all others stand on the throwing line. Each player, including the chaser, has a "duck," that is, a smooth round stone slightly smaller than a baseball. To start the game the chaser sets his duck on top of the duck rock. Then the other men, taking regular turns, throw their ducks at the chaser's duck, trying to knock it off the rock. After a man has thrown his duck he must eventually get it and carry it back to the throwing line, at the risk of being tagged by the chaser. He may do this at any time, and may delay as long as he wishes, except that if a man does not have his duck ready to throw when his turn comes, he is considered tagged and trades places with the chaser. There is, however, one situation in which a thrower is most likely to attempt the retrieval of his duck. This situation arises when one of the throwers succeeds in knocking the chaser's duck off the rock, for when this happens the chaser is required to secure his own duck and replace it on the rock before he has the right to chase and tag one of the throwers. The man who knocks the duck off is immune to tagging.

To determine which man shall be the first chaser, all throw their ducks from the throwing line, each trying to cause his duck to come to rest as near the rock as possible. The one farthest away from the rock determines the first chaser; sometimes it is ruled that if two ducks "kiss," that is, come to rest in contact with each other, neither of the throwers is the first chaser.

Variation 1. The game is best played in the fields with real rocks. However, substitutes can be improvised and the game can be played with beanbags or softballs as ducks, and with a box, a stool, or even an Indian club, as the rock.

Variation 2. The duck rock is surrounded by a circle with a diameter of about 20 feet, and a thrower can be tagged only while he is within this circle.

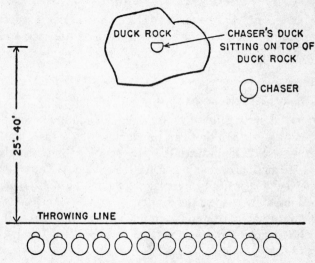

Figure 8. Duck-on-the-Rock.

Variation 3. A thrower is liable to tagging only after he picks up his rock, and accordingly may go to his duck and stand beside it until he is ready to run. This rule is sometimes varied to permit the thrower to place a foot on his duck. He is liable to tagging when he removes the foot.

Variation 4. Instead of throwing in turn, one man at a time, the throwers all throw at the same time, on a signal. Then they must all run for their ducks whether the chaser's duck is dislodged or not.

2. CIRCLE DUCK-ON-THE-ROCK

One man is chosen chaser and the others are all throwers. All, including the chaser, stand in a large circle, which surrounds the duck rock. The chaser's duck is on the rock. The others throw their ducks in turn exactly as in Duck-on-the-Rock. Nothing happens until the chaser's duck is knocked off the rock; then all throwers must run for their ducks, and each must return to his former place in the circle. The chaser must run for his duck and replace it on the rock before he can tag any thrower. Any man tagged by the chaser is the new chaser; if none is tagged, the same man is chaser again.

3. SNOWBALL DUCK-ON-THE-ROCK

This game is exactly the same as Duck-on-the Rock, except that it is played in the snow with a large snowball as the rock and small snowballs as ducks.

4. PIN DUCK-ON-THE-ROCK

This form of Duck-on-the-Rock uses as a target an Indian club that stands about ten feet from a wall, and requires each thrower to have an old softball that can be identified by initials marked on it, or otherwise. Taking turns, the players roll balls at the club and the game is continued exactly as Duck-on-the-Rock. The chaser does not have a duck; instead of replacing a duck he must replace the Indian club before chasing the runners.

Variation. Each player rolls a dumbbell instead of a ball at the club. The difficulty of making the dumbbell roll straight adds interest to this variation.

5. CENTER BASE

One man stands in the center of a circle formed by the other players, who stand facing the center. The center man has a ball, either a basketball or a softball. He throws this ball to any circle man and then flees from the circle. The circle man catches the ball, carries it to the center of the circle where he places it in a one-foot circle on the ground, and then sets out after the center man. The object of the center man is to get back to the ball and touch it without being tagged. If he succeeds he acts as thrower again, but if he is tagged, his tagger is next thrower.

6. CAP TAG

Ball Chase. Ball-in-Cap. Cap Chase.

This game requires all players to have caps, which they place upside down on the ground in two or more rows about 20 feet from a throwing line. A selected player throws a small object at the caps, continuing until the object comes to rest in one of the caps. A ball is often specified as the small object, but small stones are probably best. When the thrown object lands in a cap, the owner of the cap flees, with all the other players in pursuit, until he is tagged or until he secures immunity by returning to his cap and touching it. If the cap owner is successful he is next thrower; if not, the same thrower throws again.

Variation 1. The cap owner is chased, not by all the others, but only by the thrower.

Variation 2. Whether he wins or loses, the cap owner is next thrower. If he loses, he has a point against him and if he gets three such points he must pay a penalty.

7. PEBBLE CHASE

One player holds a small pebble between the palms of his hands and the others gather around him in an informal group, each with his hands extended forward, palm to palm. The one with the pebble goes to one player after another and passes his hands downward between the hands of the others, as in Button, Button. He must do this in such a way that the others have difficulty in knowing whether the pebble has been retained or passed on. When the other men discover that the pebble has been passed on they give chase to the new holder of the pebble, who can save himself only by returning to the one from whom he received the pebble and handing it back to him. If the one with the pebble wins the chase he becomes the one to pass the pebble for the next chase. If not, the same one passes the pebble again. The loser may be required to pay a forfeit.

8. THROUGH-THE-CIRCLE

One player stands near a five-foot circle marked on the ground, and the others stand behind a line about 30 feet away. At a signal, the player on the right of the line begins to run, with the odd man (the one near the circle) in pursuit. The runner may go anywhere, but sooner or later he must touch the circle with one or both feet and must eventually return to the starting line, all without being tagged by the chaser. If the runner wins the chase he becomes chaser, and the old chaser joins the others. If the chaser wins he is chaser again.

Division Six: No-Flight Tag

The games of this small class are all tag games, but the element of flight and pursuit has been reduced, by one restriction or another, so much as to be almost nonexistent. In about half the games, true chasing is eliminated by the fact that some or all of the players are blindfolded; in the other half by other restrictions.

Section I: One or more players are blindfolded

Except where some other method is specified (as in Tap-the-Can, for example), a player should be blindfolded by a clean handkerchief or other cloth used only for this purpose. In certain situations a player may be blindfolded with his own handkerchief. It is possible, but usually not advisable, to dispense with the cloth entirely, merely instructing the one to be blindfolded to close his eyes.

1. TAP-THE-BUCKET

One man, the chaser, is blindfolded by a bucket of suitable size placed over his head. He chases any or all of the others, who run at random and tantalize the chaser by tapping his bucket. One who is tagged trades places with the chaser.

2. BLIND HOP-TAG

The chaser is blindfolded, the others not. The chaser runs, but all others must hop. If one of the runners touches the floor with his raised foot or loses his balance and falls, he must cease traveling and stand still until he is tagged or until a new man becomes chaser. Any runner who is tagged by the chaser, either while standing or while hopping, trades places with the old chaser. This game is best played in a restricted area or with boundary lines.

3. BLIND PARTNER-TAG

This game is much like Blind Hop-Tag. The chaser is blindfolded and may run; the runners are not blindfolded and must hop. The chaser has a helper who is not blindfolded; the helper may not tag runners or interfere with them, but he gives oral directions to the chaser. A runner who is tagged becomes helper, the old helper becomes chaser, and the old chaser joins the runners.

Variation. The chaser carries a swatter and tags a runner by hitting him with it.

4. BLIND LINE-TAG

The chaser is blindfolded, the runners are not. The runners hold hands in one long line. The chaser pursues the linked runners, and one tagged by him trades places with him. If the line breaks, the one responsible is considered tagged.

5. CIRCLE BLIND-CHASE

Circle Blind-Guess. Circle Blindman's-Tag.

The chaser is blindfolded, the runners are not. The chaser stands in the center of a circle formed by the runners, who stand facing the center with hands joined. The circle men must not release hands but may run as much as possible without doing so. When the chaser tags a circle player he runs hands over him and tries to guess his identity. If the chaser makes a correct guess in two tries he trades places with the one tagged; otherwise he is chaser again.

6. CIRCLE BLIND SWAT-TAG

Circle Blind-Swat. Circle Blindman's Swat-Tag.

This game starts in the same way as Circle Blind-Guess, except that the chaser carries a swatter and tags a circle man by hitting him with it. When a circle man is hit with the swatter, he grasps one end of it and must answer three questions asked by the chaser. The latter tries to identify him by his voice. If the chaser guesses the identity of the one tagged he trades places with him; otherwise he is chaser again.

7. STILL POND, NO MORE MOVING
Still Pond. Still Water, Stop.

The chaser is blindfolded and the others, not blindfolded, gather close about him. The chaser turns around rapidly three times calling, as he finishes, "Still pond, no more moving." The other players run away as the chaser turns around, but must stand still at the command. However, any one of the runners may take one additional step at any time. The chaser tries to find any runner and identify him. When he succeeds, he and the one caught trade places. The number of turns made by the chaser and the number of extra steps allowed to the runners may be varied from those given.

8. BLIND TEN-STEPS
Blindman's Ten-Steps. Ten Steps.

The chaser is blindfolded, the runners not. The chaser turns around three times and calls "Stop." The runners, who were originally scattered at random, flee in any direction, but must stand motionless at the command. The chaser then takes ten steps, long or short, in any direction, in an attempt to tag one of the runners. If he succeeds he trades places with the one tagged; if he fails he is chaser again.

9. BLINDMAN'S BUFF
Circle Blindman's-Buff. Feeling Blindman's-Buff.

The chaser, blindfolded, is in the center of a circle formed by the others, who hold hands and are not blindfolded. The circle moves about the chaser in either direction and stops when the chaser claps his hands three times. The chaser then points toward the circle with his finger. If he points to a gap in the circle he remains chaser and the process is repeated. However, when he points to a player in the circle the latter enters the circle and the chaser pursues him. When the chaser catches the runner he must identify him by running hands over him. If the chaser does not succeed in identifying the runner he is chaser again, but if he succeeds he and the runner trade places. The chaser may be given only one chance, or he may be given two or three, to name the runner.

Variation. The identification of the runner is omitted and the chaser must only tag the runner.

10. BLIND BELL
The Belled Cat. Bell-the-Cat.

In this game there is only one runner and all the other players are chasers. All the chasers are blindfolded, but the runner is not. The runner has a bell, which he carries in his hand or on a string around his neck and which he must keep ringing continuously. The chasers all try to tag the runner and the one who does so trades places with him.

11. JACK AND JILL
Jacob and Jacobine. Jacob and Rachel.
Ruth and Jacob.

Only two players are active at any time; they are in the center of a circle formed by the others holding hands. The circle players should stand close together to make the circle rather small. Of the center players, Jack is blindfolded but Jill is not. Jack, trying to tag Jill, calls out repeatedly "Where are you, Jill?" and Jill must always answer promptly. When Jill is caught she is blindfolded, a new Jack is chosen by her or by the leader, and the game is repeated, this time with Jill trying to tag Jack. This game is intended for mixed groups of boys and girls, with the part of Jack always taken by a boy and that of Jill by a girl. It can, of course, be played by an unmixed group using the same names, or different names can be used, so as to correspond to the sex of the players; for example, Jack and Jim, or Ruth and Rachel.

Variation. Both players are blindfolded.

12. RATTLESNAKE

Only two players are active at one time; they are in the center of a circle formed by the others. Of the two in the center, the hunter is blindfolded and the rattlesnake is not. The rattlesnake carries a can containing pebbles and must keep it rattling constantly. When the hunter catches the snake, he joins the circle, the snake becomes hunter and a new snake is selected from the circle players.

Variation. Two or more hunters chase the snake, instead of only one.

13. DEER STALKING

Only two men are active, a hunter and a deer, and both are blind-folded. The game requires a large table of some sort. The two players take places at opposite ends of the table with hands on the table. At a signal, the hunter moves at will around the edge of the table and the deer evades him by also moving about the table; neither may leave the table. When the deer is tagged he becomes hunter, the old hunter withdraws, and a new deer is appointed.

14. BLIND NUMBERS-CHANGE

Blindman's Number-Change. Change Places. Exchange.
French Blindman's-Buff.

A chaser, blindfolded, stands in the center of a circle formed by the other players, standing and not blindfolded. Each player has a number. The center player calls any two numbers and the players with these numbers must immediately trade places. If the chaser can tag either of them as they exchange, he trades places with him; otherwise he calls two other numbers.

Variation 1. The circle players sit in chairs.

Variation 2. The chaser may call either two or three numbers.

Variation 3. The chaser carries a swatter and tags a runner by hitting him with it.

15. BOSTON

Same as Blind Numbers-Change, except that the center man may, when he wishes, call "Boston," instead of calling two numbers. When he does so, every circle player must find a new place; in this case, the chaser may win either by tagging one of the moving players or by getting one of the places. This game requires well-marked places for the circle players and is therefore most conveniently played with the players sitting in chairs.

Section II: No players are blindfolded

As already explained, the games of Division Six are games of tag, but the element of flight and pursuit is restricted to the point where it scarcely exists. In the games just described in Section I, either the chaser or the runner is blindfolded; a blindfolded man may chase another in a fashion, but the chasing is so restricted that it justifies a special classification of the games. There are a few other games in which none of the players is blindfolded, but in which there is no true flight and pursuit; these games are described in Section II.

1. STOOPING HEADS-AND-TAILS

Black and White. Blue and White. Day and Night.
Heads and Tails.

Players are divided into two equal teams, distinguishable from each other, and all are scattered at random over the play area. One team is designated heads, the other, tails. A neutral leader tosses a coin and, according to its fall, calls loudly either "Heads", or "Tails." The team with the name called is immediately subject to tagging by the other team, but can become immune to tagging by stooping low. For example, if the leader calls, "Heads," then the men of the tails team immediately rush at those of the heads team, tagging as many as possible before they stoop. At the same time, the men of the heads team try to evade tagging by stooping deeply; they are not permitted to run. Each man tagged counts one point for the tagging team. Scores are kept and compared at any time selected by the leader, provided the number of chases has been the same for the two teams.

This game is the same as Heads and Tails (page 63), except that players escape tagging by stooping instead of by flight. Variations in the method of scoring or in other procedures can be used as described for Black and White (page 61).

2. HUNT-THE-SLIPPER

All players but one sit in a circle close together, with feet drawn up and knees raised so as to form a tunnel under the circle of knees. They pass a slipper or other object from one to another under the knees, trying to keep it hidden. The odd player stands outside the circle; he tries to keep track of the slipper and to tag the player who has it. When he succeeds he trades places with the one tagged.

3. RING-ON-THE-STRING

One man stands in the center of a circle formed by the others, who sit or stand. The circle players have an endless piece of cord, and each one holds it with both hands. On the cord is a ring, which the circle players pass from one to another, trying to keep its location concealed from the center man. The latter tries to locate the ring and to tag the one who is holding it at the moment. When he succeeds, the one tagged becomes center man and the tagger joins the circle.

4. CIRCLE TAG

One man stands in the center of a circle formed by the others, who stand facing the center. The circle players have a ball which they throw from one to another at will; a basketball is most commonly used but a medicine ball is good, and any ball at all may be used. As the circle men pass the ball the center man tries to tag any one of them while he is holding it. When he succeeds, the one tagged becomes center man and the old center man replaces him. If the ball is dropped and a man is tagged as a result, the leader decides whether the fault was with the catcher or with the thrower, and the one at fault is considered tagged. With skilled players, the circle tends to have too much advantage over the center man and this advantage should be reduced by an adjustment in the game. The easiest method is to use a medicine ball, which is handled more slowly than a basketball. An alternative is to restrict the passing; it may be ruled that the pass must be to the first or second man and not farther, or even that it must be to the first man only, either right or left.

5. SWAT-THE-FLY

One man is within a circle formed by the others, who stand facing the center, shoulder to shoulder, and with hands behind their backs. The circle men have a swatter which they pass from one to another behind their backs, trying to keep its location hidden from the center man. When possible, circle men hit the center man with the swatter. The center man tries to keep track of the swatter and to tag the circle man who has it. When he succeeds, the man tagged becomes center man and the old center man replaces him.

6. STOOP TAG
Floor Tag

One man is within a circle formed by the others. The center man tries to tag any one of those in the circle, but a circle man is immune from tagging when he is in the squat or stoop position. The circle men must remain in place. The center man trades places with a circle man whom he tags.

7. CHARLEY-OVER-THE-WATER

One man, Charley, is within a circle formed by the other players. The circle players join hands and dance around Charley, reciting or singing this rhyme:

> Charley over the water,
> Charley over the sea.
> Charley catch a blackbird,
> Can't catch me.

At the word *me,* Charley rushes at the circle players and tries to tag any one of them. The latter can become immune to tagging by assuming the squat or stoop position. Any one tagged by Charley before stooping trades places with Charley. This game is merely a dramatic form of Stoop Tag.

8. FROG-IN-THE-SEA
Frog-in-the-Middle

One player, the frog, sits on the floor with his legs crossed and does not leave this position. The other players tantalize the frog by coming as close as they dare, dancing and milling around, and calling "Frog in the sea, can't catch me," or "Frog in the ocean, frog in the sea, frog in the middle, can't catch me." Without leaving his seat the frog tries to tag one of the others. When he succeeds, the two trade places. Like many other games, this one is completely dependent for its success on the readiness of the players to run risks in tantalizing the tagger.

9. SLING-THE-MONKEY

One man, the monkey, has one end of a rope tied about his waist and the other end attached to an overhead support, so that his weight is largely upheld by the rope and his feet barely touch the ground. The other players run in and out, slapping the monkey as often as they dare, and the monkey tries to slap one of them. When he succeeds, the one slapped trades places with the monkey.

Variation. All use swatters.

10. WINK

Chairs are arranged in a circle. Every chair has a player standing behind it, and every chair except one has a player sitting in it. The player who stands behind the empty chair winks at any sitting player and the latter tries to slip out of his chair and into the empty one without being tagged by the player behind him. If he is tagged he must remain in the old chair, if not he sits in the new one. The guards behind the chairs must keep hands at sides until the wink is given.

Class II

RUNNING GAMES WITH NO TAGGING

The games thus far described all have the distinctive element of flight and pursuit, one man trying to tag or capture another. Most running games are of this kind, but there are other running games that, while they have much in common with the tag games, do not include tagging. Such running games constitute Class II.

Division One: Freeze-Out Games

In a freeze-out game, the players run to secure or to exchange objects, spots or partners; but there is always one player too many and consequently one must be unsuccessful. He is "frozen out."

Section I: All rush to secure objects, spots, or partners

In these games there is no odd man or chaser. At the start no man has an object, spot, or partner, but at a signal all rush at the same time, each trying to obtain one. One player must be left or frozen out; he is penalized or eliminated and the game is repeated.

Group A: All Rush to Secure Spots

1. CIRCLE RUSH

The Hunter. Huntsman. Jack Be Quick. Music Rush. Porpoise and Fishes. Rushing-the-Spots.

Circles or spots are marked on the ground, one circle fewer than the players; they may be placed at random, or in a single or double row. All players march in single file around the circles. A neutral leader blows a whistle or gives some other signal, and all rush for the spots, the first man to touch a spot with either foot being entitled to it. One man is necessarily left without a spot; he has a point scored against him and the game is repeated. When a man has three points against him he must pay a penalty. The signal may be "Bang," in which case the game is called The Hunter or Huntsman. The players may pretend to be fish, in which case the game is called Porpoise and Fishes and the signal will be "Dive in!" or "A whale is coming." The players may be required to trot rather than to walk.

Variation 1. The loser, that is, the man left without a spot, is eliminated from the game, one of the spots is removed, and the game continues until only one man is left. This is probably the more common form of the game, but it is not recommended.

Variation 2. The players march or trot in time to music and rush for the spots when the music stops; this variation is usually called Music Rush.

2. SITTING CIRCLE-RUSH

Exactly the same as Circle Rush, except that a player must sit on a spot in order to claim it.

3. MUSICAL CHAIRS

Going-to-Jerusalem. Last-One-Out. Marching-to-Jerusalem. Music Rush.

Chairs are placed in a single row with the even-numbered chairs facing in one direction and the odd-numbered chairs facing in the opposite direction. The number of chairs is one less than the number of players. All march in single file around and around the row of chairs, to the music of a piano, phonograph, or other instrument. Suddenly the music stops and each player tries to sit on one of the chairs. The one who is left without a chair has a point scored against him and the game is repeated with all players participating. When one has three points against him he must pay a forfeit.

Variation 1. The player left without a chair is eliminated from the game, one chair is removed and the game is repeated until only one player is left.

Variation 2. The chairs may be placed in a double row, back to back, or they may be placed in a circle, facing outward.

Variation 3. With a large group of players, two chairs may be removed each time.

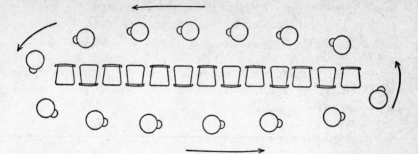

Figure 9. Musical Chairs.

4. MOUNTED MUSICAL-CHAIRS

This game is the same as Musical Chairs except that it is played by men on horseback. Chairs are used and when the music stops each man must dismount and sit in a chair, holding his horse by the reins.

5. TREE RUSH

Squirrels in Trees

About two thirds of the players stand in pairs facing each other and holding hands, thus forming trees. The other players are the only ones who are active, and they must be exactly one more than the number of trees. The active players march or trot around the trees, in single file, and when a signal is given each tries to get into a tree. Any signal may be used, but it is best if the players march to music and use the stopping of the music as the signal. The one who is left without a tree has a point scored against him and pays a forfeit when he has three points; or the player left out may be eliminated, as in Circle Rush. This game is the same as Circle Rush except that trees are used instead of circles or spots. Each player who gets into a tree should trade places with one of the tree players.

6. COME WITH ME

Come Along

All players except one stand in a circle facing counter-clockwise, with right arms extended sideward. The odd man walks around outside the circle, grabs an arm, and says, "Come with me." The player whose arm is grabbed falls in behind the odd man and the two continue around the circle. The second man grabs an arm of a circle player and the latter falls in behind. This continues, the rear one of the marching group grabbing an arm and thus adding to the group. Suddenly a neutral leader calls, "Go home!" and all the players in the marching group rush for the vacant places in the circle. Since there is one spot too few, one player is left without a spot. He is odd man for the next game, and, in addition, may be required to pay a forfeit.

Variation. The circle players sit on the floor.

GROUP B: ALL RUSH TO SECURE OBJECTS

1. SNATCH-A-PIN
Snatch-a-Club

Indian clubs, one less than the number of players, are placed upright in a small circle on the floor. The players march in single file around the clubs, keeping step with any available kind of music. When the music stops, each man dives for a club. The man left without a club is eliminated or has a point scored against him. If the music is not available, players may march without music and any signal may be used. Other objects may be used instead of Indian clubs.

2. MUSICAL MARBLES

All players march to music, in bare feet, around a circle in which are placed marbles or jacks, one less than the number of players. When the music stops each man tries to pick up a marble with his feet; he may use either foot, or the right or left may be specified. The game is continued as in Snatch a Pin.

3. OBJECT RUSH
Cap Rush. Club Rush. Pin Rush.

All players stand on a starting line. Some distance away, on a line parallel with the starting line, are Indian clubs, old softballs, or other objects, one less than the number of players; all the objects need not be the same. At a signal, all run for the distant line and each tries to secure one of the objects. Two players may struggle for one object, but when one obtains definite possession of it, it may not be taken away from him. The player left without an object is eliminated or has a point scored against him.

4. MARCHING OBJECT-RUSH
Odd-Man-Out

Players stand in two lines, back to back, with a row of objects between them. At a signal all march forward. The leader must see that the two lines of players are straight and that they advance at the same rate. When the lines have become well separated, the leader blows a whistle and all break ranks and rush back for the objects. The game is continued in the same way as Object Rush.

5. OBJECT RUSH (Team Form)
Grab Ball. Odd Bag.

This game is Object Rush with the team method of scoring. The players are in several teams, each team in single file with its front man on the starting line. A row of objects, one fewer than the teams, is placed on a distant line that is parallel with the starting line. At a signal, the front men of the respective teams run forward for the objects, exactly as in Object Rush. After this race the first runners step aside, the objects are replaced, and the second men run, then the third, and so on until all have run. Each loser scores a point against his team and the team with the low score wins.

Variation. All men form a single line, side by side, all the members of each team together. Each team numbers off. The leader calls out any number and his call is the signal for all those with this number to run as in Object Rush. Then other numbers are called until all have run, and the game is scored as above. Care must be taken to spread out the objects so that all will have an equal chance at them.

6. ELIMINATION OBJECT-RUSH
Club Chase

This game may appear to be a team form of Object Rush, but it is not. It is an individual game run in heats, with elimination of players. The players form in a column of eights (or any other desired number). The men of the first rank run a heat of Object Rush exactly as in the basic game, and the loser is eliminated from the game. The men of the second rank then run a heat, and so on until all ranks have run. The survivors take their original places, thus forming the original column of eights except that there is one gap in each rank. The ranks close in to the right, thus forming a column of sevens. The men in the column of sevens repeat the whole process from the beginning, so that they finish with a column of sixes; the column of sixes reduces itself to a column of fives, and so on until only a single file is left. These men then form on the starting line and run a series of heats, with one man eliminated each time, until only the champion is left.

7. DUCK-ON-ROCK OBJECT-RUSH

Goal Duck-on-the-Rock. Spot Duck-on-the-Rock.

A circle 40 to 60 feet in diameter is marked on the ground with a large rock or other elevated object in the center. All players stand toeing the circle and facing the center. Each player, except one odd man, has a stone somewhat smaller than a baseball, the odd man being empty-handed. A tin can, block of wood, or other object easily distinguished from the stones, is placed on top of the rock to serve as a "duck." The circle men, except the odd man, throw their stones one at a time and in regular order, trying to knock the duck off the rock. When one succeeds, all who have thrown, and also the odd man, rush for the stones, each trying to obtain one. Since the number of runners is one greater than the number of stones, one player is necessarily left without a stone, and he is odd man next time. Beanbags or other objects may be substituted for the stones.

GROUP C: ALL RUSH TO SECURE PARTNERS

1. FIRE-ON-THE-MOUNTAIN

All players except one stand in two concentric circles, with the odd man in the center. The center man calls out "Fire on the mountain, run, run, run!" At this signal the inner circle remains standing and the outer circle runs at a brisk trot around the other in a counterclockwise direction. Suddenly the center man blows a whistle or gives some other signal, and at the same time jumps in front of one of the men in the inner circle. Each man in the outer circle rushes to do the same thing, that is, to jump in front of one of the men in the inner circle. The one who fails is odd man for the next game.

2. MERRY-GO-ROUND

All players except one are in two concentric circles, with the odd man in the center. Keeping time to music, the inner circle marches in one direction and the outer circle in the opposite direction. Suddenly the music stops. Whereupon each man tries to grasp right hands with any player in the other circle; at the same time the odd man tries to grasp right hands with any man of either circle. The player left without a partner is odd man next time.

3. GROUPS

Players are scattered at random. A neutral leader calls out any number by which the number of players is not exactly divisible, and then all players rush to form groups of the number called, each group in a circle with hands joined. The one or ones left out are eliminated or have points scored against them.

Section II: Players exchange places or partners

In games of this section, each player except one has a place or partner, and, usually on a signal, he must leave his place or partner and get another. But, as in a game of Section I, there is always one place or partner too few, and one player is left out.

GROUP A: ALL EXCHANGE AT SIGNAL

1. ALL CHANGE

Change All. Goal Tag.

All players but one stand in a circle, each with his place marked by a stone, circle, or the like, the odd man standing in the center of the circle. The center man calls "All change!" and at this signal each circle man must leave his place and get another, the center man also trying to get a place. The man left without a spot is the next center man. He may also have a point scored against him and be required to pay a penalty for three points.

Variation. The players may sit in chairs and change seats.

2. SQUIRRELS IN TREES

Squirrel and Trees. Squirrel in the Trees. Squirrel in
Tree. Squirrel in Trees. Squirrels in the Trees.

All players except one stand in groups of four, three forming a
tree by placing hands on one another's shoulders, the fourth standing
inside as a squirrel. The groups may be scattered at random or may
be in a circle. The odd man is a squirrel without a tree. At a signal
from the odd man or from a neutral leader, each squirrel must leave
his tree and try to get another, the odd man also trying to get a tree.
The one who is left without a tree is odd man next time. At frequent
intervals, one of the tree men should trade places with the squirrel.

Variation. Each tree is formed by only two players instead of three.

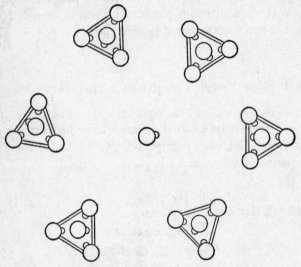

Figure 10. Squirrels in Trees.

3. CHANGE RIGHT OR LEFT
Boston

The same as All Change, except that the signal is either "Change
right" or "Change left," and each player must move in the direction
called for by the signal.

4. POISON SPOT
Poison Seat

This game is the same as All Change, except that there is no odd man. All stand or sit in a circle, each with his place marked. Then one of the occupied places is marked somehow to indicate that it is "poisoned." The signal for exchanging places is given and each man must find a new place, but no one may take the poisoned place. Since there is no odd man in this game, it is usually played by eliminating the one who is left out and continuing until only one is left. It is recommended, however, that it be played with the penalty system.

5. BACK-TO-BACK

All players except one are in pairs scattered at random, the two members of each pair standing back to back with elbows hooked. The odd man calls "Change," and each man must find a new partner and hook elbows with him, back to back. The odd man tries to get a partner, and if he succeeds, the man left out is odd man next time.

6. VIS-À-VIS

All players except one stand in pairs scattered at random. The odd man gives commands which the others must follow, such as "Face to face," "Knee to knee," "Hands on hips," "Back to back," "Join right hands," "Join both hands." Sooner or later, the odd man calls "Vis-à-vis," and then each man must find a new partner and join hands with him. The odd man tries to get a partner, and the player left out is odd man next time.

7. THE CAR WAS WRECKED
The Boiler Burst

Same as All Change, except the signal. The odd man makes up a story, which he tells to the others. Sooner or later he includes in the story the words, "The car was wrecked." This is the signal for all to trade places, the odd man trying to get one of the places. Other words, such as "The boiler burst," may be agreed upon instead of the ones given.

8. STAGECOACH

An odd man stands in the center of a circle formed by the other players sitting in chairs. Each player has the name of some part of a stagecoach, of its possible contents, or of something else likely to be connected with a stagecoach journey. The odd man tells a story to the others, frequently including one of the names given to the players. When a player's name is called he must immediately rise, turn around once, and then sit down, and one who fails or is too slow has a point against him. If the odd man includes the word "stagecoach" in the story, all must rise and turn around. Sooner or later he includes the words "the stagecoach upset." This is the signal for all to trade places and for the odd man to try to get one of the places.

GROUP B: TWO OR THREE EXCHANGE AT SIGNAL

1. NUMBERS CHANGE

By the Numbers Change

All players except one stand in a circle facing the center, with the odd man standing in the center. Each man has a number. The odd man calls any two of these numbers and the players with the numbers called must trade places. The odd man also tries to get one of the places. The man left without a place is the next odd man.

Variation 1. Players sit in a circle, either on the floor or on chairs.
Variation 2. Three numbers are called instead of two.

2. HOPPING NUMBERS-CHANGE

Same as Numbers Change, except that all men must travel only by hopping.
Variation. The odd man must hop, but the others may run.

3. TRIPLE CHANGE

All players except one stand in a circle with the odd man in the center. The circle players count off by threes. The center man calls "One," "Two," or "Three," and all with the number called try to trade places while the odd man tries to get one of the places. The one left out is the new odd man, the old one taking the place and number of the loser.

Variation. There are three men in the center and they count off. The number one center man calls "One" and he (not the other two center men) tries to get a place as the "ones" in the circle trade places. Then the number two center man calls "Two" and the number three center man calls "Three."

4. MAILMAN
Parcel Post

The same as Numbers Change, except that the circle players have the names of cities, instead of numbers. The center man calls the names of two, or three, cities, and the men with these names must try to trade places as the center man also tries to get one of the places.

5. FRUIT BASKET
Parcel Post

All players except one stand in a circle with the odd man in the center, each man having the name of some fruit. The center man calls the names of any two fruits and tries to get one of the places as the players called trade places. Occasionally the center man may call, "Fruit basket upset" and then all must trade places.

Variation 1. Players have names of cities, as in Mailman, instead of fruits. The center man calls the names of two cities, or, as a signal for all players to trade places, "Parcel Post."

Variation 2. Players sit in the circle instead of standing. They may sit on the floor or on chairs.

GROUP C: PLAYERS EXCHANGE AT WILL

1. FINDING-A-HOUSE
The First of May. House-Hiring. Puss-in-the-Corner.

Each player except one has a corner, post, tree, or other identifiable spot or place; it could be merely a circle on the ground, or a chair. The odd man wanders about at will and the other players, without signal, trade places whenever they care to. If the odd man succeeds in getting one of the places, the one left out is next odd man.

2. PUSS-IN-THE-CORNER
Puss-in-a-Corner. Pussy Wants a Corner.

The formation is the same as for Finding-a-House. The odd player, Puss, goes from one player to another saying "Pussy wants a corner," and receives the reply "Go to my next-door neighbor." As Puss goes about, the others exchange places at will. If Puss can get one of the places, the player left out is next Puss. Occasionally, Puss may call "All change," and then every player must find a new place.

3. CHAIR SCRAMBLE

All players except one sit on chairs in a circle, with the odd man in the center. The circle of chairs includes one empty chair in addition to the ones on which the players sit. The odd man rushes for the empty chair, but as he does so, one of the others sits in it; then the odd man rushes for the one just vacated, and so on, the odd man always trying to sit in the empty chair and the others trying to prevent his doing so by sitting in it themselves.

Division Two: Racing Games

The Racing Games are in most cases very similar to certain Tag Games, but the tag element is missing. Instead, two or more men race in an effort to see which can be first to reach a certain spot or goal. It is true that the games of Division One are racing games in a sense, but they are complicated by other factors that seem to justify classifying them separately.

Section I: Players race for a gap in a circle

In any one of these games, a number of men, usually two, race around a circle formed by the other players, each trying to be first to reach and occupy a gap in the circle. Each of these games has its counterpart among the Tag Games, the point in the latter being for one man to tag the other before the gap is reached.

1. FILL-THE-GAP

Flying Dutchman. Fox. Herr Slap Jack. Hopaway. Skipaway.
Slap Jack.

All players except one stand in a large circle facing the center. The odd man trots around the outside of the circle in a counterclockwise direction and slaps one of the circle players on the back. The odd man then reverses direction and runs around the circle clockwise, and the one slapped immediately starts to run around counterclockwise; in other words, the slapper reverses his direction and the one slapped runs in the slapper's original direction. Each tries to be first to reach and step into the gap left by the circle man, and the one who fails is next odd man.

2. COUPLE FILL-THE-GAP

Partner Skipaway

Same as Fill-the-Gap, except that all players are in pairs, holding hands. The odd pair runs around the circle and slaps both members of a circle pair on the back.

3. DROP-THE-HANDKERCHIEF (Variation)

Same as Fill-the-Gap, except that the odd man carries a handkerchief and drops it behind one of the circle players instead of slapping him on the back. The basic game of Drop-the-Handkerchief (page 66) is the same as this variation except that it is a tag game.

Variation. Each circle player holds his hands behind his back and the odd man drops the handkerchief into the hands.

4. HOCKEY-DRIBBLE FILL-THE-GAP

Circle Hockey-Dribbling Race

This game uses the same formation as Fill-the-Gap, except that every player has a field-hockey stick and ball. The odd man runs around the outside of the circle and touches a circle player. Then he drops his ball to the ground, reverses direction, and dribbles the ball around the circle. The one slapped drops his ball and dribbles it in the other direction. The winner is the first one to complete the circle and dribble his ball through the gap.

5. ZIGZAG FILL-THE-GAP

Circle Zigzag. Hop-to-the-Gap.

Same as Fill-the-Gap, except that each of the two runners must travel by weaving in and out of the circle, passing in front of and behind the circle players alternately.

Variation. Same, except that both runners travel only by hopping.

6. DOUBLE-CIRCLE FILL-THE-GAP

All players except one stand in two concentric facing circles about three feet apart. The odd man runs around between these two circles and touches simultaneously any two facing circle players. These two then race around between the circles of men, each one starting to his right, to see which one can first reach the gap. Otherwise the same as Fill-the-Gap.

7. RUN FOR YOUR SUPPER

All players but one stand in a circle facing the center. The odd man runs around outside the circle and at will holds a hand between two players and calls "Run for your supper." The two men race around the circle, outside, for the gap. It should be noted that this game differs from Fill-the-Gap in that the odd man is not one of the racers.

Variation. The racers may be required to travel by hopping, skipping, or some other restricted method.

8. GOOD MORNING

Same as Fill-the-Gap with this addition: When the two runners meet they must shake hands, bow, and say "Good morning." After this they resume their running. The game may be varied by omitting the words, leaving only the handshake and the bow, or by saying "Good morning" three times.

9. SWING AROUND

Come With Me. Filling-the-Gap. Skipaway.

Same as Fill-the-Gap, except that when the two runners meet they hook elbows, swing around once, and continue running.

Section II: One player chases and swats another

In the few games of this section, one man chases another and swats him as many times as possible until he reaches a position of safety. There is no clear-cut victory or defeat.

1. SWAT TO RIGHT

Beater Goes Round. Beat-the-Beater. Beat-the-Beetle. Swat Tag.
Swat-the-Bear. Swat-Your-Neighbor. Towel Tag. Whip Tag.

All players but one stand in a circle facing the center, each with his hands held behind his back and with his eyes straight to the front. The odd man walks or runs around the outside of the circle, carrying a swatter. At will, he places the swatter in the hands of one of the circle players. The one who receives the swatter immediately begins to pommel his right-hand neighbor with it. The latter flees around the circle to the right, that is, counterclockwise, and is free from further swatting when he regains his former place in the circle. In the meantime, the original odd man has fallen into the place vacated by the swatting runner. The man with the swatter then goes around outside the circle and leaves the swatter in the hands of a circle man, and the game continues as before. It is important that the circle men look straight ahead. If they do so, and if the man with the swatter uses care in leaving it in the circle man's hands, the one to be swatted will not know of his election until he feels the first swat.

Variation 1. The man who receives the swatter may swat and chase either of his immediate neighbors.

Variation 2. The man to be swatted may run either to the right or to the left.

Variation 3. Each circle man bends forward and extends one hand backward between his legs; the swatter is placed in the extended hand.

2. FIND-THE-SWATTER

Hot Butter and Blue Beans

While all the other players close their eyes at a designated goal, one man takes a swatter a reasonable distance away and hides it. When he gives the signal the others search for the swatter and when

one man finds it he chases the others to the goal, swatting them as
they run.

Variation. The signal given by the odd man for the others to hunt
the paddle is "Hot butter and blue beans." He aids the searchers
by calling "Warm," "Warmer," and "Hot" for various degrees of
closeness; or "Cool," "Cold," "Colder," and "Freezing" for various
degrees of distance away from the swatter. When a player finds the
swatter, he calls "Roasted" as he begins the chase.

3. CENTIPEDE

All players but one sit on the floor in a rough circle with feet
stretched out and mixed up into a tangled pile, so that the owners of
the various feet can be identified only with difficulty. The feet are
usually shod but they might be bare. The odd player touches a
foot and calls upon one of the players to identify the owner of the
foot. The one called upon makes his guess. Then the guesser and the
true owner of the foot disentangle themselves and one chases the
other to a distant safety line, swatting him as often as possible. If
the guess is correct, the guesser does the chasing; if incorrect, he is
the object of the chase. The original odd man joins the pile and the
chaser is next odd man.

4. COCK STRIDE
Walk, Moon, Walk

This game was originally played with boys' caps, but in the
present hatless age a substitute must usually be used; a ball of
crumpled paper does quite well. One player is the cock. He is blindfolded and stands erect with his feet wide apart. Behind him at a
distance of ten feet or somewhat less is a throwing line. The other
players throw their caps, one or more at a time, from this line, each
trying to throw his cap between the legs of the cock and as far
forward as possible. When all have thrown, the blindfolded cock
walks slowly forward with very small steps until he steps on one of
the caps. The owner of the cap immediately begins to flee for a
distant safety line, with all the others in pursuit, pommelling him
with the flats of their hands until he reaches the line. The owner of
the cap is the cock for the next time.

Section III: Players race when a hider is found

In these games, players race for a goal, and the signal for the beginning of the race is the finding of a hidden player.

1. HIDE-AND-SEEK
Hide-and-Go-Seek. I Spy.

All players except one run and hide while the odd man covers his eyes and counts to a prescribed number. As soon as the count is completed the odd man, with or without calling "Coming," goes in search of the hiders. When he sees one he calls "I spy————," and the two race for home, that is, for the place at which the odd man did the counting. The same man then goes in search of other hiders and the game continues until all hiders have run home. The first of the hiders to lose his race with the odd man is odd man next time. Any man in hiding may run home without waiting to be spied, if he believes he can make it before the odd man.

The count that the odd man makes while the others hide may be to any prescribed number and may be by ones but is more often by fives, for example, to one hundred by fives.

2. THROW-THE-STICK
Green Wolf. Yards Off.

This game is essentially the same as Hide-and-Seek, with the counting replaced by throwing and retrieving a stick.

All gather around a tree or other goal against which it is possible to lean a short stick. One player is selected as odd man and any other player takes the stick in his hand and throws it as far as he can. All except the odd man immediately run and hide, as in Hide-and-Seek, but the odd man must run for the stick, bring it back, and lean it against the goal; then he goes in search of the hiders. From this point on, the game is the same as Hide-and-Seek, except that this feature is usually added: Any hider who beats the odd man in the race to the goal may pick up the stick and throw it; then the odd man must again retrieve the stick before proceeding with his search for hiders.

Variation. The stick, four to six inches long, is leaned against the goal and hit with a longer stick, instead of being thrown.

3. KICK-THE-CAN
Kick-and-Hide. Kick Hide-and-Seek.

All gather around an old tin can placed on the ground inside a two-foot circle. An odd man is selected and one of the other players kicks the can as far as he can. The odd man retrieves the can and places it in the circle while the others run and hide, and then he goes in search of them. When he spies one he calls, "I spy————," and the two race for the can. The first to reach the can kicks it as far as possible, the other racer immediately becoming odd man. As he retrieves the can, any who have come out of hiding run and hide again. Thus the game continues indefinitely. Of course an old ball or some other object can be substituted for the can.

4. RUN, SHEEP, RUN

The players are divided into two equal teams, each with a captain. All members of one team close eyes at the goal and count, while all of the other team, except the captain, run and hide. After the count, the counting team goes in search of the hiders, the captain of the hiders being free to accompany the searchers or to go wherever he pleases. When one of the searchers spies any one of the hiders he notifies the captain and the latter calls "Run, sheep, run!" at which signal all race for the goal. The first man to reach the goal wins for his team. The game may be continued with the roles of the two teams reversed, or with the losing team as hiders. If the captain of the hiding team considers it wise, he may give the call "Run, sheep, run" at any time, and then the chase is on as before.

Variation. The winner of a race is determined, not by the first man to reach the goal, but by the last man. In other words, the winner is the first team to get all of its men to the goal.

5. STATUE HIDE-AND-SEEK
Go Stop. Ten Steps.

This game is Hide-and-Seek with an element of the game of Statue (see Class V) added. As in Hide-and-Seek, the odd man covers his eyes and counts, but he counts only to ten and then opens his eyes. As he counts, the others move toward, but do not need to reach, places of hiding. When the odd man opens his eyes the others must either be in hiding or else motionless, for any one seen to move must return to the goal and make a fresh start. Again the odd man covers his eyes and counts to ten, and the process is repeated until all have hidden, any man seen to move always being required to make a fresh start. When all have reached places of hiding, the odd man seeks them and the game from here on is the same as Hide-and-Seek. In some situations, it will be found better to place a limit on the number of times that the odd man is to count, and any man who has not reached a place of hiding then is considered a loser. If the number of counts is limited, the last one should be longer than the others, say twenty-five instead of ten.

6. BEAR HUNT

This is a Hide-and-Seek game with only one hider, all the rest of the players being seekers. One man, the bear, runs and hides while the others close their eyes at the goal and one of them counts as in Hide-and-Seek. When the count is completed they call "Coming," and go in search of the bear. When any one of the seekers spies him, he calls "Bear," and all players race for the goal. The first one to reach the goal is bear next time.

Variation 1. All who reach the goal after the bear does are eliminated. The game is repeated until only one survives, each time with the first arrival at the goal as the bear.

Variation 2. Same as the basic game, except that the last man to reach the goal, rather than the first one, is Bear next time.

7. MOUNTED BEAR-HUNT
Mounted Hide-and-Seek

The same as Bear Hunt, except that it is played by men on horseback. In this form the distances are large and the hider must have considerable time to hide, say three or four minutes.

Section IV: Miscellaneous racing games

1. LAST-MAN-OVER
Last-Man-Across. One-Over.

All players stand toeing one of two parallel lines. At a signal, they all race for the other line. There is no reward for being first.

but the penalty for being last is elimination from the game. During the run it is legal for one man to interfere with another by blocking, bucking, or pushing, but not by holding. After the loser of the first race has been eliminated, the survivors run again, this time back to the first line. The race is continued, the loser being eliminated each time, until only the winner is left.

Variation. The players are divided into two equal and distinguishable teams, the teams alternating at the start. The game is played exactly as in the basic form, except that it continues only until all members of one team have been eliminated, the other team being the winner.

2. HUNTSMAN
Come With Me. Hunter.

At the start, each player has a spot that is marked so that he can distinguish it from the others. The spots can be in a line, in a circle, or at random. All players fall in behind a leader and follow him in single file wherever he goes; he may march or trot. Suddenly the leader calls "Bang!" and each player must rush for his own spot. The first one to reach his spot is next leader.

3. BROTHERS

Players stand in two concentric circles, facing in opposite directions, and the two who are side by side are brothers. At a signal, both circles march forward, one clockwise, the other counterclockwise. At a second signal, each player must find his brother, join hands with him, and sit on the floor. The first pair to sit scores a point, or the last pair scores a negative point.

Division Three: Object-Scramble Games

1. CAP SCRAMBLE
Team Cap-Scramble

This game, like a number of others, originated at a time when boys wore caps, the caps being used in the game. Since caps are almost unknown among modern boys a substitute will usually be needed; that is, each player must have some object which he can identify as his own. A block of wood marked with the initials of the owner is satisfactory. The caps, or substitutes, are piled up on a line, and all the players make ready to run from a second line parallel to the first. At a starting signal all run to the line on which the caps are piled, and each player gets his own cap and runs back with it to the starting line. The game can be scored in various ways. A point can be scored by the man who gets back first; a negative point can be scored by the one who is last, with a penalty for three points; or the last man can be eliminated and the race continued until only one is left.

Variation. The players are divided into two equal teams and the teams alternate on the starting line. The team that first gets all of its men back to the start is the winner.

2. OBJECT SCRAMBLE

Players are in two equal teams. Each team forms a straight line, the two teams being back to back with a line marked on the ground between them. On this line are a number of objects of any kind, the more variation in the objects the better. The number of objects should be less than the total number of players, probably about equal to the number on one team. At a signal all start marching forward, the teams thus separating from each other. At a suitable time, the leader blows a whistle and all players turn around and rush for the objects, no man being permitted to get more than one object. The team that obtains the larger number of objects is the winner.

3. CORK SCRAMBLE (Aquatic)

Cork Retrieve

Corks, small blocks of wood, or other small objects that will float, are thrown into the water. At a signal all players dive or jump into the water and each man gets as many corks as possible, the one with the largest number being the winner.

Variation 1. Each man has a certain position at the edge of the pool, marked by a one-foot circle. At a signal all jump into the water and each man brings back corks one at a time, placing them in his own circle. When all corks have been retrieved the man with the largest number in his circle is the winner.

Variation 2. Players are in two equal teams, one at each side of the pool. At the signal each man jumps into the pool and gets as many corks as possible, the team with the largest total being the winner.

Variation 3. Same as Variation 2, except each man may recover only one cork in one trip, as in Variation 1. Each of the two teams has one circle for the whole team.

4. TREASURE SCRAMBLE (Aquatic)
Sunken Treasure. Water Mine.

A large number of pennies are thrown into the pool so that they are scattered on the bottom. At a starting signal all players dive into the pool and each man recovers as many pennies as possible. He may come to the surface and dive again but must keep his pennies in his hands and not lay them down. When all pennies have been recovered, the man with the largest number is the winner.

Variation 1. Each man has his own circle marked on the floor at the edge of the pool. He recovers pennies one at a time and places them in his own circle.

Variation 2. Players are in two equal teams, one team on each side of the pool. At the signal, all dive and recover as many pennies as possible, and, as in the basic game, the team with the largest total is the winner.

Variation 3. Same as Variation 2, except that each man may recover only one penny at a time, as in Variation 1. Each team has one circle into which all pennies must be placed.

5. WEIGHT SCRAMBLE (Aquatic)
Weight Retrieve

This game is the same as Treasure Scramble, except that other objects are used in place of coins. Any metallic objects may be used: tin plates, cups, spoons, for example. The game may be played with any of the variations described for Treasure Scramble.

6. FIND-THE-COIN (Aquatic)

Players are in two equal teams. The leader throws a penny into the water and two men, one from each team, dive into the pool, each trying to recover the penny. The one who succeeds scores a point for his team. The process is repeated until all have had a try, the team with the larger number of points being the winner.

7. WATERMELON SCRAMBLE (Aquatic)

A large watermelon is placed in the water some distance from the shore of a lake. At a signal all players dash from the shore toward the melon, each one trying to secure the melon and bring it ashore. Anything is permitted except ducking or extreme roughness, and it is of course permissible to take the melon away from one who holds it. The man who steps ashore with the melon in his possession is the winner.

Class III

DODGEBALL GAMES

A DODGEBALL GAME IS ONE THAT IS BASED ON ONE MAN'S ABILITY TO hit another by throwing a ball at him, while the one thrown at dodges to avoid being hit. The words *throwing a ball* are not strictly accurate because in two or three games the ball is not thrown but is otherwise propelled, and in one or two games an object other than a ball is used. There are a few games in which one man throws a ball at another, but the latter has no chance to dodge; these games are not included in this class but are considered to be Target Games and accordingly are placed in Class VI. The Dodgeball Games are arranged in five divisions on the basis of the amount of freedom of motion given to the dodgers.

Division One: Spot or Line Dodgeball

In a game of this division a man at whom the ball is thrown is more limited in his dodging than in a game of any other division. He must keep at least one foot in contact with a certain spot or small area, or else in contact with a certain line.

1. CROWN-THE-KING

A 30-foot circle is marked on the ground and a stool is placed in its center. The king stands on the stool, his helper moves at will within the circle, and all other players stand outside the circle. The ones outside the circle have a soft ball which they throw at the king. They may pass the ball about among themselves and may enter the circle to retrieve the ball, but must throw only from outside the circle. The helper tries to prevent the ball's hitting the king, but he is permitted only to block the ball or bat it away, not to catch it. When the king is hit with the ball, he joins the throwers, the guard becomes king, and the thrower who has hit the king becomes guard.

Variation. Under some conditions the game is better with two guards, or with two guards and two balls.

2. HOT RICE

One man with a softball and bat stands with one foot on a 12-inch square or circular base. All other players are scattered at will around him. The batter starts the game by hitting the ball fungo-style as hard as he can or wishes. The fielder who recovers the ball, whether it has struck the ground or not, must immediately throw it from the spot of recovery and try to hit the batter with it. The batter may dodge the ball, or he may hit it with the bat; in the latter case he may choose merely to deflect the ball so that it will not hit him, but if he thinks he can he will try to hit it solidly and knock it far afield. In any case the batter must keep one foot or the other in contact with the base. Whenever the batter is hit by a throw, or whenever he takes both feet off the base, the game is interrupted, the batter and thrower trade places, and a fresh start is made with a fungo hit by the new batter. Until the batter is put out, the game is continuous, the ball always being thrown at the batter by any fielder who recovers it, and always from the spot of recovery. It should be noted that the batter is not out on a caught fly ball.

Variation. Any fielder who catches two fly balls from the same batter puts the batter out and trades places with him.

3. LINE DODGEBALL

The playing field is marked with three parallel lines at intervals of from 20 to 30 feet, the distance varying with the age of the players and the nature of the ball used. One player stands on each of the outer lines and the other players stand on the middle line. Each of the two outer players has a ball, which he throws at the players on the middle line. The throwers may throw at a signal from the leader, but it is probably better if they get together by signaling each other; in either case they throw simultaneously. When a thrower misses he throws again, but when he hits a man he leaves the game, being replaced by the one whom he has just hit. The game is continued until only one man, the winner, remains on the middle line. The middle line should be of limited length and should be

shortened by appropriate marks as the number of remaining players
becomes smaller. The original two throwers are really not in the
game, since they have no chance to win.

4. COLUMN DODGEBALL

A line of indefinite length is marked on the ground, and all
players but two stand facing in any desired direction, each with at
least one foot touching the line. Across this line two throwing lines
are marked, each some distance beyond the line of men, and each
of the two extra players stands behind one of these throwing lines.
One of these men has a ball and throws it at will, trying to hit one or
more of the men in the line. The other odd man recovers the ball
and throws at the line, and so on, the odd men throwing the ball
alternately, always from their original positions. Any man hit with
the ball, before or after it strikes the ground, replaces the man who
hit him; this man leaves the game, and the process is repeated until
only one man remains in the line. In eluding the ball, a man may
twist, stoop, or jump into the air, but if he ever touches the ground
without having one foot on the line, he is considered hit.

Variation. A man who is hit trades places with the one who hit
him, and there is no elimination of men.

5. CALL DODGEBALL

Two equal teams, each numbered off, line up on base lines 50 to
60 feet apart. A neutral leader stands midway between the two
lines, tosses a ball into the air, and calls a number. The two opponents with this number rush for the ball, each trying to get in. The
one who succeeds immediately throws it at the line of opponents,
each of the latter being required to keep at least one foot on the
line. Whether the thrower succeeds or fails, both men return to their
respective lines and the game is repeated with different numbers.
The throwing team scores one point for each throw that hits an
opponent.

6. WALL SPUD

This game requires a solid wall about 20 feet high from which a
ball can be bounced. All players stand behind a line marked on the
ground parallel with the wall and 15 to 20 feet from it. One of the
men has a handball or tennis ball. He drops the ball to the ground

and as it rebounds he strikes it with open or closed hand so that it strikes the wall and rebounds as far as possible. As he does this, he calls the name of one of the other players. The one called recovers the ball and at the same time the others rush to the wall, each placing one hand on it. As soon as he recovers the ball the man called throws it at the men at the wall, the latter being permitted to move along the wall so long as one hand is kept in contact with it. Any hit counts, including one after a bounce from the ground or wall. Whether he hits or misses, the thrower puts the ball into play next time. One who makes an unsuccessful throw, or one who is hit, has a point scored against him and one with a predetermined number of points pays a penalty.

Variation. A man who is hit is eliminated. This variation has no satisfactory and logical termination and is not recommended. The game may also be played by eliminating a man who is hit and also a man who makes an unsuccessful throw.

Division Two: Restricted-Area Dodgeball

In games of this division, the defenders, or men thrown at, are confined within a prescribed area which the attackers do not enter. In the first of the two sections into which the games are divided, each man is at any moment either thrower or dodger, but not both. In the other section every man is thrower and dodger at the same time.

Section I: Men thrown at do not retaliate

In these games a defender can only dodge the ball and try to avoid being hit; he can never throw the ball back at his attackers.

Group A: All Players are Independent

1. ONE-MAN DODGEBALL

Bounce Dodgeball. Center Dodgeball. Dodgeball. Individual Dodgeball. Simple Dodgeball.

One man runs at will within a circle formed by the others, who stand facing the center. The circle players have a basketball or volleyball that they pass about among themselves and, when they choose, throw at the center man. A circle man who hits the center man trades places with him. Sometimes the regulation is that a man who *misses* the center man trades places with him, and this raises an interesting question. It can be argued that to be given the center position is a penalty and that the method recommended penalizes the circle man for success. The answer to this contention is that in fact the center position is considered desirable; in this game a player shows his skill, and gets his satisfaction, not so much by hitting a center player as by being center player and holding the position for a long time without being hit.

Variation 1. To put the center man out a throw must bounce from the floor at least once before hitting him.

Variation 2. To put the center man out a hit must be not higher than the knee.

2. TRAIN DODGEBALL

Chain Dodgeball. Locomotive Dodgeball.

Five men are within a circle formed by the others. The five are in Fox-and-Geese formation; that is, each man has his arms wrapped about the waist of the one just in front of him. The circle men have a ball that they pass about and at will throw at the rear man of those in the center. Hitting any man other than the rear one is disregarded, counting nothing. The front man has the right to bat the ball away, but not to catch it. When the rear man is hit, he replaces the one who has hit him, the latter becoming the head of the formation and the others moving back one place.

3. CUMULATIVE DODGEBALL

A circle, say 20 feet in diameter, is drawn on the ground. One man stands outside the circle, all others move at will inside. The outside man has a ball that he throws at the others; if he misses, he must recover the ball himself, and he continues to throw until he hits one of the men in the circle. The man who is hit goes outside the circle and becomes a second thrower. The two throwers now cooperate in hitting the others, and may pass the ball from one to the other as much as they wish. As soon as a center man has been hit, he joins the throwers, so that the number of throwers constantly increases and the number of center men constantly decreases. The game continues until only the winner is left in the circle. Since the first thrower is likely to have some difficulty in making a hit, it may be well to start with two throwers.

GROUP B: PLAYERS ARE IN TEAMS

1. DODGEBALL
Circle Dodgeball

Players are in two teams, one within and the other without a circle about 30 feet in diameter. The men of the outer team have a ball that they pass about at will and throw at the center team whenever they wish. A man of the throwing team may enter the circle to retrieve the ball, but must never throw it except when outside the circle. When a man is hit by the ball, he immediately leaves the circle and the game. The game continues until all the inner players are eliminated. Then the two teams reverse positions and the game is played again. Time is kept and the winner is the team that eliminates its opponents in the shorter time. If preferred, each half inning may be for a prescribed time and the winner determined by comparing the numbers of survivors at the expiration of the time.

Variation. A man who is hit is not eliminated, but remains in the game. Each team throws at the other for a predetermined time, and the number of hits made is counted. The winning team is the one with the greater number of hits.

2. WATER DODGEBALL

This is not a separate game, but merely Dodgeball played in water about waist deep. Of course, a waterproof ball must be used.

3. KICK DODGEBALL
Soccer Dodgeball

Same as Dodgeball, except that the ball is kicked, not thrown. A soccer ball should be used, and it should be kept rather soft.

4. TRAIN DODGEBALL (Team Form)
Fox-and-Geese Dodgeball. Mother Carey's Chickens.

Players are in several teams of four or five men each. All except the members of one team stand in a circle facing the center, with the odd team inside. The odd team assumes the Fox-and-Geese formation; that is, each man wraps his arms about the waist of the man in front of him. The circle men pass a ball about, and, at will, throw it in an attempt to hit the rear center man. Hits on any man except the rear one are disregarded, but when the rear man is hit he leaves the circle at once. The game continues with the new rear man as target, until the center team is entirely eliminated. The time required is noted and the game is repeated with another team in the center. When each team has been in the center, the times are compared, the winner, of course, being the team that survived for the longest time.

Variation. There is no elimination. Each team plays in the center for a prescribed time and the number of hits on the rear man determines the winning team.

5. CHAIN DODGEBALL

This game is a special form of Train Dodgeball, with only two teams. All the members of one team form as prescribed, and the other team surrounds them in a circle. The winner is determined by comparing times required for elimination of the opponents or by comparing the number of times that the rear men are hit.

6. HEN AND CHICKENS
Mother Goose

Players are in two teams. All but five of one team form a circle and all but five of the other team form a separate circle. The odd five of each team are within the circle formed by the opponents. They have no formation, but one of them, the hen, has a special status. The circle players throw a ball trying to hit and thus eliminate the opponents in the center. Any player who is hit, except the hen, immediately leaves the circle. The hen cannot be eliminated, and she may protect the others by blocking and warding off the ball. The game continues until one circle or the other has eliminated all the opponents, except the hen, and this team is the winner.

7. PROGRESSIVE DODGEBALL
Three-Team Dodgeball

This game requires a long rectangular field with two cross lines forming three equal courts. Players are in three equal teams, one in each court. In the first round, the two end teams cooperate in throwing a ball at the center team. When a man is hit he leaves the game and the time is noted for the elimination of his entire team. Then a second round is played with another team in the middle court serving as the target of the throws, and finally a third round with the remaining team in the middle court. The team that survives longest before all its members are eliminated is the winner.

Variation. No one is eliminated. Each team plays in the middle court for a prescribed time, and the hits are counted and compared.

Section II: All men throw

In the games thus far described in this class, the men have been divided into throwers and dodgers, and a dodger has been helpless to do anything beyond running, jumping, or squirming, to avoid being hit. We now come to games in which every man is a thrower and a dodger at the same time. No one need be satisfied with avoiding the shots of the enemy; he can fight back.

1. BATTLEBALL
Bombardment. Square Dodgeball.

The game is played on a rectangular field with a middle line dividing it into two equal courts, each about 30 feet square. Players are in two teams, one in each of the courts. One team has a ball that it throws at the other. Only direct hits are valid and only one hit can count from one throw. It should be noted that the ball must not be caught, since catching it would cause the catcher to be hit. (See, however, *Variation 1.*) Any man hit with the ball immediately withdraws from the game. Whether or not the first throw is successful, the opponents of the throwing team retrieve the ball and throw it back at the first-throwing team. Thus, the ball is thrown back and forth until all members of one team or the other have been eliminated. Since retrieving the ball is likely to slow the game, the time required for retrieving should be reduced as much as possible. The best way is to play the game in a room small enough so that the whole room can be the playing field. Lacking this, the eliminated players should be stationed out of bounds to recover the ball.

Variation 1. A man who catches the ball is not considered hit. However, the catch must be a clean one, for one who muffs the ball is considered hit.

Variation 2. Same as the basic form except there is no elimination. The hits are counted, and scores are compared at the expiration of a set time.

Variation 3. Two or three balls are kept in play.

2. MACHINE-GUN FIRE

This game is the same as Battleball except that it adds this important and interesting feature: A defensive man who catches the ball is not considered hit; on the contrary, his catching the ball eliminates the thrower.

3. HOTBALL

Players are in two teams, one in each half of a rectangular field, as in Battleball. A variety of balls is used, at least eight and preferably sixteen or more in number. The game starts with the balls divided equally between the two teams. At a signal, all start throwing at the opponents, trying to eliminate them. But a man is eliminated only when hit by a throw while he is holding one of the balls. When a man holding a ball is hit by another ball he is out, and the game continues until all of one team or the other have been eliminated.

4. FOUR-COURT DODGEBALL

A rectangular field is divided into two equal parts by a middle line. Players are in two teams, and each of the two teams is itself divided into two equal parts. One half of each team occupies one of the two courts; the other half stands beyond the farther end line. Thus, the two halves of each team are separated by one half of the other team. Each team has a ball with which it tries to hit the opponents, any opponent being eliminated when hit with the ball. The game continues until one team or the other is completely eliminated.

Variation. A man is eliminated only when hit by the ball on the first bounce.

5. THREE-COURT DODGEBALL
Progressive Dodgeball. Triple Dodgeball

A rectangular field, about 20 by 60 feet, is divided by two cross lines into three equal courts. Players are in three equal teams, one in each court. The two end teams cooperate in throwing a ball at the center team, but do not throw at each other. The center team also tries to hit men on either of the end teams. The game continues for two minutes and a scorekeeper keeps track of the hits on each team. Any hit counts, but only one hit can count from one throw. After two minutes a second team takes the center court for two minutes, and finally the third team. At the end of the three periods, the scores are totaled and compared.

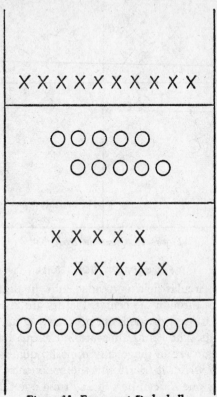

Figure 11. Four-court Dodgeball.

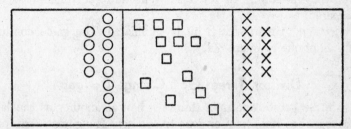

Figure 12. Three-court Dodgeball.

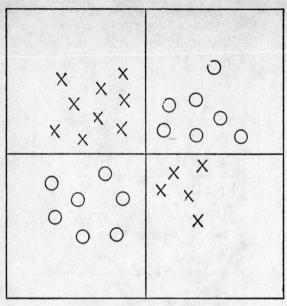

Figure 13. Quadrant Dodgeball.

6. QUADRANT DODGEBALL

A square or circular field is divided into quadrants by two perpendicular lines through the center. Players are in two equal teams and each team is itself divided, not necessarily equally, between two of the quadrants. The teams alternate in the quadrants, so that the parts of one team are in diagonally opposite quadrants. Each team has a ball with which it tries to hit the opponents. Only direct hits count, and only one hit can be counted from one throw. Any player may move from one to the other of his team's quadrants at any time. Play is continued for a set time and the numbers of hits compared.

Variation. A man who is hit is eliminated. The game continues until all of one team are out.

Division Three: Goal-Change Dodgeball

In these games one man throws a ball at another as the latter runs from one line, spot, or goal, to another. The games correspond more or less to the Goal-Change Tag Games included in Class I-B.

Section I: All run simultaneously or at will

1. SNOWBALL POM-POM-PULLAWAY

This game must be played on a field covered with snow. One man stands near the center of a rectangular field about 60 feet square, all others on one of the end lines. The man in the center calls "Pom-Pom-Pullaway, come away or I'll pull you away!" At the last word of this call, all on the end must rush for the opposite line, and as they do so the center man tries to hit one of them with a snowball. Any man hit by the center man joins him on the next chase, so that there are now two throwers. The game continues, the runners going back and forth, and the number of throwers increasing until all have been put out. The last man to be hit is the winner. This game is the same as Pom-Pom-Pullaway (see page 39) except that throwing snowballs is substituted for tagging.

2. THROWING POM-POM-PULLAWAY
Dodgeball

The formation for this game is the same as for Pom-Pom-Pullaway or for Snowball Pom-Pom-Pullaway, except that it is not played in the snow. The center man has several soft balls that he throws one at a time, trying to hit the runners as they change goals in response to his cry. In this game, a man who is hit trades places with the center man and becomes thrower next time; there is no accumulation of throwers as in the last game.

3. MAT TAG

Small gymnasium mats are scattered at random on the floor. A thrower tries to hit the other players with a ball as they run from one mat to another. They run at will and any number of them may be on a mat at the same time. When a runner is hit while not on a mat he trades places with the thrower.

Section II: Only one or two men run at a time

1. FIELD DODGEBALL

The game is played on a field about 40 by 60 feet with a turning post in the middle of one end line. Players are in two teams, one scattered at will within the field, the other behind the end line that does not have the turning post. The former team is the throwing or fielding team and has a softball or other ball for throwing at its opponents. The latter team is the running team and must have an established running order.

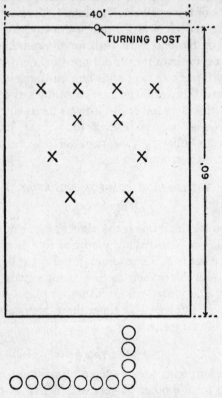

Figure 14. Field Dodgeball.

At the start of the game, the ball is held by a fielder in the center of the field. Two runners take positions anywhere on the end line, and at a signal both start to run. Each of them tries to run to the far end of the field, around the turning post, and back over the starting line, without being hit with the ball; he may run anywhere and in any direction, so long as he stays in bounds. The fielders try to hit the runners with the ball. Fielders may not run with the ball in their possession but may pass it from one to another in order to get into better throwing position. The instant a runner is put out, the next runner starts. As soon as a runner crosses the finish line without being hit, the next runner starts. In other words, the running team always has exactly two runners in action. Even though a man has been put out, he takes his next turn at running.

One team continues to run until three of its men have been put out, and scores a point for each run made before the third putout. Then the teams reverse positions and the other team runs until it has three men out. The game continues for any number of innings agreed upon.

Variation 1. In each inning, each team continues to run for two minutes, regardless of putouts.

Variation 2. In each inning, each team is in until all of its members have run once, regardless of the number of putouts.

2. STOP THIEF

Two parallel base lines are marked about 60 feet apart and a third line between them 20 feet from one line and 40 feet from the other. Players are in two teams, one on each of the base lines. On the third line stands an Indian club with a soft ball on the ground beside it. At a signal two players run, one from each team. The man from the line nearer the club picks it up and runs back to his base line. The opposing player, arriving at the third line later than the other, picks up the ball and throws it at the fleeing runner. The process is repeated with two other men until all have run. Then the two teams exchange places and the whole thing is done again. At the end of the double round, the team with the larger number of hits to its credit is the winner.

3. PIN PICKUP

This game is played on a small baseball diamond, with an Indian club standing on each base except home. One man stands at home, the others are scattered in the field at will. The man at home places a soccer ball on the plate and kicks it as far afield as he can. He then runs and tries to pick up all three of the pins and bring them home. He may take the pins in any order and may carry them all at once; further, he is not restricted in his running, and may go anywhere he chooses. The other men, meanwhile, try to recover the ball and, passing it from one to another as much as they wish, to throw it and hit the runner. A fielder may not run with the ball in his hand. When a "batter" is put out, he takes the last place in the field and the others move up one place. A man cannot be put out by a caught fly ball.

Section III: Pairs of runners trade places

1. THROWING NUMBERS-CHANGE
Numbers Change

One man, the thrower, has a ball and moves at will. The others are scattered at random, but each has his place clearly marked, and each has a number. The thrower calls any two numbers and the two men with these numbers must exchange places, the thrower trying to hit one of them as they do so. If he hits one he is thrower again, but if he misses, the one missed is the next thrower.

2. PASS-AND-CHANGE

A thrower with a ball or beanbag stands in the center of a large circle formed by the other players. The thrower calls the names of any two players and at the same time tosses the ball to a third. The two men whose names are called rush to exchange places. The one to whom the ball is tossed immediately throws it back to the first thrower and the latter then tries to hit one of the runners who are in the process of exchanging places. If he hits a runner he is thrower again, but if he misses, the one missed is next thrower.

3. BALL PUSS

Each player except one occupies a "home," which is a corner or other well-marked base. Players beckon to one another and trade places at will. As they do so, the odd man tries to hit one by throwing a soft ball or beanbag.

4. OFF-THE-SPOT
Ball Puss-in-the-Corner

The thrower with a ball is in the center of a large circle formed by the other players. Each circle player must have his spot well marked. The circle players trade spots at will, and as they do so the thrower tries either to hit one of the runners with the ball or to secure a vacant spot. If he succeeds in either attempt the man hit or the man left without a spot is the next thrower. The game is the same as Ball Puss except for the added feature that the thrower can win by obtaining a place.

Division Four: Flee-and-Throw Dodgeball

The games of this division include a variety of devices by which one man is selected to be the thrower. While he is securing the ball, or preparing to throw, or going through some other prescribed preliminary activity, the other players run away from him. Then the thrower throws the ball at the others in an attempt to hit any one of them. In many of the games the thrower, when he is ready to throw, calls "Halt," or its equivalent, and the runners must stop in their tracks until the throw is made. The games are in three sections on the basis of the method by which the thrower is selected.

Section I: The thrower is predetermined

1. ALL RUN

The thrower stands with a ball, the other players gathered close around him. The thrower tosses the ball into the air and catches it himself, the others all fleeing as he does so. When the thrower catches the ball, he throws it at the runners. A runner hit with the ball trades places with the thrower. If the thrower does not hit anyone he is thrower again, but has a point against him and pays a penalty for three such points.

Variation. When the thrower catches the ball he calls "Halt." The runners must then stand still.

2. COUNT-AND-THROW

The thrower stands in the center of a circle formed by the other players. He selects any even number and announces it. He throws the ball to any one of the circle men and receives a throw in return. He then throws it to other players in turn, counting all throws, both from and to him, until the announced number is reached. Then he throws the ball at the circle men as they flee. One who is hit trades places with the thrower.

Section II: The thrower is one whose name or number is called

1. SPUD

*All Run. Ball Stand. Catch-and-Run Ball. Catching Spud.
Days of the Week. Numberball. Number Tag. Soak About.
Standball. Wall Spud.*

One man has an old softball and the other players gather informally around him. The man with the ball tosses it into the air calling the name of another player as he does so. The man whose name is called rushes for the ball, catches it if possible, and, in any case, recovers it as quickly as he can. Then he calls "Halt," and the others, who have fled meanwhile, stop in their tracks. The ball is then thrown at any of the other players. If a man is hit by the throw he recovers the ball, calls "Halt," and throws it at any other player, the players meanwhile having fled from him. This is repeated as long as the throws are successful. When a throw is unsuccessful and does not hit anyone, play starts as at the beginning of the game, the thrower who has failed to hit a runner being the one to toss the ball and call the name of the next thrower.

Variation 1. The ball, instead of being tossed into the air, is thrown against a wall. This variation is called Wall Spud.

Variation 2. The call "Halt" is omitted and a thrower throws the ball as soon as he can get it.

There is really no need for a scoring system in this game, but it is sometimes played with the penalty or dud system, that is, with a point against a man for failure and a penalty for a prescribed number of such points. A point may be scored against a man for being hit, for missing a throw, or for either.

2. WATER SPUD

This is the same as Spud, except that it is played by men in water waist deep. A cork or rubber ball is used. A player is not permitted to duck under the water.

3. DRIBBLE SPUD

This form of Spud uses a basketball and consequently must be played indoors, or at least on a hard floor that permits basketball dribbling. A man tosses a basketball into the air and calls a player's name as in Spud. The one called recovers the ball as the others flee. There is no call of "Halt." The thrower may throw at once or he may make a legal basketball dribble and continue as long as he wishes, then throw. Otherwise the rules are the same as those for Spud.

4. PARTNER SPUD

The formation is the same as for Spud except that the players are numbered and each number is given to two men, the two with the same number being partners. The ball is tossed into the air and a number called. One of the two men with the called number gets the ball as the others flee. There is no call of "Halt." The man with the ball may throw it at once, or, if he prefers, may throw it to his partner and let the partner throw. Only one throw may be made between the two. Otherwise the game is the same as Spud.

Section III: Thrower is selected by some other method

1. PICKABACK SPUD

Horse-and-Rider Spud. Mountball. Mounted Spud. Riderball.

Players are in horse-and-rider pairs, that is, one man rides on another's back with legs firmly wrapped about the waist just above the hips. The pairs are formed in a large circle. The riders toss a ball from one to another at random, and the horses try to make them miss. To do this the horses may twist and squirm, but must remain in place. Riders continue to pass the ball among themselves until one of them misses a throw. Then the riders dismount and flee. The ball must be recovered by the horse of the rider who missed it. When he recovers the ball he calls "Halt" and throws at any of the riders. If any rider is hit by the throw the horses and riders trade places and the game is played as before with the new riders in possession of the ball. If no rider is hit, the game is repeated with the same riders.

2. POISON SPUD

Poison Circle

All players lock elbows in a circle, facing the center. Inside the circle stands a group of Indian clubs, and an old softball is on the ground at the center of the group of clubs. At a signal all push and pull each other, each one trying to make some other player knock down one of the clubs. As soon as a man knocks down a club he picks up the ball and throws at the others, who have fled meanwhile. A point is scored against a thrower who misses or a runner who is hit, and one with three such points pays a penalty.

Variation. No clubs are used, but a circle is marked on the ground. One who steps into the circle becomes the thrower.

3. ANTE-OVER

Antony-Over. Fox and Ball. Haley-Over.

This game requires a shed or other building over which a ball may be thrown by two teams standing on opposite sides. The teams throw the ball back and forth over the building, each team trying to catch the throws of the other. When the ball is not caught it is recovered and thrown back over the building. When a man catches the ball he does not throw it back but runs around the building and throws it at the opponents, scoring a point for each hit.

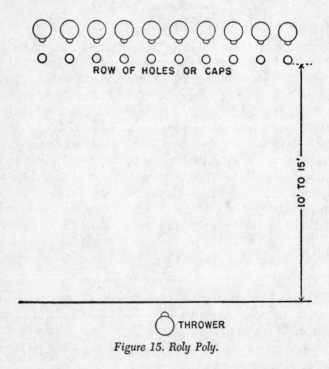

Figure 15. Roly Poly.

4. ROLY POLY
Cap-roll Ball. Hatball. Holeball.

This game was formerly played with boys' caps, but it is now usually played with shallow holes dug in the ground. The holes are in a straight line, about one foot apart, and are one fewer than the players. One man stands on a line parallel with the row of holes and 10 to 15 feet away. The other men stand beyond the holes, each by a hole that he identifies as his own. The man at the rolling line rolls an old softball, trying to make it lodge in one of the holes; if he fails, the ball is returned to him and he continues until he is successful. When the ball lodges in a hole, the owner of the hole recovers the ball and the other men all flee. When the owner of the hole gets the ball he calls "Halt." The runners must stop in their tracks, and the ball is thrown at them. A man who is hit by the throw, or a thrower who misses, becomes next roller, and has a point against him; he is required to pay a penalty for three such points.

5. KETTLE DRIVE

The kettle is a shallow hole, or merely a circle marked on the ground, about a foot in diameter. Surrounding the kettle is a circle of smaller holes, each hole four or five inches in diameter, and the circle of holes five or six feet in diameter. The number of small holes is one less than the number of players. Each man has a gymnasium wand or similar stick. One man, the "driver," has a large ball, such as a volleyball, and takes his position, with ball and stick, outside the circle of holes. Each of the others takes possession of one of the small holes and places his stick in it. The driver now hits or pushes the ball with his stick, trying to drive it inside the circle of holes and into or over the kettle. If he succeeds in doing this, he picks up the ball and throws it at any of the others, all of whom have fled meanwhile. A thrower who misses, or a man who is hit by the throw, is driver next time and has a point scored against him.

While the driver is trying to drive the ball into the circle and across the kettle, the other players, of course, try to prevent his doing so. Whenever a player removes his stick from the hole in order to block the ball, the driver may grasp the opportunity to place his stick in the hole thus vacated. In such a case, the man whose hole has been stolen immediately becomes driver and the game continues without interruption. Thus, there may be any number of different drivers before one of them succeeds in driving the ball across the kettle.

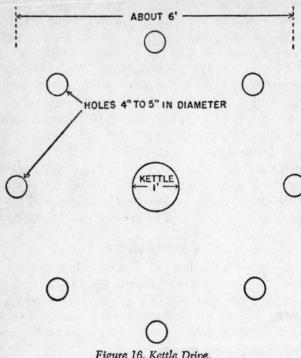

Figure 16. Kettle Drive.

Division Five: Free-Run Dodgeball

In the Dodgeball Games already described, the runners are restricted in various ways: in Divisions One and Two they are restricted to certain spots, lines, or relatively small areas; in Division Three they may run only from one line or goal to another; and in Division Four they may flee from the thrower only at certain times. In Division Five there is for the first time in this class an element of continuous flight, and the runners run at random, being vulnerable at any time. The games are described in three sections, which, like those in Class IV, are based on the method by which the thrower is selected.

Section I: Man who is hit becomes thrower

These games closely resemble Simple Tag. One man is thrower. He chases all the other players and throws until he hits one. Then the one who is hit immediately becomes thrower and the game continues without interruption.

1. BALL TAG

This game is the same as Simple Tag except that the chaser carries a softball and may tag a runner either by touching him with the ball while holding it in the hand, or by throwing the ball and hitting him with it. All players run at random and the chaser is permitted to run with the ball. Any hit counts, whether direct or on the roll or bounce. The game has one serious weakness in most situations: when a throw is made and missed, the retrieving of the ball causes an undesirable slowing of the game. This weakness is eliminated when the game is played in a relatively small room so that the ball will rebound from the walls. Where this is impossible the game is best played with two throwers as in Variation 1.

Variation 1. Two throwers work together. This variation greatly reduces the chasing of the ball. The throwers may pass the ball from one to the other as often as they wish before making a throw. A man who is hit trades places with the one who hits him.

Variation 2. Only direct hits count, not rolling or bouncing hits. This variation is recommended for use with Variation 1, but not with the basic game.

2. SNOWBALL TAG

Same as Ball Tag except that snowballs are used. Hits above the shoulders do not count.

3. KICK BALL-TAG
Football Tag. Soccer Tag.

Same as Ball Tag except that a soccer ball is used and it is kicked as in Soccer, not thrown. The game should be played in a relatively small court, enclosed if possible, otherwise with boundary lines. Runners must stay in bounds and one who steps out is considered tagged; the chaser is not required to stay in bounds. One man kicks the ball about, following Soccer rules, until he tags a runner by hitting him with a kicked ball. Then the one hit immediately takes over as kicker (chaser). A kicked ball that hits above the chest does not count.

Variation. Same, except that the penalty idea is added. A runner scores a negative point when he is hit with the ball not above the chest. The chaser scores a negative point when he touches the ball with his hands or hits a runner above the chest. One with three such points pays a penalty.

4. HOOP TAG
Automobile Tag

The chaser has a hoop or old tire that he rolls about. He tags a runner by hitting him with the tire. Otherwise, the same as Ball Tag.

5. CANOE TAG (Aquatic)

This game is played by men in several canoes, two or more men to each canoe. The men in one canoe are chasers; they have an old, soft, waterproof ball. They chase the other canoes and, at a suitable opportunity, throw the ball with the object of making it land in one of the canoes. The men in the fleeing canoes must not interfere with the ball and may do nothing in defense except speed away. If a throw is unsuccessful the throwers recover the ball and continue trying until they succeed.

Section II: One who can get the ball becomes thrower

1. FREE-BALL TAG

Players run at random within boundary lines, preferably in a closed room. One man has a ball that he throws at the others. The ball is recovered by any player who can get it, whether or not it hits a runner. The ball may not be caught before it strikes the floor or a man, because in this case the catcher would be considered hit. A man is not permitted to run with the ball. This game has no chaser and may possibly appear to be pointless. In fact, it is very popular and successful, and needs no motivation beyond the desire to hit another player and to avoid being hit. However, it may be played with the penalty system; that is, a man may be required to pay a penalty when he has been hit three times.

2. ELIMINATIONBALL

This is the same as Free-Ball Tag, except that a man who is hit by the ball is eliminated from the game, the game continuing until only one man survives.

3. CRACKABOUT

Same as Free-Ball Tag with this addition: when a man gets the ball he must throw it into the air and catch it again, calling "Crack-about" as he does so, before he throws it. When played in a closed room, it may be required that the ball be thrown against a wall. In a gymnasium with overhanging balcony, the ball may be thrown against the balcony. The thrower may run with the ball before he throws and catches it, but not afterward.

Section III: Men pass ball about and then throw

Two or more men are chasers. They may not run with the ball but may pass it about as much as they wish before throwing. Chasers and runners run at will, except that the game should always be played with boundary lines, preferably in a closed room.

1. DOUBLE SPUD

Each player has a partner, but partners run independently and do not work as a unit. One pair of partners have a ball with which they try to hit any other player. They may run at will while throwing the ball back and forth, but must not run with the ball. They chase the others in this manner and throw the ball at the runners whenever they choose to do so. If the throw is unsuccessful, the throwers recover it and continue until they are successful. When a man is hit he and his partner get the ball and proceed in the same way as the original throwers. Thus the game continues without interruption and without any necessary termination. No scoring system is necessary for this game, but the penalty system may be used, a point being scored against a man for being hit. Negative points may also be scored for traveling with the ball, for dropping a throw from one's partner, or for failing to hit a runner with a throw.

2. LONE BANDIT

All men except one are scattered within the playing field and travel at will. The odd man stands in the center of the field with a ball. He tosses the ball straight up into the air and then runs anywhere within bounds. One of the other players recovers the ball and then all of them work together in an attempt to hit the original odd man. They may throw the ball from one to another as often as they wish, but no one may travel with the ball. If the odd man is hit he must be odd man again, but any one of the throwers becomes odd man if he travels with the ball, if he misses a throw, or if he throws at the odd man and fails to hit him.

3. TEAM SPUD

Players are in two equal and distinguishable teams, all scattered at random in a court about 50 feet square. The men of Team A have a ball that they pass at will among themselves and, when they choose, throw at Team B. If the throw fails, Team A keeps the ball and tries again. When a man of Team B is hit with the ball, Team B takes the ball and proceeds as Team A did in the beginning. If a scoring system is desired, a point may be scored against a team for each unsuccessful throw; also for running with the ball or going out of bounds.

Class IV

COMBAT GAMES

As explained in the first chapter, a combat is a fight or struggle in which one man tries to achieve mastery over another, for instance, by hitting him, throwing him to the ground, or forcing him into or keeping him out of a designated area. The combat element is basic and dominant, and achieving mastery over an opponent is the principal and final objective of each player. The games of this class are in four divisions.

Division One: Line-Charging Games

In a game of this division, a man charges against a line formed by other men, and tries to force his way through the line. In some games only one or two men charge the line at one time, in others one whole team charges a line made up of another team.

Section I: One or two men charge

1. HITTING-THE-LINE
Forcing-the-City-Gates

Players are in two teams. One team forms a straight line with hands joined. One player from the other team tries to break through the line. He is allowed three tries and may climb over, crawl under, or break through the hands. If he wins he scores one point for his team. Then the second team forms a line and the first team sends a man to try to break through. The two teams alternate until every man has had a try, and the team with the larger number of successes is the winner. Since there is a strong tendency for the charger to direct his charge at the center of the line, it is well for the men to rearrange themselves after each charge.

2. BREAK-THE-RING

One man stands within a circle formed by the others, who hold hands as firmly as possible. The center man charges the circle in an attempt to break out, which he may do by going over, under, or through the pairs of hands. When he succeeds in breaking out, the man at the right of the place where he got through trades places with him.

Variation. Two men are in the ring at the same time. They operate independently and are not allowed to hit the same place at one time. When either man breaks out, both center men join the circle and are replaced by the two men between whom the breakout was made.

3. BREAK-THE-RING (Partner Form)

Battering Ram

All players but two join hands firmly in a circle. Of the odd two, one is inside the circle, the other outside. The one inside tries to break out exactly as in Break-the-Ring and the one outside tries to help him escape; he may do this by pulling on his partner, giving him a lift, pulling hands apart, or in any other way. When the center man breaks out both he and his partner join the circle and are replaced by the two between whom the breakout was made.

4. BREAK-THE-RING (Team Form)

Players are in two teams. All but one man of each team form a circle by joining hands firmly; that is, there are two separate circles. The odd man of each team is inside the circle of the opponents. At a signal, each center man tries to break out of the circle as in Break-the-Ring. The first center man to escape scores a point for his team. Play is then halted, the circles formed again with different center men, and the game is continued until every man has had a turn in the center.

5. BULL-IN-THE-RING

The bull is inside a circle formed by the other players, who hold hands firmly. The bull charges the pairs of hands until he breaks through. When he does so he flees with all the others in pursuit. The man who catches him is the next bull and the old bull joins the circle. The bull must break through the hands, and is not allowed to go over or under them. It may be asked what happens in case the bull is unable to break out of the ring. The only satisfactory answer is that the game should be so played that the bull will eventually break through. Players of games like this one usually have the spirit of giving a man a chance. If the center man has difficulty they naturally tend to ease up a bit. If this spirit is lacking it should be inculcated by the leader.

This game, as well as the three games immediately following, includes chasing and tagging and might, with considerable logic, be classified among Tag Games. They are not so classified here but as Combat Games instead, on the ground that the combat element is basic and of primary importance, and that the chase is quite incidental, serving chiefly as a method of determining who will be the next runner.

Variation. It is common for the bull to approach two of the circle players, take hold of their joined hands, and ask in a tantalizing tone, "What is this?" The boastful answer is "Steel," "Solid rock," or the like. Of course the bull may double-cross the enemy by suddenly lunging at a different part of the circle.

6. HERE I BUY, HERE I BAKE

This game is Bull-in-the-Ring with a dramatic element added. The bull touches a pair of hands, saying "Here I buy." He moves to a second pair of hands and touches them, saying "Here I bake," then a third pair with the words "Here I make my wedding cake." Suddenly he lunges at a fourth pair, saying "Here I break through." If necessary he repeats the process, and when he does break through he is chased by the others as in Bull-in-the-Ring.

7. BEAR-IN-THE-PIT

This game is identical with Bull-in-the-Ring, except that the bear has more ways of escaping than does the bull in the other game. The bear may break through the hands, but he may also climb over or crawl under the hands, or even dive between the legs of a circle man.

8. BULL-IN-THE-RING (Partner Form)

Same as Bull-in-the-Ring, except that the Bull has a partner. The partner is outside the circle and he helps the escape of the bull in any way possible. This may be done by pulling on the bull, by pulling arms apart, or by any other method that the partner chooses to use. When the bull escapes, both he and his partner run, pursued by all the others. The one who tags the bull becomes the new bull and the one who tags the helper becomes the new helper.

Section II: A whole team charges

1. OVER-THE-TOP

Hitting-the-Line. Holding-the-Line. Taking-the-Trench.

A defensive team stands between two parallel lines about ten feet apart; the attacking team stands on a third parallel line about ten feet away; in other words, there are three parallel lines at ten-foot intervals, one team standing on one of the outside lines and the other team between the other two lines. The court should also have side lines just far enough apart to accommodate either team when standing with hands joined. At a signal the attacking team rushes forward and each man tries to break through the defensive team and beyond the farthest line. He is considered to be through the line when he touches the floor with either foot beyond the farthest line. The struggle continues for 30 seconds; then the teams reverse positions and repeat. The winner is the team that gets the larger number through in the 30-second period.

2. STORMING-THE-FORT

The fort is a line of gymnasium horses, bucks, parallel bars, or similar obstacles over which men may climb. The obstacles should not be too high and should, where necessary, be covered with mats. The court should have side lines and the row of obstacles should extend from one side line to the other. Players are in two teams, one standing on a line about 20 feet from the obstacles and the other just beyond the obstacles. At a signal, the attacking team (the more distant one) rushes forward and tries to climb over the obstacles. The attackers must go over the obstacles, not under or around them, a man being considered over when he touches the floor with either foot on the far side. The defending team tries, of course, to prevent the attackers' getting over the obstacle. To do this they may go anywhere they choose: they may stay on the far side with the idea of

pushing climbers back; they may climb to the top of the obstacle; or
they may go clear over to the attackers' side. In any case, any kind
of holding or pushing is permitted, anything, in fact, except hitting
or other forms of excessive roughness. The attackers are given a predetermined amount of time, say one minute; then the two teams
reverse positions and repeat.

3. CHAIN BREAK

Jail Delivery. Ten-Second Chain-Break.

One team joins hands in a circle. The other team joins hands in a
second circle within the first. The outer team faces inward, the
inner team outward. At a signal, the outer circle moves in a clockwise direction and the inner circle in the opposite direction. At a
second signal, both circles stop moving, the men of the inner circle
release hands and charge the outer circle in an attempt to break
out. After ten seconds a third signal is given; all stand still and the
inner circle is given one point for each man who has escaped. Then
the teams form again with positions reversed, the game is repeated
and scores compared.

Variation. Players can be divided into three, or even more, teams
instead of two. One team forms the inner circle, all the others the
outer circle. Teams take turns in the inner circle and scores are
compared.

4. HOP ACROSS

Two parallel base lines are marked about 25 feet apart. Each team
stands on one of these lines, the teams facing each other. At a signal
each man starts toward the opposite line, with arms folded, hopping
on one foot. Each man tries to get to the opposite line without being
forced to put down his free foot or to unfold his arms; if he does
either of these things he is immediately eliminated from the game.
Any player may charge an opponent but must not hold him. Play
continues until every man reaches the goal or has been eliminated.
Then the team with the larger number over its goal is the winner.

Division Two: Wrestling and Sparring Games

Section I: One man strikes another

1. HAT FIGHT

All players are in one large circle, each wearing a hat, real or improvised. For fairness all should have the same kind of hat and for this reason paper hats are best; an ordinary paper bag is probably best of all. Each man tries to knock the hats off the others. When a man loses his hat he leaves the ring and play continues until only one man is left.

2. HAT FIGHT (Team Form)

Same as Hat Fight, except that players are in two distinguishable teams and play continues until all members of one team or the other are eliminated.

3. HANDS UP

Hand-Slapping Tag. Hand-Slap Tag. Hand Tag. Slap Catch.

An odd man is inside a circle formed by the other players who stand, shoulder to shoulder, facing the center. Each circle man extends his forearms forward, palms up, keeping his elbows fixed firmly at his sides. The center man moves about inside the circle, trying to slap the hand of any one of the circle men. The latter evades the blow by moving his forearms, but may not move his elbows or his feet. The center man darts about until he succeeds in hitting one of the hands and then trades places with the player whom he has hit.

4. BALLOON BATTLE

Balloon Battle-Royal

All players are within one large circle, each one with a toy balloon hanging to a string tied to his waist. At a signal each man tries to break the balloons of the other players. When a balloon is broken, its owner leaves the circle and the game continues until only one man survives.

5. BALLOON BATTLE (Team Form)

Same as Balloon Battle, except that players are in two distinguishable teams and play continues until one team is entirely eliminated.

6. TAIL FIGHT
Tail-Snatching

All players are in one large circle, each with a piece of cloth hanging from his belt in the back. At a signal each man tries to snatch the cloths from the belts of the others. When a man loses his cloth he leaves the game, which continues until only one man is left.

7. TAIL FIGHT (Team Form)

Same as Tail Fight, except that players are in two distinguishable teams and play continues until one team is eliminated.

Section II: One man throws or unbalances another

Included here are games in which each man tries to make others lose their balance so as to fall to the ground, touch a raised foot to the floor, or topple from a perch. In most cases play is confined within boundary lines and one who goes out of bounds is considered unbalanced. Also included are games based on wrestling, the term being interpreted broadly so as to include any struggle of a wrestling nature.

1. ROOSTER FIGHT
Bear Battle. Free-for-all Cock Fight.

All players are within a large circle. Each man raises one foot behind him and holds it in either hand, folding the other arm on his chest. At a signal, men begin pushing and bucking each other, each trying to make any other lose his balance. A man who touches the floor with any part of the body except the foot on which he is hopping, or who goes out of bounds, is eliminated from the game. The last survivor is the winner.

2. ROOSTER FIGHT (Team Form)

Same as Rooster Fight, except that men are in two teams, distingushable from each other. Each team tries to unbalance the other and play continues until all of one team have been eliminated.

3. LEG FIGHT

All players form a large circle, each man standing on one foot with arms folded on chest. Each man tries to unbalance any other by pushing or bucking him, or by tripping him with the free foot. Anything is allowed except kicking, use of the hands, or excessive roughness. This game is the same as Rooster Fight except that the use of the free foot is permitted.

4. LEG FIGHT (Team Form)

Battle of Legs

Same as Leg Fight, except that players are in two distinguishable teams and play continues until one team is eliminated.

5. DUCK FIGHT

Barnyard Battle-Royal. Rooster Rumpus.

This game is the same as Rooster Fight except for the position assumed by the players. Each man squats fully and grasps his ankles with both hands.

6. DUCK FIGHT (Team Form)

Same as Duck Fight, except that players are in two distinguishable teams and play continues until one team or the other is completely eliminated.

7. SHOULDER SHOVE

Out-Hopping Game. Shoulder Push.

Five men are within a circle. Four of the men fold arms on chests and hop on one foot; the fifth man is unrestricted. They all engage in a combat with the four hopping men against the other man. The hoppers try to push or shoulder the fifth man from the circle, but the latter tries to remain in the circle and at the same time to unbalance the hoppers. A hopper who unfolds his arms or touches the free foot to the floor must leave the game. If the fifth man can eliminate all of the others he wins, but if they eject him from the ring they win. Each man takes his turn as odd man and the winner is the one who eliminates the largest number of opponents before being pushed from the ring.

8. KNIGHTS' COMBAT

Cavaliers' Combat. Knights. Rough-Ride Roughhouse.

Players are in horse-and-rider pairs; that is, one man rides on the back of the other with legs wrapped around him just above the hips. Each rider tries to force any other rider to lose his balance and touch the floor. Each horse helps his rider by maneuvering but must not use his hands. When a rider touches the floor he and his horse are eliminated and play continues until only one pair remains.

9. KNIGHTS' COMBAT (Team Form)

Same as Knights' Combat, except that players are in two teams, each team of course trying to unbalance the other. Play continues until one team or the other is completely eliminated.

10. WATER KNIGHTS'-COMBAT

Water Knights

Same as Knights' Combat except that it is played in water waist deep.

11. HOG TYING

Players are in two distinguishable teams, all inside one large circle. A supply of three-foot lengths of old clothesline or similar rope is available. At a signal, each team, its members combining in any way desired, begins to try to tie together one or more pairs of opponents' ankles. When a man's ankles are securely tied together he leaves the game. The game continues until one team is completely eliminated except that a time limit should be set and the winner determined by comparing the numbers surviving if neither team has been eliminated.

Variation. Players are in two teams. Two circles are drawn and all but one of the members of each team occupy one of the circles. The odd man of each team is in the enemy's circle. At a signal each team catches the enemy in its circle and proceeds to tie his ankles together with a three-foot piece of rope and to tie his hands together behind his back with another piece of rope. The first team to complete tying its prisoner is the winner. Kicking or hitting is not permitted.

12. WRESTLE ROYAL

All players are within one large circle. At a signal, each man tries to throw any other to the ground. Anything legal in wrestling is permitted, but a man need not be pinned to the mat; he is down when he touches the ground with any part of the body other than the feet. Any number of men may combine against one other. When a man is down he leaves the game and play continues until only one is left.

13. WRESTLE ROYAL (Team Form)

Same as Wrestle Royal, except that players are in two distinguishable teams and play continues until all members of one team or the other are eliminated.

14. MOUNT-THE-BRONCHO
Crawl-the-Dragon. Riding-the-Broncho.

All players but one form a broncho in this way: one stands erect with his back to a wall; the others face him in single file; and each bends forward and wraps his arms about the waist of the man in front of him. The odd man mounts the broncho by a straddle vault from the rear and tries to crawl up to the head of the broncho and to touch the head of the front man, that is, of the man who stands with his back to the wall. The men forming the broncho try to interfere with the rider and to shake him off. They may shake and wiggle as much as they choose, and may move their feet about, but they must not straighten up or release their grasp. After the first man has had his try he takes the rear place in the broncho, all others move one place forward, and the man at the head becomes next to try. The man who travels farthest forward on the broncho is the champion. If several go all the way, they may play off the tie.

15. MOUNT-THE-BRONCHO (Team Form)
Crown-the-Dragon. Saddle-the-Nag.

Same as Mount-the-Broncho, except that players are in two equal teams. The teams take turns in forming the broncho, the members of the other team taking turns in trying to get to the head. The team with the larger number to succeed is the winner.

16. BRONCHO BUSTING

Bucking Broncho

Players are in two teams. One team forms a broncho as in Mount-the-Broncho. The men of the other team, without interference from the broncho team, all mount the broncho, sitting astride and facing the head. At a signal the broncho men proceed to try to shake the others off; to do this they may do anything except release their grasp or straighten up. The game is continued until all riders have been dislodged. Then the process is repeated with the teams reversed, and the times are compared. If experience shows that the riders cannot be dislodged, they should be restricted to a certain method of holding on. For example, they may be prohibited from wrapping their arms about the broncho, or even from holding on with their hands at all.

Division Three: Fight-for-Object Games

In the games of this division players struggle to secure possession of an object or to move it to a certain place. Some of them show considerable similarity to Goal games (see Class XI), and a case could be made for classifying them as such. They are here classed as Combat Games because in all of them the real struggle is an attempt to move men rather than objects, and the objects are merely the means by which the men are moved. This should be clear in the case of a game based on a tug of war with a rope. In a sense, the two sides struggle for the rope, but to obtain it, one side must pull the other bodily in a direction in which it tries not to go. It seems then that the Fight-for-Object Games of Division Three are basically much the same as the Fight-for-Position Games of Division Four.

Section I: Men fight for a rope

1. ROPE RUSH

Rope Pull. Rush Tug-of-War.

Players are in two teams, each behind one of two parallel goal lines about 30 feet apart. Midway between the lines a heavy rope is placed on the ground, perpendicular to the lines, and with the middle of the rope clearly marked. At a signal, all rush for the rope, grasp it and start to pull, each man pulling toward his own base line. If either team pulls the middle of the rope over its goal line within two minutes, that team is the winner; if neither team succeeds in doing this, the winner is the team with the middle of the rope nearer its goal line at the end of the two minutes.

2. ROPE PUSH

Two teams, each in line, face each other about two feet apart, with a line marked on the floor between them. Each man has both hands on a heavy rope, the two teams alternating in positions. At a signal all push on the rope. The team with the larger part of the rope in enemy territory after three minutes of play is the winner.

Variation. Teams form on base lines each about 15 feet from the center line, with the rope laid on the ground on the center line, that is, parallel with the goal lines. At a signal, all rush for the rope, grasp it, and push. Thus the game is the same as Rope Rush, except that the rope is pushed rather than pulled.

3. LINE TUG-OF-WAR
Go To It

Same as Rope Push, except that the men pull on the rope instead of pushing.

4. WHALE (Aquatic)

This is a tug-of-war game played by swimmers. Instead of a plain rope, the game uses a log with a rope at each end, the log floating in deep water. The log should be about eight feet long and eight to ten inches in diameter. A hole is bored through the log near each end and a ten-foot length of rope is tied through each hole. Men are in two teams, and each team grasps one of the ropes. At a signal all start to pull, each team toward its own base line. The team with the log nearer its line at the end of two minutes is the winner.

5. BOAT WHALE (Aquatic)

A log with a rope at each end is used as in Whale. The players, however, are in boats, each team in a boat at a distance of 50 feet from the whale. At a signal each team propels its boat to the whale. Even though a rowboat is used, the players should have paddles, not oars. Men may get their boat to the whale by any method desired: they may paddle, or they may go into the water and push or pull. Arriving at the whale, each team must tie its boat to the whale and then proceed to move the whale toward its base line. Again, players may stay in the boat or they may get into the water and help the movement in any way. To win, a team must move the whale entirely across its base line.

Section II: Players fight for an object other than a rope

1. SACK RUSH

Two teams form on parallel goal lines about 50 feet apart. Midway between the goal lines is a heavy sack filled with old paper and firmly tied. At a signal all rush for the sack and each team tries to carry it back to its own goal line. Any player has a choice between trying to advance the sack toward his goal and engaging with the enemy team so as to keep it from advancing the sack.

Variation. An old gymnasium mat is used instead of a sack.

2. CORNER MAT-RUSH
Four-Mat Tug-of-War

Players are in four teams, each in one of the corners of a square court. In the center of the court are four small gymnasium mats, each assigned to one of the teams. At a signal, each team rushes for its mat and tries to take it back to its corner, the first to arrive with its mat being the winner. Any player may work on advancing his own mat or on hindering the opponents. The game offers a chance for considerable planning and strategy.

3. DETHRONING-THE-KING

Players are in two teams, Royalists and Revolutionists, each team behind one of two parallel goal lines. The Royalists have a king sitting in a chair. At a signal, they pick up the chair with the king in it and try to carry him to the opposite line. The Revolutionists try to prevent this. If any part of the king's body touches the floor his team loses, but if he arrives at the opposite line his team wins.

4. RUSH-THE-POLE
Rush-the-Stick

Players are in two teams, each on one of two parallel goal lines about 40 feet apart. Midway between the lines, on the ground, is a pole. A pole eight to ten feet long and two to three inches in diameter is best, but a baseball bat will do. At a signal, all rush for the pole and get as many hands as possible on it. At the end of one minute (or any other period set in advance) the leader blows a whistle and all must hold their positions so that the hands can be counted. The team with the larger number of hands on the pole at the whistle is the winner.

Division Four: Fight-for-Position Games

The games of this division are those in which men grasp others and try to force them to move. They may try to eject the others from a certain area, to push or pull them across a certain line, or to force them into an area or against an object.

Section I: Men eject others from a certain area

1. CLEAR-THE-FORT
Rough-and-Tumble

The players are in two equal and distinguishable teams, all inside a single circle 12 to 15 feet in diameter. At a signal each team tries to force its opponents out of the circle. A man is out when he touches the floor on or ouside the circle. A man who is out immediately withdraws from the game, and play is continued until all members of one team or the other are out. Anything is permissible execept hitting or other forms of extreme roughness.

2. STORMING-THE-HEIGHTS
Storming-the-Fort

In the center of the playing field is a ten-foot square. If possible, this area should be elevated; a gymnasium mat may be used indoors. Players are in two teams and line up on opposite parallel lines a short distance from the center area. At a signal, all rush for the center area, each man trying to remain in the area and to keep out, or throw out, the opponents. At the end of a period agreed upon in advance, the leader blows a whistle and the team with the larger number of men in the area is the winner.

3. BATTLE ROYAL

King-of-the-Mountain

All players stand on a large gymnasium mat or other elevated area. At a signal each man tries to force others off the mat and to remain on the mat himself. A man is considered off when he touches the floor with any part of his body. The game continues until only one man is left on the mat, and he is, of course, the winner.

4. WATER BATTLE-ROYAL

Same as Battle Royal, except that it is played by swimmers on a raft. The swaying and tilting of the raft add to the fun. The playing of this game must be permitted only under close supervision.

5. KING-OF-THE-MOUNTAIN

Players are in two teams, each team with a king who is distinguishable from the other players. One team stands on a large gymnasium mat with its king in the center. The other team attacks and tries to force the defending king from the mat. The attacking team wins when the defending king is off the mat, provided the attacking king is on the mat. If both kings are off at the same time, the game continues, the two kings trying to get back on the mat, and ends only when the attacking king is on, and the defensive king off, the mat.

6. MASTER-OF-THE-RING

Dog-in-the-Manger

All players stand on a large gymnasium mat, or within a circle or rectangle marked on the floor, with arms folded on chests. Each man tries, by bucking and pushing, to eject any one of the others from the mat. One who touches the floor off the mat, or falls or unfolds his arms, leaves the game. The game continues until only one man is left.

7. MASTER-OF-THE-RING (Team Farm)

Same as Master-of-the-Ring except that players are in two distinguishable teams. Each team tries to force the other off the mat, and play continues until one team or the other is completely eliminated.

8. OUT-OF-THE-RING

This game is a variation of Master-of-the-Ring. Four circles are marked on the floor with diameters of eighteen, twelve, nine, and five feet. Play begins in the largest circle, as in Master-of-the-Ring. When a man is eliminated from the largest circle he goes immediately to the second circle, where the same game is played. When he is eliminated from the second circle he goes to the third, and when eliminated from the third, he goes to the fourth. Play is continued until there is only one man in each circle. The winners score four, three, two, and one for winning in the respective circles.

Section II: Men force others over a line

1. DITCH TUG

Catch-and-Pull Tug-of-War. Ditch Pull. French and English. Line Tug. Line-Wrestling. Pull Across Line. Rough-and-Tumble.

Two teams face each other separated by a line on the floor between them. At a signal, members of each team reach over the line, trying to grasp opponents and pull them over the line. A man is over the line when he is touching the floor with any part of his body on the far side of the line and not touching it with any part of the body on the original side of the line. Any number of men may combine against one opponent or pull on a teammate who is in the grasp of an opponent; the game is very definitely not played one against one. When a man is over the line he leaves the game. Logically, the game continues until one team is completely eliminated, but since the final stages of the game are likely to be slow, it is usually better if played for a predetermined time (for example, two minutes), and the winner determined by counting the survivors at the end of this time.

Variation. When a man is pulled over the line he becomes a member of the opposing team and play continues until all are on one side. This form of the game is illogical and provides no sound method of scoring. Nevertheless, it provides vigorous and fascinating activity and is very much enjoyed by the players.

2. BASE-LINE TUG
Carry to Base

Two teams line up exactly as in Ditch Tug, but two other lines are marked on the floor, one on each side of the center line, parallel with the center line and ten feet from it. The game begins like Ditch Tug, but a man is not considered captured until he is carried entirely over the base line at the rear. The game is continued and scored like Ditch Tug.

3. BASE-LINE TUG (Variation)

The field is marked with three parallel lines, two of them five feet apart, and a base line 30 feet away. Players are in two teams, an attacking team behind the base line, and a defending team in the five-foot zone between the other two lines. At a signal, the attacking team rushes forward and proceeds to force the defenders beyond the base line. The defenders must work individually, and are not permitted to help one another in any way. The attackers, on the other hand, may combine in any way. When all the defenders have been forced over the base line, the two teams reverse positions and the game is repeated. Time is taken in each case and the winner is the team that captures all of its opponents in the shorter time.

4. BASE-LINE PUSH
Push Across the Line. Shove Struggle.

Three parallel lines are marked on the floor at ten-foot intervals. Two teams face each other across the center line. At a signal, each team begins to push the opponents, trying to force them back over the farthest line. Players may push, but not hold or pull. When a man is forced over the base line he is eliminated, and the game continues until all members of one team or the other are out. The game may be varied by having a man join the opponents instead of being eliminated, as in Ditch Tug. Thus, this game is the same as Base-Line Tug except that pushing is substituted for pulling.

5. COPS AND ROBBERS
Robbers and Soldiers

This is a combat game that includes the hide-and-seek element. Players are divided into cops and robbers, but three-fourths or four-fifths of the group should be cops, and all the others should be robbers. The cops gather at a goal and close their eyes while the robbers run and hide; two or three minutes should be allowed for hiding. The cops then go in search of the robbers, and when they find one they must bring him in by force, the robber fighting all the way. When a robber is brought to the goal he must stay there. The cops continue until they have brought in all the robbers. The game is repeated with different men as cops.

6. SCOUTS AND INDIANS

Two parallel lines are drawn about 25 feet apart. Players are in two teams, one behind each of the lines, with a neutral zone between them. One team is called Scouts and its territory is the stockade; the other team is the Indians and its space is the Indian village. The men of each party, either singly or in groups of any size, make raids into the neutral zone and there try to capture enemy players and bring them back to the captors' territory. The team with the larger number of captives after five minutes of play is the winner. This game depends for its success on the readiness of the players to venture into the neutral zone and to take chances by engaging with the enemy. It will be a complete failure if players try too hard to play safe.

7. BUCCANEER (Aquatic)

Players are in two teams, one team at each end of a swimming pool. At a signal, all dive into the water and each team tries to pull opponents back to its base line. Any number of men may combine against one opponent, the play in general being the same as in Base-Line Tug. A man who is forced to the opponents' base line leaves the game, and the team with the larger number of survivors after two minutes is the winner. This is a game for good swimmers and even good swimmers should take care to avoid excessive ducking.

Section III: Men force others into an area or object

1. POISON SNAKE

Indian-Club Circle Pull. Indian-Club Wrestle. Knock-'em-Down.
Poison. Poison Stake. Poison Sticks.

Players all join hands in a circle. Several Indian clubs are placed
within the circle, about as many clubs as players. The clubs should
not be in a compact group, but should be spaced so that it is possible, but very difficult, for a player to step between them. At a
signal the players begin to pull and push each other, each trying to
make the others step into, and thus knock down, one or more clubs.
As soon as a club is knocked down, play is halted momentarily, the
guilty player withdraws from the game, and play is resumed. The
game is continued until only one man is left. It is sometimes ruled
that the original number of clubs is the same as the number of
players, and that when a player is eliminated he takes a club with
him. This procedure is probably not the best, but clubs should be
eliminated arbitrarily as the number of survivors decreases.

Variation 1. Players are not eliminated, but one who hits a club
has a point scored against him and pays a penalty for three such
points.

Variation 2. Sometimes it is better for players to hook elbows
instead of joining hands, or for each one to place his arms behind
the backs of his immediate neighbors and join hands with the second
men to his right and his left.

2. POISON SNAKE (Team Form)

Into-the-Ring. Team Poison-Stake.

Players are in two teams, but all form a single circle; the odd
numbers are one team and the even numbers the other. Each man
places his hands behind the backs of the opponents next to him and
join hands with his nearest teammates; that is with the second men
to the right and left. Indian clubs are placed within the circle as in
Poison Snake. Players pull and push, trying to make the opponents
hit the clubs and knock them down. There is no elimination, but
play is continued for a set time and scores are compared.

Variation. The same game can be played with three teams, or
even more.

3. POISON

Circle Tug. Cushion Dance. Poison Circle. Poison Spot.
Pulling-in-Circle. Pull-into-Circle.

Same as Poison Snake, except instead of using Indian clubs a circle is drawn on the floor within the circle of players.

Variation 1. A large cushion is placed within the circle of players and each tries to make others touch the cushion.

Variation 2. Same, except that a box or stool is used.

Variation 3. Same, except that the object in the center is a piece of rope coiled in imitation of a snake.

4. WATER POISON

Same as Poison, except that it is played in the water, either by players standing in shallow water or by swimmers in deep water. The object in the center of the circle of players is a board or any other floating object anchored to the bottom.

Class V

STUNT AND ALERTNESS GAMES

THIS CLASS OF GAMES IS BASED ESSENTIALLY ON SUCCESS OR FAILURE of the players' attempts to perform prescribed stunts without interference from other players. It also includes games that test the players' alertness in performing stunts or movements in response to commands or signals. Finally, it includes a few games in which winning or losing depends on a player's ability to make a correct guess, or even on chance.

Division One: Stunt Games

Section I: Player throws and catches a ball

Most of the games that are based on the successful throwing and catching of a ball are included in Class VII as Propel-and-Catch Games, and only a few are listed here as Stunt Games. The distinguishing characteristic of the games so listed is that a player always throws the ball and catches it himself, never throwing it to another player. Thus, the throwing and catching is itself in the nature of a stunt. In addition, the throwing and catching are nearly always accompanied by the performance of some other movement or activity of a stunt nature.

1. STUNT-CATCH ELIMINATION

The leader designates a stunt. Each player in turn throws a ball into the air, performs the stunt, and catches the ball before it touches the floor. After all have had a turn, the ones who have failed are eliminated, the survivors try again with a different stunt, and the game is continued until only one player survives. The stunts should be very easy at first and should become progressively more difficult. A few of the many possible stunts are: clap the hands one or more times; turn around half way or all the way; kneel and rise; roll forward; crawl under a bar or other obstacle.

2. WALL STUNT-CATCH
Wall Ball-Drill

Same as Stunt-Catch Elimination except that the ball is thrown against a wall and caught on the rebound.

3. O'LEARY

O'Leary is a game for girls only, since it involves the use of a skirt, but it could be adapted to play by boys. The girls take turns in batting a ball against the floor with the hand while repeating a little poem and performing a prescribed stunt. There is a whole series of stunts and each performer goes as far down the list as possible before missing.

To start the game, one girl takes a tennis ball or another similar ball and bounces it continuously against the floor while repeating these lines:

> One, two, three, O'Leary,
> Four, five, six, O'Leary,
> Seven, eight, nine, O'Leary,
> Ten, O'Leary, Postman

While repeating the first three lines she bats the ball at each word, and on the word *O'Leary* she swings her right leg over the ball, outward. On the last line she does not do the stunt and bats the ball only once, then catches it and rests for a moment before starting the second stunt. She continues, taking the stunts in the prescribed order, until she misses the ball or fails in the stunt. Then she steps aside while the other girls have their turns. If any girl succeeds in going through the entire list of stunts without a miss, she wins the game. However, it is much more likely that every girl will miss without having completed all the stunts. In this case, after every girl has had her turn, the first one has a second turn. This time she begins with the stunt on which she missed the first time. The game is continued until one girl finishes the list of stunts; all players should have the same number of turns.

The stunts to be used can be varied but in any particular game it must be understood just what the stunts are to be. The following list is suggestive only:

Stunts [4]

1. Swing right leg outward over the ball.
2. Same with left leg.
3. Swing right leg inward over the ball.
4. Same with left leg.
5. Let ball drop through skirt.
6. Let ball pass upward through skirt.
7. Touch right heel, then toe, to the ground.
8. Same with left heel and toe.
9. Touch right heel, then toe, then swing right leg outward over the ball.
10. Swing leg over ball on each count.

4. STUNT BALL-CATCH

Each player in turn begins a series of stunts, each of which consists of throwing a ball into the air and catching it, both throw and catch being according to specifications; in some stunts a simple movement comes between the throw and the catch. The first player goes as far down the list of stunts as he can without missing. When he misses, the next player takes a turn. After every player has had a turn, the first player starts again, this time with the stunt on which he failed the first time. The first player to complete the series is the winner, except that all must have an equal number of trials. Among the many possible stunts are the following: throw with one hand, catch with two; throw with two hands, catch with two; throw with two hands, catch with one; throw with one hand, catch with the other; throw to the ground and catch on the rebound, using all the variations above; bat ball upward before catching it; throw the ball upward or to the ground and before catching it do one of the following: clap hands, bow, kneel, jump upward, jump with turn.

5. POTS

Same as Stunt Ball-Catch, except that the ball is thrown against a wall and caught on the rebound.

---

[4] For a more complete list, see: *88 Successful Play Activities,* pp. 12-14. New York: National Recreation Association, 1946.

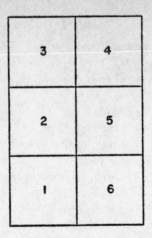

ROLLING LINE

Figure 17. Pavementball.

6. PAVEMENTBALL
Roly Poly

This game is based partly on O'Leary, but it also contains elements of Hopscotch. Like O'Leary it is played by little girls.

A paved surface is marked with a rectangle divided into six squares, each about 30 inches on a side, the squares being in two rows of three each. Three-foot squares are satisfactory and can often be found already marked in concrete sidewalks. Six or eight feet from one of the narrow sides of the rectangle is a "rolling" line. The squares are numbered in a clockwise direction beginning with the nearest one on the left.

The first girl takes her place at the rolling line with a small rubber ball. She rolls the ball toward square number one and must then run after the ball and pick it up while it is inside square number one. If she succeeds in this she throws the ball down to the ground inside the first square and catches it with both hands on the rebound. She then steps into the second square and bounces the ball there as she did in the first square. She steps into the other squares in order, bouncing the ball once in each. After she recovers the ball in the first square and while she is bouncing it in the squares successively she must not step on any line and must not let the ball touch any line. All this is called "Onesy." If she completes "Onesy" without a miss, she proceeds to "Twosey."

The girl now returns to the starting line, from which she rolls the ball toward the second square. She runs after the ball and picks it up inside the second square, stepping in the first square on the way. She now throws the ball to the ground so that it lands in the second square, bats it downward again as it rebounds, and catches it with both hands on the second rebound. Then she goes through the remaining squares in order, bouncing the ball twice in each one. That is, "Twosey" differs from "Onesy" in that the ball is bounced twice instead of once and play begins on the second square.

"Threesy" is the same, except that the ball is rolled to the third square where it is recovered by the girl, who is required to step into the first two squares on the way. The ball is bounced three times in the third, fourth, fifth, and sixth squares.

"Foursy," "Fivesy," and "Sixy" follow in the same way.

Now comes "Stampsey." This includes the entire progression of roll, recovery, and bounce from "Onesy" through "Sixy" with the addition that each time the ball is bounced on the ground the player stamps one foot.

After "Stampsey" is completed, "Clapsey" is begun. The same progression is used but this time the girl claps her hands together at each bounce.

Any desired number of additional stunts can be used and many suggestions can be found in the game of O'Leary. A few suggestions are:

1. Combine stamping and clapping.
2. Knuckles. After each bounce the ball is struck upward by the back of the hand and then batted downward.

The first girl starts at the beginning and continues to do the activities in order until she misses; she may miss by failing to recover the ball in the proper square, by stepping on a line, or by making an incorrect bounce. The other girls take turns, each going as far as she can with the series. After all have had a turn, the first one starts again, this time with the stunt on which she missed the first time. The first one to complete the series or the one who has gone farthest at the expiration of the time set is the winner.

7. JACKSTONES [5]
Jacks

Jackstones is played with a solid rubber ball, about as large as a golf ball, and six jacks. A jack is made of cast metal and is in the shape of three rods or bars three fourths of an inch long intersecting at their centers and each at right angles to the other two. The game consists of throwing the ball into the air and catching it, usually after a bounce, meanwhile performing various specified stunts with the jacks, such as picking up and laying down the jacks either singly or in groups of various sizes. As in other games just described, each player goes as far as possible through the series of stunts until he misses. After everybody has had a turn, he begins his second trial at the point where he missed.

Rules for Jackstones have been formulated in detail by the National Rules Committee on Athletics and Games of the National Recreation Association. Of course, the series of stunts can be, and often is, simplified and reduced considerably from those given.

Section II: Player catches a falling object

1. CATCH-THE-CANE
Catch-the-Staff. Catch-the-Stick. Falling Stick.

All players are numbered. One of them stands in the center of a circle formed by the others. The center man has a gymnasium wand or similar stick which he holds upright on the floor by placing a finger on the upper end. Suddenly he removes his finger and at the same time calls a number held by one of the players. The one whose

---

[5] For complete rules and list of stunts, see: *88 Successful Play Activities,* pp. 19-23. New York: National Recreation Association, 1946.

number is called dashes out and tries to catch the wand before it falls to the floor. If he succeeds he trades places with the center man; if he fails the same center man repeats.

Variation. The man whose number is called trades places with the center man whether he succeeds or fails. If he fails a point is scored against him.

2. ARITHMETICAL CATCH-THE-CANE
Mathematical Catch-the-Cane

Same as Catch-the-Cane, except for the method of calling the number. In this case the center man does not call a number directly but indicates it with an addition or subtraction. For example, he calls "Six plus three" or "Eight minus four," indicating that number nine or number four is to catch the cane.

Variation. Multiplication and division are used in addition to addition and subtraction.

3. CATCH-THE-CANE (Team Form)

Players are in two teams, but all form a single circle with each half circle constituting one team. Each team is numbered consecutively so that the two opponents with the same number are opposite each other in the circle. A neutral leader holds a cane in the center of the circle and releases it, as in Catch-the-Cane, calling a number as he does so. The two opponents with the number called rush for the cane and the one who gets it scores a point for his team, provided of course that he gets it before it falls. If neither man gets the cane before it falls no point is scored. If both catch it at the same time no point is scored.

4. SPIN-THE-PLATE
Spin-the-Platter

All players are numbered consecutively. One stands in the center of a circle formed by the others. The one in the center has a tin plate or pan which he spins, calling a number. The one whose number is called tries to catch the plate before it falls to the floor; if he succeeds he trades places with the center man. The game can also be played by counting a point against one who fails and making him pay a penalty for three points.

The center man should vary the speed of the spin given to the plate, or vary the delay in calling the number, so that the one whose number is called has barely sufficient time to catch the plate.

5. SPIN-THE-PLATE (Team Form)

Team Spin-the-Platter

Same as Catch-the-Cane (Team Form) except that the spinning plate is used instead of the falling wand.

6. CATCH-THE-BALLOON

Same as Catch-the-Cane except that the center man has a toy balloon that he drops as he calls a number. He must adjust the height from which the balloon is dropped so as to give the one called just enough time to catch the balloon before it strikes the floor. If necessary, he can give the balloon a slight upward toss.

7. CATCH-THE-BALLOON (Team Form)

Same as Catch-the-Balloon, except that it is played by two teams as is Catch-the-Cane (Team Form).

Section III: Player jumps, hops, or vaults

GROUP A: PLAYER JUMPS OVER A MOVING OBJECT

1. JUMP-THE-SHOT

Circle Jump. Hopping Circle. Hopping Toads. Jumping Circle. Jumping Jack. Jumping-the-Shot. Rope Skip.

One man is in the center of a circle formed by the others. The center man has a rope with a soft weight at one end, such as those often used for high-jump standards. He swings part of the rope in a circle and gradually increases the swinging part of the rope until it reaches the feet of the men in the circle, and then increases it still more until the circle men must jump over the rope to avoid being hit by it. The center man of course has considerable choice as to the speed and the height of the rope and it is up to him to adjust both so as to produce the right degree of difficulty for the circle men who jump over the rope. When a circle man is touched by the rope or the weight at its end a point is scored against him and he trades places with the center man.

Variation. A man who is touched by the rope is eliminated. The center man continues to swing the rope until all are eliminated, the last one becoming center man next time.

2. JUMP-THE-SHOT (Team Form)
Jumping Circle

Players are in two teams, all in a single circle with teams alternating. A neutral man swings a rope as in Jump-the-Shot. Each time a man is hit by the rope the opponents score a point. The game is continued with the same center man until one team has scored ten points.

3. JUMP-THE-STICK
Circle Jump

Same as Jump-the-Shot, except that the center man swings a bamboo stick instead of a rope.

4. ALL-FOURS JUMP-THE-SHOT

Same as Jump-the-Shot, except that the circle men take the all-fours position and jump over the rope on all fours.

5. PICKABACK JUMP-THE-SHOT
Horse-and-Rider Circle Jump

Same as Jump-the-Shot, except that the circle men are all in horse-and-rider pairs, that is, one rides on the back of another, the "rider" with his legs wrapped about the body of the "horse" just above the hips. The center man swings the rope, and each horse, with his rider, must jump over it. When a horse fails he becomes center man, each original rider becomes a horse, and the old center man becomes rider in place of the new center man.

6. JUMP-THE-CANE

This game is an adaptation of the well-known jump-stick relay. All players except two stand in single file about three feet apart. The odd two men have a gymnasium wand or similar stick. They stand in front of the column, facing the rear and holding the stick between them. They run rapidly from the front of the column to the rear, one of them on each side of the column. As the stick moves down the column the men must jump over it, and any man who fails to jump over the stick is eliminated. Then the column faces to the rear and the same two men carry the stick in the other direction. The game is continued until all are eliminated. As in Jump-the-Shot, the men with the stick must adjust their speed and the height of the stick so as to produce just the right amount of difficulty for the jumpers.

GROUP B: PLAYER HOPS

1. HOPSCOTCH

The *scotch* of Hopscotch has nothing to do with Scotland, but is a noun that in this case means a line on the ground, so that the name correctly suggests a game in which a player hops over lines. The lines form a diagram with several compartments, and the player hops from one compartment to another in a prescribed order. Before beginning his series of hops, he tosses a puck out into one of the compartments. When he reaches the puck he must kick it out of the diagram. The game varies a great deal and the diagram and rules suggested here are subject to unlimited variation. The puck is any available flat object about three inches in diameter; a rubber shoe heel is often used.

To begin the game, the first player stands, on one foot, behind the base line and tosses or drops the puck into square number one; the puck must come to rest within the square without touching any line. The player hops over the base line into the square and then, using the hopping foot only, he must kick the puck over the base line and out of the diagram. Having done this he hops over the base line to the starting position, where he may put his raised foot down and rest for a moment before beginning the second part of the game.

Standing on one foot as before, the player tosses the puck into square number two. He hops into the first square and from it into the second. Then he kicks the puck across the base line and hops from the second square to the first and from the first over the base line to the start, where he may again take a rest.

Whenever the player makes an error he must drop out and make way for the next player. He can make an error by failing to toss the puck into the proper compartment, by allowing his raised foot to touch the ground, by failing to hop to the compartments in proper order, by touching the ground on a line, or by failing to kick the puck across the base line. It is also an error to hop more than once in any compartment except that containing the puck; in that one, any number of hops are allowed.

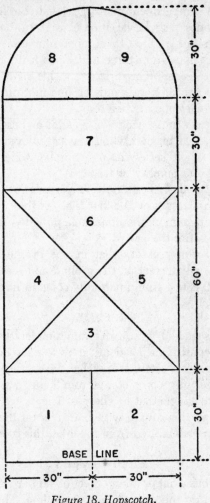

Figure 18. Hopscotch.

So long as he does not make an error, the player continues, throwing the puck on each round to the compartment with the next higher number, and always hopping to the compartments in numerical order and back the same way. Thus on the fifth round he tosses the puck to triangle number five, hops to one, two, three, four and five in order, kicks the puck back over the base line, and then hops back through four, three, two, and one, to the start.

Starting with compartment number six and continuing through all the remaining ones, a slight variation is used. In these cases he does not hop from number three to number four and then to number five; instead, he hops from three and lands in four and five simultaneously, with his left foot in four and his right foot in five. He jumps from his two feet and lands on one foot only in number six, from which he continues as before.

The players take turns, each going as far as possible before missing. The game is at an end when any one player has successfully completed the whole series through number nine, and all players have had the same number of trials.

As the game is described above, a player must always kick the puck out of the diagram on the first trial. As the game is sometimes played, he may take more than one kick, provided the puck does not rest on any line after the first kick.

Another variation provides that in one of the compartments a player may place both feet on the ground and rest. In the diagram as given here, this rest would naturally come in number seven.

2. POTSY

This game is played with a diagram simpler than that used for Hopscotch; it consists of 20 identical rectangles in two rows. Play is the same as in Hopscotch, except that this feature is added: When a player successfully completes a round, he marks his name or initials in any rectangle that he chooses. Thereafter he has the privilege of resting in this square with both feet on the ground, but all other players are prohibited from touching this rectangle at all.

3. HOP-THE-HATS

Each player has a hat or other object of similar size and shape. All hats are placed on the ground in a single line. The first man hops over the hats, one at a time, from one end of the line to the other, and then hops back over the hats to the start. Then he makes a second round trip, still hopping only, but this time he hops to the right of the first hat, to the left of the second, and so on. Arriving at the start he bends forward, places his hands on the ground, picks up his hat with his teeth, and throws it backward over his head. If he misses at any point, or touches any hat, he must pay a penalty. Whether he succeeds or fails, he places his hat at the far end of the row and the man who owns the next hat takes his turn.

4. HOP-THE-BLOCKS
Chicken Hops. Chinese Chicken.

Ten to 20 blocks—three-inch cubes are about right—are placed in a row two feet apart. The first man hops on one foot from one end of the row to the other, hopping over each block as he comes to it. He hops over the last block and then, with the hopping foot, kicks this block so that it stops at least three feet from its former position. Then he hops back over the blocks to the start and, without putting down his raised foot goes down the row again as before, this time kicking away the block that was originally second from the end but is now the last one. He continues this process until all the blocks have been kicked away; if he does so without touching a block except in the prescribed kicks, and without touching the ground with the raised foot, he succeeds. One who fails may be required to pay a penalty. The game can also be played with the elimination principle or, best of all, with players in two equal teams. The team with the larger number of members successful is the winner.

GROUP C: PLAYER VAULTS OVER ANOTHER

1. FOOT-AND-A-HALF
Par. Par and Leader.

A starting line is marked on the ground. One man is selected to be "down"; he makes a "back" about two feet beyond the line. To make the back, he plants his feet firmly on the ground moderately far apart, bends forward with his hands firmly on his knees, and bends his head forward. Sometimes the elbows are placed on the knees, but the method described is probably best. The other players line up in single file behind the starting line, the one in front being the leader. The leader calls "Straight over" and then proceeds to do a straddle vault over the back; that is, he runs, lands with feet together just behind the starting line, jumps or dives forward from

both feet, places both hands on the back with legs spread, and lands
on the ground beyond the back. The other men all do the same thing,
each taking his turn. This first stunt is easy and no man is likely to
fail. When all have vaulted, the back is moved forward a foot and a
half, measured not with a ruler but with the leader's foot. The whole
process is repeated again and again, the "back" moving forward a
foot and a half each time. The vault must always be made with both
feet behind the starting line.

Before long the distance from the starting line becomes so great
that the leader doubts his ability to vault over from the starting line,
and then he calls for a step, hop, leap, or jump between the starting
line and the vault. In a step, one springs from one foot and lands on
the other; in a hop, he springs from one foot and lands on the same
one; in a leap, he springs from one foot and lands on both feet; in a
jump, he springs from both feet and lands on both. Sometimes the
distinction between the leap and the jump is not made. Then the leap
as just defined is called a "jump" and the jump as defined is not
used at all.

Suppose now that the leader calls "One hop and over." Then he,
followed by the others, runs to the starting line, springs from one
foot behind the line, lands on the same foot between the line and the
back, and does the straddle vault. The leader may call for any one
of the springs mentioned, or, as the distance becomes still greater,
any combination of two or more of them.

If a player at any time fails, by stepping either on or over the
line, or by not making a good vault, he replaces the old back, the
latter becomes leader, and the old leader takes his place just
behind the new one. Any player other than the leader may at any
time try to do the vault with one step less than called for by the
leader; for example, if the leader calls "One step and over," a player
may try to vault straight over without the step. If he succeeds, the
leader is considered to have failed and becomes back.

2. LEADER AND FOOTER

The formation for this game is the same as for Foot-and-a-Half
and the play is the same with this important addition: The man at
the head of the column of vaulters, called the leader, has no particular function. The man at the rear, called the footer, is the one who
calls the method of vaulting. The footer calls "Straight over," "One

step and over," or the like, and all try, the footer coming last. At any time any player in the line may challenge the footer to do the vault himself in the prescribed way. If the footer succeeds, the challenger becomes "back," but if he fails he becomes back himself, the challenger not being required to do the stunt in either case.

3. DOUBLE FOOT-AND-A-HALF

· In this game there are two backs, one in front of the other, and no starting line. At the beginning of the game the backs are close enough together that players can easily vault over one after the other with no steps between. For the next vault the nearer back retains his original position but the farther one is moved a foot and a half farther away. The game is played in the same way as Foot-and-a-Half except that the first vault may be taken from any desired point behind the first back and that the steps or other springs called for by the leader are taken between the two vaults.

4. DOUBLE LEADER-AND-FOOTER

Leader and Footer

Same as Double Foot-and-a-Half except that the method of vaulting is called by the footer as in Leader and Footer.

5. SPANISH FLY

Stunt Leapfrog

In this game, one man forms a back and the others in turn vault over him as in Foot-and-a-Half, but there is no starting line, all vaults being made from any desired point behind the back. The stunts consist of different methods of vaulting or of doing certain prescribed tricks during the vault. The leader announces a certain vault, usually beginning with "Straight over," and all follow him in turn. Then he calls another and another. One who misses the stunt is the new back, exactly as in Foot-and-a-Half. Vaults sometimes used are: straight over; from left foot; from right foot; left hand only; right hand only; vault on knuckles; pinch "back" on way over; slap "back" on way over; vault straight over but land with half turn right; same left or with greater or smaller turn; leave cap, handkerchief, or cloth on back.

Section IV: Player does miscellaneous stunts and combinations

1. WAND-BALANCE ELIMINATION

All men stand inside boundary lines, each with a gymnasium wand or similar stick. At a signal, each man balances his wand on one finger. As soon as a man loses the balance of his wand he leaves the game, the last survivor being the winner. During the game all walk about at will and may bump against one another but may not hold.

2. MUMBLE-THE-PEG
Mumblety-Peg

Mumble-the-Peg is played with a folding pocket knife with one blade fully open. The National Recreation Association rules specify a Boy Scout knife with the leather-punch blade open, but any ordinary knife can be used. There is no reason why a sheath knife should not work quite well.

Each player in his turn takes the knife and starts on a series of stunts, each stunt being a method of throwing the knife so that it will land with the blade sticking in the ground. If he succeeds in one stunt he goes to the next, and continues until he misses. When each man has had his turn, the first one begins again with the stunt on which he missed the first time. The first man to finish the whole series of stunts, all having had the same number of trials, is the winner.[6]

3. MUMBLE-THE-PEG BASEBALL
Mumblety-Peg Baseball

This game requires a folding pocket knife with two blades, a large one and a small one, at the same end; a Boy Scout knife is very satisfactory. The game is played on a board of very soft wood; it is not satisfactory when played on the ground. The small blade of the knife is opened all the way and the large blade only half-way.

The first man places the knife with the large blade sticking in the board and the small blade touching, but not sticking in, the board. He places his index finger under the free end of the knife and flips it upward so that the knife turns end over end in the air. The position

---

[6] For list of stunts, see: *88 Successful Plays Activities,* pp. 23-25. New York: National Recreation Association, 1946.

in which the knife lands determines the success of the "batter" with each "pitch," as follows:

1. Knife resting on its side: batter out.
2. Resting on its back: strike.
3. Large blade in wood with end of knife touching wood: single.
4. Both blades in or touching the wood: two-base hit.
5. Large blade in wood, rest of knife not touching wood: three-base hit.
6. Small blade in wood, rest of knife not touching wood: home run.

Each player keeps the knife until he has three outs and then passes it to the next player. The game is not restricted to two teams, but can be played by any number. That is, each man can represent a team. It is better, however, with several players, to divide them into two teams, letting one man bat until he is out and then letting one of his teammates bat.

When a runner is on base he can advance only on a hit and then only the exact number of bases of the hit; a runner on second base cannot score on a single but may advance only to third base.

4. ALPHABET

Players are in two teams, each man with a card at least six inches square, with a large letter on it. The two sets of cards are identical and letters are selected that will make any of a number of words. Each team is assembled at a designated place, and some distance away are two lines on the floor, one for each team. The leader calls out a word that can be spelled with the letters and each team rushes to its line, lining up so as to spell the word. The first team to complete the word is the winner.

5. DRIVING GAME

Driving Contest

A large plank, marked off into equal sections, is laid on the ground. Several men, each with an ordinary hammer and ten large nails, are distributed along the plank. At a signal, all begin to drive nails into the plank. This is very difficult on account of the bouncing motion of the plank. The first man to drive in all his nails, or the one with the largest number successfully driven in, is the winner.

6. FOLLOW-THE-LEADER
Follow-my-Leader

One man is selected as leader. He starts off at a dog trot and all other players follow him in single file. The leader runs wherever he wishes, but seeks hazards as in an obstacle race; he jumps over ditches, vaults fences, squeezes through narrow openings, and so on. He may also travel by hopping, running backward, or any other method, and may do rolls and other stunts. In short, he may go anywhere and do anything, and the other players must all follow him and do what he does. When a player fails in any way he goes to the foot of the line and the game continues without interruption; if the leader fails in anything that he tries he goes to the foot.

Variation. A man who fails is eliminated and the game continues until only one remains.

7. WATER FOLLOW-THE-LEADER

Same as Follow-the-Leader except played in the water.

8. STUMP-THE-LEADER
Stunt Elimination

One man steps out from a group of players and performs a stunt of any kind—he may do a roll, upstart, or other tumbling stunt, or he may chin himself or do anything at all that may be classed as a stunt. The other players in turn try to perform the demonstrated stunt. Then the second player sets a stunt that all try, and the others in turn do the same thing. A man who fails goes to the foot of the line or is eliminated.

Division Two: Alertness Games

In most of the games of this division a player is expected to make quick and accurate response to commands or signals. In a few games the player has no signal but is expected to move at certain times and not at others. None of the games involves difficult stunts, but all require players to do the right thing at the right time; in other words, they require him to be alert.

Section I: Players respond to commands and signals

GROUP A: PLAYERS RESPOND TO ALL COMMANDS

1. CIRCLE SQUAT

Players run, skip, or march, as directed, in a circle around the leader. When the leader blows a whistle all must immediately assume a full squat position. A player who is last to stoop, or who is clearly slow in his response, is eliminated. Play is continued until only one is left. If music is available the game can be played by having the players march or run to music and stoop when the music is interrupted.

2. COMMAND DRILL
Quick Commands

Players are in open formation as for calisthenics, with a leader in front. The leader gives commands and each man must obey instantly and with great speed. Any one who makes a mistake or is too slow is eliminated or pays a penalty. The commands are not for calisthenic movements but for more extensive and vigorous movements. Examples are: sit; stand; kneel; squat; lie front; lie back; roll right.

3. MARCHING COMMAND-DRILL

Same as Command Drill, except that players march in a circle around the leader. After each command has been executed the leader calls "March," whereupon all jump to their feet and resume marching until the next command.

4. ELIMINATION DRILL
Attention. Drill Elimination.

Men are in open formation ready for calisthenics. A leader gives standard commands for facing, marching, and calisthenics, but gives them with exceptional speed and snap. A man who makes an error or is obviously too slow is eliminated and the game continues until only one man remains. This game is the same as Command Drill except for the nature of the commands.

5. I SAY STOOP

Players are in open formation as for calisthenics or, if there are only a few, in one straight line. A leader stands before the group and gives commands in quick succession, the commands being restricted to "I say stoop" and "I say stand." At the former command each player must do a full squat and immediately return to a stand, but at the latter command he must remain motionless. The leader, as he gives the commands, tries to mislead the players by himself performing actions which are sometimes different from the commands. That is, he may command "I say stand" and then may stoop and rise; or he may command "I say stoop" and remain standing, in the hope that some player will imitate him rather than follow his command. One who makes a mistake is eliminated or has a point scored against him.

6. I SAY

Players are in open formation or in a straight line. A leader gives commands, each preceded by "I say," and at the same time he performs some movement that may or may not be the one commanded. For example he may say "I say hands on hips" and at the same time place his own hands on his shoulders. One who makes an error is eliminated or has a point scored against him. This game is the same as "I say stoop" except that any command or movement may be used instead of stooping.

7. CONTRARY CHILDREN

A leader stands before the other players and gives commands. Each player must respond to each command by doing the opposite of the command. For example to the command "Right foot forward" each one extends the left foot forward. To the command "One step forward" he takes one step backward, and so on. Sometimes there may be more than one correct response. One who makes an error is eliminated or has a point scored against him.

8. HOLD FAST AND LET GO
Opposites

This game is like Contrary Children in that the players are expected to do just the opposite of the movement commanded. All players but one gather around a square piece of cloth and each grasps it with one hand. The odd player, the leader, calls either "Hold fast" or "Let go" and always the players must do just the opposite. One who makes a mistake trades places with the leader. Other commands may be added, particularly "Drop it," "Pick it up," and "Let it lie."

Variation. Players form a circle, each one holding one end of a handkerchief in each hand, the other end being held by his next neighbor. Otherwise same as above.

GROUP B: PLAYERS RESPOND TO CERTAIN COMMANDS ONLY

(a) All respond to commands that include certain words

1. DO THIS, DO THAT

A leader stands before the other players. He goes through various movements or exercises. As he does each movement he calls either "Do this" or "Do that." If the movement is accompanied by the command "Do this" all must imitate the movement, but if it is accompanied by the command "Do that" all must remain motionless. One who makes an error trades places with the leader.

Variation. One who makes an error is eliminated or has a point scored against him.

2. SIMON SAYS

O'Grady Says. Old Grady. Kelly Says. Tony Says.

One player stands before the others and gives commands for facing, marching, or calisthenics. The leader himself obeys all the commands, but the others are expected to obey them only when they are preceded by the words "Simon says." For example, the leader calls "Simon says, hands on hips—place" and executes the command himself; all others should also place hands on hips. But if the leader says "Forward—march" and steps out, the others should remain motionless. One who makes an error, either by making a movement when he should not, or by being too slow, trades places with the leader; or he can be eliminated or have a point scored against him.

The same game is played with other prefixes, as "O'Grady says," "Old Grady says," "Kelly says," or "Tony says."

3. WATER SIMON-SAYS

O'Grady in the Water

Same as Simon Says, except that it is played by men in water chest deep. The water gives opportunity for commands different from the usual ones, for example, "Duck" or "Surface dive."

4. SIMON SAYS STOOP

The leader says, "Simon says stoop" or "Simon says stand." These commands must be obeyed, but any command without the prefix "Simon says" must not be obeyed. The game is identical with Simon Says except that the movements are restricted to stooping and standing.

5. SIMON SAYS THUMBS UP

Simon Says

Players all sit around a table, each with both hands on the table, fists doubled up, and thumbs extended upward. One player, selected as leader, gives the following commands, mixing them up to suit himself: "Thumbs up," "Thumbs down," and "Wiggle waggle." Sometimes he prefixes the commands with "Simon says" and sometimes not; in the former case the commands are to be obeyed, and in the latter case not. The leader himself executes all the commands in an effort to confuse the others. One who makes an error trades places with the leader. If preferred, he may be eliminated or have a point scored against him.

(b) All respond to commands that are appropriate

1. BIRDS FLY

One player stands before the others, who are in open formation, and calls "——— fly," naming any animal, or any other object he chooses. At the same time he raises and lowers his arms in imitation of flying. If the call of the leader names an animal that actually flies, then all the players must raise and lower their arms, otherwise not. The leader, of course, does not need to obey the rules and tries to confuse the others by moving his arms at the wrong time. One who makes an error trades places with the leader, is eliminated, or has a point scored against him.

2. DUCKS FLY

One player, the leader, stands before the others, who are in open order. The leader calls the name of any animal or object, followed by a verb indicating any kind of activity. If the activity named is one performed by the animal or object, then all must do their best to imitate the activity; but if the activity is not appropriate, then all must remain motionless. The leader tries to confuse he others by making motions at the wrong time. One who makes an error trades places with the leader, is eliminated, or has a point scored against him.

3. HORNS

All players sit around a table, each with both forefingers extended downward and touching the table. A leader calls "Cat's horns up," or "Cow's horns up," or "——— horns up," naming any animal. If the animal named is one that has horns, all must lift their forefingers and point them upward, but if the animal does not have horns, all must remain motionless. The leader tries to confuse the others by raising his fingers at an inappropriate time. The leader may also call "All horns up," and then all must raise their fingers. One who makes a false motion or is too slow in making a correct one trades places with the leader.

4. CROWS AND CRANES

All except a leader are in open formation and divided into two teams, the teams alternating. One team is called crows, the other cranes. The leader gives standard commands for facing, marching, calisthenics, or other movements, but instead of the usual command of execution he uses either the word "Crows," or the word "Cranes," always prolonging the first part of the word, as "Crrrrows." Only the team called must execute the command. A point is scored against the teams for each error, and play is continued until one team or the other has accumulated a specified number of points.

Section II: Players advance at certain times only

This section includes the game of Statues and several others that are modifications of it. The point of the games is that players try to advance from one place to another, but are permitted to advance at certain times and not at others; usually they may move while one

player is not looking at them but must be motionless (hence the
name *Statues*) while he is looking.

1. STATUES

Advancing Statues. Red Light. Sculptor. Step. Steps.

The field is marked with two parallel lines about 50 feet apart.
All players but one stand on one of these lines, facing the center,
and the odd man stands on the other line. The odd man turns his
back to the others, counts to ten, and then turns again to face the
group; he may count rapidly, slowly, or by jerks. While his back is
turned, the other players advance toward the opposite line, but
when the odd man turns around after counting he must not see
anyone move. Any man seen moving is set back to the starting line.
The game is continued until one man succeeds in crossing the line;
he is the winner and trades places with the odd man. Another method
is to continue until all have crossed the line; in this case the last one
across is next odd man.

Variation. The object of each player is to touch the odd man,
rather than to cross the line.

2. SILENT STATUES

Advancing Statues. Statues. Steps.

Same as Statues, except that the odd man does not count. He may
turn at any time.

Variation. Players are divided between two base lines, the odd
man standing midway between them. The odd man turns first one
way and then the other, trying to give equal opportunities to the two
groups. Any man may advance while the odd man's back is turned.
Otherwise, it is the same as Statues.

3. ONE-FOOT STATUES

Same as Statues, except that men must stand on one foot while
the odd man is looking at them.

4. STATUES (Team Form)

Same as Statues, except that players are in two teams. The first
team to get ten men across the line or to touch the odd man is the
winner.

Division Three: Guess or Chance Games

As explained in the introduction to Stunt Games, the small group of games based on guess or chance is included here only by doing some violence to logic. They are not Stunt Games in any strict sense of the term, but they do seem to show some affinity to Stunt Games and are included here as a matter of convenience.

1. HOT HAND

This strenuous and somewhat painful game is popular with boys of college age. One man bends forward with his eyes closed and hands on knees, or, better, he leans on a table with his head on his arms. The other players gather around, and, after appropriate preliminaries, one of them gives a very vigorous swat with the palm of his hand to the rear of the man who is down. The latter then rises and tries to guess the identity of the man who has hit him. If the guess is correct the two trade places; if not, the same man is down again. Players develop various clever ways of confusing the down man, with remarks and changes of position. The game should be conducted so that the man down has a reasonable chance of making a correct guess. For this reason he should be given two or even three guesses whenever the group is large. However, it is best for the group not to be large; a group of more than six or seven should be divided between two games.

2. PAIRED HOT-HAND
Hot Hand

Same as Hot Hand, except that the swatters line up in a column of twos and the pairs take turns in swatting. That is, the first two step up, and one of them hits the man who is down, so that the latter has only to guess which one of two did the hitting. Next time the second pair steps up and one of them swats, and so on.

3. HOAX HOT-HAND

Hoax Hot-Hand is not a real game, but a trick played on an innocent victim. After the standard game of Hot Hand has been played for awhile, it is suggested that Double Hot-Hand be played, with two men down instead of just one. One man who is in on the hoax volunteers to be one of the men down and the victim is appointed to be the other. It is explained that the game is the same as the standard one, except that two men are swatted at the same time, each guessing independently. In fact, the victim is always swatted, not by one of the men gathered around him, but by the other man who is down. The latter is swatted in the usual way and in fact is engaged in a standard game of Hot Hand, except that he is perhaps treated with surprising leniency. The poor victim never seems to guess correctly. He is likely to catch on soon; if not, the usual method of terminating the hoax is for the players intentionally to become more and more careless until the victim cannot avoid getting the point.

4. BUCK

One man takes a firm stance and leans forward slightly so as to be able to support another man on his back. The others gather around and one of them jumps onto the back of the first man, extends any number of fingers of one hand and says "Buck, Buck, how many fingers are up?" If the guess is correct the two change places; if not, the same man is down again. Players should take turns in jumping on the back of the man who is down.

5. POISON CARPET

Crossing-the-Lake. Magic Carpet. Poison Areas.

On the floor is a gymnasium mat or an area of similar size marked with lines. Players march in single file and in step, travelling in a circle and walking across the mat. A leader blows a whistle and any player on the mat at the time is eliminated, the game being continued until only one is left. The leader with the whistle should turn his back to the group so that elimination will be determined by chance. Several areas may be used instead of only one.

6. WHISTLEBALL

Passball

Players are in a circle and pass a ball about at random. A leader, with his back to the group, blows a whistle from time to time and anyone holding the ball when the whistle blows is eliminated. The game is continued until only one is left. More than one ball may be used.

7. PAPER, STONE, AND SCISSORS

This is a game for two players only. It is usually considered a guessing game, but experience shows that some players develop surprising ability to use cleverness and for them it is partly a game of strategy and not one of pure guessing. Each of the two players doubles up one fist. The two count, together, "One, two, three," and at each count both swing the fists upward. At the third count, each man swings his fist upward and keeps it there in any one of these three positions: palm open to represent a sheet of paper; two fingers extended to represent a pair of scissors; or fist clenched to represent a stone. Now with two of these articles one is always superior to the other: paper is better than stone because it can wrap up the stone; stone is better than scissors because it can break the scissors; and scissors are better than paper because they can cut the paper. If the two players extend their hands in the same position, there is no play and they start again, but if they extend the hands in any two of the three possible positions, one is always better than the other and is the winner. The loser bares his wrist and the winner strikes it as hard as he can with two extended fingers. Of course, this last feature can be omitted and the game played with simple score keeping.

Class VI

TARGET GAMES

IN A TARGET GAME, A PLAYER THROWS OR OTHERWISE PROPELS AN object, nearly always a ball, at a target of some kind, his success being measured in one of several possible ways. There is never any interference from an opponent in the actual throwing of the ball, and hence a target game is very similar to a contest. As explained in the introduction, a game is distinguished from a contest by some complication or added feature that prevents its being a simple and valid measure of skill. In some target games this feature is interference by an opponent, but the interference comes after and not during the throw. In other cases it is a complicated scoring system, such as the one in Bowling. The class Target Games has five divisions: Pin Bowling Games; Gradual-Approach Target Games; Proximity Target Games; Diagram-Target Games; and Hit-or-Miss Target Games.

Division One: Pin-Bowling Games

Pin-Bowling Games include the standard game of Bowling, other games that are played on standard bowling alleys, and a few informal games that are played with improvised equipment.

1. BOWLING
Tenpins

In terms of players, rather than of spectators, Bowling is probably the most popular indoor game in the United States. It is estimated that 15,000,000 people bowl with more or less regularity each year. Rules that are universally accepted as official are formulated by the American Bowling Congress and published annually.

In Bowling, a player rolls a large ball down a wooden alley at a target that consists of a group of ten wooden pins standing in the form of a triangle with its apex toward the bowler. His object is to knock down as many of the pins as possible. The scoring system is unique and ingenious, and is the feature that makes Bowling a game and not a simple contest.

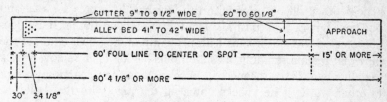

Figure 19. Bowling.

The bowling surface or bed is made of strips of wood set on edge, dressed to a perfectly flat and smooth surface, and finished with varnish or shellac. Its length from the foul line to the center of the first pin is sixty feet, and from the latter point to the pit approximately 2 feet, 10 1/8 inches. The approach to the foul line is 15 feet or more in length and the pit is 2 1/2 feet from front to back, so that the entire length required for an alley is more than eighty feet. The alley bed is 41 to 42 inches wide. The bed, not including the approach, is bordered on three sides by a depression, a gutter on each side, and a pit at the far end. At the pit end of the alley are ten spots for the pins, arranged in the pattern of an equilateral triangle, each spot 2 1/4 inches in diameter. Measured from center to center, the distance from one spot to the next is 12 inches, and the entire triangle is therefore 36 inches on a side. The rear row of four spots is 3 inches from the pit edge of the alley and the front or head-pin spot is 60 feet from the foul line.

A pin is made of hard maple. It must weigh not less than three pounds nor more than 3 1/2 pounds. Its height is fifteen inches, its diameter at the base 2 1/4 inches, and its diameter at the widest point 4 49/64 inches. The ball must be spherical, with a circumference of 27 inches or less, and a weight of not less than 10 nor more than 16 pounds. It may be made of any material, but is now almost always of composition. The ball has either two or three holes drilled in it for insertion of the bowler's fingers.

A game consists of ten innings, known as *frames*, for each player, the players bowling in turn. At the start of a frame the ten pins are set up on their spots and the bowler, holding the ball, takes a position at any desired point behind the foul line. He takes as many steps as he wishes and releases the ball with a swinging motion so that it rolls down the alley toward the pins. He must not step on or over the foul line; if he does so, the roll counts for nothing. If he knocks down all ten pins with the first ball he scores a *strike* and does not bowl again until his turn for the second frame. If he does not knock down all the pins with his first ball, he bowls again at the pins that remain standing, all fallen pins having been removed from the alley bed. If the second ball knocks down the remaining pins, or in other words if he knocks down all ten pins with two balls, he scores a *spare;* whether he does so or not he is through for the first frame and awaits his turn for the next frame.

If, in any frame, a bowler knocks down fewer than all ten of the pins his score for the frame is simply the number that he does knock down, but if he gets them all the situation is entirely different. When a player makes a spare, his score for the spare is ten plus the number of pins that he will knock down with the next ball that he bowls. Since this next ball will not be bowled until the following frame, it is obvious that the player who has just bowled a spare must wait until the following frame to know his score for the spare. Accordingly he indicates the spare by a diagonal line in the upper right hand corner of the proper space on the score pad; when he has bowled the first ball in the next frame he computes the score for the spare and writes it down. For example, if he gets eight pins with the first ball in the frame following the spare, his score for the spare is eighteen. The spare has no influence on the score for the following frame. If, in the example just given, the bowler gets a total of eight pins in this frame, the score for the frame is simply eight; if he makes a strike or spare the score is computed as for any other frame.

For a strike, a bowler scores ten plus the number of pins knocked down on the next *two* balls bowled. When he makes the strike he marks an "X" in the corner of the scoring space and waits until he has bowled two more balls before he can write in the score. These two balls will be bowled in the following frame unless the first of them results in another strike, in which case the second will not be bowled until the second frame after the original strike.

When a player makes a spare or a strike in the tenth frame, he bowls one or two extra times in order to determine the score for the spare or strike, the pins being set up for this purpose. A spare followed by a strike, or a strike followed by a spare, counts twenty points. A strike followed by two other strikes scores thirty, and a perfect game, consisting of nothing but strikes, has a score of three hundred.

2. DUCKPINS

There are two games of Duckpins. One uses pins made entirely of wood and allows three balls to a frame; the other uses pins that have rubber bands around the center and allows only two balls to a frame. The former is the basic or "regulation" game and is the one to which the term Duckpins, without qualifying adjective, is applied.

The game of Duckpins is played on the same alley as the standard game of Bowling, and with the same pin spots, but with smaller balls and smaller pins. Also, three balls are bowled in each frame, unless of course all pins are knocked down with the first one or two. Strikes and spares are scored exactly as in Bowling; ten pins with three balls count just ten, with no extra count as in a spare. Otherwise, the game is the same as Bowling.

Pins are made of maple and have the same shape as those used in Bowling. They are 1 3/8 inches in diameter at the base and 4 1/8 inches at the thickest part. They are 9 13/32 inches high. The ball has a maximum diameter of 5 inches and a maximum weight of 3 3/4 pounds. It does not have finger holes.

3. RUBBER-BAND DUCKPINS

The game of Rubber Band Duckpins uses pins that are the same as those of the hard-pin game except that each pin has a heavy rubber band around it at the thickest part, which makes it considerably easier for the bowler to score strikes and spares. In this game the bowler is allowed only two balls to a frame instead of three, as in the other form of Duckpins. In other words, this game is played and scored exactly like Bowling except for the different pins and balls.

4. COCKED HAT

Cocked Hat is played on a standard bowling alley. It is played with three standard pins and with Duckpin balls. The three pins are set up at the three corner spots 36 inches apart from center to center.

Two balls are bowled in a frame and the scoring is exactly as in standard Bowling, except, of course, that the score for a strike is three, instead of ten, plus the count on the next two balls, and the score for a spare is three plus the count on the next one ball. Thus, three strikes in succession count nine and a perfect score is ninety.

5. COCKED HAT AND FEATHER

This game is a modification of Cocked Hat. Four pins are set up, three at the corners, as in Cocked Hat, and the fourth on the center spot. Play and scoring are identical with those in Cocked Hat with this very important addition: The bowler tries not to knock down the center pin and scores nothing at all in any frame in which he does knock this pin down.

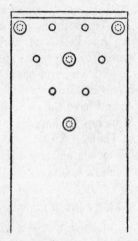

Figure 20. Cocked Hat and Feather.

6. CANDLEPINS

Candlepins is played on a standard bowling alley, but with duck-pin balls and special pins unlike those used in other bowling games. The pins are not well standardized but are about 15 inches high and almost cylindrical, their shape being suggestive of candles. The diameter is about 2 inches at top and bottom but about 2 3/4 inches in the middle. Three balls are permitted to a frame and the play and scoring are the same as in Duckpins.

7. SETBACK

Setback is a bowling game played on a standard alley, with five standard pins and Duckpin balls. The five pins are set up on the back row of spots, that is, on spots 7, 8, 9, and 10. In each frame a player bowls three balls, unless he knocks down all pins with one or two. The pins are numbered 1, 2, 3, 4, and 5, from left to right. A player's score is the sum of the numbers of the pins knocked down, provided pin number one is knocked down. If number one remains standing the player's score is negative. Strikes and spares are scored as in Duckpins.

8. SKITTLES

Skittles is an ancient game no longer played to any extent. It is played on an alley similar to a standard bowling alley but smaller and of indefinite demensions. Since the game is damaging to the alley surface the game is played on crude and perhaps improvised alleys. Standard pins or cylindrical sticks may be used, and they are set up as in Bowling. No ball is used, but, instead, a wooden disk about 5 inches in diameter and 1 1/2 inches thick. The player has the option of sliding the disk along the floor or of tossing it with an underhand motion. Scoring is as in Bowling.

9. SKIDDLES

Skiddles is an outdoor game, not played on an alley, in which sticks are thrown at a group of five upright pins. The pins are cylinders about 2 inches in diameter and 6 or 8 inches long. They are arranged with four in a 30-inch square and the fifth in the center, with the diagonal of the square in line with the throwing path. The pins are numbered, and scored according to their numbers; the pin nearest the thrower is number one, the center pin is number 10, and the others are, in clockwise order, 3, 4, and 2. Each player in turn throws three sticks at the pins, unless, of course, he knocks down all pins with one or two throws. The sticks are about 2 inches in diameter and 15 inches long. Players throw in turn and the first to score 100 points wins the game.

Variation. To win, a player must score exactly 100 points. If he scores more than 100 he must start again at zero.

10. IMPROVISED BOWLING
Informal Bowling

Bowling pins or substitutes are set up as in the standard game but on any smooth floor, such as that of a gymnasium. Players bowl at these pins with a basketball, scoring as in Bowling.

11. IMPROVISED DUCKPINS
Bowling in the Gymnasium. Informal Duckpins.

Duckpins or substitutes are set up on a gymnasium floor, as in the standard game of Duckpins. Players bowl at these pins with softballs, scoring as in the standard game.

12. KICK BOWLING

Bowling pins or substitutes are set up in a gymnasium. Players kick a soccer ball at these pins, scoring as in the game of Bowling.

13. SNOWBALL BOWLING
Snowball Tenpins

Sticks of wood are set up like bowling pins. Players throw snowballs at these pins from a line thirty feet distant, scoring as in the game of Bowling.

14. TIRE BOWLING

Bowling pins or sticks are set up as in Bowling. From a line 25 feet distant, players roll old automobile tires at these pins, scoring as in Bowling.

15. ROB-O-LING

This game was invented by Mr. Marion F. Robinson of Knoxville, Tennessee. It uses standard bowling pins set up in the usual way, but does not require an alley. It is played in a gymnasium, corridor, or any other room with a smooth floor. Instead of a ball, the game uses an object called a *skull*, which is slid along the floor; the skull is a modified hemisphere with finger holes. The bowling or sliding distance is variable but considerably shorter than that in Bowling. Scoring is the same as in the standard game of Bowling.

Division Two: Gradual-Approach Target Games

In a gradual-approach game, a player drives a ball toward a target, not expecting to hit the target on the first trial, but only to come as close to it as possible. He takes as many additional shots as necessary, each from the spot at which the last one came to rest, until finally the ball strikes, or drops into, the target. In most of the games the ball is driven by striking it with a stick or club, as in Golf, but in some of them the ball is driven by an entirely different method.

Section I: A ball is driven with a stick or club

This section includes Golf and other gradual-approach games in which a club is used to propel a ball. The games are in two groups: first, those in which standard golf balls and clubs are used; second, those in which other balls and clubs are used.

GROUP A: GAME USES GOLF BALLS AND CLUBS

1. GOLF

The game of Golf consists of driving a small ball, by means of specially constructed clubs, into a series of holes in stipulated succession. The player first drives the ball from a designated starting place and thereafter strikes it as many times as necessary, always from the spot at which it last came to rest, until it drops into the hole, using as few strokes as possible in the process.

The most famous golf club in the world is the Royal and Ancient Golf Club of St. Andrews in Fife, Scotland. Although a private club, the Royal and Ancient formulates rules and makes decisions that are accepted throughout the world, except in the United States, where the governing body is the United States Golf Association. The rules of these two governing bodies, while not identical, are generally in agreement; the most important conflicts that existed at the time were eliminated in May, 1951, by agreement between the two organizations.

The ball. The ball with which golf is played is made of hard rubber. Until 1921 it was not standardized, but beginning in that year it was everywhere required that the weight be not greater than

1.62 ounces and the diameter not less than 1.62 inches. The specifications still hold outside the United States, but here they have been changed twice. In 1931 the USGA increased the minimum diameter to 1.68 inches and decreased the maximum weight to 1.55 ounces. In 1932 the maximum weight was restored to 1.62 ounces, the size remaining unchanged. These specifications are still official, so that the United States ball has the same weight as the Royal and Ancient ball, but a larger size. However, the agreement of May, 1951, makes both balls legal in the United States. Effective in 1942 a USGA rule restricted the resilience of the ball, decreeing that it shall have an initial velocity of not more than 250 feet per second when tested at 75 degrees F. on a machine especially designed for the purpose. The ball has a dimpled surface, and is covered with white enamel.

Clubs or sticks. Each player has a collection of clubs or sticks that he carries, or a caddy carries for him, in a bag made for the purpose. The number of clubs carried by a player varies considerably but the tendency toward more and more has resulted in a rule that limits the number to fourteen. Each club consists of a straight shaft formerly made of hickory but now almost universally of steel, with the upper part enlarged and covered with leather to form a grip or handle, and a head, made of wood in the case of certain clubs and steel in others; clubs with wooden heads are called *woods,* those with steel heads, *irons.* A player may use any club that he chooses for a particular shot, his choice depending on the distance to be covered, the nature of the ground on which the ball lies, obstacles or hazards to be avoided, and the amount of roll desired after the ball strikes the ground. Clubs have both names and numbers, the numbers being of comparatively recent origin but rapidly replacing the names, especially for the irons.

The heads of wood clubs are usually made of persimmon, and are more or less disk-shaped, with the striking surfaces trimmed so that they are flat or slightly convex. They are the long-distance clubs. There are four standard wood clubs, although the fourth is much less common than the others. The number 1 wood is the driver. It has a heavy head, a long shaft, and a nearly vertical striking surface. It is used only for the initial strokes on those holes where the maximum possible distance is desired. The number 2 wood is the brassie, so called from the protective brass plate with which its sole is shod, although all woods nowadays have such plates. The brassie is used when the maximum possible distance is desired on any shot after the first one, provided the ball lies on the grass in a favorable position. It is very similar to the driver, but its driving face is less nearly perpendicular, so that it gives the ball more loft. The number 3 wood is the spoon. It is smaller and lighter than the brassie and gives the ball considerably more loft. It is used when the desired distance is slightly less than that given by the brassie, when the position of the ball is less favorable, or when more loft is desired. The number 4 wood is the baffie. In nature and use the baffie has the same relation to the spoon as the latter has to the brassie. The baffie is not a very common club and many players consider their sets of clubs complete without it.

There are nine standard, numbered irons in addition to the putter. The nine constitute an orderly, related series, the amount of loft becoming gradually greater, the weight greater, and the shaft shorter, as the numbers increase. Thus the number one iron has the longest shaft of all and the most nearly vertical face while number nine has the shortest shaft, the greatest weight and the largest amount of loft. The higher the number of the club the less distance it will drive the ball, the greater the height of the ball's trajectory, and the less the amount of roll after the ball strikes the ground. The names formerly used for these clubs, but now in rare use, are as follows:

Number 1—Driving iron, or cleek
Number 2—Midiron
Number 3—Mid mashie
Number 4—Mashie iron
Number 5—Mashie
Number 6—Spade mashie
Number 7—Mashie niblick
Number 8—Pitching niblick, or lofter
Number 9—Niblick

The putter is sometimes called the number 10 iron, but this designation is illogical and misleading since the putter does not fit at all into the series with the other irons. It has a nearly vertical face and is used only for rolling the ball along the ground when it is on the green. Putters vary a great deal in form, some of them having broad heads resembling those of woods, and some being made of material other than steel. Certain nonstandard irons are sometimes used, the most common one being the sand iron, sand wedge, or blaster, which resembles the number 9 iron but is even heaver; it is used for pitching the ball to the green from a sand trap. The jigger resembles a number 1 iron but has a short shaft; it is used to strike the ball from a position near the green so that it will roll into the desired position.

The course. Golf is played on a stretch of open country called a *golf course;* the term *golf links* [7] was formerly used but is not often heard at present. A golf course requires a much larger area than does the ground for any other well-recognized game, a full course of eighteen holes occupying at least 100 acres. Scattered over the course is a numbered series of holes, each consisting of a steel cylinder 4 1/2 inches in inside diameter, sunk flush with the ground and located in an area of closely cut and carefully cultivated grass called a *green.* The green is smooth and free from imperfections, but not necessarily level. Projecting upward from each hole is a bamboo shaft with a flag, on which the number of the hole is marked. The flag serves to locate the hole for players at some distance and is removed as the players arrive at the green. The construction and maintenance of good greens are difficult and very expensive and for this reason many unpretentious courses use sand as a substitute for grass and have therefore what are called, somewhat illogically, *sand greens.* For each hole there is an area called a *teeing ground,* or less correctly a *tee,* from which the initial stroke must be made. The distance from the teeing ground to the hole varies at the will of the architect of each course, and may be as short as 75 yards or as long as 650 yards. The sum of the distances for a good course is likely to be something like 7,400 yards, or more than four miles; in playing a round of golf, even a good player walks farther, and a poor one considerably farther, than this. The nature of the land not included in the greens and teeing grounds varies greatly. Some of it is covered with grass that is short and smooth—although not so much so as that on the greens—on which a ball can be found easily and played without difficulty; such areas are called *fairways.* Other parts may be covered with long and coarse grass, ditches, swamps, thick underbrush, or large trees, all very effective in giving a miserable time to the poor golfer whose ball goes among them. In addition, there are to be found built-up ridges, pits full of loose sand, and other "hazards." The favorable and unfavorable areas are distributed so that the golfer whose shots are straight and of the proper length will do his playing on the fairways and greens, while the one whose

---

[7] The word *links,* while plural in form, is usually construed as singular.

shots are poor is likely to make many of them from the "rough", from sand traps, or from behind trees.

Scoring. There are several methods of scoring in Golf, but they are all based on one or the other of two principles, "match play" and "stroke play." In match play, each hole is a unit in scoring; that is, a point is given for the low score on each hole, and the side with the larger number of points at the end of the match is the winner. In match play there are many ties on individual holes; a hole on which the score is tied is said to be "halved." Stroke play is sometimes less correctly called "medal play." In such play there is no scoring at the individual holes, but only for the entire round, the winner being the one who completes the round in the smaller number of total strokes.

The game may be played by two, three, or four players, any larger number being prohibited by the rules in order to prevent interference with other matches. For three players, the rules recognize three methods of scoring, each of them applicable to match or stroke play, although perhaps better suited to one than to the other: (*a*) Each man may play and score for himself. In match play a player must beat both of his opponents in order to score. This method is called a *three-ball match.* (*b*) Best-ball match—one player competes with the other two and his score is compared on each hole with the better of the two opponents' scores. Thus, if *A* competes against *B* and *C*, he wins with a three against two fours, loses with a four against a three and a six, and halves the hole with a four against a four and a six. (*c*) Threesome—one man competes with the other two and the two play only one ball; in this case the partners alternate in striking the ball from the tees and play the ball alternately after each tee shot. Thus, *A* strikes the ball from the teeing ground on the odd-numbered holes and *B* on the even-numbered ones; when *A* takes the first shot on any hole, *B* takes the second, *A* the third, and so on until the ball is in the cup.

With four players there are four recognized methods of scoring: (*a*) Best ball match—one player competes with the other three, comparing his score with the best of the opponents' scores. (*b*) Foursome —two players compete with the other two, each pair playing only one ball, as in the threesome. (*c*) Four-ball match—two players compete with the other two, each pair comparing its better ball on each hole with the better ball of the opponents. This is the only method of scoring recognized by the USGA rules, but it is more common, at least among average players, to count one point for the best ball and one point for the low total; for example, if partners A and B score three and five against their opponents' two fours, A's side gets one point for low ball and neither side scores for low total, whereas if A and B get three and six against two fours, the hole is halved since each side gets one point.

The standing in match play is indicated by giving the number of points by which the leader is ahead and also the number of holes remaining to be played; for example one may say that A is "one up and three to go," meaning that A is one point ahead and that three holes remain to be played. A player is said to be "dormie" when he is as many holes up as there are holes to be played, so that he cannot do less than halve the match and must win if he can win or even halve any one of the remaining holes.

Scores made by players are commonly compared with *par*. It is often said that par is the score made by one who plays perfectly, but this cannot be true since good players frequently beat par, not only for individual holes, but even for entire rounds. Par is, nevertheless, a high standard for all but a few players.

While there are exceptions for special cases, par is usually three for a hole with a length up to and including 250 yards, four up to 445 yards, five up to 600 yards, and six for lengths greater than 600 yards. One who makes a hole in par is said to *par* the hole, a score one less than par is a *birdie*, and a score two less than par is an *eagle*.

A few rules of play. For a game essentially simple, Golf provides an astonishing variety of situations and has, accordingly, a complicated set of rules. No attempt will be made to explain or digest these rules here, but a few of the more basic ones will be mentioned. At the beginning of a match the order of hitting the ball from the teeing ground is determined by lot. The player who wins a hole must be first to play the next hole; he is said to "have the honor," and he keeps the honor until he is defeated. If he has a partner, both he and his partner play before either of the opponents, but the two may play in either order; that is, if A wins the honor, then on the next hole either A or his partner may play first, the other following before the opponents play. Except for the tee shots, the player whose ball is farthest from the hole always plays next.

On a tee shot a player may elevate his ball on a *tee*, a small wooden peg. Not so many years ago little piles of moist sand were used for tees, but they have disappeared entirely. After the tee shot, a ball must always be played from the spot at which it comes to rest; it may not be lifted or moved for any purpose or at any time, except in a very few unusual situations provided for by the rules. It is true that in informal games on courses without proper fairways, local rules sometimes permit a slight adjustment of the ball.

A player is always penalized when his ball goes out of bounds, is lost, or is unplayable.

Since the agreement of May, 1951, a player making a putt has a right to an unobstructed shot at the hole, and any ball which may obstruct his shot is temporarily removed. Before that time there were certain conditions under which an obstructing ball was not removed, and the player making the putt was obliged to do the best he could in spite of the obstruction. The situation in which one ball lay in another ball's path to the hole was called a *stymie*. Even before the rule was changed, the stymie was played only under certain conditions; only in strict match play and even then with certain exceptions. As it is usually stated, stymies were formerly played, under certain conditions, but now stymies are not played under any conditions.

2. PUTTING GOLF
Midget Golf. Miniature Golf. Tom-Thumb Golf.

Nine or eighteen holes are laid off on the smoothest grass available, in irregular order, and numbered so as to provide the most interesting series of shots. Players use only putters and play the holes in order, the first shot being from the last hole to the first. Commercially operated courses of this type have had occasional periods of great popularity. Such courses are usually covered with some material more durable than grass, and are provided with hazards of great variety, including bridges, tunnels, loop-the-loops, ski jumps, and the like.

3. CLOCK GOLF

Clock Golf is a special form of Putting Golf, the holes being arranged in a circle and suggesting the numbers on a clock face. The holes are not numbered in order, but each one is directly across the circle from the preceding one; that is, the holes are numbered 1, 3, 5, 7, 9, 11, 13, 15, 17, 2, 4, 6, 8, 10, 12, 14, 16, 18. There are no teeing grounds, but the first shot at each hole is taken from a position within one foot of the preceding hole. Sometimes twelve holes are used in conformity with the clock idea.

4. ONE-HOLE CLOCK GOLF

As the name implies this game uses only one hole. The hole is surrounded by markers for the starting shots. It is better for the hole not to be in the center of the circle.

GROUP B: GAME DOES NOT USE GOLF BALLS AND CLUBS

1. GOOFY GOLF
Tennis Golf

A small golf course is improvised and tin cans are sunk in the ground for holes. Players use improvised sticks and old tennis balls.

2. HOCKEY GOLF

Same as Goofy Golf, except that the players use field-hockey sticks and balls.

3. CROQUET GOLF

Same as Goofy Golf, except that the players use croquet mallets and balls.

4. POST GOLF

Goofy Golf or any other improvised form of the game can be played by using posts instead of holes, each post extending a foot or so above the ground. A hole is made when the ball hits the proper post.

5. GOPHER GOLF

Gopher Golf is a proprietary name. The game was originated by Mr. G. H. Winfrey of Richmond, Virginia. In principle, the game is identical with Golf, but it uses different clubs, balls, and even holes. The ball is about the size and weight of a standard baseball. Each player uses only one club, a mallet quite similar to a polo mallet. The holes are not sunk below the ground but are in ready-made sheet metal devices, each a low, truncated pyramid with a hole at the top, the ball being rolled up the slight incline of the pyramid and into the hole. These targets are very similar to the ones used in the older game of Codeball-on-the-Green.

6. CROQUET

Croquet appears to have originated in France and to have come to the United States by way of England about 1870. Since that time the game has had its ups and downs, but has never ceased to be a well-known and popular game, especially on home lawns, where it is the family game par excellence. A more formalized set of rules has had some slight success, and a still more formal version is played under the name of Roque. But Croquet is essentially an informal game in which the basic idea is clear enough, but in which details of the rules and layout of the court are variable. The description given here applies to the standard game played according to the most common rules.

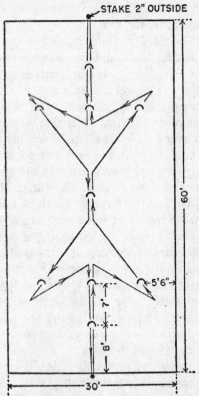

Figure 21. Croquet. All dimensions are suggestive only and may be varied at will. Boundary lines are commonly omitted.

Croquet can be played on almost any surface but is usually and most satisfactorily played on grass. The court should be level, or nearly so, but a slight roll does no harm; it can be of variable size, 30 by 60 feet being about average. Each player plays with his own ball, which is made of wood and is 3 3/8 inches in diameter. He drives this ball with a wooden mallet through a series of nine wire arches (through five of them twice), and against two wooden posts, one at either end of the court, following an irregular path as he does so. The game can be played by two, three, or four men, each for himself, or by two, three, or four pairs of partners. A croquet set, accordingly, consists of two stakes, nine arches, eight mallets, and eight balls, the balls being in four colors. Custom requires that each stake be painted with four circles in the four colors of the balls, and that the order in which the balls are played shall be same as that of the circles, beginning at the top.

The arches or "wickets" are laid out as in Figure 21.

Players draw lots for color, and hence order of play, and the first man prepares to play. He sets his ball on the ground between the first stake and the first wicket and strikes it with his mallet. Unless he is a very poor player the ball will travel through the first two wickets. A basic rule of the game is that a player is entitled to another shot for every wicket through which his ball travels or for each time that he strikes another ball (friend or enemy) with his own. Accordingly, the first player, having driven his ball through two wickets, has two shots to play. He will probably use them in an attempt to drive his ball through the third wicket. He uses the first shot to drive the ball to a position in front of the wicket. If this shot is a good one he uses the remaining shot to drive the ball through the wicket and into position for the next one. He continues until he has used up the shots available to him and then waits for his turn to come again. The second player, an opponent, now plays from the starting position. For him the situation is different than for the first man because he always has the right to drive his ball against that of the first player. This is a very important play and gives the one who makes it unusual privileges.

When a man has hit another ball (friendly or enemy) with his own, he has his choice of four different plays: (*a*) he may play his ball as it lies, in this case getting only one shot; (*b*) he may place his ball a mallet head's distance from the other in any direction and take two shots; (*c*) he may place his ball so that it touches the other, step firmly with one foot on top of his own ball, strike his ball with the mallet so as to drive the other ball away, and then take one additional shot with his ball; (*d*) he may place his ball so that it touches the other, as in (*c*), and then without stepping on his ball hit it so as to drive both balls away.

Some other rules of importance are these: A man is never more than two shots ahead; for example, if a man has two shots and on the first one goes through a wicket and also hits a ball it might seem that he now has four shots, one left from the original two, one for the wicket and two for hitting the ball, but he is always limited to two. When a man hits the ball of another player he may not hit this same ball again until he first goes through a wicket or hits a stake; in the meantime he is said to be "dead on the other ball." In a game with partners, a player who is in position to hit the final stake and thereby finish the round may, if he chooses, refrain from finishing the round and become a *rover* instead. This means that he drives his ball into the field of play in the hope that the chance to play on it and thereby get additional shots will be of greater benefit to his partner than to the opponents.

7. ROQUE

The word *Roque* is, of course, manufactured from Croquet by omitting the first and last letters. The game is a formalized version of Croquet, adapted for more skillful play. The court is 30 by 60 feet but is octagonal rather than rectangular. Sometimes, but not always, the court is surrounded by a low wall from which the balls may be carromed in play. The wickets are smaller and heavier than those used in Croquet and each man plays two balls instead of one. There are many refinements in the rules, but the game does not differ in its essentials from Croquet.

Section II: Ball is not driven with a stick or club

1. CODEBALL-ON-THE-GREEN

Codeball-on-the-Green was devised in 1929 by William E. Code, M.D. of Chicago. The same man devised another game to be played in a handball court, called *Codeball-in-the-Court*. The two

Codeball games cause some confusion but they have nothing in common except the use of the feet.

Codeball-on-the-Green is patterned after Golf. It is played with a specially made inflated rubber ball six inches in diameter, and the ball is propelled by kicking. The holes are not sunk in the ground but are in movable metal "bowls," each bowl being a truncated cone seven and one-half inches high and 42 inches in diameter at the base. The hole, at the top of the bowl, is 18 inches in diameter. The bowls can be set out, and the game played, on a field of almost any size, but it is recommended that the distances from teeing ground to hole shall vary from 50 to 300 yards.

2. ARCHERY GOLF

Archery Golf requires a course about the size of a golf course and, in fact, is sometimes played on a golf course out of golf season. Instead of driving a ball with a club the player shoots an arrow with an archery bow. The principle is the same as that of golf, the player taking a tee shot and then making successive shots, each from the spot of recovery, until he "holes out," which he does by hitting a target with his arrow. It is obvious that the gradual-approach principal breaks down somewhat as the player approaches the target, and that this part of the play presents some difficulty.

In one form of the game the target is a bale of straw with a disk marked on each of the four vertical faces; the player shoots until he hits the bale and is assumed to have holed out if he hits one of the disks. He is charged with an extra shot if he hits the bale but not the disk. In another form of the game, the target is two-faced, each face smaller than a standard target and having only three circles. The target is in the center of a 20-yard circle marked on the ground. Usually the player shoots until his arrow comes to rest at some point within the circle; he then goes to any desired point on the circumference of the circle and shoots at the target, his success in this shot determining the number of "putts" needed. A shot into the bull's-eye counts one putt, into the next circle two putts, and into the third circle three putts. If he does not hit any of the circles he shoots again from the circumference of the circle. A player has the right to shoot at the target from a point outside the 20-yard circle. He then has the option of counting his score on the basis of this shot, or of counting the shot as merely the one required to get into the circle; in the latter case he goes to the circumference of the circle and shoots as described above.

3. MARBLE GOLF

In this game, ordinary marbles are shot in the "knuckles-down" position at holes made by very small tin cans sunk in the ground. The course is laid out on clay or other fairly smooth ground; the holes may be up to 60 feet in length and hazards of all sorts can be improvised.

4. HOPSCOTCH GOLF

In this golf-type game, a cubical wooden block two or three inches on a side is used instead of a ball. To advance the block the player hops on one foot and kicks the block with this same foot. Holes may be made of tin cans sunk in the ground, and the distances may vary from three or four yards to 20 yards. Sometimes the holes are laid out in a circle, as in Clock Golf.

Division Three: Proximity Target Games

In a Proximity Target Game, players throw or otherwise propel balls or objects toward a target, with the purpose of causing them to come to rest as near the target as possible. The principle of scoring is the same for all games in the group, namely, a side (individual player or team) scores a point for each of its objects that is nearer the target than the closest of the opponent's objects. The objects may be thrown or they may be rolled or slid, and the games will be described in two sections corresponding to these two methods of propulsion.

Section I: Object is thrown

1. HORSESHOE PITCHING

Horseshoes

In the game of Horseshoe Pitching, players throw horseshoes, either real ones or modified ones made for the purpose, at stakes driven into the ground. The player's purpose on each throw is to make a "ringer," in which the shoe encircles the stake, or failing this, to cause the shoe to land and remain very close to the stake. The

National Horseshoe Pitchers' Association makes rules that are accepted as official.

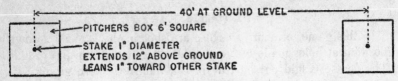

Figure 22. Horseshoe Pitching.

The character of the game as played by experts was changed radically as the result of the example set in 1920 by Mr. George May of Akron, Ohio. Until that time even a good player scarcely expected to make a ringer when making a throw at the stake. The difficulty was that the shoe had an uncontrolled spin in flight. Even when aimed perfectly it was likely to hit the stake with the closed end and bounce off. It was largely a matter of chance when the shoe arrived at the stake with the open end forward. Mr. May changed all this. He found that he could control the spin of the shoe so that it always rotated the same number of times and always, or nearly always, arrived at the stake with the open-end forward. Since an expert player has relatively little difficulty in throwing a shoe so as to hit the stake, Mr. May was able to score ringers a large part of the time. The result has been that, among the best players, ringers are decidedly the rule and not, as formerly, the exception. The tournament record is held by Guy Zimmerman who, in the national championship tournament of 1940 played thirty games and scored 86.1 ringers for each one hundred throws. In 1934 Guy Zimmerman and Dean Brown threw twenty-eight consecutive double ringers in a singles match.

The game uses two iron stakes driven into the ground 40 feet apart at ground level. Each stake is one inch in diameter and extends 12 inches above the ground, leaning on inch toward the other stake. Each stake is in the center of a *pitcher's box* which is six feet square and filled with moist clay, the surface of the clay being not more than one inch above the general level of the ground. The horseshoes that are used in this game are noticeably different from those actually worn by horses, being seven inches wide by seven and a half inches long and weighing two and a half pounds each.

The game may be played as singles, with one player opposing

another, or as doubles, with two partners opposing two others. Whether the game is singles or doubles, four shoes are used, two by each side. In singles, the two players stand at one stake and throw for the other, one player throwing both his shoes and the opponent then throwing his. They then walk to the stake at which they have just thrown, decide the score, and throw the shoes back at the first stake; they continue thus, throwing the shoes at the stakes alternately until the end of the game.

In doubles, the players do not walk from one stake to the other, but each man throws always from the same place and at the same stake. One man and one of his opponents stand at each stake; these two throw the shoes to the other stake and the other two players throw them back. Thus each man in a sense competes against only one of his opponents and a doubles game may be thought of as a combination of two games of singles.

The pitcher always stands inside the pitching box. At the beginning of a match the first pitcher is determined by lot. The loser of any game is first pitcher in the next game. After the beginning of any game, the first pitcher is the one who made, or whose side made, the last score.

The score is determined by the relative positions of the shoes after all four have been thrown. In general, the shoe that is closest to the stake scores one point, and if both shoes thrown by one side are closer than either of the two thrown by the other side they score two points. In other words, a side scores one point for each shoe that is closer to the stake than the closer shoe of the opponents. However, when a shoe that scores is a ringer, it counts three points instead of one. Thus in any half-inning only one side can score, and the score can be one, two, three, four, or six. If two shoes are tied, neither one scores. All ringers are considered equal and accordingly in the frequent cases in which all four shoes are ringers, there is no score at all. A "leaner" or "hobber" (a shoe leaning against the stake but not encircling it) is not recognized in the official rules and is merely a close shoe that scores one point, if anything. A rule commonly disregarded except in expert play is that no shoe can score if it is more than six inches from the stake.

It is usually said that a game is won by the side that first makes 50 points, but this is not strictly accurate. More precisely, the winning side is the one with the larger score at the end of the half-inning

206 **Target Games**

in which either side reaches 50 points. If both sides have the same
score, play is continued until the tie is broken.

2. INFORMAL HORSESHOE-PITCHING

For inexpert players, Horseshoe Pitching is often played with
rules somewhat different from the official rules. The box is commonly dispensed with and the stakes driven into any level piece of
ground. The ground may be dug out gradually by the impact of the
shoes until there is a saucer-like depression surrounding each stake.
The distance may be estimated rather than measured accurately.
Several variations in scoring have been common, most common of
all being that a game ends with 21 points instead of with the official
50. Sometimes a ringer counts five, and quite commonly a "leaner"
counts three or two. Another variation provides that if one ringer
tops one or more other ringers, then the top one counts the score of
all put together. All these variations tend to disappear from use as
the official rules become better known. It is here recommended that
even for informal play the stakes be placed according to the official
rules and that the official scoring system be used, but that the box
and its surrounding clay be dispensed with and that a game be 21
points instead of 50.

3. QUOITS

Although Quoits has been played rather extensively in the past, it
is now almost unknown in the United States and there are no generally accepted rules for it. On the few occasions when it is played
the rules may be almost exactly those of Horseshoe Pitching, or they
may include various rules from the traditional game.

The quoit, that is, the object that is thrown, is shaped like a
doughnut except that one surface is flat and the other convex; the
inside diameter is four inches and the outside diameter nine inches,
so that the rim is 2 1/2 inches wide. If an attempt is made to follow
traditional rules rather than those of modern Horseshoe Pitching, the
principal differences are likely to be something like this: The pins
project from the ground only one inch and are about 50 feet apart.
(Some rules say eighteen yards.) A ringer counts three points and a
hobber or leaner two points. If two or more ringers are thrown, the
top one counts the scores of all of them, as in Informal Horseshoe-
Pitching. A game ends at 21 points.

4. BLOCK HORSESHOES

This game is an adaptation of Horseshoe Pitching and is played on a horseshoe court, but uses blocks of wood instead of horseshoes. Cubical blocks about two inches on a side are recommended, but in any case they should be uniform. Of course other objects, stones for example, can be substituted. Play and scoring are the same as in Horseshoe Pitching, except that there are of course no ringers or leaners.

5. MASS BLOCK-HORSESHOES

Three or more men play this game, each for himself. Each man has a block of wood that can be identified as his. All stand at one stake of a horseshoe court and throw the blocks in turn. When all have thrown, the one block that is nearer than any other scores a point for its thrower.

Variation. Instead of throwing in turn, all players, at a signal, throw at the same time.

Team Variation. Either the basic game or the variation can be scored on a team basis, the players being divided into two equal teams and one of them scoring a point for each block that is nearer the stake than the nearest block of the opponents.

Section II: Object is rolled or slid

The games in this section are basically the same as those in Section I, and a good case could be made for grouping the two sections together. The only important difference is that in Section II objects are rolled or slid instead of being thrown.

1. LAWN BOWLING

Bowling-on-the-Green. Bowls. Lawn Bowls.

There is a question whether the game listed here is correctly called Bowls or Lawn Bowling. The game is directed in the United States by the American Lawn Bowling Association, which in its constitution declares as its purpose "to foster, promote and safeguard the game of Lawn Bowling (or 'Bowling on the Green')" and "to adopt and uphold the laws of the game of Lawn Bowling..." But the American Lawn Bowling Association, in the same book that contains its constitution, publishes as the Association's laws of the game those adopted by the International Bowling Board, and these laws make it clear that the name of the game is Bowls. The British Associations connected with the game all use the word *bowling* (but not *lawn*) in their titles, but they sponsor a periodical

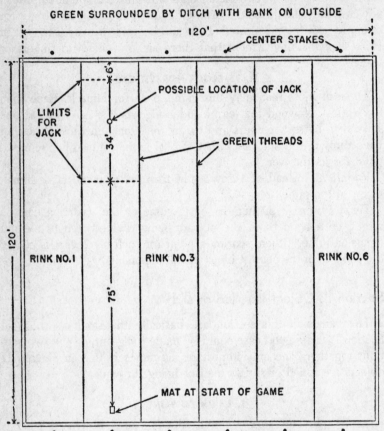

Figure 23. *Lawn Bowling. A standard green of six rinks.*

called *The Bowls News*. In British usage, a man who plays the game is a *bowler* and the playing is called *bowling*, but when the game is given a name it is consistently Bowls. There is no question that in the United States the term *Lawn Bowling* is more frequently used and that it has definite official sanction. The conclusion of the author is that in British or international usage the game must be called *Bowls* but that in the United States, the better name is *Lawn Bowling*.

Although Great Britain is the home of the game, it is played in many other countries and is more common in the United States than is usually realized. According to Menke [8] there were, in 1947, more than 150 lawn bowling clubs in the country and many thousands of greens, with six alleys to the green, patronized by at least 2,000,000 regular or occasional players.

Lawn Bowling is based on exactly the same principle as Horseshoe Pitching: Players propel objects toward a target, and one side scores a point for each of its objects that is nearer the target than the nearest one of the opponents. It differs from Horseshoe Pitching chiefly in these ways: (*a*) The player rolls a ball along the ground instead of throwing a horseshoe; (*b*) The target is not a stake but a small ball; (*c*) There can be no such thing as a ringer or a leaner; (*d*) The target itself is likely to be moved during play; (*e*) Striking an opponent's ball so as to move it is an important play in Lawn Bowling, while moving an opponent's shoe in the other game is much less important.

The game is played on a piece of smooth and level ground called a *rink*. Rinks are nearly always laid out in groups of six, side by side. The whole area for the six games is called a *green*, a term that is heard much more frequently than rink and is occasionally used in error instead of the latter term. Bowling greens have traditionally been covered with grass, the best of them having beautifully kept bent grass that is equal to that found on the finest golf greens. It has lately been found that the game can be played very successfully on greens without grass and many greens now used in this country are made of marl (a clay mixture), covered with a fine layer of sand. Marl is the usual material in Florida, where there are a great many greens and clubs, including the St. Petersburg Club which claims to be the largest in the world.

A bowling green for six rinks is square; the rules prohibit a size larger than 132 feet, and 120 feet is most common. The six links that comprise the green are not indicated by any permanent markings but only by temporary corner stakes and by green linen threads that serve as the side lines; the center line of each rink is indicated by

[8] Frank G. Menke, *The New Encyclopedia of Sports.* New York: A. S. Barnes Company, 1947, p. 678.

two stakes that are beyond the limits of play. The entire green is surrounded by a ditch at least six inches deep and ten to fifteen inches wide. A bank extending at least nine inches above the level of the green surrounds the ditch. In order to reduce the unequal wearing of the turf the direction of the rinks is changed occasionally, sometimes every day; that is, if the rinks are laid out North and South they are changed to East and West and then later back to North and South again.

The target of the bowlers is a white ball with a diameter of two and one-half inches and a weight of ten ounces. It was traditionally, and is still commonly, made of porcelain, but is now sometimes made of composition. This ball is called the *jack*.

The balls that are bowled at the jack are called *bowls*. Until about 1920, bowls were universally made of lignum vitae, a very hard and heavy wood, and most of those in use in Great Britain today are still of this material, but in the United States the composition bowl is much more common. The diameter of a bowl must not exceed 5 3/16 inches and may be as little as 4 7/8 inches. There is a maximum legal weight for each diameter, the weight ranging from three pounds and eight ounces for the largest legal ball, down to three pounds and two ounces for the smallest. A bowl is never spherical but has a lop-sided quality called *bias*, which is obtained by taking a spherical ball and turning part of it until it becomes a portion of a sphere with a radius different from that of the rest. The rules specify a minimum bias but balls are often used with a bias greater than the minimum. Bowls used by serious players are made with great precision and are quite expensive. Each bowl must be individually tested and stamped to indicate its legality; the approval indicated by the stamp is good for ten years and then the bowl must be re-tested. Bias causes the ball to roll in a curve.

A game of Lawn Bowling is played by two sides of one, two, three, or four men each, and is called accordingly, a *singles game*, a *doubles* or *pairs game*, a *triples* or *trebles game*, or a *rink game*. The number of bowls used by each man is four in singles, four in doubles, three in triples, and two in the rink game. Regardless of the number of players, all bowl one inning from the same end of the rink, then cross over to the other end and bowl from it, and so on, alternately; this is in contrast to Horseshoe Pitching where two partners stand at opposite ends. Thus the number of bowls involved in the play and in the scoring of each inning is eight in singles, eighteen in triples, and sixteen in doubles or the rink game.

In bowling, a player stands on a mat 14 by 24 inches in size. At the start of the game the mat is placed three feet from the ditch that is behind the bowler. In any subsequent inning, it is placed, at the option of the first bowler, anywhere between the ditch and the position of the jack at the close of play, except that it must be on the center line and not less than three feet from the ditch.

At the beginning of a game the player who is to bowl first stands on the mat from which he is about to bowl and throws the jack toward the opposite end of the rink. The jack should come to rest on the rink not less than six feet from the ditch and not less than 75 feet from the front edge of the mat; if it does so the throw is proper, the jack is moved laterally to the center line, and play begins. If the throw is less than six feet from the ditch but otherwise proper it is simply moved out until it is six feet from the ditch, but if it is too short, or if it goes into the ditch or out of bounds, the thrower loses his turn and the jack is thrown by the opposing team. It is seen that in a good throw there is a latitude of 34 feet, since it can be as little as 80 feet or as much as 114 feet from the ditch behind the bowler.

Players always bowl in pairs, each pair consisting of opposing men. The two bowl alternately, one bowl at a time, until they have delivered their two, three, or four balls, and then make way for the next pair. For example, the first bowler of Team *A* delivers one ball, then the first of Team *B* delivers one, then the first man of Team *A* delivers his second ball, and so on, until these two men have finished their bowling for the inning, which in this game is not called an *inning*, but an *end*.

A game lasts for a certain number of ends. There is no legal restriction on this number, but in practice it is nearly always 15, 18, or 21.

An important fact in the game is that the jack is often moved from one place to another by one of the bowls. If the jack is thus moved beyond a side line or entirely over the bank at the far end, then play ceases, play that has taken place in the end is nullified, and the end is begun anew. However, if the jack is driven into the ditch it is still in play, and in this connection the *toucher* must be noted. A bowl that on its delivery touches the jack is designated a *toucher* and the fact is indicated by marking the bowl clearly with chalk.

Now any toucher is good and in play even when in the ditch, although it is of course removed from play if it goes entirely out of bounds. A nontoucher, on the contrary, is not good when it goes into the ditch, and is removed from play.

There is a great deal for a player to learn about Lawn Bowling, both in skill and in strategy, and the best players show remarkable finesse in both. It is seen at its best in the rink game, the form that is by far most common and that is used in most important competition. The four players of a team are known as a *rink*.

Since there is a great difference in the play demanded of the first, second, third, and fourth bowlers, they all tend to become specialists and to play always in the same position. The four men of a rink are known respectively as *lead, second man, third man* or *vice-skip*, and *skip*. As in the game of Curling, the skip is the leader and director and his orders are to be followed by his teammates. He stands at the target end of the rink and directs the other three as they bowl and then crosses over to do his own bowling under the direction of the vice-skip.

The Game of points. The so-called *game-of-points*, which is often mentioned as a variation of Lawn Bowling, is here not considered as such. In fact, the game of points, while derived from elements of the game of Lawn Bowling, is not a game at all, as the game is defined in this book, but is simply a contest, or group of contests, in bowling for accuracy. It has a definite point-scoring system and each man scores on the basis of the system without regard to what an opponent may do. There are four separate contests, each with its scoring; they are called: *drawing, guarding, trailing,* and *driving*.

2. LAWN BOWLING (The Crown-Green Game)

The Crown-Green Game is played to a considerable extent in certain parts of England and Wales, although it is far overshadowed by the standard flat-green game, and is probably declining in popularity. It has never secured a foothold in the United States. In Great Britain it is governed by the British Crown Green Association.

The green, as its name suggests, is not flat, but crowned; the center of the green is elevated above the edges by as much as 18 inches. The bowls are similar to the standard ones but narrower; that is, they have less bias. Otherwise the rules are almost identical with those of the regular game.

3. IMPROVISED LAWN-BOWLING

Carpet Bowls. Indoor Bowls.

This game is merely Lawn Bowling, or a game as close to it as possible, played on any area and with any balls that happen to be available. Any ball that is easily distinguishable from the others can be used as the jack. Croquet balls make excellent bowls.

Variation. The game can be played with three or more players on a nonteam basis. In such case, the scoring system can be changed so as to count all places except last. For example, with four players, the nearest ball counts three, the next, two, and the next, one.

4. PIT BOWLING

Players roll balls along the ground at targets made of holes dug in the ground, each trying to cause his ball to come to rest in the hole. The game is played and scored like Horseshoe Pitching, counting three points for a ball that is in the hole at the end of an inning. Croquet balls are very good but many other kinds of ball will serve satisfactorily. The holes should be 40 feet apart and shallow enough to make it possible for a ball in a hole to be dislodged.

5. CURLING

In the game of Curling, players slide heavy stones along an ice surface toward a fixed target called a *tee*. Otherwise it is very similar to Lawn Bowling, so much so that it has been called *Lawn Bowling on the Ice*. While the game may have originated elsewhere, it is in its present form a product of development in Scotland, where it has a history of at least 300 years. It was introduced into Canada and the United States early in the nineteenth century and is now widespread in the former country, whereas in this country it is known only in the northeast and in the Great Lakes region. Originally played only on natural ice, it has lately moved indoors and is played largely on artificial-ice rinks.

Like all games, Curling was played during most of its history under diverse rules. Now, however, the rules have become standardized under the leadership of the Royal Caledonia Curling Club of Scotland. This organization, which is really not a club but rather an association of many clubs, is recognized throughout the world as the governing body for the game and the rules that it formulates are obeyed without question.

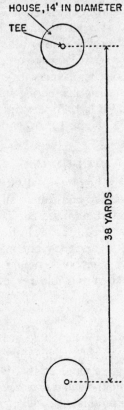

Figure 24. Curling. Diagram of rink.

The game is played on a strip of ice called a *rink* with two targets 38 yards apart, one near each end of the rink. The ice surface is prepared with great care and sometimes it is sprinkled with warm water to produce a slightly beaded or "pebbled" surface. The rules do not specify the nature of the tee. Sometimes it is a depression cut in the ice, and at other times it may be a small iron plate with a protruding spike. In any case, the tee is always surrounded by a 14-foot circle called *the house*. No stone can score unless it is inside the house.

The propelled implements were originally made of stone with no limit to size or weight. For some time, Americans and Canadians used metal implements of weights occasionally exceeding 100 pounds. Now, however, the size and weight are limited by the rules, and stone is used almost universally. The maximum weight is 44 pounds, the maximum circumference 36 inches, and the minimum height 4 1/2 inches. The stone is provided with a handle which projects upward from the top and is bent horizontally. It is also reversible, so that either surface of the stone can be used as the sole. The two surfaces are finished differently, one being suitable for hard and smooth ice, the other for ice that is relatively soft or rough.

Although Curling can, of course, be played by sides of one or two men each, it is officially recognized only for teams or rinks of four men each. Each player has two stones and alternates his throws with those of one of his opponents, exactly as in Lawn Bowling. Scoring also is exactly the same, except that a stone that is outside the house cannot score. A stone on the line is considered to be inside the house. One of the four players in each rink is the skip, and he has, perhaps even more than in Lawn Bowling, complete authority over his rink, each man being expected to play and otherwise act completely according to orders from the skip.

As a player delivers a stone he can impart a rotation to it that causes it to curve, and this curve is likely to be of great importance in making the most effective shot. It is believed by some that this twist explains the name of the game.

A conspicuous and unique feature of the game is the use of the broom, or besom. When it is desired to prolong the distance over which a stone slides, a player may sweep the ice ahead of it until it reaches the tee; beyond the tee the broom may be used only by an opposing player. All sweeping is of course done under orders from the skip. This sweeping is very much practiced and the players must have perfect confidence in its effectiveness, but there may be some question as to the explanation of its value. The usual explanation is that the sweeping helps by removing small particles of ice or snow. At least one authority, however, states that the sweeping motion produces a partial vacuum and thus helps the stone along.

A game may last for any number of ends that is agreed upon in advance. This number is usually 10 or 12, but may be any smaller or larger number.

It is sometimes stated as an amusing feature of the game that when his stone breaks a player must finish the game with the largest fragment of the broken stone. The rules do not say this, but merely that when a stone breaks the score for the stone is determined by the position of the largest fragment. The player is required to resume the game with a whole and legal stone.

6. LINE SHUFFLEBOARD
Shuffleboard

Players slide disks along a smooth surface and score on the basis of relative proximity to a target, exactly as in Lawn Bowling or Curling, except that in this case the target is a straight line that extends across the alley or playing surface. A side scores one for each disk closer to the line than the closest one of the opponents, except that if a scoring disk touches the line it counts three. If two opposing disks touch the line they cancel each other, one touching the line being as good as any other, even though one barely touches it while the other lies directly on it. This game is played on various types of surface and on alleys of various sizes. It is also played with disks of various sizes and different methods of propulsion. However it is usually played on an elevated surface about waist high, made of wood, and with iron disks that are propelled by hand. Many commercial establishments have equipment for this game that is used by customers who pay a fee. Such equipment usually includes a table about 15 feet long with a playing surface made of polished and waxed heavy maple, like a bowling alley, and disks that weigh about a pound each, made of nickel-plated iron. Usually a game is ended when one side has scored 21 points.

7. DISCO

Disco is one special form of Line Shuffleboard. It is played on the floor with five and one-half-inch wooden disks each having a wooden handle projecting upward at an angle of 45 degrees. It can be played with one or two men on each side. In either case, each side has four disks instead of the usual two; one side plays two of the four, then the other side plays two; the first side plays its other two and the second side does the same. Scoring is the same as in other forms of the game.

8. TUMBLE SHUFFLEBOARD

This game may be considered a special form of Line Shuffleboard, but in this case the line is the far edge of an elevated playing surface. Any disk that travels too far will cross the line, tumble off the alley, and be worthless.

Division Four: Diagram-Target Games

In any of the "Proximity Target Games," the target is a single and simple object. In a diagram-target game the target is more complex, consisting of an area divided by lines into several sections, to each of which a score is assigned. Accordingly, the score is determined not by relative proximity to a simple target, but by absolute position on the diagram that serves as a target. The simplest and most obvious target is the one marked by concentric circles, as in the archery target. Such a target will be found among those used in the games described in this group, but it is not common because its use is likely to be in a contest rather than in a game. Most diagrams are more irregular and of such nature as to introduce game elements of a novel kind.

1. SHUFFLEBOARD

There are several games to which the name *shuffleboard* has been applied, but the one listed here has come to be played so much more than any other that it seems right to say that it has pre-empted the name. Although a game much like modern Shuffleboard was played in England for several centuries and was well known in this country early in the nineteenth century, the continuous development of the present game began in the 1870's, when it began to be played on shipboard. It quickly became and has always remained a prominent feature of life on the decks of passenger liners, and the modern game ashore almost certainly was borrowed from the ships. The game is played very widely, both indoors and outdoors, but is most prominent in Florida, where courts are to be found everywhere and where there are many thousands of players. In St. Petersburg alone there are more than 300 courts. The National Shuffleboard Association, founded in 1929, is accepted as the governing body for the game; it publishes rules and holds national tournaments.

Shuffleboard is played on the floor or ground on a surface that must be flat and reasonably smooth. The best surface is probably a wooden one like that of a bowling alley, but by far the larger number of the courts are outdoors and are made of concrete. The alley or playing surface is 52 feet long and six feet wide. Courts are commonly laid out in batteries of several side by side. Near each end of

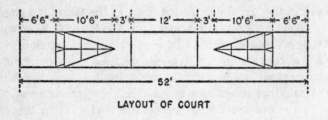

NOTE: ALL MEASUREMENTS FROM CENTERS OF LINES. LINES 3/4" WIDE

LAYOUT OF COURT

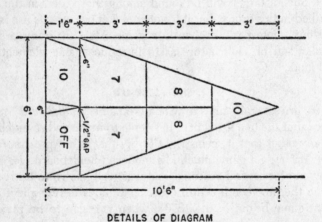

DETAILS OF DIAGRAM

Figure 25. Shuffleboard.

the court is a diagram target in the shape of a modified triangle. The game consists of propelling, by pushing with a forked stick called a *cue*, six-inch disks along the floor at these targets. Each diagram is marked off into six areas with a score indicated for each. One area counts ten, two of them count eight each, two count seven each, and the remaining area counts minus ten or "ten off." In order to score, a disk must be entirely within one space, not touching any line. Scores are counted, of course, after all shots for an inning have been made. Displacing an opposing disk is relatively easy and is more important in this game than in other games, Lawn Bowling for example.

The disk is made of wood or, more commonly, plastic; it is six inches in diameter and 1 inch thick. The cue was formerly provided with a crescent-shaped head but nowadays is made with a heavy wire fork of which each tip has a plastic knob or button attached to it. The game may be played as singles or doubles, and eight disks are used in either case, each side playing four.

Disks played by one side are colored red, by the other, black. Playing positions are as in Horseshoe Pitching, that is, in singles the opponents play from one end and then walk to and play from the other end, while in doubles two opponents play from each end and remain there throughout a game. The order of play differs from that of Horseshoe Pitching in that each player plays only one disk at a time, always alternating with an opponent. In other words, the order of play is like that of Lawn Bowling, not Horseshoe Pitching. The first play in a game is always made by red and is always from the right-hand side of the ten-off area. Red and black alternate until the eight disks have been played. In singles the players walk to the other end and then black plays first and they continue, red always playing first at one end and black at the other. In doubles the rule is slightly different. Here, the first red player plays first and at the other end the red player also plays first, that is, red plays first for a complete round, then black plays first for a complete round. A small point should be noted. The red disks are always played from the right side of the head of the court (the end from which play is begun) and from the left side of the foot of the court, and, of course, vice versa for black.

A game ends at fifty points, but an end or half-round is never left uncompleted, so that it is possible for a side to score 50 and still be defeated by a larger score.

2. CIRCLE SHUFFLEBOARD

On the floor or ground are marked two sets of five concentric circles, each set having diameters of one, two, three, four and five feet and the two sets being about 30 feet apart. Men play with standard shuffleboard disk and cues, propelling the disks at the targets from a distance of 30 feet. Score is computed as the disks lie after all have been played, the circles counting five, four, three, two, and one. A disk touching a line does not count, but there is no negative score. This game is sometimes played on ice.

3. *LONDON*

London is a sidewalk game in which tin-can tops or similar disks are thrown at a target marked on the walk. The target is about three

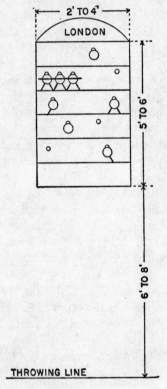

Figure 26. London.

feet wide and six feet long and the throwing line is about eight feet away. It is best played with four players, but can be played with other numbers. Players take turns in throwing one disk at the target, and each scores immediately after his throw. If a disk lands entirely within one of the spaces, the thrower marks a circle in the space to indicate the head of a man. If he later gets a second disk in this same space he adds a larger circle to represent the trunk of the man. He then tries to add first one leg and then the other. Having completed a man, except for his arms, the player tries to draw a second and third man in the same space. If he has three men (again except for the arms) in one space, the next time he gets a disk in the space he is entitled to draw one horizontal line, which supplies arms to all three of them at once. The first player to do this wins the game. One space has a curved edge and is called *London*. No men are drawn in this space, but when a man gets his disk in it he is entitled to make a mark in every one of the spaces.

4. DART BASEBALL

In Dart Baseball, players throw the same darts that are so widely used in the contest of throwing at a circular target, but they throw them at a specially designed diagram target instead. There are no generally accepted rules for the game nor for the target, and the latter varies a great deal, but the basic idea is always the same: Spaces are marked off to represent everything that can happen to a batter—ball, strike, out, single, double, and so on. The first batter takes a collection of darts and throws them one at a time at the diagram, continuing to throw until he is out or safe on base. Then the second batter of his team comes up, and so on, the team batting until three men are out, when the opposing team comes to bat. The game is very fascinating and is played intensively in some localities.

5. OTHER DART GAMES

Many other games are played by throwing darts at a diagram target, but none is established well enough to be described here. They are nearly always based on other well-known games, as is Dart Baseball. For example, one can set up a diagram representing a golf course and play Dart Golf. It would not be difficult to devise Dart Bowling. There is even Dart Poker, in which the diagram is formed by tacking up real playing cards.

Division Five: Hit-or-Miss Target Games

In a hit-or-miss target game there is a simple target that the player tries to hit, and the score is based, in any of a variety of ways, on his success in doing so. There is no gradual approach and no credit for proximity. All the games resemble contests, and it is likely that some of them should be so classed, but many of them have at least some elements that make them games, without question. Some of the doubtful ones are included in order to make the collection complete. Nearly all the games in this group are games of throwing a basketball at a goal.

Section I: The target is a basketball goal

All these games are similar and are based on contests, often in relay form, but also include added elements. Several of them are sometimes given names that include the word *golf*, but this word is misleading since none of them includes the gradual approach that is the distinguishing feature of Golf.

GROUP A: PLAYER THROWS FROM A SERIES OF SPOTS

1. SPOT-POINT BASKET SHOOT

Several spots are marked on the floor around one basketball goal, and different numbers are assigned to them. The spots may be all about the same distance from the goal or at varying distances. Players throw in turn from spot number one and then from the other spots in order, each man having only one shot from each spot. When a throw is successful, the thrower scores according to the number of the spot, a goal from spot three counting three points, for example.

2. BASKETBALL GOLF

Nine spots are marked on the floor, at varying distances from a basketball goal. Players throw in turn from spot number one, each man following up his shot when he misses and continuing to shoot from the spot of recovery until he makes the basket. His score is the number of shots required to make the basket. When all have "holed out" from the first spot, they repeat the same process from the other spots in turn.

3. LONG-SHOT BASKETBALL GOLF

Same as Basketball Golf, except that there is no follow-up. A man who misses continues to shoot from the same spot until he makes the goal.

4. RELAY BASKET-SHOOT

This is a relay basket-shooting game played for speed. A team may have as few as three men and should not have many more, since the amount of action for each man is greater with smaller teams. Three teams are probably best, but the game works very well with two teams or with more than three. At least three baskets are needed and more are better. For each basket there is a throwing line clearly marked about 20 feet out or at any other distance that is suitable to the ability of the players.

To start the game, each team lines up in single file behind the first throwing line, except that the rear man leaves the line and takes his place near the basket, ready to recover and return the ball. Each team has its own ball, held by the front man. At a signal from a leader, all throw at the same time and at the same basket. From this point each team, without regard to the others, proceeds thus: The man under the basket recovers the ball, whether the goal is made or not; he throws it to the second man of his team, the latter having stepped up to the throwing line; then he returns to his place in the line. The man who has thrown at the basket runs down to the basket and replaces the man who was there originally. Thus the front man throws, runs to the basket, recovers and returns the throw made by the next man, and takes his place at the rear of his file. However, as soon as a throw goes through the basket, the throwing team leaves this basket and moves over to the next one, without interruption. This procedure is followed by each team and continues until one team or another has made the prescribed number of baskets. On a floor where six baskets are available, the prescribed number of goals should probably be one in each of the six baskets. With fewer baskets, the teams should be required to go around more than once. There may be some overlapping, but this merely adds to the fun. The game can be played, although less satisfactorily, with only one basket; in this case, there should be several throwing lines, the teams moving from one line to another but always throwing at the same basket.

5. AROUND-THE-WORLD

Several baskets are used, the more the better, each with its own throwing line. Players line up in single file behind the first throwing line. The front man shoots at the basket; if he makes a goal he moves to the second throwing line and throws at the second basket; if he succeeds again he moves to the third, and so on until he misses, after which he stands behind the line from which he missed. As soon as the front man has finished his turn, the second man does likewise, and so on until every man has had a turn, each one stopping at the line from which he missed. Then they throw again in the same order, each man resuming where he left off. The required round may consist of one goal in each basket or it may require going around them more than once. The game can be played with only one basket and several throwing lines, the men moving from one line to another.

6. FREEZE-OUT AROUND-THE-WORLD

This game is the same as Around the World with one added feature that changes the game radically. Half of the throwing lines are marked "Safety"; the other half are unmarked. When one player moves up to a throwing line on which another man is already standing, one or the other must leave the line and return to the start. If the line in question is one of those marked "Safety," the original occupant stays, but if it is not so marked, the new arrival freezes out the old and the latter must return to the start.

GROUP B: PLAYER TAKES LONG SHOT AND FOLLOW-UP SHOT

In each of these games, a player makes a long shot at the goal and he, or his partner, rushes in to recover the ball and shoot again from the spot of recovery. All of the games are variations of Twenty-One, so called because the game is usually set at twenty-one points.

1. TWENTY-ONE
Basketball Twenty-One

Twenty-One is a basketball goal-throwing game for two men only. The two men stand behind a throwing line at any desired distance from a basket, say 20 feet; in fact, the line is usually imaginary, the men merely standing together at a suitable distance. One of the men throws the ball at the goal and then runs in to recover it and shoot again from the spot of recovery. He scores two points for a successful long shot and one point for a successful short or follow-up shot. When he has completed his turn he throws the ball to his opponent who takes the same shots. The players take turns in throwing first. As soon as either man has scored 21 points the game is over, except that both men must have had the same number of shots; thus, if the first thrower in any inning scores 21 points the second player still takes his turn (provided he has a chance to win or tie). A common difficulty arises when, after the long shot, the ball is recovered beyond the end line where it is impossible to shoot at the basket. Sometimes the player is permitted to dribble the ball to a position where he can shoot but it is recommended, instead, that a player lose his shot unless he can make it without violating the basketball rule against traveling with the ball. The following variations in the game are common.

Variation 1. Each of the two men has a ball. They make their long shots simultaneously, one of them counting, "One, two, go." This leads to some interesting complications.

Variation 2. To win a game, a man must score exactly 21 points, rather than 21 or more, as in the basic game. If he scores more than 21, his score reverts to zero.

Variation 3. The short shot is not taken unless the long one is recovered before it has bounced twice.

Variation 4. A successful long shot counts three instead of two.

Variation 5. The short shot is not taken, except when the long one is missed. If this variation is used, it is suggested that three points be counted for a long shot.

2. TWENTY-ONE (Partner Form)

Same as Twenty-One, except that it is played by two partners against two others; one of the partners takes the long shot, the other the follow-up, the two alternating in the starting position.

3. TWENTY-ONE (Team Form)

This is the same game as Twenty-One, except that the several players are divided into two equal teams, the team score being the sum of the individual scores.

4. THREE, TWO, AND ONE

Same as Twenty-One except for a variation in the scoring. A long shot counts three and a follow-up shot recovered before the ball strikes the floor counts two. Any other follow-up shot counts one. This game should be played with the throwing line somewhat closer than usual, to facilitate recovery of the ball.

5. THREE-SHOT TWENTY-ONE

Same as Twenty-One, except that a man who misses the long shot and also the follow-up shot gets still a third chance. Score three, two, and one. He always takes two shots, but takes the third only when he misses both of the first two.

6. TEN-SHOT TWENTY-ONE

The player takes a long shot and then nine follow-up shots, taking all ten whether he succeeds or fails, always shooting from the spot of recovery. He scores one point for each goal made, with no extra credit for the long shot.

7. TWENTY-ONE FOR SPEED

This form of the game is played by two or more pairs of players. At the start, one man from each pair stands behind the throwing line, with his own ball, while his partner stands behind him. At a signal, the throwers all shoot for the basket and each takes his follow-up shot; he then throws the ball to his partner, who has stepped up to the line. The two partners play alternately, each taking two shots. Play continues until one pair has 21 points or more, the first to do so being the winner. Thus, this is a game based on speed in scoring.

8. FOLLOW-THE-MISS

Players line up behind a throwing line. The front man takes a shot at a basketball goal. If the shot is successful the ball is returned to the line and thrown by the second man. But if it is unsuccessful the second man must recover it and shoot from the spot of recovery. Likewise, if the second man succeeds, the third man shoots from the line, but if he fails, the third man shoots from the spot of recovery. The game continues thus, the men shooting in turn, each successful shot being followed by a throw from the line and each unsuccessful one being followed by a shot from the spot of recovery. Play continues until one player has scored ten points.

GROUP C: PLAYER THROWS UNTIL HE FAILS

1. FOUL-LINE TWENTY-ONE

In this game, all throws are made from the foul line. The first man throws at the goal from the foul line and continues to shoot until he misses. Then the other players get their chances in order. One point is scored for each goal made and the first to score 21 is the winner.

Variation. The first basket in any series scores one, the second two, the third three, and so on.

2. FREE-THROW TWENTY-ONE

This game is for two men only. The first man tries a basketball free throw and continues to throw until he misses. When he misses, his opponent recovers the ball and shoots from the spot of recovery. If the second man is successful with the follow-up shot, he goes to the foul line and starts as the first man did; but if he misses the follow-up shot the first man must recover it and shoot. Thus the two opponents follow up each other's shots until a basket is made; then the one who has made the basket goes to the foul line and shoots until he misses as at the beginning of the game. The winner is the first to score 21 points, counting one for any basket.

3. SCRAMBLE TWENTY-ONE

This game is for four or five players, each playing for himself. One player tries a free throw at the basketball goal. If he makes the goal he throws again from the foul line and continues until he misses. When he misses, the other men all scramble for the ball. The one who recovers it tries for a basket; if he misses they all (including the first thrower) scramble again and continue to throw and scramble until a goal is made. Then the one who has made the goal goes to the foul line and the game continues as at the beginning. Every basket counts one point and the first player to get 21 points is the winner.

Section II: Target is other than a basketball goal

This small section includes only six games and in five of them the target of the thrower is another player. Since the player who is the target is not permitted to dodge, the games are not classed with the "Dodgeball Games."

1. CROSS-COUNTRY BOWLING
French Bowls

This is an interesting game for two players where a considerable expanse of reasonably smooth ground is available. Each man has a ball—almost any kind will serve but a softball is most commonly used. The first man rolls his ball along the ground in any direction and to any distance. Then the second man rolls his ball from the same place. Thereafter they bowl in turn, always from the spot where the ball lies, and a man scores one point each time that his ball strikes the other one. There is more to the game than may appear at first. For example, a player may choose not to try to hit the other ball but to make a short roll and let the opponent take a longer one.

2. TARGET PRACTICE
Range Practice. Shooting Gallery.

Players are in two equal teams and each team stands on one of two parallel lines about 40 feet apart. The men of one team stand with their backs to the other and bend forward slightly, placing hands on thighs but keeping knees straight. Then any one man from the other team throws an old, well-worn softball, trying to hit one of the opponents. A thrower who does not hit an opponent, or a man who is hit, withdraws from the game. The game is repeated, the teams throwing in turn, until all of one team have been eliminated. Since the usual tendency is to throw at men near the center of the line it is well to shuffle the teams; this can be done by moving two men from the center of the line to the ends each time that a team is to be the target.

Variation 1. Men are not eliminated, but a point is scored for each hit. Men must be shuffled as explained above, and the men of each team must throw in turn. The game is completed when each man has had one throw.

Variation 2. Same as the basic game, except that elimination is only for being hit, not for missing a throw.

3. FREE SHOT

One man, selected to be the first target, stands close to and facing a wall; he leans forward slightly, with hands on thighs but knees straight, as in Target Practice. The other players are in an informal column of twos and are beyond a throwing line about 40 feet to the rear of the target man. The first pair of the column steps up to the throwing line and one of them throws a ball at the target man. If the throw misses, the thrower immediately trades places with the target man. If the throw is successful, the target turns around and guesses which one of the two made the throw. If this guess is correct the two trade places, but if not, the same man must be target again for the next pair of throwers, the old pair going to the rear of the column.

4. GUESSBALL

The same as Free Shot, except that the thrower may be any one of the players, instead of either of two. In this case the guess is, of course, much more difficult.

Variation. When the throw misses, the thrower and target do not automatically trade places, but the target must guess the identity of thrower; this time, however, he has three guesses instead of only one. If he guesses correctly he trades places with the thrower, if not he must be target again.

5. SHARP SHOOTING

This game is the same as Guessball, except that it adds an interesting method of selecting the thrower. The target man takes his position and then counts in a loud voice from one to ten. At each count the ball is thrown from one man to another and the man who receives it at the count of ten is the thrower.

6. GUESSBALL (Team Form)

Players are in two equal teams and each team stands on one of two parallel lines about 40 feet apart. The men of one team stand with their backs to the other and bend forward slightly, placing hands on thighs but keeping knees straight. Any man of the other team throws a soft ball, trying to hit one of his opponents. If the throw misses, the thrower loses; if it hits an opponent the one hit tries to guess the thrower and wins if he guesses correctly but loses if he guesses incorrectly. In any case the loser is eliminated from the game and the game continues until all members of one team have been eliminated. Thus this game is the same as Target Practice with the guessing element of Guessball added. It can be played with either of the variations described under Target Practice.

Class VII

PROPEL-AND-CATCH GAMES

THE GAMES INCLUDED IN THE PRESENT CLASS ARE THOSE IN WHICH throwing and catching are the basic and essential elements. A successful throw or catch is the true objective of each player, and the way in which he scores and helps to win the game. Throwing and catching may be very important elements in many games not included in this section, but they are not the final objectives, as they are here. Included in the preceding class ("Stunt and Alertness Games") are a few games of throwing and catching, but in these games a man throws a ball and catches it himself, and for this reason the activity is considered a stunt and the games classed accordingly. In every game of the present class a man tries to catch a ball thrown by another man, or perhaps to interfere with an opponent's attempt to catch it.

The words *throwing* and *catching* are used somewhat loosely. It is true that in most of the games men actually throw and catch a ball; but in a few of them the men propel the ball by kicking or by other methods, and they may in rare cases not actually catch the ball but control it with the foot. This class consists of five divisions: Single-Catcher Games, Keepball, Captainball, Scrambleball, and Drives.

Division One: Single-Catcher Games

In games of this group, a ball is thrown to a certain man, who has only to catch it and perhaps throw it to another man. There may be competition between the thrower and the catcher, but never between two catchers.

Section I: One player throws to all the others

GROUP A: BALL IS THROWN TO PLAYERS IN ORDER

1. TEACHER AND CLASS

One player, the teacher, stands facing the others, who stand in an arc of a circle. The teacher throws the ball to the others in turn, starting with the one on the right. Each player catches the ball and throws it back to the teacher. If a player misses the ball he goes to the left of the line. If the teacher misses a throw he goes to the left of the line and the one on the right becomes teacher. If the teacher does not miss while the ball goes twice around, he falls in just to the right of the players who have missed, and again the one at the right takes his place.

2. STEP-BY-STEP

All players but one sit side by side on the bottom of a flight of steps. The odd player stands some distance in front of and facing the others. He throws a ball to the others in turn and they throw it back to him, exactly as in Teacher and Class. If the odd man misses a throw, he is replaced by the thrower. There is no penalty for a miss by the other players, but a man who does not miss moves up to the next step. The first man to reach the top step is the winner, but all must be given an equal number of chances. If two or more reach the top at the same time, the others are eliminated and the winners play off the tie, starting at the bottom again.

Variation. A catcher who misses is eliminated from the game; otherwise the same as the basic form.

3. CIRCLE MISSBALL

One man stands in the center of a circle formed by the others. The center man has a basketball and one of the circle men has another. At a signal, the circle man with the ball throws it to the center man and simultaneously the center man throws his ball to the circle man who is at the left of the first thrower. Throwing is continued rapidly and without hesitation, going around the circle to the left; a circle man who receives a ball returns it immediately to the center man and the center man always throws his ball to the man at the left of the circle thrower. This continues until the center man fails to catch a throw; when he does so he trades places with the thrower.

There is no penalty for a miss by a circle man; accordingly, the center man makes his throws so that they can be caught easily. On the other hand the circle men throw in such a way as to make them difficult to catch. The speed of the throws must not be overdone, and may require some restraint from the leader. Sometimes a particular style of throw is specified, often a style taken from Basketball, as a push-shot, and so on. When the center man loses his place for missing a throw, it is assumed that the throw is one that he should be expected to catch; if it is not, the center man must not be charged with a miss.

GROUP B: BALL IS THROWN TO PLAYERS AT RANDOM

1. CALLBALL

Catchball. Catch Numberball. Ring Callball.

One man stands in the center of a circle formed by the others, who may or may not be numbered. The center man tosses a ball into the air, calling as he does so the name or number of one of the circle players. The one called tries to catch the ball before it strikes the ground. If he succeeds he is next center man; otherwise the same man repeats. The game may be played with the penalty system, a man scoring a negative point when he misses the ball.

Variation 1. Players do not form a circle but gather informally around the thrower.

Variation 2. For small children the ball may be caught on the first bounce.

2. SCHOOLBALL

One player stands in the center of a circle formed by the others. The center man throws a ball to any one of the circle men and the latter immediately throws it back. The center man continues to throw to the others at random, the exchange being made as rapidly as possible. When the center man misses he trades places with the thrower. When a circle man misses he keeps his place but has a point scored against him and pays a penalty for three such points. Sometimes a man will fail to catch a throw because the throw is poor. In such a case, the leader or the players must decide who is at fault and charge him with the miss.

3. DOUBLE-PASS SCHOOLBALL

Same as Schoolball, except that a circle man who catches a throw from the center man throws the ball to a second circle man and this one throws it to the center.

Section II: Players throw to one another

1. CIRCLE PASSBALL

All players stand in a single circle at intervals of three feet or more, the interval depending on the kind of ball and the ability of the players. A ball is thrown from one man to another, entirely at random, as quickly as possible. When a man makes a bad throw or fails to catch a good one, he is eliminated and the game continues until only one is left. A throw is considered good if the catcher is able to touch it with both hands. The game can be played without elimination, using negative scores and a penalty. A man who is eliminated may be required to sit on the ground in his place, or to turn around to face the rear.

2. SITTING CIRCLE-PASSBALL

Same as Circle Passball, except that all players sit on the ground.

3. REVERSE CIRCLE-PASSBALL

All players stand in a single circle. They pass a ball but always either to the next man or to the second man. At the start, the ball is passed in a clockwise direction, but soon the leader blows a whistle and the direction is changed. Each time the whistle is sounded the direction is changed again. A man is eliminated for a bad throw, an incorrect throw, or missing a catch. Otherwise the same as Circle Passball.

4. VARIETY CIRCLE-PASSBALL

Same as Circle Passball with this exception: players face in a prescribed direction and pass the ball in a prescribed way, the prescription being changed frequently by a call from the leader; the call may be supplemented by a demonstration. Examples: throw with left hand, throw between legs, face out, face left, push throw.

5. ALL THROW

All players stand in a circle facing the center, at intervals of five or six feet. Each man has a ball or other object that can be thrown and caught. Medicine balls are very good but not often available in sufficient number. The objects may be all of the same kind, but a different and possibly better game results from having as much variety as possible. A leader stands in the center of the circle and counts slowly. At each count, every man throws his object to the next man on his right and of course catches the object thrown by the next man on his left. When a man makes a bad throw or fails to catch a good one, a point is scored against him and a man with three such points pays a penalty.

Variation. A man who misses is eliminated from the game and the game continues until only one man survives.

6. MEDICINE CATCHBALL
Battleball

Two teams form parallel lines about eight feet apart. A medicine ball is thrown back and forth, the throws being made as hard as possible. When a man fails to catch a good throw, or makes a poor one, he is eliminated or has a point against him.

7. PICKABACK PASSBALL
Mountball

All players form horse-and-rider pairs; that is, one man rides on the back of another, the rider with his legs about the body of the horse just above the hips. All form a circle. The riders have a ball with which they play Circle Passball, except that the horses twist and squirm, trying to make the riders miss. When the ball strikes the floor, each horse trades places with his rider and the game continues.

Division Two: Keepball

A keepball game is one in which men throw a ball about among themselves, trying to do so in such a way that it cannot be caught, or perhaps cannot be touched, by another man or group of men. The games of this division are in two sections: those in which one man tries to secure a ball that is passed about by all the others; and those in which players are in two equal teams, one of which tries to keep the ball away from the other.

Section I: One man opposes the others

1. CIRCLE TOUCHBALL

Ball Tag. Center Catchball. Center Touchball. Circleball.
Circle Chaseball. Circle Tagball. Object Tag. Tagball.
Touchball.

One man is within a circle formed by all the others. The circle men have a ball that they throw from one to another at random, trying to prevent its being touched by the center man. The center man tries to touch the ball and when he does so he announces which man he thinks made the error that permitted him to touch the ball; he and this man then trade places. The chances of the center man to touch the ball vary greatly with the kind of ball and the ability of the players; for this reason the game should always be adjusted so that any center man can succeed in touching the ball within a reasonable time. Probably the best way is to use a medicine ball. Another way is to restrict the method of throwing or to limit the men to whom a man may throw; for example, it may be ruled that the ball must be passed always to the next man or second man, or that every pass must bounce on the floor. In any case, a ball that is missed and touches the floor as a result should be considered as if touched by the center man.

Variation 1. Two men are in the center at the same time.
Variation 2. Circle men sit on the floor.

2. WATER CIRCLE-TOUCHBALL

Water Circleball

Same as Circle Touchball, except that it is played by men standing in water waist deep. Of course a waterproof ball must be used.

3. KICK CIRCLE-TOUCHBALL

Foot Tagball. Kick Circleball. Soccer Centerball.

Same as Circle Touchball, except that the circle men have a soccer ball and kick it about from one to another, the center man trying to touch it with his foot.

4. GET-THE-CAP

Odd Man's Cap

Same as Circle Touchball, except that each man, including the center man, has a gymnasium wand or similar stick, and, instead of a ball, the circle men have a cap that they pass or throw with the ends of their wands. The center man tries to get the cap on the end of his wand and when he does so he trades places with the one who makes the error.

5. CAGEBALL CIRCLE-TOUCH

Same as Circle Touchball, but played with a large cageball. The ball may be thrown but is usually rolled.

6. OUTSIDE TOUCHBALL

Outside Tagball. Touchball.

Same as Circle Touchball, except that the odd man is outside the circle, instead of inside, so that he is behind the circle men and not in front of them. This gives the odd man some advantage, since it is harder for the circle men to keep track of him.

Variation. The circle men face outward and the odd man is inside the circle, behind the circle men.

7. CHANNEL TOUCHBALL

*Channelball. Channel Tag. Circle Channel-Tag.
Double-Column Channelball.*

One man is inside a circle formed by the others. The circle men face right or left, as agreed or directed, and all stand with feet wide apart. They pass a basketball or other ball from one to another between their legs and the center man tries to touch it. Otherwise the same as Circle Touchball.

8. TWENTY-ONE TOUCHBALL

Same as Circle Touchball except for this addition: The circle men count aloud as each successful pass is made. If they succeed in making 21 good passes without a miss the center man must pay a penalty.

Section II: One team opposes another

GROUP A: PLAYERS ARE NOT RESTRICTED

1. KEEPBALL

Keepaway. Keeping Away. Keep-the-Ball.

Players are in two distinguishable teams, all scattered at random within boundary lines, such as those of a basketball court. The men of one team have a basketball that they pass about among themselves while the other team tries to get the ball. Touching the ball means nothing; actual possession of the ball is required. The rules of basketball apply except that dribbling is not permitted. There is no scoring in this game.

2. NUMBER KEEPBALL

Keep-the-Ball. Number Keepaway.

Same as Keepball, except that each time a man catches a throw from a teammate he counts aloud to indicate the number of catches from the time that the team gets the ball until the time that it loses it again. When the opponents get the ball they do the same, and the team with the larger score for the inning scores one point. The same thing is done for subsequent innings.

3. TEN CATCHES

Same as Keepball, except that the catches are counted as in Number Keepball. When the count of ten is reached, a point is scored and the count is begun again with one.

4. BALLOON KEEPBALL

Same as Keepball, except that the ball is a rubber balloon and the opponents of the team with the ball are required not merely to catch the ball but to burst it. When they succeed a new balloon is given to them for their turn.

5. WATER KEEPBALL

Water Ten-Catches

Same as Keepball or Ten Catches, except that it is played in deep water by swimmers.

GROUP B: METHOD OF THROWING IS RESTRICTED

1. VARIETY KEEPBALL

Keep Away. Keepaway. Keepball. Variety Keepaway.

Same as Keepball, except that only a specified method of throwing the ball may be used. The method is changed frequently, at the direction of the leader.

2. DRIBBLE KEEPBALL

Dribble Keepaway

Same as Keepball except that each circle player must bounce the ball on the floor and catch it before throwing it to the next man.

3. SOCCER KEEPBALL

Soccer Ten-Kicks

Same as Keepball or Ten Catches, except that the circle men kick a soccer ball and the center man tries to touch it with his foot.

4. HOCKEY KEEPBALL

Hockey Ten-Passes

Same as Keepball or Ten Catches, except that it is played with a field-hockey ball and sticks, the center man trying to get the ball with his stick.

5. VOLLEY KEEPBALL

Ten Volleys. Volley Keepaway.

Same as Keepball or Ten Catches, except that it is played with a volleyball that is batted from one to another, not caught and thrown.

GROUP C: PLAYERS ARE RESTRICTED TO CERTAIN AREAS

1. THREE-COURT KEEPBALL

Same as Keepball except that the players are restricted as in Three-court Basketball. The playing area is divided into three equal parts and each team is divided equally among the three courts. Each player is required to remain in the court to which he is assigned.

2. SIX-COURT KEEPBALL
Passball

The playing area is divided into six equal rectangles and each of the two teams is divided among them. Otherwise, it is the same as Keepball. That is, the game is the same as Three-court Keepball, except that it uses six courts instead of three.

3. NINE-COURT KEEPBALL
Nine-court Ten Catches

Same as Keepball or Ten Catches, except that players are restricted to the areas used in Nine-court Basketball.

4. KNOCKING DOWN

The play area is divided into two courts with a five-yard neutral zone between them. Players are in two teams and each team has half its members in each of the two courts. Thus, each court contains half of one team and half of the other team. One team has a basketball and passes it from one to another, but always to a man in the other court. Otherwise the game is the same as Keepball.

Division Three: Captainball

The distinctive feature of Captainball Games is that a team can win by throwing a ball so that it is caught by certain designated members of the team. In true Captainball, a team wins a point only when one certain man, called the *Captain*, catches a ball thrown by one of his teammates. In the "Endball Games," which are a part of this division, a team can win if any one of a group of men catches the ball. Between the "Endball Games" and the true "Captainball Games" are a few in which the ball can be caught by either of two men.

Section I: Only one catcher can score

1. CAPTAINBALL

A rectangular field about 30 by 60 feet is divided into two equal courts by a center line. In each of the courts several two-foot circles are marked on the floor, the number of circles being half the number

of players on one team. The circles are arranged in a semicircle with
the open side toward the center line. Ten players is a good number
for a team, but the number can be as small as six or as large as 20,
or possibly more. Half the players on each team occupy the circles
in one of the courts, one man to a circle; the other half run at will in
the other court. Thus, each court has half of one team in the circles
and half of the opposing team running at random. The men in the

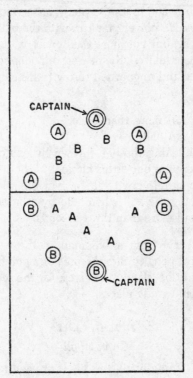

Figure 27. Captainball.

circles are basemen, the others guards. One of the basemen—the one
in the circle farthest from the center line—has a special status, and
his circle should be marked in a distinctive way, say by a double
line. This man is the captain. A baseman must remain in his circle
and a guard must remain in his own court, not crossing the center
line.

The game is played with a basketball and is started with a center jump by two opposing guards at the center of the field. The ball is passed about among the men, each team trying to score and, of course, to keep the ball from the opponents. A team scores when its captain catches the ball thrown by one of his basemen. It is illegal for a guard to throw the ball to his captain; he must throw it to a baseman and the latter may then throw to the captain or to another baseman. Basemen may pass the ball among themselves as much as they wish, throwing to the captain for a score when a good opportunity arises. No player may run with the ball. He may bounce it once on the floor, but not more than once.

When a foul is committed, the nearest opponent of the one making the foul has a free and unguarded throw to his captain. The following are fouls:

1. Bouncing the ball more than once.
2. Running with the ball.
3. The captain touching the ball thrown by one of his guards.
4. A baseman stepping out of his circle with both feet.
5. A guard stepping into any circle or over the middle line.
6. A guard touching the ball when held by a baseman.
7. Holding the ball more than three seconds.

A successful throw from a baseman to the captain scores two points; a successful penalty throw scores one point.

The game should be played in halves; for the second half, guards and basemen should trade places.

2. CENTERBALL

Captainball

In this form of Captainball, the bases of each team are arranged in a circle with the captain's base in the center. The game is the same as Captainball, except that it includes an additional method of scoring: If a baseman can get the ball and pass it to the next baseman, and the ball is thrown from one baseman to the next until it has gone entirely around the circle, two points are scored. That is, in this game, one point is scored by a successful penalty throw and two points by a successful throw from a baseman to his captain or by a complete circuit of the bases in order.

3. PROGRESSIVE CAPTAINBALL

This game is the same as Captainball, except that the players of each team rotate positions after each point is scored, as in Volleyball. Players rotate clockwise, each baseman moving to the next base, except that the last baseman becomes a guard and one guard becomes a baseman. The same system can, of course, be used for Centerball.

4. BASKET CAPTAINBALL
Captain Basketball

This game is played on a basketball court. It is the same as Captainball except for this addition: Any baseman may at any time throw the ball at the basketball goal; if the goal is made two points are scored, and if not, the ball remains in play.

5. POSTBALL

Near each end of a rectangular court are two concentric circles, with diameters of three and six feet. Players are in two equal teams; one man of each team stands inside one of the smaller circles and the others run at random over the court. The men inside the circle must remain there and the other players must not enter either of the larger circles. The game is started and played according to the rules of Basketball, except that a goal is scored whenever the man in the circle catches a throw from one of his teammates, and that it is a violation for a man in a circle to step out of it or for any other man to step into one of the larger circles. The game can be based on basketball rules for girls or on those for men with dribbling prohibited. It is not well adapted to standard men's rules with dribbling.

Section II: Two or more catchers can score

1. CORNERBALL
Corner Keepball

A rectangular field about 30 by 60 feet is divided into two equal courts by a middle line. In each corner of the field is marked an eight-foot square or a quarter of a circle with a radius of about eight feet. The size of this corner area is rather critical and should be determined by experience in each particular situation. It must be small enough to make a successful catch moderately difficult but not small enough to make it impossible even with good defense. Players are in two teams. Of each team, all but two occupy one of the two courts, and the other two occupy the boxes in the two farther corners, one in each. The game is played with a basketball and started with a center jump. Thereafter the ball is passed from one to another, no man being permitted to cross the center line. A score is made when a man succeeds is throwing the ball from behind the middle line to a teammate who is in a far corner, assuming of course that the ball is caught.

2. ENDBALL

A rectangular field is divided into two equal courts by a middle line. About five feet inside each end line and parallel with it is another line, making an end zone five feet wide. Players are in two teams. Two thirds of each team is in one of the main courts and the other third in the farther end zone. The best size for a team is from 12 to 18 men. The game is played with a basketball and started with a center jump. The ball may be passed at will among the men in the main court, but no running with the ball or dribbling is permitted. When the situation seems favorable, a man with the ball throws it to his teammates in the end zone, and if the throw is caught two points are scored. When a player commits a foul one point is given to the opponents. It is a foul to step over a restraining line, to dribble the ball, to travel with the ball, or to hold the ball more than three seconds. If the ball goes out of bounds it is recovered by the nearest man and thrown back to the field with no interruption of play. A score can be made only by catching a ball on the fly.

3. WATER ENDBALL

Same as Endball, except that it is played in the water. It can be played by men standing in water waist deep, or by swimmers in deep water.

Division Four: Scrambleball

In a scrambleball game, a ball is thrown and two or more men compete for possession of it. A point is scored as soon as a player secures the ball.

1. SCRAMBLEBALL
Toss-Up

One man stands in the center of a circle formed by the others. The center man tosses a ball into the air and then gets out of the way. The circle men all try to catch the ball. If the ball strikes the ground it is dead and the same man throws it again, but if any man can secure the ball before it strikes the ground he is next thrower. In scrambling for the ball men may push or otherwise interfere with others, but must not hold them.

2. SCRAMBLEBALL (Team Form)

Same as Scrambleball, except that the players are in two teams, alternating in the circle. A player who secures the ball scores a point for his team.

3. WALL SCRAMBLEBALL

All players stand in a random group near a wall. One man throws a ball against the wall so that it will rebound into or near the group. All except the thrower scramble for the ball and the one who secures it before it touches the ground is next thrower.

4. BEANBAG SCRAMBLE
Beanbags-Over-the-Head

All players but one stand in a random group. The odd man stands in front of the group with his back to it. He throws a beanbag backward over his head so that it lands among the group. Otherwise it is the same as Scrambleball.

5. NUMBER SCRAMBLEBALL
Catchball. Number Catchball.

Players are in two teams, but all are in a single circle, each half circle being one team. Each team numbers off from right to left, so that each number is held by two opponents who are opposite each other in the circle. A neutral leader stands in the center of the circle and throws a ball into the air, calling a number as he does so. The two players with the number called scramble for the ball and the one who gets it scores a point for his team.

Variation. Same, except that players sit in the circle.

Division Five: Drives

In a drive, a ball is kicked, thrown, or otherwise propelled back and forth between two teams, each team trying to send the ball as far as possible and in such a way that the opponents cannot catch it. The ball is kicked or thrown from the spot of recovery, or, when it is caught, usually from a specified number of steps ahead of the spot of recovery. If one team is superior to the other the ball will gradually move down the field, and when it has moved far enough the advancing team wins the game.

1. PUNT DRIVE
Driveball. Punt Back.

The game is commonly played on a regulation football field, but a somewhat smaller one may be better, certainly for younger players. In any case, goal posts are not used. Players are in two teams, each scattered at will in one half of the field. One team has a football, and one man from this team takes the ball and punts it toward the opponents from a line marked in his half of the field. This line is commonly about 15 yards from the center of the field, but its exact location should be determined by trial; it should be so located that a good kick will carry the ball just as far from the middle of the field as is the kicking line. The opponents of the kicker try to catch the ball on the fly. If they succeed they advance the ball three steps and kick it from there; if not, they kick from the spot where the ball is recovered. In any case, the ball is not necessarily kicked by the man who recovers it, but is always kicked by the men in order, each one taking his proper turn.

The ball is kicked back and forth, each team trying to move toward the opponents' goal, until one team or the other is able to kick the ball so that it strikes the ground, or is caught, beyond the opponents' goal line and thus wins a point. Since one team is almost sure to have some advantage in the location of the first kicking line, a game should never be decided by a single point, but after the first point is scored, the teams should change goals and play again.

Variation 1. Another method of scoring that is just as good as the one described, and perhaps better, is this: A point is scored by a team that succeeds in catching the ball in the opponents' half of the field.

Variation 2. The game is nearly always played, as described, with a bonus for catching the ball, the bonus being usually three steps, but sometimes five. Certainly five steps, and possibly three steps, gives too much advantage to the catching team, since catching the ball in itself gives a team the ball in a much better position than if it missed it. Accordingly, it is likely that the best rule would be to give no bonus at all but to have the ball always kicked from the point of recovery.

2. DROP-KICK DRIVE

Same as Punt Drive, except that all kicks must be drop kicks and that to score, a team must drop-kick the ball over the goal posts.

3. KICK DRIVE

Same as Punt Drive, except that each kicker has the option of punting or drop-kicking. Scoring is as in Punt Drive.

Variation. Score only by drop-kicking the ball over goal posts.

4. VARIETY-KICK DRIVE

Same as Punt Drive, except that the ball is punted, drop-kicked, or place-kicked, as ordered by the leader. When a given kick is directed for the first-kicking team, it is also used by the next kicker of the opponents, so that both teams use the same number of each kind of kick.

5. THROWING DRIVE
Forward-pass Drive

Same as Punt Drive, except that the ball is thrown, instead of being kicked. Any kind of ball may be used, but a softball or football is suggested.

6. KICK-OR-THROW DRIVE
Kick-and-pass Drive

Same as Punt Drive, except that each player has the option of punting, drop-kicking, or throwing the ball. Scoring is by sending the ball over the goal line, and varies with the method, as follows: drop kick, three points; forward pass, two points; punt, one point.

7. BATTING DRIVE
Driveball

Same as Punt Drive, except that a baseball or softball is advanced by striking it with a bat.

8. VOLLEY DRIVE
Hand Batball

Same as Punt Drive, except that a volleyball is used, and it is advanced by batting it with the fist or open hand.

Class VIII

BANDY GAMES

IN A BANDY GAME TWO SIDES PROPEL A BALL, OR, RARELY, SOME
other object, back and forth from one to the other, each trying to
propel the ball properly, but so that the other side will be unable to
do the same. The best-known bandy games are Tennis, Volleyball,
and Handball. Since these games and most others of the class use
either a net, as in Tennis, or a wall, as in Handball, the whole class
of games is sometimes called "Net and Wall Games." This term
seems unacceptable for two reasons: (a) Some few games that unquestionably belong in the class do not use either a net or a wall;
(b) It seems better to use a class name based on the basic principle
or objective of the game, but the term in question is based only on
the equipment used. The term *bandy*, while it may be somewhat
fanciful, does suggest the essential nature of the games and gives a
workable guide for logical classification. The principal meaning of
the word, according to Webster, is "to give and receive reciprocally;
to exchange." It is interesting to note that an obsolete meaning of the
word is "an old form of tennis; also a stroke or return of the ball in
this game, or the ball when struck."

Division One: Net and Line Games

In most bandy games the two opposing parties are separated and
face each other across a net, rope, line, or zone. The ball (or other
object) may be propelled in one of three ways—by throwing, by
batting with the hand, or by striking with a racket or bat. These
games comprise Division One; they are subdivided into three sections
corresponding to these three methods of propulsion.

Section I: A ball or other object is thrown

1. NEWCOMB
Netball. Volley Newcomb.

Newcomb is essentially the same as Volleyball, except that the ball is caught and thrown instead of being batted. The ball must always be caught cleanly. If a player misses or juggles the ball, his team loses. The best way to play the game is to follow closely the rules of Volleyball, for men or for women. Newcomb was devised and is often used as a lead-up game for teaching Volleyball. It is not suited to skillful players.

Variation 1. The player who catches the ball when it comes over the net must return it over the net; in other words, passing to a teammate is prohibited. This variation is undesirable if the game is used as a lead-up to Volleyball.

Variation 2. Same as the basic form, except that play is always started with a Volleyball serve.

2. CATCHBALL
Groundball. Newcomb.

Same as Newcomb, except that a neutral zone is used instead of a net. The court is divided into three equal parts, the middle part serving as the neutral zone.

3. FOOTBALL NEWCOMB
Forward-pass Newcomb. Pass Newcomb.

Same as Catchball, except that a football is used instead of a volleyball.

4. FENCE NEWCOMB
Fenceball

An ordinary fence is used instead of a net. In this game the court should be as wide as possible and much shallower than a Volleyball court, so that the players will run rapidly back and forth along the fence. In most cases it should be played without the passing to teammates and in some situations it will be wise to have a neutral zone extending a short distance from the fence.

5. GOAL-POST NEWCOMB
Newcomb Over-the-Goal-Posts

This is merely Newcomb with a football goal for a net, the ball being thrown over the crossbar between the uprights. A football or volleyball may be used. Boundary lines should be located by experiment and for some players they may be omitted entirely.

6. MEDICINE-BALL NEWCOMB
Cabinetball

Same as the basic form of Newcomb, except that it is played with a medicine ball as heavy as the players can handle well. This game is said to have been originated by Herbert Hoover while he was President and to have been played by him and his Cabinet on the White House lawn. In this game a serve by throwing from the base line is likely to be difficult. For this reason the serve should be made from a line midway between the net and the base line, or, if preferred, the serve made from the base line and one assist permitted.

7. CURTAIN NEWCOMB
Ante-over. Curtainball. Kitty-Ki-Over.

This game requires an opaque curtain, wall, or high fence, the higher the better. The game does not have much point unless the curtain is at least seven feet high. Play is exactly as in Newcomb.

8. BLIND MEDICINE-BALL NEWCOMB
Blind Medicine-Ball Tennis

This game is a combination of Medicine-Ball Newcomb and Curtain Newcomb. In other words, it is the same as Medicine-Ball Newcomb except that it uses an opaque curtain, wall, or fence, as in Curtain Newcomb.

9. OVER-THE-HOUSE
Newcomb Over-the-Tent. Over-the-Shed.

This game is a special form of Curtainball and is the same as Curtainball except that the ball is thrown over a house, shed, or tent.

10. FIFTH COLUMN

Teams form as for Newcomb with the important exception that each team has one man on the opponents' side of the net. Play is as in Newcomb, except that the one man among the enemy tries to catch the ball and scores a point if he does so.

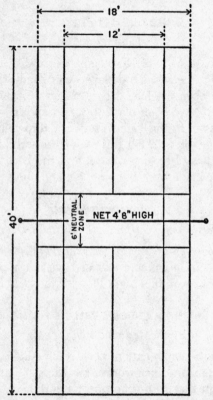

Figure 28. Deck Tennis. Combination court for singles and doubles.

11. DECK TENNIS

Quoitennis. Tenikoit.

Deck Tennis owes its name to the fact that, like Shuffleboard, it was first played extensively on board ship. The game is based on

Tennis and is like the latter in principle, but instead of a ball it uses a doughnut-shaped "ring" or "quoit" that is usually made of sponge rubber but sometimes of rope; its inside diameter is six inches. The quoit is not batted but is caught and thrown, and the throw must be made with an underhand or tossing motion. Like Tennis, it may be played with sides of either one or two players each, or even with one against two. The rules vary somewhat, but the following are in fairly general use:

The court for singles is 12 by 40 feet; for doubles a three-foot alley is added to each side, making the court 18 feet wide. The top of the net is four feet and eight inches high, and is in the middle of a six-foot neutral zone. Each half-court is divided into two equal service courts by a line parallel with the side lines. A quoit that touches a line is in, but the neutral zone is out of bounds. The server has only one chance on each serve, not two as in Tennis, but a serve that touches the net and lands good is a let and does not count either way. Rotation of servers and of the service courts follows the rules of Tennis. The scoring system, however, is similar to that in Volleyball or Handball. That is, only the serving side can score, and the immediate objective of the receiving side can be only to put the serving side out and thereby obtain the right to serve and score. The winner is the first side to reach a score of 15, provided it is ahead by two points or more. Accordingly, if the score gets to be 14 all, it is deuce, and either side must win two points in succession in order to win the game. A player loses for his side if he holds the quoit more than three seconds, touches it with both hands, allows it to touch his body, or juggles it.

12. DECK TENNIS (NSWA Rules)

The National Section on Women's Athletics of the American Association for Health, Physical Education, and Recreation publishes rules for Deck Tennis in its biennial publication, *Official Recreational Games and Volley Ball Guide*. These rules differ in the following respects from the ones given above:

The width of the court is 14 feet for singles and 17 feet for doubles. The top of the net is five feet high.

Either side can score, and the scoring system is exactly the same as in Tennis.

13. SWORD TENNIS

This game is played like Deck Tennis, with the deck-tennis quoit, but each player has a gymnasium wand with which he must catch and throw the quoit.

Section II: Ball is batted with the hand

This section includes net or line games in which a ball is smacked or batted with the hand. In some of the games, such as Volleyball, the ball must not be permitted to touch the floor, while in others there is no such provision. The games are in two groups, depending on whether a bounce is permitted.

GROUP A: BALL MUST BE HIT ON THE FLY

1. VOLLEYBALL

Volleyball was invented in 1895 in the YMCA of Holyoke, Massachusetts, by William G. Morgan, the physical director. Like Basketball and unlike almost all other well-known active games, it was deliberately invented at a definite time. Other games have histories but they have no known beginnings. The game has, of course, undergone changes, but its essentials are those of the original game. It is now one of the most popular and widespread games in the world. For a good many years the game was governed by the YMCA, but since 1929 the controlling body has been the United States Volleyball Association.

In Volleyball two teams bat a ball with the bare hands from one to the other across a net, each trying to drive the ball over in such a way that the opponents are unable to make a good return. The court is 30 by 60 feet, so that each half-court is 30 feet square. The net is stretched tight with the middle eight feet above the floor; it is made of heavy cord woven into four-inch mesh.

A team consists of six men, and each one is assigned to one of six equal areas into which the half-court is divided by imaginary lines. Each man is required to be in his area when the ball is put into play, although he may leave his area to play the ball provided a man in the back court does not go to the net and spike or block the ball. The rule requiring a man to have his own area was made to distribute the play among all members of a team and to prevent specialization. Another rule made for the same purpose is the one requiring rotation. Whenever a team wins the serve from the opponents its members all "rotate" before the serve; they circle in a clockwise direction so that, of the three men in the front line, the one on the left moves to the middle, the one in the middle moves to

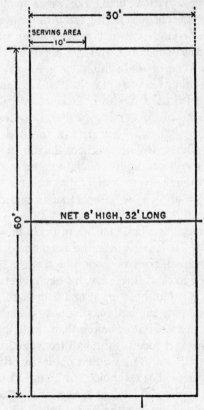

Figure 29. Volleyball. Plan of court.

the right side, and the one on the right moves to the right of the rear row. Likewise in the rear row, the one on the right moves to the middle, the one in the middle to the left, and the one on the left to the left of the front line.

The ball is spherical, consisting of a rubber bladder in a leather case. It has a circumference of from 26 to 27 inches and a weight of from 9 to 10 ounces.

Each play is started with a serve, made by a man in the right rear space on the serving side. To serve the ball, the server stands behind the end line not more than ten feet inward from the right corner. He tosses the ball with one hand and strikes it with the other without touching the floor on or over the line. The serve must go over the net without touching it (there being no let as in Tennis), and the server has only one chance. If the serve falls short of the net, or touches the net, or lands out of bounds without being touched by an opponent, the server is out and the opposing team serves next. If the ball does none of these things, it is in play, and it is up to someone on the other team to play it. The best and most common way to do this is to strike it with both hands simultaneously, using the palms and heels of the hands, but the rules are very liberal and permit striking the ball with any part of the body not lower than the knees. Sometimes, usually without intent, the ball is played with the chest, the head, or the back, and such a play is entirely legal. The important requirement is that the player must bat the ball and not catch and throw it; and that he must not hit it twice in succession.

When a man receives a ball that has just come over the net he has a perfect right to bat it back over the net immediately, and this is exactly what inexperienced or poor players are likely to do, but he is not required to do this. He has his choice between batting the ball back over the net and batting it to a teammate. The rule on this is that on any one play the ball may be passed among the members of a team once or twice, but not more than twice, before it is batted over the net. Thus if A receives the ball from the opponents he may bat it to teammate B and B may either bat it over the net or bat it to C; in the latter case, C has no choice, for he must bat it over the net. Incidentally, B could bat it back to A and let A drive it over the net, for while a man may not hit the ball twice in succession he has a right to hit it twice on one play. Among good players, the ball is only rarely batted over the net by the one who first receives it from the opponents. Good players use the system of setting up the ball and spiking it. In this system the man who receives the ball strikes it so as to send it with little force to one of the men at the net; the latter then bats it so that it floats gently upward considerably higher than the top of the net without crossing over it, and in good position for the next net man to jump into the air and hit the ball downward. This final downward blow is the spike. Good spikers are usually tall, and the best of them can hit a good set-up so that it is next to impossible for the opponents to do anything with it. Volleyball without spiking is not the real thing and should be discouraged in every possible way. Where the height or ability of the players makes the net seem too high it should be lowered.

In Volleyball only the serving team can score. When a team wins in a play started by the opponents' serve, it does not win a point but only the right to serve. A man continues to serve until his side loses; when the serving team loses on a play it is called side out. Until 1947 the game was always played in 15-point games with the deuce system. That is, the team that scores 15 points wins the game, provided it is two points ahead. If a team gets to 15 and is only one point ahead, play continues until one team or the other has a margin of two points. This is the same principle that is used in Tennis and some other games. Starting in 1947, the rules have permitted games to be played by time instead of points, provided both teams agree in advance. Under this system a game lasts for eight minutes of actual playing time, the watch being stopped when the ball is not in play, and the deuce system is not used.

An important principle of the game is that each player must always remain on his own side of the net. Accordingly, it is an error, resulting in a point or side out, for a man to touch the net, to reach over it, or to move under it. Even if a man is standing still and the net is driven against him by the ball, he loses for touching the net.

It is understood of course that the ball never touches the floor or ground; the game gets its name from the fact that it is played entirely in volleys, that is, fly balls.

It has been said that a server loses if the served ball touches the net. After the serve, however, a ball that touches the net is still in play. If it strikes the top of the net and goes over, it is up to the team on the other side to do the best it can with it. If the ball strikes the net and rebounds it is still in play and can be recovered and played like any other ball provided, of course, that it is not struck more than three times, or twice in succession by one man, on the one play, including the play before and after the ball strikes the net.

2. VOLLEYBALL (Women's Rules)

Rules formulated by the National Section on Women's Athletics of the AAHPER are generally accepted as the official rules of Volleyball for play by girls and women. These rules, while following the men's rules in general, differ from them in several important ways. The important rules for women that are different from those for men are as follows:

1. The top of the net is seven feet, six inches high.
2. A team consists of eight players.
3. The *let* principle applies to the serve. That is, a serve that strikes the net but is otherwise good counts nothing and the server is permitted to try again.
4. A player may hit the ball twice in succession. Furthermore, two hits in succession count as only one play. The ball may be played only three times before going over the net, exactly as in the men's rules, but a player who hits the ball twice in succession is considered to have played it only once. Thus the ball can be struck six times in being played three times.
5. The game is always played by time, not by points. A game consists of two halves of 15 minutes each. Generally, tie scores stand, but it is not illegal for a tie game to be played off.
6. Players do not necessarily rotate. That is, each player must take her turn at serving, but may otherwise play in the same position throughout the game. Teams may agree in advance either to use or not to use rotation of playing positions. If no agreement is reached, then one half of the game must be played with each method.
7. By advance agreement an assistant may be permitted on the serve. If the assist is used, a served ball may be struck once by a teammate of the server before it goes over the net. As with rotation, the teams should agree in advance whether the assist is to be used, and if no agreement is reached one half shall be played with, and the other half without, the assist.

3. MODIFIED VOLLEYBALL

Volleyball is sometimes modified in various ways to meet special situations, without changing its essential nature. The official rules specify a net seven feet, six inches high for play by women, and it is recommended that a net of this height or even lower be used whenever it seems more suited to the abilities of the players.

The game is sometimes played with more than six on a team. This is likely to result in an undersirable reduction of the activity of the players and in a tendency for the amount of activity to be unequally distributed. For inexperienced players the limit of two passes may be eliminated. It has been found a useful teaching device to *require* two passes or more.

4. SINGLES OR DOUBLES VOLLEYBALL

When four or even two confirmed Volleyball players get together and can find no others to join them they can still play after a fashion. The game must be played on a court considerably smaller than the standard one, the numerous lines on a gymnasium floor usually making this possible. With two on a side no changes need to be made in the rules, but with one on a side the rule prohibiting successive hits by one man must be eliminated. The player is entitled to two passes before driving the ball over the net, and he makes these passes to himself.

5. BALLOON VOLLEYBALL

Good fun can be had by playing Volleyball with a toy balloon. It can be played indoors in a space much smaller than the one required by the standard game. The serving line must be moved much closer to the net so as to make it possible for the server to get the ball over the net.

6. GIANT VOLLEYBALL

This is Volleyball or a game as near Volleyball as possible, played with a cageball 36 inches in diameter or as large as available. The net should be lowered to six feet or so; something sturdier than a net is better and a row of parallel bars is just right. The server has two chances and any serve may be assisted once. There is no limit on the number of passes. There is also no limit on the number of players on a team; six is hardly enough and the game does very well with 20.

7. WATER VOLLEYBALL

Volleyball can be adapted to play in the water, using a waterpolo or sport ball. It can be played in water only chest deep, the players standing on the bottom. In this case the net should be about

four feet above the water. It can also be played in deep water if
the players are good swimmers, although even then it should be
played in a pool and the players permitted to rest at the rail. A rope
should be used for a net and it should be about two feet above the
water.

8. CROSS VOLLEYBALL
Crossball

A square court is divided into quarters by two nets that intersect
at right angles. Four teams play, one in each quarter of the court.
The server may serve the ball into any of the opposing three quarters
and while in play the ball may go from one quarter into any of the
other three. If a nonserving team wins a play, it gets the serve as
usual. But when the serving team wins, a point is counted, not in
favor of the winner, but against the loser. When one team has
scored ten points the team with the lowest score is the winner.

GROUP B: BALL MAY BE HIT AFTER BOUNCE

1. BOUNCE VOLLEYBALL

Same as Volleyball, except that every time that the ball is hit it
must bounce on the floor before the next man plays it. The serve
must strike the floor on the server's side and bounce over the net.
A pass from one man to a teammate must bounce between them. A
ball that goes over the net must bounce over.

2. FIST VOLLEYBALL
Fistball

In this adaptation of Volleyball the ball must always be struck
with the closed fist of one hand, but it may always be hit either on
the volley or on the first bounce. Otherwise it is the same as Volleyball.

3. BOUNCEBALL

Bounceball is played with a volleyball, but with a net only four
feet high. It is played like Volleyball except that any ball may be
played either on the volley or on the first bounce. The low net makes
it easy for the players to make hard drives over the net, but the first-
bounce privilege makes it possible for the opponents to play such
drives. The game turns out to be not much like Volleyball.

4. HAND TENNIS

Hand Tennis is played much like standard Tennis except that the ball is struck with the open hand instead of with a racket. An old tennis ball is usually used but any similar ball may be substituted. The court is simply a rectangle with no service areas and much smaller than a tennis court; a paddle-tennis court, which is 18 by 39 feet, is about right. Play follows the rules of Tennis. The usual method of scoring Tennis may be dropped and a straight count used instead, the game going to the side that first accumulates 15 points.

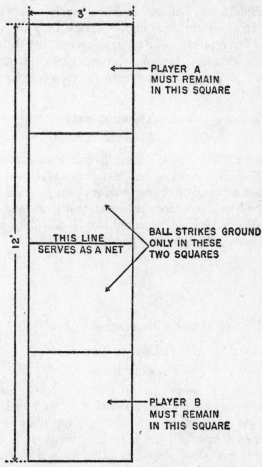

Figure 30. Sidewalk Tennis. Plan of court.

5. SIDEWALK TENNIS

This game is played on a small paved court consisting of four three-foot sidewalk squares, in a line. The middle line represents a net. One man is in, and must remain in, each of the end squares. The two opponents bat a rubber ball back and forth over the middle line, following the principle of Tennis. The ball must always go over the middle line and strike in the square just beyond it; the end squares are not used except to confine the players. The serve is made by bouncing the ball on the court and striking it as it rebounds (as in Handball). Any ball may be hit on the fly or first bounce. The same man continues to serve until he loses. Only the serving side can score. Eleven points make a game, except that the deuce principle applies; that is, if the one who gets eleven points is not two points ahead, play must continue until one man is two points ahead.

6. CIRCLE BOUNCEBALL

Circle Ball-Bounce. Spotball.

A two-foot circle is drawn on the floor or smooth pavement with a straight line through its center extending several feet beyond the circle. Two men stand on opposite sides of the line and alternate in striking a ball with the hand, always so that it hits the floor inside the circle. The game may be scored like Handball, or players may serve alternately with either one eligible to score.

Section III: Ball is struck with a racket or bat

GROUP A: BALL MUST BE HIT ON THE FLY

1. BADMINTON

Badminton is a game in which two sides of one or two men each drive a feathered object called a *shuttle* back and forth over a net, using light gut-strung rackets, the shuttle being always volleyed and never permitted to touch the floor or ground. It is the modern development of a game played in India, known as Poona. Poona was played in India by English army officers stationed there and was carried by some of them to England in the early 1870's. It became generally known chiefly through its play, beginning in

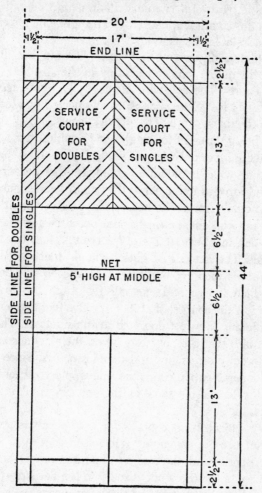

Figure 31. Badminton. Combination court for singles and doubles.

1873, on the Gloustershire estate of the Duke of Beaufort and took its name from that of the estate. England is still the principal home of the game, but many other countries have adopted it and it is now played widely in the United States. In this country the game is under the direction of the American Badminton Association, which is a member of the International Badminton Federation. Rules of the game are made by the International Badminton Federation and are published in this country, apparently with slight amendments, by the American Badminton Association.

The court naturally resembles that for Tennis, but differs from the latter in its dimensions and notably in the size and location of the service courts. The court for singles is 17 by 44 feet, and for doubles 20 by 44 feet. The game is usually played on a combination singles and doubles court. The service courts have the strange property of being different for singles and doubles, the singles court being relatively long and narrow, while the doubles court is relatively short and wide. It should be noted also that the service courts do not extend forward to the net as they do in Tennis, but only within six and one-half feet of the net, so that a served shuttle, in order to be good, not only must clear the net but also must travel at least six and one-half feet beyond it, and a serve that falls too close to the net is a fault. The amount of out-of-bounds space needed is very small, five feet at each end and three feet at each side being ample. The net, which is two and one-half feet from top to bottom, is stretched across the court so that its top is five feet above the ground at the middle and five feet one inch at the sidelines. The rules apparently require that the net posts be on the sidelines and thus be located differently on singles and doubles courts. Since this is impossible on a combination court, the rule is seldom strictly followed. The difficulty here is the same as the one discussed in connection with Tennis.

The driven object, formerly called a *shuttlecock*, is now officially a *shuttle*, but is more commonly referred to as a *bird*. The shuttle consists of a cork hemisphere one to one and one-eighth inches in diameter with 14 to 16 feathers fixed into the flat side, the feathers being two and one-half to two and three-fourths inches in length. The cork is usually covered with thin white leather. The shuttle is very light, the official weight range being 73 to 85 grains or, since a pound equals 7,000 grains, less than one fifth of an ounce. The racket is not restricted by the rules but as actually used is extremely light and slender, with a weight of about five ounces and a length of about 26 inches; it has gut stringing and except for its lightness very closely resembles a tennis racket.

The server stands within one of the service courts, not behind the base line as in Tennis or Volleyball, and is free to take any position desired within the boundaries of the service court. The server must strike the shuttle with a definite underhand stroke, since it is required that the shuttle be below the waist of the server when struck. The serve is always from one service court to the diagonally opposite service court on the other side of the net. If the shuttle touches the net and lands good, it is a let, counts nothing, and is played again. If the shuttle does not go over the net or if it goes over the net and lands on the ground outside the proper service court, the server is out and must make way for another server; he has only one chance, not two as in Tennis. Finally, if the shuttle goes over the net and is played by an opponent, it is bandied back and forth until one side or the other makes a fault. The receiver of course does not have an opportunity to know for certain whether the serve is good and accordingly is called upon to use his judgment in deciding whether to play the serve. It is understood, of course, that after the serve the entire court is used, the lines marking the service court being used only on the serve.

In Badminton, as in Handball or Volleyball, only the serving side can score. When the nonserving side wins a rally, it does not win a point but only the right to serve and the opportunity to score points. When a server wins a point he serves again and continues to serve for point after point until he loses, serving alternately from the right and left service courts. In singles, the service court from which the first serve in each inning is made is determined by the present score of the server. If the server upon beginning his inning has an even number of points he always stands in the right-hand service court and serves diagonally across the net to the opponent's right-hand court, but if he has an odd number of points he always begins his inning by serving from his left-hand court diagonally across into the opponent's left-hand court. This system, however, does not apply to doubles. In doubles, when the first server in any game has lost his turn, the right to serve goes to the opponents, but thereafter when the first server of a team is put out his partner takes a turn; this means that except for the very first inning of a game, the nonserving team in order to take the serve from the opponents must win two rallies, as in the game of Handball or Racquets. In doubles the first serve made by a side in each inning is always made from the right-hand court regardless of the score. If the first point is won by the server, he then moves to the left-hand court, his partner replaces him in the right-hand court, and he serves to the opponent who is in the opponent's left court. So long as the serving side wins points the partners exchange places for each serve. It should be noted that when the second partner serves he takes up where the first left off, so that if he begins with his side having an odd number of points for the inning he makes his first serve from the left court. It should also be noted that the members of the receiving side do not change places but each one keeps the right or left service court with which he started.

Except in the case of singles for women, the game is completed when either side has 15 points; the deuce principle is not used in this game. However, there is an important and interesting exception to this generalization. If the score becomes 13-all, then the side that first accumulated 13 points may, if it wishes to do so, "set the game to five." If this is done, the score becomes zero, or love-all, and the players begin a five-point game, which is won by the first side to accumulate five points. If the score never get to be 13-all, or if it does and the game is not set, and then comes to be 14-all, the side which first secured 14 points has the right to set the game, but in this case the game is set to three and not to five. It is permissible for players, before starting a game, to agree on a game of 21 points, but such games are not often played; in a 21-point game, the scores of five and three are set at 19 and 20. The official game for women's singles consists of 11 points; a game that reaches nine-all may be set to three, while one that reaches ten-all may be set to two.

Badminton is sometimes played outdoors, but in most climates outdoor play is seldom satisfactory since the slightest wind spoils the game. For the country as a whole, Badminton is essentially an indoor game.

2. PADDLE BADMINTON

Aerial Dart. Aerial Tennis-Dart. Modified Badminton.

Paddle Badminton is essentially the same as Badminton, except that wooden paddles are substituted for the rackets, and a considerably heavier and sturdier shuttle is used. The game can, of course, be played according to standard Badminton rules, but is usually played with modifications, in particular with a larger court and a higher net. Paddles and shuttles for the game are made by various manufacturers and some of the latter issue rules of their own and

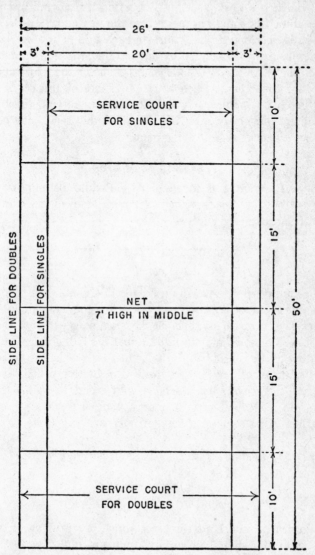

Figure 32. Paddle Badminton. Combination court for singles and doubles.

give proprietary names to the game. The following changes from the Badminton rules are in fairly wide use and have been found satisfactory:

The court is 20 by 50 feet for singles and 26 by 50 for doubles. The top of the net is seven feet high. A service line is marked parallel with each end line and ten feet nearer the net.

There is only one service court on each side of the net, not two. The service court is bounded by the end line, the side lines, and the service line. The server stands in his own service court and must serve into the other service court, any part of the service court being good. In doubles, players take turns in serving exactly as in Badminton, but not in receiving the serve; any serve may be taken by either player of the receiving team.

3. SPONGE BADMINTON

Sponge Badminton is identical with Paddle Badminton, except that it uses an ordinary sponge trimmed to a spherical shape in place of the feathered shuttle.

4. VOLLEYBALL BADMINTON
Leeball

An ordinary shuttle can be used for this game, but a sponge is much more practical. Also, paddles are recommended instead of rackets. Two teams of six each bat the sponge over the net, the members of each team being permitted to bat the ball among themselves according to the rules of Volleyball. In other words, the game is the same as Volleyball, except that instead of batting a volleyball with the hand, the players bat a sponge with a paddle. While this relationship to Volleyball suggests teams of six, it is perhaps better for the teams to be somewhat smaller; any size from two on up will work.

Variation. Leeball is the same game played with a five-inch sportball.

5. TETHERBALL
Tether Tennis

A vertical pole extends ten feet above the ground. It must be fairly rigid and should be either firmly planted in the ground or firmly attached to a heavy and broad base. A strong cord is attached at one end to the top of the pole and at the other to a ball which is commonly a tennis ball enclosed in a net cover, but which may be a leather-covered ball made for the purpose. The cord is seven and one-half feet long to the center of the ball. A line is marked around the pole six feet above the ground. A circle six feet in diameter is marked on the ground with the pole as the center, and one diameter if the circle is extended in both directions to make a line 20 feet long.

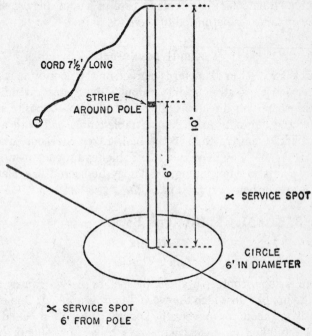

Figure 33. Tetherball.

Two service spots are marked on the ground six feet from the pole, the imaginary line connecting these spots being perpendicular to the long line and passing through the center of the base of the pole. The game was originally played with tennis rackets but is now usually played with wooden paddles such as the ones used in Paddle Tennis.

The game is for two players, each remaining on his own side of the long line. The object of each player is to strike the ball in such a way as to cause the cord to wrap around the pole above the line (the one six feet above the ground) and to continue doing so until the cord is completely wrapped around the pole.

The first server is determined by the toss of a coin, and he gets his choice of directions in which to wind the cord. He stands on his service spot and bats the ball. Thereafter either player may bat the ball whenever he can reach it without touching or stepping over the long line, or stepping into the six-foot circle. Play continues until one player has won by winding the cord completely around the pole, unless one commits a foul. In case of a foul, play is stopped and the opponent is permitted to serve the ball.

6. PADDLE BOUNCEBALL

A circle two feet in diameter is marked on the floor or on a smooth pavement, with a straight line through its center extending for several feet in both directions. Two men stand on opposite sides of the line and alternate in striking a table-tennis ball with a table-tennis paddle, always so that the ball strikes the floor inside the circle. The game may be scored like Table-tennis, each man serving for five points in each inning, or it may be scored like Handball, only the server being allowed to score.

GROUP B: BALL MAY BE HIT AFTER BOUNCE

1. TENNIS

Lawn Tennis

There is some confusion about the names of two games, related but quite unalike, to which the word *Tennis* is applied. One of these games is the modern, universally known, game often called *Lawn Tennis*, the other an ancient game which has now almost, but not quite, disappeared; the latter is described below under the name *Court Tennis*. Most authorities appear to believe that strictly correct usage requires that the term *Tennis* be restricted to the ancient game and that only the term *Lawn Tennis* be applied to the modern one. One excellent authority deviates from this usage by calling the earlier and later games *Court Tennis* and *Tennis* respectively, but explains that such usage, while realistic, is "technically" incorrect. It is not clear just what standard these authorities apply to determine strict or technical correctness, and the opinion is here ventured that the present widespread game should be called *Tennis* and the ancient game *Court Tennis,* and that such usage cannot be called incorrect no matter how technical or puristic one may become. It is conceded of course that the game of Tennis may also be called *Lawn Tennis* with perfect correctness, but this term is considered second choice.

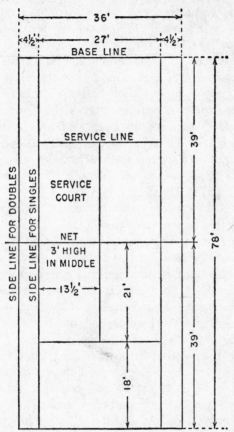

Figure 34. Tennis. Combination court for singles and doubles.

The modern game is certainly called *Tennis* most of the time by the great majority of players, teachers, officials, and other people connected with it. If it is not the technically correct name it must be that the governing body that is generally accepted for the game —in this country the United States Lawn Tennis Association—says so. But like most of the makers of rules for games, the USLTA does not take the trouble to state directly the exact name of its game, and no name for the game appears anywhere in the body of the official rules. However, there is basis for deciding what the officials of the organization consider the name to be. The USLTA publishes annually a book called *The Official Tennis Guide,* which includes the official laws along with various other material. In a recent edition of this book, the first page of text dealing with the laws is headed, "The Official Rules of Lawn Tennis," but a moderately careful examination indicates that the expression *Lawn Tennis* does not appear at any other place in the entire publication. The title page of the rules themselves is headed, "Official Tennis Rules." The title of an article by the president of the Association includes the term *Tennis.* Other headings are, "NCAA Tennis Championships," "How to Lay Out a Tennis Court," "Care and Construction of Tennis Courts." The publication includes advertisements of "tennis balls," "tennis rackets" and other "tennis equipment," but no equipment for and no books on *Lawn Tennis.*

It is true that the earlier game was called *Tennis* long before the present game was known, and this fact is probably the basis for the statement that the word must be applied to the earlier game and not to the later one, but this argument seems completely unsound. Usage does change the names of games as well as of other things, and the old tennis game has no official governing body able to preserve its name. The simple fact is that the name has been taken over by the present game and that to avoid confusion a different name must be applied to the old game. It seems clear, then, that the best name for the prevailing game is *Tennis,* with *Lawn Tennis* a perfectly correct second choice; that the best name for the older game is *Court Tennis;* and that there is no good argument against these names on the grounds of "strict correctness" or "puristic usage." Incidentally it may well be noted that the choice between *Tennis* and *Lawn Tennis* has nothing to do with the surface of the court. If the game is *Lawn Tennis* at all, it is *Lawn Tennis* whether played on grass or on concrete.

Tennis is played by two sides of one or two men each, the two sides alternately striking a ball with a racket so as to drive it over a net that is stretched like a fence between them. The game undoubtedly owes something to the earlier game which was also called *Tennis* and which is now better called *Court Tennis,* but probably should be considered a new invention rather than the development of an older game. The inventor was Major Walter Wingfield, an Englishman, and he introduced the game at a lawn party in 1874, with the name *Sphairistike*. The original court was suggestive of an hour glass, being wider at the base lines than at the net, and used a net higher than the present one. After some experimentation, the court took its present dimensions in 1877 and the net in 1880. The game was introduced to the United States very quickly, probably in its first year. For some years Tennis suffered from its lawn-party origin and was generally looked upon as a "sissy" game, but it spread rapidly nevertheless and became more rugged and strenuous as it spread. It is now, for players rather than spectators, one of the most popular games of the world. It is more highly developed in international competition than any other game or sport.

Tennis is played on a court that may be covered with grass, clay, wood, concrete, or any other suitable material. The original courts were grass-covered, but nowadays only a very small fraction are of this type. Grass courts are difficult and expensive to maintain, especially in some regions, but they are most highly rated, and are used for the leading championship tournaments. A court should be absolutely flat. For outdoor courts where some provision must be made for drainage of water it is recommended that the entire court be tilted sideward so that one side line is slightly higher than the other, the court thus being flat but not perfectly horizontal. The amount of slope needed does not exceed an inch and a half for 30 feet; such a slope apparently has no effect on play and cannot be detected by the players. The boundary lines of a court form a rectangle that is always 78 feet long, but is 27 feet wide for singles (one to a side) and 36 feet wide for doubles (two to a side). Since the ball may be struck on the first bounce as well as on the fly, and in fact is usually struck on the first bounce, players must be able to go out of bounds to recover balls that have struck the ground inside and bounced out. For this reason the actual playing area is considerably larger than that inside the lines. The rules recommend a 21-foot space at each end and a 12-foot space at each side beyond the lines, making the total area for a doubles court 60 by 120 feet. Many courts have less than the recommended allowance at the ends and where they are built in groups side by side the space between them may be as little as nine or ten feet. A doubles court is identical with a singles court except that it has a four and one-half foot alley along each side; that is, each doubles court has a perfect singles court contained within it. For this reason, nearly all courts are constructed for doubles with the idea that they can be used for singles as well.

The net is stretched tight across the middle of the court. Its top is exactly three feet high at the center and higher at the ends. According to the letter of the rule the net is to be three and one-half feet high at the posts that support it and the posts are to be three feet beyond the side lines. This means that the posts for a singles court are located differently than those for a doubles court and that when a doubles court is used for singles the height of the net at the side lines is not precisely correct; it is 1.3 inches too low.

The ball is an inflated rubber sphere with a diameter between two and one-half and two and five-eighths inches and a weight between two and two and one-sixteenth ounces; it is covered with felt. When dropped 100 inches upon a solid concrete base, it must rebound between 53 and 58 inches. The rules say nothing about the nature of the racket, but rackets in use vary but little. They are about 27 inches long, about half of the length in the handle and the other half in an oval or elliptical head filled in with a very tight network of strings. The traditional material for strings is "cat" gut.

At the beginning of each game and after each point, play is begun with a "serve," a play to which several special rules apply. The man who serves at the beginning of each game continues to serve until the end of the game. On the first serve of a game the server stands behind the right half of the base line. He tosses the ball into the air and strikes it with his racket; usually he throws the ball well above his head and hits it with a fairly high stroke, but this is not required and the notion that an underhand serve is illegal is entirely unfounded. The served ball must go over the net without touching it and strike the ground on the opponents' side of the net in a certain designated section called the service court. There are two service courts on each side of the net; their location is seen in the diagram. The serve is always diagonal, from the right side of the base line to the service court on the server's left, or from the left side to the court on his right. The first serve of a game is always from the right (and hence to the receiver's right), the second from the left, and so on, alternately. The server must be entirely behind the base line when he hits the ball. The server gets two chances for a good serve on any one point. If his first serve is good in every way and lands in the service court, it is, of course, in play, but if it is not good he tries again. A bad serve is called a fault and two of them constitute a double fault. In the case of a double fault, the server concedes a point to the opponent, moves over to the other side of the middle line and serves for the next point. Occasionally a served ball will strike the net at the top and still go over and land in the proper service court; such a serve counts nothing and the server makes another serve in place of it. It is called a *let*, not as some say, a *net* ball. The term *let*, while it is almost always used in reference to a serve, really is a broader term and refers to any play that is cancelled and replayed. For example, a let would be called if the net should suddenly fall, or if a dog should run onto the court. A served ball must be allowed to strike the ground and may not be struck, as any later ball may, before it does so.

After a good serve has been made the ball is struck by the two sides alternately until one side misses and loses the point. If the ball strikes the net it is still in play and if it goes over and lands good it is up to the receiver to return it; there is no let like the one on the serve. Any ball can be struck either after it has bounced once or before it has bounced at all. Every man must stay on his own side of the net and loses the point if he touches the net, touches the ground beyond the net, or strikes the ball by reaching over the net. It is not illegal, however, for a man to reach over the net after striking the ball, provided he strikes the ball on his own side. A player loses the point when the ball hit by him does not go over the net or when it goes over the net and strikes the ground out of bounds. Sometimes a receiver has difficulty in deciding whether a ball will strike in bounds or out. If it is to go out he can win the point by letting it do so, but if it is to go in he may need to play it before it strikes the ground. It should be noted that a ball is never out until it strikes the ground or some object that is out of bounds. When a player strikes or touches a ball that has not yet struck the ground, no matter how far past the line it has gone, he loses the point unless he makes a good return.

One of the most distinctive features of Tennis is its scoring system. A score can be made by either side on any play and is not restricted to the serving side, as it is in other bandy games like Handball and

Volleyball. A game is won by the first player to win four points, provided he wins by a margin of two points; if he is ahead by only one point, then play must continue until one side has a margin of two points. Scores are not counted as zero, one, two, three, and four, as they well might be, but in a different and apparently meaningless system. Zero score is called *love*, the first point counts 15, two points 30, three points 40. In naming the score one must always mention first the score of the serving side and then the score of the other side; there is a difference between 40-15 and 15-40. If the ball is not in play, so that there is really not a serving side, the first-mentioned score is that of the side that is to serve when play is resumed. Thus if a server wins all four points in a game, the scores are 15-love, 30-love, 40-love, and then, simply, game; if he loses four, the scores are love-15, love-30, love-40, and game. When both players have the same score the word *all* is used, as in 30-all. Other possible scores are 30-15, 40-15, 15-30, and 30-15. If the score gets to be 40-all it is not designated as such but as *deuce*, indicating the fact that to win the game either player must win two points in succession. The one to win the next point after deuce is said to have "the advantage"; if he wins again he has won the game, but if he loses, the score again becomes deuce. The only approved method of announcing the score when one side has the advantage is to call the word *advantage* and the name of the player or team that has the advantage, as "Advantage Mr. Jones." A player may say "my advantage", or "your advantage." In very informal play the contraction *ad* is sometimes used and the word *in* and *out* are used in reference to the server and receiver respectively, resulting in the expressions "Ad in" and "Ad out". There is no limit to the number of times that the score can revert to deuce before the player with the advantage wins another point and the game. Deuce is not officially recognized until the score reaches 40-all but it is interesting to note that it exists in fact at 30-all. With this score, a player must win two points in succession in order to win the game and it would make no difference whatever in the outcome if 30-all were called deuce and treated exactly like 40-all. Competition is never in terms of games but always of sets, the winner being the first to win two or three sets, or possibly the first to win one set. A set is won by the first player to win six games, except that here again the deuce principle operates to prevent the winning of a set by a margin of less than two games. Thus a set can be won by six games to four but not by six to five. When the games are five to five it is called deuce and from this point play continues as long as necessary until one man has a margin of two games.

The United States Lawn Tennis Association, founded in 1881, is recognized as the governing body for the game in this country. The Association is a member of the International Lawn Tennis Federation, the latter body formulating the rules that are standardized throughout the world. Tennis is a great game for tournaments and each year hundreds of tournaments of varying importance are held. Reference will be made here to three tournaments that are most widely known.

Undoubtedly the tennis matches with the greatest prestige are the international Davis Cup matches for teams representing nations. The cup was donated in 1900 by Dwight F. Davis, who, at the time, was an undergraduate student in Harvard University and who became Secretary of War under Coolidge and later Governor General of the Philippines. Any nation in the world may enter a team in the competition. All nations except the one that last won the cup must compete among themselves for the right to challenge the defending nation. For this preliminary competition the world is divided into two zones, called American and European. A nation must first win the championship of its zone and then meet the champion of the other zone. The winner of this interzone match then challenges the defender and the whole thing culminates in the "Davis Cup Challenge Round" between the defending nation and the one that has earned the right to challenge it, the round always taking place in the country of the defender.

The competition between two teams is called a tie, and a tie in this case includes five matches, four in singles and one in doubles, each counting one point. A team includes two singles players, each playing against each of the two opposing singles players, and one pair of doubles players. Since doubles players may or may not be singles players also, the number of men actually competing for a team may be two, three, or four.

The world of Tennis, like that of Golf, is full of championship tournaments purporting to cover geographical units of all sizes: United States, England, Canada, Colorado, New England, Cook County, and so on. These "championships," as they are called,

are not, as one might expect, restricted to players within the area
covered, but are open to all comers, so that the French Championship can be won by a Spaniard and the Wisconsin Championship
by a man from Texas. Apparently the sponsors of the various championships hope for as many entries as possible from outsiders and
measure the standing of their tournaments partly by the number of
outsiders entered. One championship has achieved greater success
than any other in attracting outstanding players; that is the so-called
Wimbledon Tournament, really the Championship of Great Britain.
This tournament attracts the greatest players from the entire world
and does it so well and so consistently that it is recognized as the
tournament for the championship of the world. It includes matches
for men's and women's singles, men's and women's doubles, and
mixed doubles.

The USLTA conducts the United States championships for men's
singles and women's singles at the West Side Tennis Club in Forest
Hills, Long Island, New York. The mixed doubles championships are
held at the same time and place. These tournaments all attract a
considerable number of leading foreign players, but not to the
extent that the Wimbledon matches do. It is understood that all
the tournaments thus far mentioned are played on grass courts.
The USLTA conducts a separate tournament for the clay-court
championships, as it does for indoor play and for men's doubles.

2. PADDLE TENNIS

Paddle Tennis was devised about 1920 by Frank P. Beal of New
York City. It has spread quite widely and is played on many play-
grounds throughout the country. The rules for the game, as well as
for Platform Paddle Tennis, which was derived from it, are made by
the United States Paddle Tennis Association.

The game is simply Tennis played on a small court and with
special balls and rackets designed to slow the flight of the ball. Two
sizes of court are recognized, the junior and the senior. The junior
court has all dimensions exactly half those of a standard tennis
court, that is, the doubles court is 18 by 39 feet, and the singles
court 13 and one-half by 39 feet. The total playing area including
the part that is out of bounds should be 30 by 60 feet. Each service
court is eight by 12 feet. The net is 30 inches high at the center and
32 at the posts. The paddle, which substitutes for the racket used in

Tennis, is made of laminated wood with no stringing, and has a maximum length of 17 inches; it looks like an oversized table-tennis bat except that the head is rectangular. All playing rules are iden-

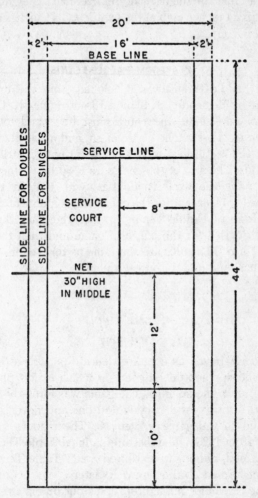

Figure 35. Paddle Tennis. Court for the senior game.

tical with those of Tennis. The ball is the same size as a tennis ball but is made of solid sponge rubber.

For the senior game, the court and paddle are larger and the net is higher. The rules are the same with the single exception that in the senior game only one serve is allowed on each point. The total area is 36 by 74 feet, the marked court is 20 by 44 feet for doubles and 16 by 44 feet for singles. The service court is eight by 12 feet, and the net is 34 inches high at the center and 41 inches at the posts.

3. PLATFORM PADDLE-TENNIS

Platform Paddle-Tennis was developed from the original form of the game by Fessenden S. Blanchard and James K. Cogswell. In this form of the game, the court must be completely enclosed, usually with tightly-stretched wire mesh, and a ball that strikes the enclosing walls is still in play, not being out until it strikes the floor out of bounds. The size of the enclosure is 30 by 60 feet. The principle of playing the walls is identical with that in Handball or Squash. The court, except for the enclosure, is identical with that for the senior form of Paddle Tennis; in fact, the court dimensions as given were devised for the platform game and then transferred to the earlier form. The rules are the same as for Tennis, except that the server has only one try on each point.

4. TABLE TENNIS
Ping-pong

Table Tennis began as a rather delicate parlor pastime but has developed into a true athletic game in which expert play demands great speed, skill, and stamina. The game was formerly called *Ping-Pong*, but this term was a copyrighted one and never should have been applied to the game in general. The modern standardized game dates from 1926, when the International Table Tennis Federation was formed, although the United States Table Tennis Association was not formed until a few years later.

The game resembles miniature Tennis but differs from Tennis in several important respects. The players stand on the floor but play the ball on the top of a table that measures five feet by nine feet and is 30 inches high. The table is made usually of plywood and is painted a dull green with a three-fourths inch white stripe around the edge of the top. There is also a white stripe running lengthwise in the middle, but this stripe is used only in doubles. The net is six inches high. The ball is very light and is a hollow celluloid sphere four and one-half to four and three-fourths inches in circumference. The ball is struck with a paddle or bat that may be plain or covered with sandpaper, cork, or other material, but is nearly always covered with beaded or stippled rubber.

The game, and also each point, begins with a serve. The server strikes the ball so that it hits the table on his side of the net and bounces over the net to hit the table on the other side; his bat must strike the ball behind the base line, that is, behind his end of the table. As in Tennis, a serve that touches the net but lands good is a let and is played again without counting for either side; but after the serve a ball that touches the net is still in play. In singles there

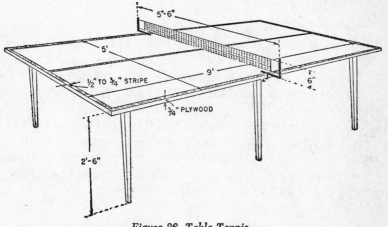

Figure 36. Table Tennis.

is no service court and the serve is good in any part of the court, just like any other ball. In doubles, the ball must be served diagonally into the proper service court, a service court being half of the entire area on one side of the net. There is no volleying in this game, and every ball must be hit only on the first bounce. The ball is struck by the two sides alternately until one side misses and a point is made. Score is not kept as in Tennis but by simple count. A game is 21 points, but the deuce principal is used. Hence, if the score is tied at 20-all play must be continued until one side is two points ahead.

The first server continues to serve until five points have been scored by the two sides together, and then the other side serves for five points; the serve alternates after each five points except that after a score of 20-all or deuce the serve changes after each point. Either side may score on any play.

In doubles it is required that partners alternate in hitting the ball, and for this reason the game is quite different from singles. The server always serves all of his five points to the same opponent and in the same service court. The serve alternates between the two sides and between partners.

5. COURT TENNIS

Tennis. Royal Tennis.

Court Tennis is the game to which the name *Tennis* was originally applied, and that many people now insist is the only game to which this name can be applied with strict correctness. As explained in connection with Tennis, this contention seems unfounded and the position is here taken that the earlier game should be called *Court Tennis*.

The game is played in a large enclosed court of very complicated design. The ball is struck with a racket over a net, but also against the walls. The courts are very costly and only a few are in use anywhere in the world, although the game is played regularly by a small group of people in a few cities.

Division Two: Wall Games

In each of the bandy games thus far described the two competing sides are separated by a net—or by a line or zone that serves the same purpose—and bandy the ball or other object back and forth over this net. In the Wall Games, which constitute Division Two, the two sides occupy the same area, and bandy the ball by striking it alternately against a wall from which it rebounds. The Wall Games are divided into two sections, those in which the ball is struck with the hands (or in one game with the feet), and those in which the ball is struck with a racket or bat.

Section I: Ball is struck with the hand or foot

1. FOUR-WALL HANDBALL

In Handball, two sides, of one man or two men each, alternately bat a ball with their hands against a wall, each trying, of course, to make it impossible for the other to make a fair return. The handball court is completely enclosed and has no boundary lines, so that while there is one wall (the front wall) from which the ball must rebound, there are three other walls and a ceiling against which it may rebound and still be in play.

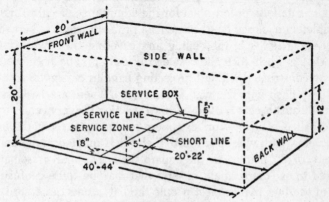

Figure 37. Four-wall Handball. Y.M.C.A. rules.

The game originated in Ireland in the tenth or eleventh century, and has never ceased to be very popular in that country. It was introduced to the United States about 1883 by Irish immigrants. About 1900 the game was changed in several important respects. In the first place, the old ball, which was a hard leather-covered one, much like a small baseball, was replaced by a rubber ball. In the second place, playing the ball with the foot, which had hitherto been permitted, was abolished. In the third place, the court, which had been from 50 to 60 feet long, was made considerably smaller. The game has flourished in the United States under the leadership of the YMCA and of the Amateur Athletic Union. The two organizations publish rules that are now identical except for a slight difference in the size of the court.

There is really no standard size for the handball court. The AAU rules specify a length of 46 feet, a width of 23 feet, and a height of 23 feet, but specifically state that even championship matches may be played on courts of other sizes. The YMCA rules specify a length of from 40 to 44 feet, a width of 20 feet, and a height of 20 feet. Actual courts vary considerably, and much high-class play takes place on courts with sizes considerably smaller than either of those mentioned. Nevertheless, the game cannot be played at its best on a court that is too small. Dimensions of 40 by 20 by 20 feet are suggested, and a court of this size should satisfy even the most expert players. Since the upper part of the rear wall can hardly be reached by the ball, it is often omitted and replaced by a spectator's gallery, or left open for the admittance of light. Lighting a completely enclosed court presents a problem which is best solved by recessing lights in the ceiling and covering them with durable glass that is flush with the rest of the ceiling. The entrance door must be constructed without projecting handles or hinges, so that it is entirely flush with the wall when closed. There are no lines in a handball court except those used for restricting the service.

The ball is a hollow rubber sphere one and seven-eighths inches in diameter, with walls one-fourth inch thick, inflated to the unusual pressure of 35 pounds to the square inch. This ball is sometimes referred to as "the softball," a term that may be quite confusing in view of the fact that to most people the ball seems quite hard. It is soft only in comparison with the old Irish leather-covered ball mentioned in the first paragraph. No other equipment is used except gloves, which are optional. Many of the best players use their bare hands, but some of the best, and probably the great majority of ordinary players, wear gloves, which must be soft and without any webbing connecting one finger with another or with the thumb.

Two parallel lines five feet apart are marked on the floor across the court; the front line is the service line, the rear one the short line, and the space between them the serving space. The short line should be across the middle of the court, that is, it should divide the court into halves. The server stands in the serving space wherever he chooses, drops a ball to the floor, and strikes it with his hand on the rebound. The serve is subject to several restrictions that do not apply to other parts of the game. In the case of some of these restrictions, a violation puts the server out and causes him to lose his turn; in the case of others, a violation on his first attempt at a service gives him another chance. In other words, sometimes a server gets a second chance on a given serve as he does in Tennis, and sometimes he does not, the distinction being based on the nature of the error made. The server is out and loses his turn if: (*a*) he strikes at the ball and misses it entirely, (*b*) he bounces the ball on the floor more than three times before striking it, (*c*) he serves the ball so that it strikes the floor, either side wall, or the ceiling before striking the front wall. The server gets a second chance when: (*a*) a serve that is otherwise good rebounds from the front wall and strikes the floor on or in front of the service line; (*b*) a serve that is otherwise good, strikes the rear wall before it strikes the floor; (*c*) a serve that is otherwise good strikes both side walls before it strikes the floor; (*d*) in doubles, the server's partner leaves the "box" in which he is supposed to stay, before the serve crosses the service line. The first of these errors is, quite naturally, called a short ball, but each of the others is sometimes, not so naturally, also called a short ball. If the server serves a short ball on a first attempt, the opponent has the option of playing it and the ball is in play when the opponent "accepts" it. It follows that if the server or his partner should try to interfere with a short ball, because of the expectation of serving another, the server is out. The server is also out, of course, if he serves two short (or long) balls in succession.

Each end of the serving space has a zone 18 inches wide marked off by a line parallel with the side lines. This zone is called a *box* and is used only in doubles. In doubles, while one man is serving, his partner must stand in this box with his back flat against the wall and must remain there until the serve has crossed the service line; as noted, a short serve is called if the partner leaves the box too early. There is only one service court and that is the entire floor area behind the service line. The server may take his position at any point within the serving space and may drive the ball to any point behind the service line, which means that in doubles there is no necessary alternation in receiving the serve and it is not illegal for several serves in succession to be sent to, or to be accepted by, the same man.

Throughout the game, on the serve or later, any ball may be played on the fly or on the first bounce. After the serve it makes no difference how often the ball hits the side walls or rear wall or

ceiling, since it is required only that the ball strike the front wall
before it strikes the floor.

As in Volleyball or Badminton, only the serving side can score,
and all that the receiving side can do immediately is to put the
servers out. The rotation of the serve in doubles is also the same as
in Badminton; that is, at the beginning of a game only one partner
serves, and when he is out the opponents serve. But after the first
half-inning, a side that gains the serve keeps it until both partners
have been put out. A game is 21 points and the deuce principle does
not apply; the first side to accumulate 21 points wins the game.
Handball has one rule that is extremely difficult to apply and that is
the "hinder" rule. The basis of this rule is the principle that every
player is entitled to a free and unobstructed opportunity to play the
ball. If a player intentionally interferes with an opponent he loses
the point or serve, but if he unintentionally interferes with him, a
hinder is called, the ball is dead, and the whole play is cancelled
and begun again. This rule is interpreted quite liberally in favor
of the one hindered. A hinder may be called in a man's favor even
though it seems to all concerned that the ball was "killed" so that he
had no real chance of returning it. A hinder is also called in his
favor even though it appears that his partner is the logical one to
play the ball. A different type of hinder occurs when a player
strikes the ball and it hits an opponent before it gets to the front
wall; of course if it hits a partner it loses. Still a different hinder
occurs in doubles when a served ball strikes the partner of the server
while he is in his proper position in the box.

2. ONE-WALL HANDBALL

One-wall Handball is an American adaptation of the four-wall
game that has become very popular in some regions and for which
rules are published by the Amateur Athletic Union.

The court has only one wall, the front one, and consequently,
unlike the four-wall court, has boundary lines. These lines and the
base of the wall form a rectangle 20 feet wide and 34 feet long; the
wall is 16 feet high. The short line is only 16 feet from the wall, and
the serving space is *behind* the short line. The service line, nine feet
farther from the wall than the short line, is not drawn across the
court but only indicated by two short marks at the side lines. The
ball and gloves are the same as in Four-wall Handball.

The server must stand between the side lines and between the
short and service lines. In doubles, the server's partner has no box

but is required to stand out of bounds. A short or long ball on a server's first try gives him a second chance, provided it lands between the side lines, but any served ball that strikes the floor outside the side lines puts the server out. The side lines must be prolonged beyond the base line so that a long ball can be judged in or out. After the serve, any ball that strikes the ground outside the side lines or beyond the base line is dead and results in a point or side

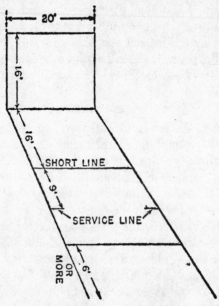

Figure 38. One-wall Handball.

out. There is no reason why the rules, with these exceptions, should not be identical with those of the four-wall game. In fact, however, the rules as published by the AAU show a few differences, the most important one referring to the hinder. The one-wall rule states that a player cannot be guilty of a hinder if, after striking the ball, he stands perfectly still. This is a rule that many players erroneously consider to apply to the four-wall game. The only other difference of any importance is that in the one-wall game it is not permissible for a player to accept a short ball.

3. TWO-WALL AND THREE-WALL HANDBALL

Handball is sometimes played quite successfully following the official rules except for obviously necessary minor changes, on courts that are neither four-wall nor one-wall; in fact any combination of walls can produce a very satisfactory game. Perhaps the most common of the variations is the three-wall game played on a court with a front wall and two side walls, but no rear wall or ceiling. The game has been played on a court with one front wall and one side wall, or with one front wall, one side wall, and one rear wall.

4. FIVES

Fives is a form of Handball played in England, notably at Rugby School. The ball is a hard one similar to the old Irish handball. The game is not well standardized and varies from place to place. The courts are outdoors and have either three or four walls. The rules are essentially the same as those of handball with some additional complications.

5. CODEBALL-IN-THE-COURT

Dr. William E. Code has invented and given his name to two entirely different games, thus creating a certain amount of confusion. Codeball-on-the-Green is a game of the Golf type and has already been described in Section VI, "Target Games." Codeball-in-the-Court is essentially Handball in which the ball must be kicked instead of being batted with the hand. It is played in a regulation handball court. The ball is a special one made for the two Codeball games; it is six inches in diameter and is made of inflated rubber.

The rules are almost identical with those of Handball, there being only two significant exceptions: (*a*) The ball may be kicked on the *second* bounce, as well as on the fly or first bounce; (*b*) A ball may be kicked twice in succession by a player or by two partners, provided it does not touch the floor or any wall between kicks. Thus if in doubles a player kicks the ball weakly his partner might be able to kick it again before it touches the floor.

Section II: Ball is struck with a racket or bat

1. RACQUETS
Rackets

In the game of Racquets a ball is struck with a gut-strung racket and driven against the walls of an enclosed court. The basic principles are identical with those of Handball, except that the court is much larger and that the ball is not played against the ceiling. The statement is sometimes made that the game was played by the ancient Greeks and Romans, or, more often, that it was originated in the seventeenth century by inmates of a debtors' prison in London, but such statements are hardly defensible. If the game is considered to have originated when players first batted a ball against a wall, then there can be no such thing as a traceable beginning, but the game as it is now known, with a four-wall court and definite rules, probably originated early in the nineteenth century. The game quickly became standardized and a number of courts were built in England, notably in the public schools. It was imported into the United States soon after the middle of the century. The game has

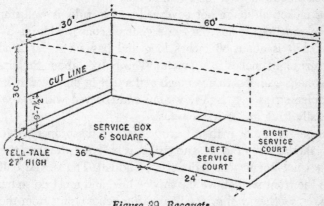

Figure 39. Racquets.

never been played widely, on account of the great cost of the courts, and has lost considerable ground in recent years, so that now there are only six or eight courts in the whole United States, these being maintained by exclusive and expensive clubs of which the best known is the Racquet and Tennis Club of New York City. Racquets has given rise to, and has been largely replaced by, other games that require less expensive courts, especially Squash Racquets.

The Racquets court is not completely standardized but is usually 30 feet wide, 60 feet long, and 30 feet high. The rear wall, like that in a handball court, need not be so high as the others and usually has a spectators' gallery in the upper part. The court is covered with a roof but the ball is not played against the ceiling. The floor is made of concrete and the walls of concrete or stone, both floor and

walls having an extremely smooth finish. The lower part of the front
wall, extending 27 inches up from the floor, is made of wood so constructed and installed as to make an easily distinguishable sound
when struck by the ball; this wooden portion of the wall is often
called a *tell-tale*. A line called the *cut line* or *service line* is painted
on the front wall parallel with the floor and nine feet seven and one-
half inches above it. A *short line* is marked across the court about
thirty-six feet from the front wall and the space between the short
line and the back wall is divided into two equal service courts by a
line down the middle. Two service boxes, each about six feet square,
are laid out in the angles between the short line and the side lines,
the boxes being in front of the short line.

The racket, although not governed by any rule, is well standardized in practice. It has the same general construction as a tennis
racket, but is about 30 inches long and has a circular head only
seven or eight inches in diameter. The ball is about the size of a
table-tennis ball, less than an inch and a half in diameter. It is made
of woolen strips very tightly wound and covered with leather; it is
unusually hard and extremely fast.

The server stands with at least one foot in the proper service box,
tosses the ball into the air, and strikes it before it drops to the floor;
he does not bounce the ball as in Handball. The served ball must
strike the front wall above the service line, and must do so before it
strikes any other wall or the floor. After rebounding from the front
wall, the ball may hit any other wall or walls provided only that
when it first touches the floor it be in the proper service court, that
is, in the one opposite the box from which the serve is made. The
server is immediately out and must make way for the next server if
the served ball strikes the 27-inch board or tell-tale, if it strikes the
floor or any other wall before the front wall, if it goes into the spectators' gallery, or if it strikes the ceiling. If the serve does not do
any of these things, but strikes the front wall below the service line
or strikes the floor not in the opposite service court, it is a fault and
the server gets a second chance as in Tennis or Handball. Of course,
two successive faults put the server out. The receiver has the option
of playing a faulty serve, and if he accepts it the ball is in play as
if the serve had been good.

The first serve in any inning may be made from either box, regardless of the score or of previous serves. When a point is won by the serving side, the same man serves again and continues to do so until his side loses the rally, but he must always serve from the two boxes alternately. Only the serving side can score; when this side loses a rally, the opponents do not score a point, but only win the right to serve. In doubles, the rotation of the serve is the same as in Handball; that is, when the first server in any game is put out, the serve goes to the opponents, but thereafter when a team wins the serve it keeps it until both partners have been put out, one after the other. The man who is serving at the end of a game remains the server to begin the next game.

A game is won when one side has 15 points, except that the score can be "set" as in Badminton. If the score comes to be 13-all, the side that is to receive next can set the score to five or three, in which case the first side to score five or three additional points is the winner Also, if the score comes to be 14-all without having been set at thirteen-all, the side that is to receive next can set the game at three. Hinders are played as in Handball, except that a hinder is called a *let*. That is, every man has a right to a free and unobstructed chance to hit the ball, and if an opponent unintentionally interferes with this chance, the let is called, the play counts for nothing, and the point is started again. Intentional interference is, of course, a foul and is penalized by loss of point or of serve.

2. SQUASH RACQUETS
Squash. Squash Rackets.

Two games, Squash Racquets and Squash Tennis, have resulted from the adaptation of Racquets to a smaller and simpler court. The term *Squash* is often applied to whichever of the two games the speaker or writer has in mind. Such usage is permissible when no confusion can result, but it must be understood that there really is no game called simply *Squash*.

Squash Racquets was originally the game of Racquets played in a small court and with a soft ball. Since the extremely lively ball of Racquets would fly around the walls of the small court so fast and so far as to make the game impracticable, the players adopted a larger, softer, and therefore slower ball that made a "squashy" sound as it hit the walls, instead of the sharp click of the racquets

ball. Hence the name *Squash.* The game in the small court was first
played in England about 1850 and in the United States about 1880.
It has developed rapidly in both countries, as well as in several
others, but has diverged considerably. The English tend to keep the
game much like Racquets and the Americans to introduce more
changes. It is now even more popular in the United States than in
England, and is widely played in clubs and colleges. In some colleges and universities it attracts more players than any other game.

The court in the United States is 18½ by 32 feet, with walls 16
feet high. All markings are the same as those in the Racquets court,
but the dimensions are necessarily different. The tell-tale, commonly

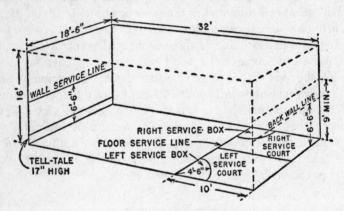

Figure 40. Squash Racquets.

made of metal instead of wood, is 17 inches high, and the service
line, marked on the front wall, is six and one-half feet above the
floor. The short line, sometimes called the *floor service-line,* is ten
feet from the rear wall. The service boxes are quarter circles instead
of squares, and are *behind* the service line, in the angles between
this line and the side lines, not in front of the service line as they
are in Racquets.

The ball is somewhat like a handball, made of inflated black rubber, but is softer and slightly smaller, with a diameter of one and
three-fourths inches. The racket is about 27 inches long and has a
circular head about seven inches in diameter.

The rules of play are, for the most part, identical with those already explained for Racquets, but there are some differences. The most conspicuous difference is in the scoring, since in Squash Racquets either side may score on any play. A game is always for 15 points. Another difference is that a served ball may strike one or more side walls before striking the front wall. It is not required to hit the front wall first as in Racquets.

The English court is 21 by 32 feet with walls 15 feet high. The tell-tale is 19 inches high, the service line six feet above the floor, and the short line 14 feet from the back wall. The English rules retain the Racquets rule that only the serving side can score. The English ball is different from the one used here and is not so well standardized, but in general is smaller and more lively.

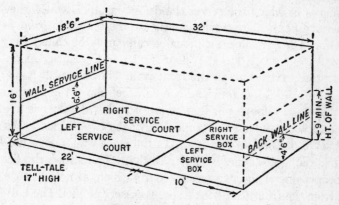

Figure 41. Squash Tennis.

3. SQUASH TENNIS

Squash

Squash Tennis was originally Squash Racquets played with a tennis ball and tennis rackets, but has undergone considerable change, so that now the two games, although identical in basic principle and played in courts of the same size, differ in a number of important respects. Squash Tennis is played extensively in some parts of the country, notably in New York City, Philadelphia, and Boston, and other places in the East, but farther west is pretty much neglected in favor of Squash Racquets.

The game is played in a court with the same size as that for

Squash Racquets. The markings are different in some respects but markings for both games can easily be made on one court. The ball is of the same size as a tennis ball but is more highly inflated and is covered with green webbing to facilitate spin. The racket is of the same shape as a tennis racket but is slightly smaller. By far the most important difference between the two squash games is in the racket and balls, since this difference results in markedly different play even when the rules are identical. The squash-racquets ball is slow and the squash-tennis ball is very fast.

The court has a center line running all the way from the front wall to the back wall, thus dividing the whole court into four parts. The two areas behind the cross line, that is, the ones that are service courts in Squash Racquets, are here not service courts at all, but are the spaces in which the server stands, or, in other words, they are the service boxes. The service courts are the spaces *in front of* the cross line. The cross line, incidentally, can hardly be called the short line and is referred to as the "floor service line" instead, in distinction to the service line on the front wall. The rear wall is marked with a horizontal line four and one-half feet above the floor, and a ball that strikes above this line before it strikes the floor is bad.

The server stands in the proper one of the two service boxes and must serve the ball so that it strikes the front wall, above the line, before striking any other wall, and so that it first strikes the floor in the proper one of the two service courts which, as noted above, extend from the front wall back to the floor service line. The ball may strike other walls after the front wall and before striking the floor; that is, the served ball may not strike any other wall on the way up to the front wall but may do so on the way back. Except as noted above, the game does not differ in any important respect from Squash Racquets.

4. ONE-WALL SQUASH

There is no standardized and recognized one-wall game for Squash as there is for Handball, but such a game can be improvised and has been quite popular where tried. Recommended dimensions are 16 by 35 feet with a floor service line 20 feet from the wall. Rules could be adapted from either of the squash games but are more likely to be from Squash Tennis, since the improvised game will probably be played with regular tennis rackets and old tennis balls.

5. PADDLE SQUASH

Paddleball

This game is simply Squash Racquets played with paddle-tennis equipment.

6. WALL TENNIS

One half of a tennis court is marked on the ground in such position that a wall, from which the ball may be bounced, is in the position of the net. The outline of a tennis net is marked on the wall at the official height. The server stands behind the base line and strikes the ball so that it hits the wall above the "net" and rebounds into the service court on the other side. Play continues exactly as in Tennis, except that the ball is always driven against the wall instead of over a net. A ball that strikes the wall below the top of the "net" is considered not to have gone over.

7. BATTLEBOARD TENNIS

Battleboard Tennis was invented by Miss Mary K. Browne. It is a special form of Wall Tennis, but the court is so much like that used for Squash Racquets that the game may be considered a one-wall adaptation of this game. The court is 18 feet wide and 30 feet long, and the board, or wall, is 18 feet wide and 12 feet high. The wall is covered with thick Celotex and the lowest 50 inches of it are inclined at an angle of 12 degrees. A tennis net of regulation height is hung parallel with the wall and five feet in front of it. The two service courts, which are nine feet wide and ten feet deep, are in the part of the court farthest from the wall, as in Squash Racquets, not nearest the wall, as in Tennis. The service boxes are quarter circles in the angles between the service line and the side lines, but they are behind the service line, not in front of it; that is, the service boxes are in the forward outer corners of the service courts.

The server stands in one of the service boxes and makes a legal tennis serve that strikes the wall and returns into the opposite service court, passing over the net, of course. Play and scoring are exactly as in Tennis, the game having been invented as a means of giving practice to tennis players.

8. JAI ALAI
Pelota

Jai Alai, pronounced "hi-a-li" or commonly "hi-li," is a Spanish term that means literally *merry festival*. The word *pelota* is simply Spanish for ball, and using it for the game is analogous to speaking of baseball simply as *ball*.

Jai Alai is a handball-type game played in a court nearly 200 feet long, in which a ball is not batted but is caught and thrown with a unique wicker implement attached to the hand of the player. The game was originated by the Basques and from them spread through Spain and then to various other countries, especially in Latin America, including Mexico and Cuba. It has been introduced to various cities in the United States but now is apparently played only in Miami, Florida. It is very much a game for spectators, rather than players and is played by only a small class of professionals. It attracts large numbers of spectators and probably owes its appeal largely to the betting that is promoted in connection with it, as in connection with horseracing.

The court has three walls, front, rear, and one side, the other side being left open or covered only with a screen so that spectators can see the game. The size is not standard, but the courts are very large, from 150 to 200 feet long and about 40 feet wide, with the front wall 35 or 40 feet high. The ball is about two inches in diameter and is covered with leather. Each player has strapped to one hand an implement called a *cesta* (Spanish for *basket*). The *cesta*, made of wicker, is narrow and two feet or more in length. It is curved both lengthwise and sidewise, so as to provide a long curved channel. The ball is not batted but is caught in the cesta and immediately thrown again. The principles of the game are the same as those in Handball, and the rules are the same in general but not in all details.

Class IX

BASEBALL GAMES

NEARLY EVERY GAME IS BASED ON A SINGLE AND SIMPLE IDEA OR principle. There is no difficulty in seeing and explaining the basic principle of Golf, Tennis, or Soccer Football, but to find and explain the basic principle of Baseball is a different matter. In fact, the game is composed of three different elements: (1) competition between a pitcher and a batter, in which the batter tries to hit the ball successfully in spite of the pitcher's efforts to prevent his doing so; (2) competition between a batter and one or more fielders, in which the fielders try to catch the ball hit by the batter or to recover it and throw it to a base before the batter gets there; (3) competition between a base runner and the fielders, in which the base runner tries to advance to the bases in order and eventually to home.

In selecting games to be included in the class with Baseball, one finds many games that are similar to Baseball in general but which nevertheless do not include all three of the elements just mentioned. Instead of a batter there may be a man who kicks the ball, or throws it, or hits it with his hand, and he may do any of these things without a pitcher throwing the ball to him. Further, there are games that are obviously closely related to Baseball but in which there is no base running. The one element that is never missing is that of fielding the ball, and the following classified list of "Baseball Games" is based on the assumption that the *sine qua non* of such games is the fielding. Many of the games have been devised by modifying the standard game, but many of the apparent modifications were actually in use before Baseball was played in its present form. The list includes many games, but only three are major games with standardized rules: Baseball, Softball, and Cricket. The games are in three divisions: (I) Games played on a diamond; (II) Games with no base running; and (III) Long-base games.

Division One: Diamond Games

The games of Division One include all those of the baseball type that are played on a diamond, the diamond serving the two functions of locating the foul lines and of locating the bases to which the players run. It must not be thought that all games of the baseball type require or use a diamond, for this is by no means true. Division Two consists of games in which there is no base running at all and hence no diamond. Division Three consists of games that are played on a rectangular field with a base on each end line.

The diamond games are numerous and highly varied; they include many variations that can be combined in an almost unlimited number of ways, so that if each possible combination of variations were to be considered a game, the number of games would be far too great to handle, as well as confusing. The problem implied in the last statement is handled by presenting the games in four sections. Section I includes only three games, those that are considered the basic games of the division, and those of which all the others are variations. These three games are Baseball, Softball, and Six-man Baseball. Section II includes the work-up games, those in which there are no teams but in which each man plays for himself. These work-up games are described only in their simplest or basic form. Section III is really a collection of variations, with the understanding that each of them can be applied to any of the basic games of Section I or equally well to any of the work-up games of Section II. The variations are given only singly or in the simplest combinations, with the understanding that other combinations can be used at will. Section IV includes a few baseball games that are played in the water or on ice; it may be that they belong logically in Section III but it seems more useful to separate them on account of their special nature.

Section I: The basic diamond games

1. BASEBALL

The origin of Baseball has been and still is the subject of considerable dispute. As with most games the development was a gradual one and it is impossible to select one event which can be taken to

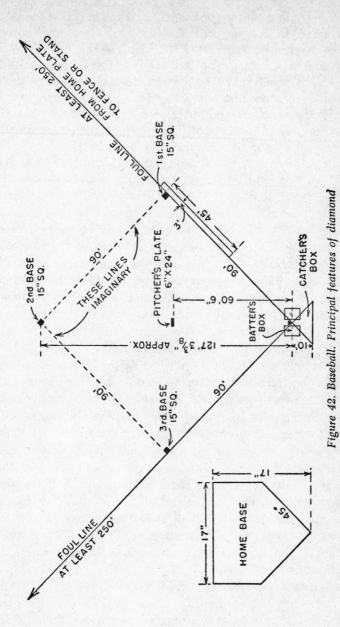

Figure 42. Baseball. Principal features of diamond

299

mark its beginning. A more or less official decision is that the game was invented in 1839 by Abner Doubleday in Cooperstown, New York, but the decision appears to have been based on only slight evidence. Certainly the game was well under way before the Civil War and expanded rapidly and continuously after the war. At first it was played only by amateurs, but before long players began to take money for their services, and in 1869 the first full-time professional team was organized in Cincinnati. The present National League was organized in 1876 and the American League in 1900.

Baseball is often called "America's National Game" but its present right to this title must be based largely on its status as a sport for spectators rather than as one for players. Although the game is played by thousands of amateur teams, its greater importance in American life today is due to the great system of business enterprises known as "organized baseball." Organized baseball includes two major leagues of eight clubs each and many minor leagues in several classifications. The games played by these teams attract each year millions of spectators who pay millions of dollars to see the games and patronize the concessions that are connected with them. The whole matter of the operation of organized baseball is quite fascinating, but too complex to be considered here.

There is only one recognized set of rules for Baseball, the one formulated for, and used by, all professional teams. The provisions of these rules have not been changed extensively for a good many years, but in 1950 the rules were completely rewritten and reorganized. Some of the rules are administrative, having to do with such things as fining players or making reports to league officials. Such rules are, of course, inapplicable to amateur games, but the rules that govern actual play of the game are accepted as the guide for baseball games everywhere. Most high school games follow the rules issued by the National Federation of State High School Athletic Associations. These rules are different in wording and organization from the professional rules, but are intended to have precisely the same effect.

The entire area of a baseball field is not fixed, and varies greatly, but it can hardly be less than 300 feet square, not counting space taken by spectators' stands. At a suitable place within this field is a square, 90 feet on a side, marked by lines on the ground; because of its orientation on the field this square is always called a diamond. In the corners of the diamond are four bases: home base (popularly home plate), first base, second base, and third base. Home plate is five-sided, made of white rubber, and sunk flush with the ground in one of the angles of the diamond. If one should place a 17-inch square in the corner of the diamond, with its sides parallel with the diagonals of the diamond and the middle of one of its sides in the exact corner of the diamond, and should then trim off the parts that extend outside the diamond, he would have the exact size, shape, and location of the home base. The other three bases are not imbedded in the ground, but lie on top of it and are removable. Each one is made of heavy white canvas in a shape like that of a thick cushion, fifteen inches square and from three to five inches thick, and stuffed with some fairly soft material. First and third bases are located inside the angles of their respective corners, but second base is located differently, its center being directly above the angle, although its sides, like those of the other two, are parallel with the sides of the diamond. The sides of the diamond that connect home plate with first and third bases are continued beyond the bases until they reach the outer limits of the field and are continued vertically up any fence, stand, or other obstruction. These lines are the foul lines and are of the greatest importance in the game.

The pitcher's plate is made of white rubber and sunk flush with the ground like home base. It is a rectangle six by twenty-four inches, and its long sides are parallel with the diagonal that connects first and third bases. The pitcher's plate is elevated fifteen inches above the level of the ground at the bases, the ground sloping gradually down from this elevation. The plate is on the line that connects home and second bases, and its nearest edge is 60 feet 6 inches from the home plate corner. A rectangular batter's box, four by six feet, is marked on each side of home plate, and certain other lines of no fundamental importance are marked for various purposes.

The ball is a sphere with a circumference of from nine to nine and one-fourth inches and a weight of from five to five and one-fourth ounces. It is made of cord tightly wound over a center of cork or rubber and is covered with white leather. The exact nature of the ball is a matter of agreement between the manfacturers and the major leagues, and many patrons and writers are convinced that it changes from time to time and that the changes have an effect on the success of the batters. The bat is made of one piece of hardwood, usually ash, with no loading. It may not be more than two and three-quarters inches in diameter at the largest part, nor more than 42 inches in length, and most bats have dimensions smaller than these maximums. Every player in the field wears a glove that, except the one worn by the catcher, is governed by certain restrictions. The catcher wears protective equipment consisting of a heavy metal mask for his face, an inflated chest protector, and shin guards that cover his lower legs and knees.

The game is played by two teams of nine men each, and at any point in the game the members of one team are "in the field," while the members of the other team take their turns at bat. A game always begins with the home team in the field, thus giving the home team the supposed advantage of batting second. One of the fielders is the pitcher, and he is required to stand at the pitcher's plate and to have one foot in contact with it when he releases the ball. The catcher must stand behind the home base. The other seven fielders are free to play wherever they wish, as long as they are in fair territory, but in practice their positions are pretty well standardized. Four of them, known as infielders, arrange themselves at roughly equal intervals between first and third bases; the first baseman stands at the left of first base, the second baseman at the right of second base, the shortstop at the left of second base, and the third baseman at the right of third base. Thus there are four men to three bases, and actually the shortstop is just as much a second baseman as the one with this name. The outfielders play out beyond the diamond and are known as left, center, and right fielder.

Before the game begins each team must submit its batting order, which lists the players' positions on the field and the order in which they will come to bat. The batting order cannot be changed except by substitution. Although it is an important rule of the game that a man who leaves the game may not return later it is always permissible to withdraw a player and substitute another who has not been in the game, and the position of the players in the field may change at any time. When a substitution is made, the new man must replace the old one in the batting order. Many strategical moves are based on this rule. For example, a pitcher who is a poor batter may be withdrawn from the game when his turn comes to bat, and replaced by a "pinch hitter"[9] who usually is not a pitcher. Then when the side is out and it is the new man's turn to pitch he is withdrawn and replaced by a third man who acts as pitcher.

As a game begins, the nine men of the home team take their positions in the field. After the pitcher has made a few warm-up throws, the first visitor in the batting order takes a bat and assumes his position in the batter's box. The pitcher throws the ball over, or at least near, the home plate and continues to do so until the batter either is out or is safe at first base. When the pitcher throws the ball and the batter makes no attempt to hit it, the umpire must call it either a ball or a strike; if he believes that the ball has passed over any part of the plate, not lower than the batter's knees nor higher than his armpits, he calls it a strike, otherwise a ball. If the batter tries unsuccessfully to hit the ball, the umpire calls it a strike regardless of the nature of the throw. Although the usual rule is that a batter who is hit by a pitched ball is entiled to go to first base, there are exceptions. If he is struck by a ball that he tries to hit, a strike is called, and if he already has two strikes he is out. If he is struck by a pitch that he does not make a reasonable effort to dodge, a ball or strike is called exactly as for any other pitch.

If the batter hits the ball, the first question is, "Is it fair or foul?" Fair territory lies between the two lines that run from home base to first and third bases and continue to the limits of the field. In general, a fair ball is one hit into fair territory, a foul ball one hit into foul territory, but in some cases a problem is created by the fact that the ball travels over both kinds of territory. In such a case: (a) A ball that travels entirely out of the playing field—over a fence or into the stands—before it touches the ground, is fair or foul according to its position when it leaves the field. (b) A ball that is on, above, or beyond first or third base when it first touches the ground, a player, or any object, is fair or foul according to its position when it does such touching. (c) A ball that is touched, or that comes to

---

[9] The term *pinch-hitter* is in general use as a metaphor, and is nearly always used incorrectly. A pinch-hitter is sent into a game because of the belief that he is a better man, in the situation at hand, than the player whom he replaces, not because the regular player is unavailable. For an after-dinner speaker to call himself a pinch-hitter, when he is a last-minute replacement for a celebrity who is unable to appear, is ridiculous; he is a substitute, not a pinch-hitter. Many other metaphors are taken from the field of games, and leaders in this field, at least, should use them correctly.

rest, before it gets to first or third base is fair or foul according to
its position when it is touched or comes to rest. (*d*) A ball that
travels to or beyond first or third base after touching the ground
but not a player, is fair or foul according to its position when it
reaches the base. Thus a ball that strikes the ground in foul territory but then curves inward and bounces over or inside of third
base is a fair ball. If a ball should first strike the ground in fair territory, then roll out and go past first base in foul ground, and finally
roll back into fair territory beyond first base, it would be a foul ball,
since it was in foul territory when it reached first base.

If the batter hits a foul ball and the ball is not caught by a fielder
before it strikes the ground, it counts a strike against him, unless he
already has two strikes. Usually a foul ball by a batter who already
has two strikes counts nothing at all and any number of foul balls
may be hit by him without changing his status. There are, however,
two exceptions to this general statement, one in the case of a bunt,
the other in the case of a foul tip.

A bunt is "a legally batted ball not swung at, but intentionally met
with the bat and tapped slowly within the infield." It must be noted
that when the batter does not hit a fair ball he has not made a bunt,
but only an attempt to bunt. Now when a batter attempts to bunt
and hits a foul ball it always counts as a strike, and if it makes three
strikes he is out.

"A foul tip is a ball batted by the batter that goes sharp and direct from the bat to the catcher's hands and is legally caught." If the
ball is not caught by the catcher it is not a foul tip, but is treated as
an ordinary foul ball. A true foul tip is not treated as a foul ball at
all, but as a ball swung at and missed. This means that a foul tip by
a batter who already has two strikes is counted as the third strike
and puts the batter out. It also means that a foul tip by a batter who
has less than two strikes is counted as an ordinary strike and does
not put the batter out as a caught fly ball ordinarily does.

Usually, but not always, a batter is out when the third strike is
called against him. He is out on the third strike provided the ball is
caught and held by the catcher. He is out whether the ball is caught
or not if there is a runner on first base and less than two men out;
this rule is designed to make it impossible for the team in the field
to profit by intentionally dropping the ball and then making a
double play. But if the catcher fails to catch the ball on the third

strike when there is not a runner on first base with less than two out, then the batter is not out but has become a base runner with the possibility of being safe on first base. It is true of course that his chances of arriving safe at first base are not very good, but they are by no means negligible.

If a batter hits the ball into the air and it is caught by a fielder before it strikes the ground, he is out. It has already been noted that a foul tip is not included under this rule. In this connection the rare but very interesting situation called the *infield fly* should be mentioned. An infield fly can occur only when fewer than two men are out and runners occupy first and second bases; there may or may not be a runner on third base. If, in this situation, a batter hits a fair fly, not including a line drive or attempted bunt, that could be caught by an infielder with ordinary effort, he has hit an infield fly and is immediately out whether the ball is actually caught or not. This rule, like another mentioned in connection with the foul tip, was made to prevent a profit by the fielders from intentional poor play.

The discussion of the methods by which a batter may be put out has thus far been concerned with what might be called unsuccessful play. In addition there are five kinds of *illegal* play by which a batter may cause himself to be called out. (*a*) If the batter delays the game by undue slowness in taking his place at bat, the umpire shall order the pitcher to proceed with his pitching; each pitch shall be called a strike whether it goes through the strike zone or not. The batter may take his position after any number of strikes, but if three strikes are called he is out. (*b*) The batter is out if he hits the ball while either foot is outside the batter's box. (*c*) He is out if he changes from one batter's box to the other while the pitcher is ready to pitch. (*d*) Under certain conditions he is out if he interferes with the catcher. (*e*) Under certain conditions he is out if he does not take his proper turn at bat. The rule on this point is very complicated and takes much more space in the rule book than any other rule. The only comment to be made here is that a batter is never out for batting out of turn, but only for not batting in turn. Thus if it is Smith's turn to bat but Jones bats instead, it is Smith and not Jones who may be called out.

There are four possible outcomes of a player's turn at bat: (*a*) He may be put out without ever becoming a base runner, that is, without a chance even to try to get to first base. (b) He may get the right to try for first base "in jeopardy," but may fail and be put out without arriving safe at first base. (c) He may get the right to try for first base, with liability to being put out, and may arrive safe at first base. (d) He may get the right to go to first base without jeopardy, that is without any possibility of being put out. There is some confusion about a player's status during his transition from batter to base runner[10] but the classification as given here will probably be acceptable. The discussion of the batter has thus far been concerned with (a), that is with the methods by which a batter may be put out without having a right to try for first base. They can be summarized by saying that the batter is out when:

1. He hits a fair or foul fly ball (not including a foul tip) that is legally caught by a fielder.
2. His third strike is caught by the catcher.
3. His third strike is not caught by the catcher but there is a runner on first base and fewer than two men are out.
4. With two strikes against him his attempted bunt results in a foul ball.
5. He is hit by a pitched ball that makes a third strike.
6. He hits an infield fly.
7. He delays the game by not taking his turn at bat.
8. He hits the ball while not properly in the batter's box.
9. He shifts from one batter's box to the other while the pitcher is ready to pitch.
10. Under certain conditions, he interferes with the catcher.
11. Under certain conditions, he does not take his proper turn at bat; that is, he permits another player to take his turn.

The rules list one additional case, which involves an attempted steal by a runner on third base, but so far as it affects the batter, this case is covered by (5) above.

There are just two situations in which a batter tries to run to first base with liability to being put out. The first is when he legally hits a fair ball that is not caught by a fielder and not called an infield fly; an exception is a home run over the fence, or other long hit that

---

[10] A comment made by the rules committee and included with the official rules contains these words, "This code frequently refers to this person as the 'batter' when a better term would be 'batter-runner'."

gives the batter a certain number of bases without jeopardy. The second situation occurs when a third strike is not caught by the catcher provided either that first base is unoccupied or that two men are out. In either situation the batter runs as fast as possible toward first base, as the fielders recover the ball and try to put him out. Usually the man who recovers the ball throws it to a teammate who is waiting at first base to receive it. In any case the batter is out if any fielder holds the ball securely in his hand while touching the base with any part of his body (usually the foot) before the runner arrives at the base. If the runner arrives before the ball does, he is safe. In this case he is permitted to run past the base without being put out, provided he returns immediately and directly to the base. A fielder can also put the runner out by touching him, before he gets to first base, with the ball, or with his glove holding the ball. There are several less common ways in which the runner can be put out, the complete list, including the ones already mentioned, being as follows. The runner is out when:

1. The ball is held by a fielder who is touching first base, before the runner arrives at the base.

2. A fielder touches the runner, before he arrives at first base, with the ball or with a glove that holds the ball.

3. The runner, after hitting the ball with his bat, hits it a second time, either while in the batter's box or while on the way to first base.

4. The runner, while running to first base, deflects the ball in any way.

5. The runner, after running past first base, does not return to the base directly and immediately.

6. He leaves the three-foot lane that is marked at the second half of the base line; there are certain exceptions to this rule.

7. Under certain rare conditions, a fielder intentionally drops a fly ball. (This is not the infield-fly rule.)

8. Under certain conditions, a preceding base runner interferes with a fielder.

There are five situations in which the batter has the right to occupy first base without liability to being put out on the way. He has this right when:

1. Four balls are called by the umpire. This is by far the most frequent of the five situations.

2. The batter is struck by a pitched ball that he tries to dodge and that is not called a strike.

3. The catcher interferes with him.

4. With certain exceptions, he hits a fair ball that touches an umpire or a fielder. If the ball hits a base runner, the runner is out but the batter is safe on first base.

5. He hits a long fair ball of certain kinds. A fair fly ball that goes over a fence or into the stands gives the batter a home run without jeopardy, provided the fence or stand is not less than 250 feet from home plate. Certain other kinds of hits give the batter two bases. In either case the batter must run to the bases in order and touch them.

When a batter has reached first base safely and has thereby established himself as a base runner, he hopes to get to second base, then third, and finally to arrive safe at home and thus score a run. Of course the best way for him to get beyond first base is to hit the ball hard enough or well enough that he can go to second or third, or even all the way home, before the fielders can get the ball into position to put him out. If, as in the great majority of cases, the batter stops at first base or another base without getting all the way to home, then there are several ways in which he can advance to the next base. In the first place, when a batter hits a fair ball and is entitled to try to get to first base, a runner who is on first base must run for second; he is "forced," and any man on the base ahead of him is also forced. For example, if a batter hits a fair ball while there is a runner on each of the three bases, each one must try for the next base and must run the danger of being put out. When a runner is forced he can be put out at the next base in the same way that a batter is put out at first base, except that in this case he does not have the privilege of overrunning the base; if he is touched by the ball while off the base, he is out. In the second place, when a batter or base runner is given a base without liability of being put out, as when a batter is given a base on balls, he forces any runner ahead of him and the latter is also free from liability of being put out. For example, if a batter is given a base on balls while a runner is on first base, the latter is entitled to "walk" to second base. In the third place, if the pitcher makes a *balk*, every base runner (but not the batter) advances one base without liability of being put out. The balk rule is complicated but in general, the pitcher makes a balk whenever he: (*a*) makes an illegal pitch; (*b*) makes a pitch or a throw to a base without making all the motions usually associated with such a pitch or throw; (*c*) makes any motion suggestive of a pitch or of a throw to a base without actually making the pitch or throw.

Finally, a base runner may, except in certain situations, run for the next base at any time, whether the ball is hit by the batter or not. In such a case, where the runner is not forced, a fielder can put him out only by touching him with the ball while he is not on a base, and it is not sufficient for a fielder holding the ball to touch the base ahead of him. A base runner may not advance on a foul ball that is not caught on the fly, but if he leaves his base on such a ball he is entitled to return without being put out. He may not advance on any fly ball, fair or foul, that is caught by a fielder, until after the ball is caught. A runner who is touching his base when a fly ball is caught may then run for the next base; but if he leaves the base before the ball is caught, he must return to the base and he is out if a fielder holding the ball touches the base before he gets back to it.

A rule of great importance provides that a runner cannot score on a play in which the third out is made. For example, with two men out, a runner on third base starts for home just before the batter hits the ball, and the batter is put out at first base. Even though the runner crosses home plate before the batter is out, the run does not count because it would have been scored on the play in which the third out was made.

The first team remains at bat, each man taking his place in the batting order, until three outs have been made. Then the first team takes its place in the field and the other team comes to bat. When this team also has three outs the first inning has been completed. The second inning begins with the first team back at bat, the batter being the next on the list, unless the last batter had not completed his turn at bat when the third out was made. In this case his turn does not count and he becomes the first batter in the new inning.

A normal game consists of nine innings except that either of the two games that constitute a double-header may be scheduled for seven innings. A game is never prolonged beyond eight and one-half innings if the home team is winning at that point. Thus if the team that bats second scores more runs in eight innings than the other one does in nine, the last half of the ninth inning is not played. Likewise, if the winning run is scored during the last half of the ninth inning, the game is stopped immediately. If the score is tied at the end of nine full innings, play is continued for as many additional innings as are needed to break the tie, and it is understood that both teams must have the same number of innings in which to score. Occasionally a game is stopped for some reason, usually rain, before nine innings have been played. In such a case, it does not count as a game at all if fewer than five innings have been played, but does count if five or more have been played. A game of only four and a half innings would count if the team to bat second were ahead.

In Baseball a great many records are kept and computations made that have no influence in determining the outcome of the game but that are of great importance in measuring the effectiveness of players. The most important of these is the "batting average," an understanding of which requires a familiarity with two technical terms, *base hit* and *time at bat*. A batter makes a base hit when he hits a fair ball and is safe on first base, provided: (*a*) the fielding team did not make an error, that is, a poor play without which he would have been out; (*b*) a runner is not forced by the batter and put out on the play. In other words, the batter makes a base hit only when he gets to first base through his own good play and not the poor play of his opponents, and only when his getting to first base is a net advantage to his team not offset by a teammate's being put out as a direct result. A situation that is often misunderstood occurs when a batter hits a fair ball with a teammate on first base and the opponents elect to try to put out the one who is forced to second. If they make such an attempt and fail, the batter does not necessarily get credit for a base hit, but only when the official scorer judges that the batter could not have been put out at first. A time at bat does not refer to every occasion on which a player takes his turn at bat, but only to those occasions on which he either makes a base hit or fails in an attempt to do so. He does not have a time at bat when he goes to first base because of four balls, being hit by a pitched ball, or being interfered with by the catcher. Also, he does not have a time at bat when he makes a "sacrifice hit", that is, when he bunts the ball in order to advance a teammate who is on base, and is put out at first base. The batting average is simply the ratio of the actual number of hits made by a player to the number of times at bat and is, of course, obtained by dividing the former by the latter. The quotient is ordinarily made accurate to three decimal places and the decimal point is disregarded. A batter who is technically "at bat" nine times and gets three base hits has a batting average of .333, which is, and should be, spoken of merely as 333.

2. SOFTBALL

Softball is essentially Baseball reduced to a smaller scale through the use of a smaller diamond, a lighter bat, a larger and softer ball, and restrictions on the pitcher. At least as early as 1900 an adaptation of Baseball was played indoors under the name Indoor Baseball, but the indoor game was never played to any great extent. Some time in the 1920's the game was moved outdoors and from that time on spread very rapidly in popularity, partly as a result of the encouragement of the National Recreation Association. There was no standardization of the game until 1933 and no very effective standardization until well into the 1940's. During this period the game was played under a great variety of rules and under many different names. It has been called Outdoor-indoor Ball, Recreationball, Kittenball, and Diamondball, but until the present name was accepted its most common name was Playground Baseball. In 1933 a national tournament with 20 teams entered was conducted in Chicago in connection with the Century of Progress Exhibition. After this tournament the Amateur Softball Association was formed, and this association has been conducting tournaments and making rules ever since. Its rules are carefully formulated and generally accepted as "official," although they are not universally followed. The following discussion is based on these rules.

Since the rules of Softball are for the most part identical with the baseball rules, the explanation will be concerned only with the rules in which the two games differ.

The diamond is a square with sides 60 feet long, as compared with 90 feet in Baseball. The pitching distance is 46 feet measured from the front of the pitcher's plate to the corner of the diamond at home plate. The bat has a maximum length of 34 inches and diameter of $2\frac{1}{8}$ inches. The ball is 12 inches in circumference and weighs from 6 to 6¾ ounces. It is filled with tightly-packed kapok, and the leather cover is smooth, with no raised seams. A ball with raised seams, called an *outseam ball*, has been used but is not now permitted. The rules permit the use of ordinary baseball shoes with metal spikes, but many local rules require rubber-soled shoes without spikes.

There are only two important playing rules that differ from those of Baseball, the first applying to the pitching, and the second to base-running. From the earliest days it has been required that the pitcher use an underhand throw, the original idea apparently being that he would toss it gently to the batter. But pitchers have learned to obey the rules and still throw the ball with remarkable speed. The present rule is somewhat complicated and difficult to interpret, but it is intended to require an underhand pitch. A great many people believe that in the game as now played by experts the pitcher is far too important.

The predecessors of Softball nearly always had some kind of rule to eliminate or restrict a base runner's lead off the base and stealing. The present rule requires a base runner to remain in contact with his base until the pitcher starts his pitch. A closely related rule requires the pitcher to stand, as he prepares to pitch, facing the batter with both feet squarely on the ground touching the rubber plate and with the ball held in both hands in front of him. The instant he takes either hand off the ball he is considered to have begun his pitch, and a base runner may leave his base.

A standard game of Softball consists of seven innings. There are other differences in the two games, but they are very minor ones and, except as noted, the Softball rules are largely identical in wording with the Baseball rules.

The official rules of most games are made to govern play by experts with little or no regard for average players or dubs. Fortunately, this usually makes no difference, since the average player can do as well under the experts' rules as he could under others. But in the case of some games it does make a difference, and Softball is an example of a game in which rules made for experts (and for spectators) are not well suited to ordinary players. There are several difficulties, but the most important one is that the game tends to be dominated by the pitcher. Professor A. J. Stankowski, Director of Intramural Sports at the University of Missouri, administers each year hundreds of softball games in which there is no permanent pitcher but each man may pitch for only one inning. After a short period of resistance, this innovation was accepted and is now enthusiastically supported by the players. Some of Mr. Stankowski's other rules that favor the weaker players are these:

1. No bunting.
2. No cleated shoes.
3. No windmill windup.
4. A base runner cannot score from third on a wild pitch, a passed ball, or a throw from catcher to pitcher.
5. An illegal pitch, a balk, or a pitch that hits a batter, is called a ball.
6. A batter is always out on a third strike.
7. A base runner may not leave his base until the ball has reached home plate.
8. A team consists of ten men. (The ten-man team was standard for many years, but is not now recognized in the official rules.)

3. SIX-MAN BASEBALL

Six-man Baseball is a recent development and has no standardized or official rules like those of Baseball and Softball. If the game becomes generally adopted, as it probably will, then rules will be gradually evolved that are different from and more complete than the ones given here. In a sense, Six-man Baseball, like Softball, is a variation of Baseball, but the variation is a basic one and it seems useful and logical to adopt the position that these three games are three different ones and that any diamond game to follow can be played as a modification of any one of these three.

This game is really not a diamond game at all, since it is played on a triangle and not a diamond; but since the triangle serves exactly the same purposes as the diamond it seems justified that the game be included here. The game can be played with a hard or soft ball and with the corresponding equipment and the corresponding length of base line. The rules are identical with those of Softball or of Baseball, except for the following:

Instead of a diamond the game uses an equilateral triangle with only three bases: home, first, and second. The length of base lines in the same as in the standard game.

A team consists of six players: a pitcher, a catcher, two infielders, and two outfielders.

A batter is out on two strikes instead of three and walks on three balls instead of four.

A side is retired on four outs instead of three.

Any foul ball counts one-half strike, and there is no distinction between a foul on the second strike and one on the first; thus it is possible for a batter to strike out on a foul ball.

Players in the field rotate in their positions. It has been suggested that they rotate after each out, but it is probably better for them to rotate only once in each inning. In either case the rotation is somewhat different from the one most commonly used in work-up games, being as follows: pitcher to first, to right field, to left field, to second base, to catcher, to pitcher.

A normal game consists of six innings.

Section II: Each player is independent

The games of this section are the work-up baseball games, in which there are no teams, but each man plays for himself, although there is of course a certain amount of cooperation in opposing the batters and base runners.

The games to be described here may be thought of as not games at all, but rather methods by which any of the three baseball games heretofore described may be played. In any case the work-up games will be described as variations of Baseball, Softball, or Six-man Baseball.

The work-up games are all essentially the same and are nothing more than a system by which baseball games can be converted from games for teams to games for individuals. Their obvious virtue is that they require fewer players and hence can be played when not enough men are available to make up two baseball teams.

1. ONE OLD CAT
One O' Cat. Rotation.

This game requires a diamond for the determination of fair and foul balls, but the only bases actually used are home and first. There are no teams, but each man plays for himself, and there is only one batter at any given time, the rest of the players being fielders. Ideally, then, the game requires ten men, one batter and nine fielders, but is usually played with fewer than nine fielders. Also, first base, the only one used except home, must be placed closer to home than the official distance of 90 or 60 feet. Pitching and batting are as in Baseball or Softball, but the base running is entirely different. When the batter hits a fair ball he must run to first base and back to home, and there is no such thing as being safe at first. Accordingly the usual play of the fielders is at home and not at first base. If the batter makes a run he immediately bats again and continues to do so until he is out. When the batter is out, he takes the last place in the field and each fielder moves up one position according to a definite system. The catcher always becomes batter and the pitcher becomes catcher. The other moves are not well standardized, but the most common is for the outfielders to move to the left and the infielders to the right. In this system the right fielder is in last position and the move is from this position to center field, left field, third base, shortstop, second base, first base, pitcher, catcher, batter.

In addition to being played with the variations already described, this game is often played with a few variations of its own. Sometimes the batter is out if a foul ball is caught on the first bounce, or if a pitch that he strikes at and misses is caught on the fly or first bounce. A much more common variation is that when a fielder catches a fly ball he trades places with the batter; or perhaps he becomes batter and the old batter takes the last place in the field. None of these variations seems sound and it is recommended that they not be used.

2. TWO OLD CAT

Rotation. Two O' Cat.

Two Old Cat is the same as One Old Cat except that it uses two batters instead of only one. Accordingly the base is in its normal position and a batter can be safe at first base. When a batter is put out he takes the last place in the field and the fielders all move up as in One Old Cat, and the other batter continues to bat. This game is on the whole much superior to One Old Cat, but it suffers from one basic defect. The two batters are not teammates and have no reason for cooperating, and often one suffers from the poor play of the

other. A batter safe on first base is in a precarious position because
the next batter may make an intentional or unintentional "sacrifice"
which puts the first batter out and leaves the second one in his
place.

3. THREE OLD CAT

Rotation. Roundball. Three O' Cat. Work-Up.

In Three Old Cat, all bases are used and a runner must make the
complete circuit in order to score, but there are only three batters,
and a batter who does not succeed in getting home to take his turn
at bat is out.

4. ROTATION BASEBALL

Rotation. Roundball.

In Rotation Baseball a regular diamond with all four bases is used
and there are four batters. Otherwise it is the same as One Old Cat.

Section III: Game is played with variations from I and II

The games of this section are all informal and have no fixed or
generally accepted rules. Each game can be based on Baseball,
Softball, or Six-man Baseball, except for certain cases where it is obvious that a softball must be used, but for simplicity they will be
described as variations of Softball. In a sense these games are not
games but merely variations to be applied to games, and it should
be understood that the variations can be, and sometimes are, used
in combinations beside those listed. The games are in three groups,
the groups being based on the nature of the variations.

GROUP A: VARIATION IS IN PITCHING, BATTING, OR BALL

1. PUNKIN BASEBALL

Same as Softball, except that a volleyball is used, the ball being
struck with a standard bat.

2. FUNGO BASEBALL

Same as Softball, except that there is no pitching. The batter hits
the ball fungo style. That is, he holds the bat in one hand and the
ball in the other, tosses the ball into the air, and hits it with the bat.

3. SIDE-TOSS BASEBALL

A teammate of the batter stands about six feet to one side of the batter and tosses the ball for the batter to hit. As this game is sometimes described, the ball is tossed by the opposing catcher, but this idea misses the point of the game, which is that the "pitcher" cooperates with the batter rather than opposing him.

4. HAND BASEBALL

Same as Softball, except that a tennis ball or other light ball is used and the batter strikes it with his hand or fist. The game is sometimes played with an old worn softball or with a volleyball. It is often best to prohibit bunting.

5. VOLLEY BASEBALL
Philadelphia Batball

In this game there is no pitching. The "batter" stands at home plate with a volleyball and makes a legal volleyball serve with it. A ball that does not cross a line 15 feet ahead is a foul. Otherwise, the game is the same as Softball.

6. THROWING BASEBALL

The batter stands at home plate with the ball in his hand and throws it. Otherwise, the same as Softball.

7. KICK BASEBALL
Playground Kickball

The pitcher rolls or throws a soccer ball and the batter kicks it. This game is usually played without calling balls or strikes, the batter waiting for a pitch that he likes. If it is played with an umpire who calls balls and strikes, the strike zone must be changed from that in Baseball. A strike should be any pitch that crosses the plate not higher than the batter's knees.

8. PUNT BASEBALL

The batter stands at home plate with a soccer ball and punts it.

9. PLACE-KICK BASEBALL

The batter places a soccer ball on home plate and place-kicks it.

GROUP B: VARIATION IS IN PUT-OUT

The games of this group will be described as variations of Softball and only the differences from the standard game will be mentioned. It should be well understood that these differences can be used equally well in most of the games just described under Group A.

1. TOUCH BASEBALL

Same as Softball except: (*a*) The base runner is always out when the base ahead of him is touched by a fielder with the ball in his hand; (*b*) A runner may leave his base at any time, but once he has left the base he must go to the next, and may not return. This variation is commonly used in Kick Baseball.

2. DODGE BASEBALL

Same as Softball except that: (*a*) In addition to the usual methods a base runner can always be put out by being hit with a thrown ball while he is not on base; (*b*) A fielder is not permitted to run with the ball at any time, nor to hold it; he must throw it immediately, either at a runner or to another fielder. This game of course requires a ball that is soft. It is often played with a softball that has become really soft, and sometimes with one of the other balls, and in connection with one of the variations, described above.

3. CROSS-OUT BASEBALL
Cross-Out

Same as Softball, except that a fielder may put a base runner out by throwing the ball across his path ahead of him; that is, the ball must pass between the runner and the base toward which he is running.

4. HOMEBALL

Any base runner is out if, while he is not on a base, the catcher or another fielder touches home plate with the ball held in his hand. A batter may also be put out by three strikes or a caught fly. When a batter hits a fair ground ball there is no play at first base, only at home.

5. HIT-PIN BASEBALL

An Indian club stands at each base including home. A fielder can put a base runner out only by knocking down the club ahead of him with the ball, which may be thrown or held in the hand. The club at home must stand at one side of the plate. A base runner may leave his base at any time but must then go on to the next base.

6. SKITTLE ROUNDERS

This is a special form of Hit-pin Baseball. A soccer ball is used and it is kicked by the batter. The ball is rolled or thrown under-hand by the pitcher, but it must touch the ground at least once before it gets to the home plate. An Indian club is located at each base, but the one at home is directly behind the plate. The distinctive feature of the game, borrowed from Cricket, is that the batter is out if the pitcher succeeds in knocking down the club behind him. The batter gets only two strikes but runs on the second unless the club is knocked down. A man can be put out by having the home-plate club knocked down by a pitch, by having a fly ball caught, or by having a club knocked down ahead of him, as in Hit-pin Baseball.

7. TOMBALL

This game is played with standard softball equipment. In it there is no such thing as a foul ball, but a batter must run whenever he touches the ball with the bat, no matter where the ball goes. The fielders group themselves somewhat differently than in the usual system.

8. SPEED BASEBALL
Hitball. Speedball.

This game is the same as Softball, except that not more than four batters face a pitcher in any one inning, the half-inning being completed when the fourth man has batted, regardless of the number of outs. If three men are put out before four have batted, the half-inning is completed as in the standard game. This variation can be used in connection with many of the games already described.

Variation. Some other specified number of batters is used instead of four.

GROUP C: VARIATION IS IN BASE RUNNING

(a) Batter must try for a home run

1. TWENTY-ONE BASEBALL
Baseball Twenty-one. Twenty-one.

This game is the same as Softball except for this distinctive feature: Whenever a batter hits a fair ball he must run the bases until he scores a home run or is put out, and he scores one point for each base reached. Thus, if a man hits the ball and arrives safe at first base, he continues toward second and even if he is out at second he still scores one point; a home run counts four points.

Variation. A game is not for any set number of innings, but continues until one team has scored 21 points. If this team is the one second at bat the game ends as the last point is scored, but if it is the team first at bat, it finishes its turn at bat, scoring as many additional points as possible, and then the other team takes its turn at bat.

2. BEATBALL
Baseball Overtake. Base-to-base Ball.
Bowl Beatball. Hand Beatball.

This game is the same as Softball with this important exception: When a batter hits a fair ball that is not caught on the fly he must run to first base and then to the others in order, making a home run or nothing. The fielders must recover the ball, throw it to first base and then to the other bases in order. At each base the ball must be held by a fielder who is touching the base, and no fielder may at any time run with the ball. The runner is not out until the ball gets home ahead of him; he might, for example, be apparently out at second base and then get home safe because of a poor throw or catch between second and home.

Variation 1. When the fielders seem too good for the batters, it may be ruled that any ball recovered in the infield, or, in extreme cases, any ball at all, must be played to home plate and then to first.

Variation 2. The game may be played like Hand Baseball, the batter hitting the ball, preferably a tennis ball, with his hand. This variation is Hand Beatball.

Variation 3. A soccer ball may be rolled by the pitcher and kicked by the batter. This variation is Bowl Beatball.

3. KICK BEATBALL

Kickball.

This game is a combination of Beatball and Twenty-one Baseball. It is described here as a kicking game but could just as well be played as a batting game. The pitcher rolls a soccer ball and the batter kicks it. The batter is out if he kicks at the ball and misses it entirely or if he kicks two foul balls. He is also out if he hits a fly ball that is caught. On a fair kick not caught, he runs to first base and to the others in order, while the fielders throw the ball to first base and to the others in order. When a fielder touches the base ahead of the runner with the ball in his hand, the runner is out, but he scores one point for each base reached, as in Twenty-one. Thus, the game is a kicking form of Beatball except that a runner scores for bases reached even though he does not make a run, and that he can be put out at any base.

4. HIT-PIN BEATBALL

Hit-pin Baseball

An Indian club or similar object stands at each base, the one at home being directly behind the base. In this game, as in all others that use an Indian club, it is better if the club be given more stability by a block attached to its base. The game is played with a soccer ball that is rolled by the pitcher and kicked by the batter. The batter is out if a pitched ball knocks down the club at home; balls and strikes are not counted. On a fair kick that is not caught on the fly the batter runs to first base and then to the others in order, scoring a run or nothing. The fielders recover the ball and may pass it from one to another at will, but must not run with it. The fielders must knock down the clubs in order and may do this with a throw of any length or with the ball held in the hand. They must knock down all four clubs in order, and if they knock down the club at home before the batter gets there, he is out; otherwise he scores a run. It should be noted that the runner can be put out only at home, as in Beatball.

(b) Batter need not try for a home run

1. DOUBLE-UP BASEBALL

The feature of this game is that a base runner is never forced off his base, but any number of men may occupy one base at the same

time. Fielders can put a runner out in any of the standard ways or
by hitting him with a thrown ball. This variation is sometimes used
in Kick Baseball.

2. TUMBLE BASEBALL
Tumbleball.

In this game a base runner, including one who is on his way to
first base, must do a forward roll, or other designated tumbling
stunt, on his way to each base. This variation may be used effec-
tively in Kick Baseball.

3. PEGGING FIRST

This game works well as a variation of Baseball or Softball. It is
identical with the standard game, except that no base running is
done beyond first base and that the whole team bats in each inning.
When a batter is out or arrives safe at first he withdraws and the
next batter takes his turn. Regardless of the number of outs, a team
remains at bat until each man has had his turn at bat, and scores
one point for each man who reaches first. Then the other team does
the same thing and scores are compared. Any specified number of
innings can be played.

Section IV: Game is played in the water or on the ice
1. WATER BASEBALL

This game is played by men standing in shallow water. The area
around home must have only slight depth but the rest of the "field"
can be deeper and the farthest part of the outfield may be deep
enough to necessitate swimming. Each base is a floating block of
wood or other material, about one foot square, anchored to the bottom. The ball must be waterproof and usually is made of rubber,
six inches or more in diameter. It can be played with a bat, or the
batter can hit the ball with his hand. The game is in any case very
informal, and various adjustments will have to be made to suit local
conditions.

2. RAFT BASEBALL (Aquatic)
Water Baseball

This form of aquatic Baseball requires four sturdy rafts, which
are not likely to be available except where water activity is highly
developed, as at a modern summer camp. The raft at home plate

must be large enough to accommodate a batter, a catcher, an umpire, if any, and a backstop; about 8 by 16 feet. The raft at each of the other three bases should be about eight feet square, and all four rafts must be securely anchored to the bottom. The ball must be waterproof and rather sluggish; a six-inch rubber sport ball is probably best. Pitching and batting are the same as in Softball, and after the batter hits the ball he dives from his raft and swims to the one at first base. A base runner may stand on the raft or not as he chooses, and the same is true for all fielders.

3. SWIMMING-POOL BASEBALL
Water Baseball in Pools

In this game the four bases are on the floor of a swimming pool just outside the water, and the base-runner swims from one to another. Fielders take any positions they choose in the water or on the floor outside. Home plate is at the deep end of the pool, second base at the shallow end, and the other two at the sides. To eliminate danger, each base must be covered with effective non-skid material. The ball must be a very slow one and it is recommended that no bat be used but that the ball be struck with the open hand.

4. SKATING BASEBALL
Baseball on Skates

A diamond is marked out on the ice and the game is played according to the rules of Softball, except that all players wear skates.

Division Two: Baseball Games with No Base Running

The games in this small division possibly should not be considered Baseball games at all. But although they lack the base running which is one of the important parts of baseball, they all have some of the other elements and are obviously derived from Baseball.

1. FUNGO

One player is batter, a second one is catcher, and the rest are fielders. There is no pitching, and the catcher's only duty is to receive the ball as it is thrown back from the field and to toss it to the batter. The batter holds the ball in his hand, tosses it into the

air, and bats it; this is known as fungo hitting. When any fielder
catches a fly ball or stops three grounders without muffing, he becomes catcher, the catcher becomes batter, and the batter replaces
the fielder. Commonly the game is played without base lines and
there are no fair and foul balls, but it might be better to have the
lines and to penalize the batter for hitting foul balls. Sometimes the
game is played without the catcher.

2. KNOCK-OUT

Knock-out is a team form of Fungo. Players are divided into two
equal teams, and one team takes the field while the other bats. The
members of the batting team each bat one ball; when all have batted, the teams trade places and the other team bats. Teams score
one point for each grounder cleanly stopped and three points for
each fly ball caught.

3. INDIANBALL

This game is similar to Fungo but uses a pitcher. The pitcher,
however, is a teammate of the batter and throws the ball so as to
help the latter. Players are divided into two teams, one at bat and
the other in the field. Base lines are needed, and, for small teams,
the angle between them should be narrower than normal. A batter
is out if: (*a*) he hits a foul ball that passes first or third base; (*b*)
he hits a fly ball that is caught; (*c*) he hits a ground ball that is
handled cleanly. Any other ball is a base hit, but base running is
entirely imaginary. A runner can advance only when he is forced
by succeeding hits by his teammates. When a man has made a run
in this way, he scores one point for his team. When three are out
the opponents come to bat.

Variation 1. The batter is out on the second foul ball, not the
first.

Variation 2. A hit that goes beyond a designated line and is not
caught or handled cleanly counts as a home run.

4. HIT-OR-OUT

This game is similar to Indianball, and, like that game, involves
imaginary base running. It requires a section of wall against which
the ball can be batted. Players are in two teams and alternate in

fielding and batting, as in Baseball. The ball is pitched as in the standard game, and usually is a softball pitched according to softball rules. Foul lines should be marked, and if the teams are small the lines should be closer together than the standard 90 degrees. The batter is out if: (*a*) he hits the ball over the top of the wall; (*b*) he hits a fly ball that is caught either before or after hitting the wall; (*c*) he hits a fair ground ball that is fielded perfectly. A ball that is not caught or fielded perfectly counts as a base hit, and can be only a single or a two-base hit. If it strikes the wall before it strikes the ground it is a double, otherwise a single. All base running is imaginary. A base runner can advance only by being forced by later hits made by his teammates. Innings are played as in Baseball.

5. CORKBALL

Corkball was developed in St. Louis. It is played intensively in that city and to some extent in other localities. The game was played originally with an actual cork cut to a spherical shape, and a broom handle. The ball now used is 1¾ inches in diameter; it is made of a piece of cork wound with cord and covered with leather; its weight is one ounce. The bat may not be more than 38 inches long nor more than 1½ inches in diameter. Home plate is 13 inches square and is the only base used. The only line on the field is a straight one of indefinite length with its nearest point 6 feet in front of home plate.

The game is played by two teams of five men each, a pitcher, a catcher, and three fielders. The pitcher throws the ball as in Baseball, from a distance of 55 feet, and the batter tries to hit it. Bunting is prohibited. The batter is out if he bunts or tries to bunt the ball, if he hits a fly ball that is caught, if he strikes at the ball and misses and the ball is caught by the catcher, or if he hits a foul ball. A foul ball is one that does not cross the line located 6 feet in front of home plate. Balls and strikes are not called, and the batter tries to hit the ball only when he cares to do so.

If the batter hits a fair ball and is not out he has made a hit. Base running is imaginary as in Indianball. Since all hits are singles, and since a base runner advances only when forced, it follows that a run can be scored only by four hits in one inning. Thus four hits score one run and each hit above four counts an additional run.

6. BUCKETBALL
Bucket Cricket

An old, ten-quart bucket stands inverted in the center of a circle with a diameter of from 30 to 50 feet, depending on the ability of the players. One man, holding a baseball bat, stands on top of the bucket, the other players outside the circle. The circle players throw at will, passing the ball among themselves if they wish, but all throws at the man on the bucket must be from outside the circle. The man on the bucket uses the bat to prevent the bucket's being hit by the ball. He is out if the ball hits the bucket on the fly, if he hits a fly ball that is caught, or if he falls off the bucket. This game can be played on a team or an individual basis. In the team form, batters follow a regular order and a run is counted each time the ball is hit by the bat and not caught on the fly. In the individual form there is no point to keeping score; when a batter is out he is replaced by the man who hit the bucket or caught the fly; if the batter is out for falling off the bucket, he is replaced by the one who made the last throw.

7. TIP-CAT
Bob

The cat is a four-inch section of broom handle, whittled to a gradual taper from the center to a point at each end. The bat is another section of broom handle, four feet long. The goal is a tree or post, or lacking this, a four-foot circle on the ground. No bases are used. The game could be played with baseball foul lines but is usually played with no foul lines at all. A real or imaginary straight line is drawn through the goal, and it is required only that the cat be hit forward across this line. The batter places the cat on the ground and then hits one end of it a downward blow with the bat, thus causing it to fly into the air, turning end over end. While it is in the air he hits it with the bat so as to drive it forward. The fielders, who may stand wherever they choose, try to catch the cat on the fly, and if one of them does so the batter is out. If the cat is not caught on the fly the one who recovers it still has a chance to put the batter out. To do this he stands where he recovered the cat and throws it at the goal. When the goal is a tree or post, the batter is out if the cat hits the goal or comes to rest within one bat's length of it. When the goal is a circle on the ground the batter is out if the cat comes to rest inside the circle.

The game can be played on a team basis with innings as in Baseball, a run being scored each time the batter hits the cat and is not put out, or it can be played as a nonteam game. In the latter case, it is common practice for the batter to be replaced by the fielder who puts him out, but it is recommended that the regular work-up system, as in One Old Cat, be used instead.

Division Three: Long-Base Games

A long-base game is played on a rectangular field and uses only two bases—home base at one end of the rectangle, and long base at the other. The batter runs from home base to long base and back to home. In about half the games of this division, he is required to make the round trip at once, as in One Old Cat, but in the other half he may be safe at long base and come home later. In Cricket, which is one of the games in this group, batting is done at both bases so that neither one is really home base or long base.

Section I: Batter must make a home run

1. BATBALL

German Batball

A rectangular court about 40 by 60 feet, is marked off with an improvised home plate in the middle of one end line and a turning post or marker in the middle of the other. A scratch line may be marked parallel with the home-plate line and ten feet in front of it, but in informal games this line is usually imaginary. A pitcher's plate is marked at standard softball distance or at whatever other distance seems appropriate. The game is played with a softball bat, and the ball must be soft, since it is to be thrown at runners. A very well-worn softball may be used, but any other ball that is soft enough may be used instead. The pitcher throws the ball with an underhand motion and the batter tries to hit it. A batted ball that first strikes the ground outside a side line or short of the scratch line is foul; any other is fair. When the batter hits a fair ball not caught on the fly he must run to the opposite end line, go around the turning post in either direction, and run back to touch the home plate. While he is doing this, the fielders recover the ball and try to hit the runner by throwing the ball at him. Fielders may throw the ball from one to another at will but must not run with the ball. Innings are played as in Baseball.

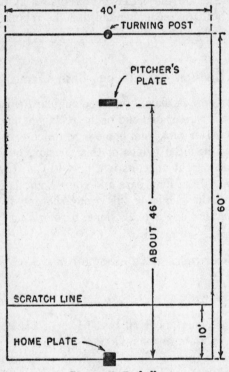

Figure 43. Batball.

Variation. If the fielders seem to have too much advantage, the runner should not be required to touch home plate but should be permitted to cross the home-plate line at any point.

2. HAND BATBALL
Batball

The pitcher throws a volleyball with an underhand motion and the batter strikes at it with his hand or fist. Otherwise this game is the same as Batball.

Variation. The pitcher must throw the ball so that it strikes the ground in front of home plate and bounces over the plate.

3. FLASHBALL

Flashball is identical with Hand Batball except for the pitching. In this case, the pitcher is a teammate of the batter and tosses the ball to him from a short distance to one side, as in Side-toss Baseball (page 317).

4. VOLLEY BATBALL

Batball. Dodge Batball. German Batball. Liberty Batball. Schlagball.

This game is the same as Batball, except that it includes no pitching. The batter takes a volleyball and makes a legal volleyball serve with it.

KICK BATBALL

Kickball. Kick Dodgeball. Long Base. Schlagball. Soccer Baseball.

This game is the same as Batball, except that there is no pitching. Instead, the batter place-kicks a soccer ball from home plate.

6. SOCCER BATBALL

In this game, the fielders do not play the ball with the hands but are required to kick it or otherwise play it, as in Soccer. Except for this, it is the same as Kick Batball.

7. PIN BATBALL

Bowl Clubball. Indian-club Baseball.

An Indian club stands in the middle of the distant line in the place of the turning post. The batter must run to the club, pick it up, and return with it. Otherwise the game is identical with Batball or with any of the variations described above.

Section II: Batter may stop at long base

Group A: Base Running Follows Baseball Rules

In these games the base runners always start at the same home plate, and a runner is forced from his base as in Baseball. The games listed here are contrasted with those in which runners are not forced from base, and with those in which the cricket system of base-running is used.

1. LONG BASE

The pitcher makes an underhand throw with a tennis ball or volleyball and the batter hits it with his hand or fist. He may make a home run or wait at the base for the next hit but is forced off base by a hit. The batter is out if a fly ball is caught or if he is hit by a thrown ball.

2. VOLLEY LONG-BASE
Dodge Batball

There is no pitching, but the batter makes a serve with a volleyball. Otherwise the same as Long Base.

Variation. A home run counts two and another run one. This variation can of course be used in any of the similar games.

GROUP B: BASE RUNNER CANNOT BE FORCED OFF BASE

1. LONGBALL
Long Base

Longball is the most popular game of the Long-base division, except, of course, Cricket. It is played with numerous variations in detail and should be adjusted to local conditions, but the basic rules are as follows.

A home plate is installed and long base, a rectangle about five by eight feet, is laid out 60 feet from it. A pitcher's plate is marked between home and long base, either at the standard softball distance of 46 feet or at any other distance that seems suitable. The game is played with standard softball bats and balls. Pitching is the same as in Softball, but the batter must run on any ball that touches his bat, no matter how slightly or in what direction it goes. He must run to long base and may stop there if he arrives safe. He may be put out only by having a fly ball caught or by being hit with a thrown ball. A man on base is not forced off by a subsequent hit but may remain there as long as he wishes, with the single and very unlikely exception that if he does not get home in time for his next turn at bat, he is out. One result of this rule is that several men may be on the base at one time and that at a favorable opportunity they all may rush for home at once. It is always understood that a base runner need not run in a straight line but may deviate from it as much as he wishes, although the game sometimes develops to the point that it is well to establish boundaries, either marked or imaginary, beyond which a runner may not go.

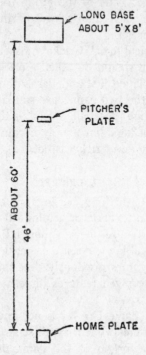

Figure 44. Longball.

2. LINGBALL

Lingball is Longball with these two variations: (*a*) The pitcher is a teammate of the batter and tosses the ball to the batter from a few feet to one side, as in Side-toss Baseball; (*b*) When a batter hits the ball he is not required to run to long base, but may wait at home for a better opportunity just as he may wait at long base.

3. SPRINTBALL

Sprintball is Longball with this variation: A volleyball is used. It is thrown underhand by the pitcher and batted with the hand or fist.

GROUP C: TWO BASE RUNNERS TRADE PLACES

This small group includes Cricket and four informal games derived from it. In the "cricket-type base running" that constitutes the distinguishing characteristic of the group there are two bases and always one runner on each, the two always running at the same time so as to exchange bases.

It is in a way illogical to call Cricket a baseball game and it might be said that Baseball should be called a cricket game instead. Certainly Cricket was played first and Baseball is in part derived from it. But in any case, the two games are similar and their basic principle is much the same. Baseball is used as the basis of comparison not for any reason of logic but merely because in the United States it is very well known and Cricket is not.

1. CRICKET

Cricket is a game of pitching, batting, and base running. It is very much like Baseball in its basic principles but differs from this game in a number of important respects. Although Baseball is derived from Cricket to a considerable degree, the exact degree is uncertain, and some of the minor games previously described herein as baseball-type games have borrowed features directly from Cricket and not from Baseball.

The origin of the name *Cricket* is not known. Various explanations have been advanced but they all seem to be guesses with no real foundation. The origin of the game itself is also unknown, partly because of a lack of historical facts and partly because of the impossibility of knowing just which stage in the development should be taken as the beginning. It is safe to say that the game in substantially its present form was played early in the seventeenth century. It is now the most popular game in Great Britain; it is played very much in Australia and to a lesser extent in some other countries. In the early history of the United States the game was played extensively but was displaced by Baseball so that now Cricket, although by no means unknown here, is rare.

There is no diamond in Cricket, and only two bases, called *wickets*. Neither wicket corresponds to home plate in Baseball; more accurately, the two alternate in serving as home plate. A wicket consists of three upright and parallel sticks projecting 27 inches above the ground, and two little sticks laid end to end across the tops of the uprights. The three uprights are called stumps; their total width is eight inches. The little cross pieces are called bails, and are intended to fall off the stumps when the wicket is hit by the ball. The two wickets are parallel with each other, 66 feet apart. A line eight feet,

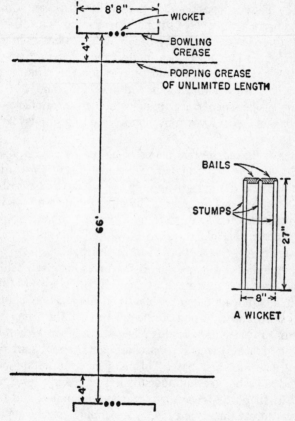

Figure 45. Cricket. Layout of field.

eight inches long is drawn on the ground through each wicket, as a continuation of the line of the three stumps. This is the *bowling crease* behind which the bowler, or pitcher, must remain as he delivers the ball. Parallel with this line and four feet in front of it, that is, four feet nearer the other wicket, is another line called the *popping crease,* behind which the batter must stand. There are no other marks on the field. There is no exact size for a cricket field, but it should be about 450 by 500 feet, with the wickets in the center.

The ball is similar to a baseball but is slightly smaller, nine to nine and one-quarter inches in circumference, and is covered with dark-colored leather, considerably thicker than that on a baseball. It is made of two hemispheres stitched together so that the stitching is a single circle instead of the figure-eight on the baseball. The bat is about 36 inches long and has a more definite handle than a baseball bat, the handle being wound with cane. The striking part of the bat is flat, with a maximum width of four and one-quarter inches. The wicket-keeper, a sort of combination catcher and first baseman, wears two gloves, but none of the other players wears them.

The game is played by two teams of eleven men each, one team in the field and the other at bat. The bowler runs forward as he throws the ball to the batter; he may run as far as he wishes but must not cross the bowling crease. The other ten men on the fielding team are not restricted as to their positions. Of course they do not scatter at random, but take certain arbitrary positions, that constitute a definite system but vary more than in Baseball.

At the beginning of a game the bowler takes his place behind the bowling crease, his teammates distribute themselves over the field, and the first batter, or batsman, stands in his position behind the popping crease and in front of the wicket. At the same time, a teammate of the batsman takes his place at the other wicket, behind the popping crease. It is as if a baseball game should start off with a runner already on first base. This is a very important point in Cricket and must be clearly understood. There is always a man on base; that is, there are always a batter and a runner, and the two must always run at the same time. Base running consists entirely of an exchange of places by the two.

The bowler takes his run and throws the ball with a motion that is strange to those accustomed to Baseball; the arm is swung overhead with straight elbow, and the ball usually strikes the ground in front of the wicket. It is legal for the bowler to send the ball over without a bounce, but since the bouncing ball is more difficult for the batsman to hit it is nearly always used. The bowling is extremely important and is developed with great variety and extreme skill. There are different styles of bowling and of bowlers: slow bowlers, spin bowlers, swingers, and so on. There are no balls and strikes; a batter never gets a base on balls and he may wait for a ball that he likes; that is, he could wait were it not for the important fact that he is out if the ball hits the wicket. Accordingly the first objective of the bowler is to throw the ball past the batter so that it will hit the wicket, and the first responsibility of the batter is to ward off with his bat any ball that would otherwise hit the wicket. In this connection a most important rule comes into play: a batter is never required to run when he hits the ball, but he runs only when he feels that his hit is good enough to take him safely to the other wicket. It naturally follows that the batter will sometimes hit the ball merely to deflect it and protect the wicket, and sometimes hit it hard with the intention or hope of being able to run. If the batter hits a fly ball that is caught he is out exactly as in Baseball; this applies of course to a hit made to deflect the ball from the wicket. If he hits any other ball and chooses to run, he may then be put out with a play similar to the one in Baseball, except that the fielders must knock down the wicket to which the batter is running. It is understood of course that when the batter runs, his teammate also runs and that a fielder can put either of them out by hitting the wicket ahead of him with the ball; he may throw the ball or hold it in his hand. There is no such thing as a foul ball, the batsman and his teammate being permitted but never required to run at any time the ball is touched by the bat, regardless of the direction in which the ball goes. Occasionally a batsman will inadvertently knock the wicket down himself by touching it with his bat or his foot, and in such case he is out.

Every time that the batsman succeeds in exchanging wickets with his partner he scores one run. It is possible for him to score more than one run on a single hit, for once the ball is hit the two men may run back and forth as often as they dare to, and the batsman scores a run for each exchange. Certain long hits count extra runs automatically, just as they would count extra bases in Baseball; a ball driven clear over the fence or "out of the park," such as would be an automatic home run in Baseball, automatically scores six runs.

There are always two bowlers in a game, and each one bowls at only one of the two wickets. When the first bowler has bowled six

times, the other bowler bowls six times at the other wicket and the
two bowlers continue to bowl alternately. A legal bowl counts as
one of the six, regardless of what happens to it. When a batsman
is put out, he is replaced by another, but his partner continues in
the game until he also is put out. Thus it is possible for a man to
score indefinitely, and it is not particularly uncommon for a good
batsman to score 100 runs before being put out.

When a team is at bat it remains at bat until ten of the eleven
members have been put out. The reason for ten instead of eleven
is that it is impossible according to the rules for a team to bat
except with two runners, so that when only one is left the side is
retired. After a side is retired it takes the field and the other team
bats; when this team is also out an inning is finished, and a game
consists of two such innings.

2. WICKET

Wicket is an informal game that bears the same relation to
Cricket that Rotation does to Baseball. There are no teams and
each man plays for himself. Two men are batters and the rest are
fielders. The fielders must have their positions numbered, the bowler
usually being number one. When a batsman has been put out he
takes the last-numbered fielding position, the bowler becomes a
batsman, and all fielders move up one position. Thus the game
becomes very much like Two Old Cat.

3. INDOOR CRICKET

This is an improvised form of Cricket designed for play in a
gymnasium, but it can be played outdoors as well. Two Indian clubs
close together constitute a wicket. The game is played with a basketball that is bowled according to cricket rules, but the ball is hit
with the bare hand and no bat is used.

4. CAN CRICKET

Can Cricket is the same as Indoor Cricket except that tin cans
are used for wickets. The cans should be relatively large; the tall
ones in which fruit juices are commonly packed are good, and
gallon fruit cans are even better. This game, as well as Indoor
Cricket, can be played like Wicket, that is, the work-up form of
Cricket.

5. CATBALL

In Catball there is a home base, a pitcher's plate at standard distance from this base, and a long base about 65 feet from home. There is only one pitcher, and he pitches always in the same direction. The game starts with a runner on long base, and base running is the same as in Cricket, always consisting of an exchange of bases by the two runners. There are no wickets, and fielders can put a runner out as in Softball or by hitting him with a thrown ball. The game may be played by teams, in which case three outs retire a side, but it is usually played as work-up.

BOMBARDMENT GAMES

IN A BOMBARDMENT GAME A TEAM OR OTHER GROUP OF PLAYERS (IN rare cases, a single player) throws, kicks, or otherwise propels one or more balls toward an objective, while the other players try to block the balls and prevent them from reaching the objective. In some games, players or teams take turns in being attackers and defenders; in other games there is no distinction, each being attacker and defender at the same time. Many of the "Bombardment Games" appear to be very similar to the "Goal Games" of Class XI, but there is a basic difference. In a goal game the two sides are intermingled, each one trying to advance the ball more or less gradually through the opponents until the goal is reached. In a bombardment game, on the contrary, the two sides are never intermingled, but each keeps its distance and, from a fixed, or at least restricted, position, throws or kicks the ball in an attempt to drive it through or past the opponents. Thus a bombardment game has a target element about it, one side trying to hit a target (or goal) with the ball, the other to block or intercept the ball on its way to the target. Sometimes the objective of the attackers is actually to hit a definite target, for example an Indian club, but at other times their objective is merely to get the ball past the defenders. About half the games are played in a rectangular court, the attackers and defenders being restricted to different parts of the court; the other half use no court at all, but players are arranged in one or more circles.

Division One: Court Bombardment Games

Section I: Attackers hit Indian club or other object

1. BOMBARDMENT

A rectangular court about 50 feet long is divided into halves by a line across the middle. It is much better if the game can be played in a closed court with a wall at each end, so that the balls can rebound from the walls; in this case, the end lines should be three to five feet from the walls. On each end line is a row of Indian clubs. It is likely to be satisfactory to have one club for each player, but the number and arrangement of the clubs should be determined by experiment, since they should vary with local conditions. Players are divided into two equal teams, and each team is restricted to one half of the court. The game is played with several balls, which may

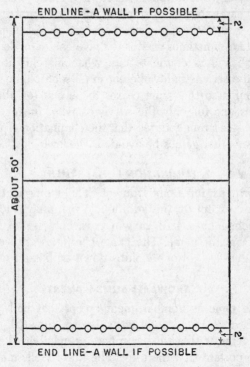

Figure 46. Bombardment.

be softballs, basketballs, or any other balls that are not hard enough to be dangerous. At least six balls should be used, and it is better to use more; it is difficult to have too many. Half of the balls are given to each team. At a signal from the leader, players begin to throw the balls, trying to knock down the clubs that the opponents guard. Any player who can get a ball may throw it at the clubs, or he may pass it to a teammate, the only restriction being that each man must remain in his own half of the court. A defender may block a ball by catching it or by stopping it with any part of his body. When a club is down it stays down, but may be slid to one side to get it out of the way. At the end of the predetermined time, the team with the larger number of clubs standing is the winner.

It is sometimes ruled that the game shall continue until one team or the other has its clubs all knocked down, but this system is very unsatisfactory and should not be used; it is readily seen that as the number of clubs becomes smaller and the number of players remains the same, the attackers have an almost impossible job. Another system sometimes used is to make one defender responsible for each club and to eliminate him when his club is down. This system has the serious fault inherent in all such eliminations: when men are eliminated the game ceases to be one for all the players and becomes one for only the survivors who, in general, are the best players. It is strongly urged that the elimination of players from this and many other games be avoided whenever possible.

2. ELIMINATION BOMBARDMENT

Teams form as for Bombardment. The game is the same as Bombardment except for this addition: A man may catch a ball but if he is touched by a ball anywhere except on the hands he is eliminated from the game. The game continues until one team or the other either has all of its clubs down or has all of its players eliminated.

3. SNOWBALL BOMBARDMENT

This is the same as Bombardment except that balls and targets are made of snow. Each target is made of a snowball, one foot or more in diameter, with a smaller sphere or cylinder of snow on top of it. It is important that the targets be fairly well standardized so that the game will be equal.

Section II: Attackers drive ball over a line

1. LINE GUARD

Each of two teams is restricted to one half of a rectangular court, as in Bombardment. Balls are thrown back and forth but there are no pins or other targets. Each side tries to cause the balls to cross the opponents' end line not more than seven feet above the floor, and scores one point whenever it does so. It is not very satisfactory to estimate the seven feet. It is possible to stretch a rope above the line seven feet high, but the best plan is to play the game in a court with walls at the ends and to mark the seven-foot lines on the walls.

2. BOUNCING LINE-GUARD

Two teams throw balls back and forth as in Line Guard, each trying to score a point by causing a ball to go over the opponents' end line. In this game, however, fly balls do not count, since it is required that the ball bounce or roll over the line. There is no height limit.

3. GROUNDERS BURN OUT

This game is similar to Line Guard, but is derived from Baseball. Only one ball is used, a baseball or softball. The thrower must throw the ball from his half of the court so that it strikes the ground on his side of the center line, the idea being to simulate a grounder, as in Baseball. If the ball goes through an opponent and crosses the end line, the throwing side scores a point; only one defender may touch the ball. The game may be played with more than one ball, but if many balls are used, the baseball element is lost.

4. KICK BOMBARDMENT
Club Kickball

The formation is the same as for Bombardment except that the clubs, instead of being on the end lines, are arranged within the court. Any arrangement will do, but it must be the same in each half court. Two teams, each confined to its own half-court, kick soccer balls back and forth in an attempt to knock down the clubs in the opponents' end of the court. Scoring is the same as in Bombardment. This game, and other forms of Bombardment also, may be played with the rule that a club knocked down must be replaced immediately. In this case, a point is scored for each club knocked down and the winner is the first to score a predetermined number of points.

5. KICK-OVER BALL
Kickit. Kickover.

Each man sits on the floor with his legs outstretched and his arms extended backward for support. Each of two teams forms a line with

its members in this position side by side, and the two lines form
with the feet of one team about 12 inches from the feet of the
other. A basketball, preferably a fairly soft one, is rolled by a leader
between the two rows of feet and each team tries to kick the ball
so that it will go over the heads of the opponents and strike the
floor behind them. The ball must not be touched with the hands.
One point is scored each time the ball goes over. A cageball may be
used in place of the basketball.

6. LINE BAT
Lineball

Each of two teams is in one half of a rectangular court. One team
scatters at will in its half, the other team forms behind its base line.
One man of the latter team takes a baseball or softball, and a bat,
and hits a ground ball from behind the base line to the opponents in
an attempt to drive it through them. Only one man on the defending
team may touch the ball; if the ball goes to the defenders' base
line or is touched by two defensive men the batter scores a point,
otherwise nobody scores. The batted ball must strike the ground
before it crosses the center line. As soon as the first man has batted,
one man on the other team bats and the two teams alternate, each
man taking his turn, until all have batted. The team with the larger
score after all have batted is the winner.

7. SHYBALL

This game requires four parallel lines, two throwing lines about 80
feet apart, and, inside these, two goal lines about 30 feet apart. Each
of two teams stands and must remain behind one of the throwing
lines, creating the strange situation of a team defending a goal line
which is 25 feet to the front. A cageball—a 36-inch one if available,
otherwise the largest to be had—is placed on the floor in the center
of the field and numerous softballs or other small balls are divided
between the two teams. At a signal, the men start to throw the
small balls at the big one, and each man is free to throw whenever
he can get a ball, except that he must throw only from behind his
throwing line. The object is, of course, to drive the big ball across
the opponents' goal line.

Division Two: Circle Bombardment Games

Section I: One man is inside a circle formed by the others

In games of this section, all players except one form a circle and the odd man is within the circle. In some games the center man is the attacker and in others the defender.

GROUP A: CENTER MAN ATTACKS

1. CIRCLE STRIDEBALL

Center Strideball. Straddleball. Throw Centerball.

All men except one form a circle facing the center, each with his feet spread, touching those of his neighbors. The odd man is inside the circle with a ball, usually a basketball or medicine ball. The center man is free to move about within the circle and he throws the ball, trying to cause it to pass between the legs of the circle players. The latter must not move their feet. They block the ball with their hands or other parts of the body, but must not catch it. When the ball goes outside the circle, the center man decides who permitted it to do so and trades places with him. If the ball goes out between two men and the center player is unable to decide which one was at fault he names the man at whose right the ball passed. Scores can be kept but the game does not need a scoring system and is usually played without one.

2. CIRCLE STRIDEBALL (Partner Form)

Partner Circle-Strideball

All players except two form a circle, as in Circle Strideball. Of the odd two, one is within the circle and the other outside. The man in the circle has a ball that he tries to throw between the legs of the circle men. When the ball goes outside the circle, the thrower trades places with the one at fault, but the odd man on the outside immediately becomes thrower, and proceeds to throw the ball in an attempt to get it through the circle from the outside. His best chance to do this is immediately after the ball has come through the circle and before the circle men can turn around.

3. CIRCLE STRIDEBALL (Team Form)
Team Circle-Strideball

Players are in two equal teams, and each team, except one man, forms a separate circle. The odd man of each team stands inside the circle of the opponents. Each circle plays a regular game of Circle Strideball until the ball goes through the circle. The first center man to cause the ball to go out of the circle scores a point for his team and play is suspended. Both center men return to their circles and are replaced by others from the circles. The game continues until every man has acted as center man, and scores are compared to determine the winner.

4. PIN STRIDEBALL

This game is the same as Circle Strideball, except that each circle man has an Indian club standing between his feet and that the object of the center man is to knock down the club with the ball.

5. KICK STRIDEBALL

Circle Bootball. Kick Centerball. Kick Circle-Strideball.
Soccer Circle-Strideball.

Same as Circle Strideball, except that the center man may play the ball only by kicking it.

6. PIG-IN-THE-HOLE

Peg Driving. Pig-in-a-Hole.

This game is quite different from the strideball games, and includes an important element not found in them, but the basic idea is the same, which is for one player to drive a ball through a circle formed by the others.

A hole is dug in the ground 12 to 15 inches in diameter and three or four inches deep. This hole is in the center of a circle formed by other holes about four inches in diameter. The small holes are one less in number than the players, and form a circle about 15 feet in diameter. Each player has a stick about one inch in diameter and three feet long, such as an ordinary gymnasium wand. The game is played with a basketball. To start the game, all players gather around the large hole and each places one end of his stick in the hole and under the basketball. Players count in unison, "One, two, three," and at "three" they all lift their sticks and thus throw the ball a considerable distance outside the circle of small holes. Immediately each player rushes for the circle of small holes and tries to place the end of his stick in one of them. Since the number of holes is just one too few, one man must be left without a hole. This man then goes after the ball and tries to drive it with his stick through the circle of players and into the center hole; the ball need not remain in the big hole. The defenders, like the attacker, may touch the ball only with their sticks, and when a defender removes his stick from the hole in order to play the ball, the attacker may seize the opportunity to place his own stick in the vacated hole. If this happens, the man newly without a hole immediately becomes attacker and proceeds without interruption.

This game is very similar to the dodgeball game, Kettle Drive (p. 131).

Group B: Center Man Defends

1. PIN GUARD
Indian-club Guard. Towerball.

All players but one stand in a circle about 20 feet in diameter. The circle can be imaginary, but it is best to have it actually marked on the floor. In the center of the circle is an Indian club, and the odd man remains inside the circle to guard the club, being permitted to move about at will. The circle men throw a basketball at the club; they may throw the ball from one to another, and may enter the circle to retrieve the ball, but may throw the ball only from outside the circle. When the club falls down, either from being hit by the ball or from being touched by the defender, the last thrower trades places with the center man and the game continues. If the center man tends to "smother" the club and thus makes it too difficult for the throwers, one of the two variations listed below should be adopted.

Variation 1. Instead of one club, three are used, and they are placed several inches apart.

Variation 2. The club is surrounded by a three-foot circle. The guard must remain outside this circle and loses if he enters it.

2. PIN GUARD (Team Form)

Players are in two teams and each team, except one man, forms a separate circle, the odd man being within the circle formed by his opponents. The center man guards a club, and play is suspended when either club is down. Each center man joins his teammates and his place is taken by another man from his team. The game continues until each man has been in the center of the opponents' circle, the throwers scoring a point for each club knocked down.

3. STOOLBALL

Stoolball is the same as Pin Guard, except that the center man guards a stool, small box, or inverted bucket. The game is played with a volleyball or other light ball that will rebound easily. The center man is out if the ball strikes the stool or if the ball rebounds from his hand or other part of his body and is caught by a circle man on the fly.

4. KICK PIN-GUARD

Same as Pin Guard, except that all players, both circle men and guard, play the ball only with the feet, or rather that they play the ball only as in Soccer Football.

5. KICK-AND-THROW PIN-GUARD

The circle players have two balls, a soccer ball and a medicine ball. They must throw the medicine ball, but must play the soccer ball as in the game of Soccer Football. A guard in the center may use any method for blocking either ball. Otherwise the game is the same as Pin Guard.

6. KICK PIN-GUARD (Team Form)
Boot-the-Pin. Team Club-Guard.

Each of two teams forms a separate circle, except that one man is inside the circle of the opponents, exactly as in Pin Guard (Team Form) (above). Circle men kick a soccer ball and the center man defends a club using only his feet. The first circle to knock down the club scores a point; play is halted and started again with new center men.

Section II: All players form one or two circles

1. CIRCLE CLUB-BOWL

All players stand in one circle facing the center, and each man has an Indian club standing on the floor behind him. A ball, usually a basketball, is thrown by any player who can get it, each trying to knock down any other player's club. A man may enter the circle to recover the ball but must return to the circle before throwing it. When a club is down, its owner has a point scored against him, the club is replaced, and the game is continued. A player with three points against him may be required to pay a penalty.

Variation. When a club is down, the club and its guard are removed from the game and play is continued until only one man survives.

2. CIRCLE CLUB-BOWL (Team Form)

Players form as for Circle Club-Bowl, except that they are in two teams and the teams alternate in the circle, that is, the even numbers are one team, the odd numbers the other. When a club is down it is replaced and a point is scored for the throwing team. Play continues until one team has a specified number of points, or for a specified time, as agreed in advance.

3. CIRCLE KICKBALL

All players form a single circle facing the center. It is best to mark two concentric circles on the floor, one in front of the men and the other behind, and to restrict the players to the space between these two circles. They have a soccer ball which they kick at will, each man trying to cause it to go out of the circle not higher than the players' heads. When the ball goes through the circle of players, the last kicker decides who was responsible; if he is unable to do so, he names the one at whose right the ball left the circle. If a man kicks the ball higher than the players' heads, he has a point against him.

Variation. The entire circle revolves slowly but continuously as the game is in progress.

4. CIRCLE KICKBALL (Team Form)

Circle Kickball. Circle Soccer.

Same as Circle Kickball, except that players are in two teams, each team forming half of the circle. When a man permits the ball to leave the circle not higher than his head, or when a man kicks the ball out higher than the heads, the opponents score a point. Play continues until one team has a specified number of points, or for a specified time.

5. GUARDING THE PINS

Players are in two equal teams. One team forms a circle as small as possible, facing outward; it guards three Indian clubs that stand inside its circle. The other team forms a circle facing inward, the distance between the two circles being about ten feet. The men in the outer circle have two or more balls, basketballs or medicine balls, which they throw in an attempt to get them past the guards and to hit the clubs. Men on the throwing team may go inside their circle to recover the balls but must not throw except from the circle. When a club is down, teams trade places and times are compared to determine the winner.

6. KICK CIRCLE

Booting the Circle

Two teams form as for Guarding the Pins, but no clubs or other objects are used. The men of the outer circle have two or more soccer balls which they try to kick through the circle of defenders. The defenders may use hands or feet. When the kicking side succeeds in getting a ball through the defending circle, the two teams trade places, the game is repeated, and times are compared.

7. CIRCLE POLEBALL

A pole about eight feet high is in the center of two concentric circles marked on the ground. The inner circle is about 20 feet, and the outer one 30 feet in diameter, but these dimensions should be adjusted in the light of experience. Players are in two teams, and each team is divided into two equal parts. One half of each team stands between the two circles on one side of a diameter that is marked on the ground; the other half stands within the inner circle but on the other side of the diameter. Thus, there are two concentric circles of players, an outer circle of throwers and an inner circle of guards, and each team forms half of each circle. The throwers have a basketball with which they try to hit the pole; the guards try to prevent their doing so. A guard may block the ball or he may catch it and toss it to one of his throwers. Play is started by a basketball toss-up between two opposing guards. Each time the pole is hit a point is scored and the ball is given to one of the guards on the nonscoring team. It is understood, of course, that the guards may not hit the pole, or at least that they cannot score.

Class XI

GOAL GAMES

GOAL GAMES, ALTHOUGH NUMEROUS AND VARIED, ARE ALL BASED ON the same single and simple principle: Each of two teams tries, against the opposition of the other, to advance a ball to one end of a field or court and to drive, carry, or throw it into a goal. There are only four ways in which one goal game can be significantly different from another: in the nature of the ball, in the method of locomotion, in the nature of restrictions on the activities of players, and in the nature of the goal. The ball is nearly always spherical, but the American football has a shape that the rule-makers call a *prolate spheroid*, and in Ice Hockey the ball has been flattened to the point where it is not a ball at all, but more like a cake of shaving soap. The diameter of the ball may be as little as two and a half inches, as in Lacrosse, or as much as six feet, as in Pushball. In most goal games the players travel on foot, but in some they swim, skate, or ride horseback. The restrictions on the players are of great variety. For example, in Basketball a player may not run with the ball and may not kick it; in Soccer he may kick it but may not touch it with his hands; in Hockey and Polo he must drive it with a stick. The goal may be all of the space beyond a line at the end of the field; most often it is a narrow segment of this space; occasionally it is something entirely different, such as the one in Basketball.

The class of "Goal Games" naturally includes a great many games that are informal and without fixed and generally accepted rules, but it also includes more of the highly organized and widely known games than does any other class. Among these games are Basketball, the three principal forms of Football, Ice and Field Hockey, Polo, Lacrosse, and Speedball.

The games are in three divisions, based on the method by which the ball is advanced: with the hand, by kicking, and by hitting or pushing with a stick.

Division One: Goal Games Played with the Hands

Division One includes goal games in which the ball may be advanced only by carrying it, throwing it, or batting it with the hand. It does not include any games in which the ball may be kicked, or advanced with the use of a stick or other implement.

Section I: Ball is played by batting with the hands

1. HAND HOCKEY

Boloball. Floorball. Scrimmageball.

Players of two equal teams scatter at will over a basketball court. A basketball, volleyball, or rubber sportball is tossed up between two opponents as in Basketball, and thereafter each team tries to advance the ball toward the opponents' goal. The ball may be played only by batting it with the open hand and no man may bat it twice in succession. The goal is a ten-foot section in the middle of the end line, marked off preferably by two uprights such as those used for volleyball nets. When a team drives the ball between the uprights it scores one point. Fouls are called as in Basketball, but the only penalty is that the opponents get the ball out of bounds.

2. DRIBBLE HAND-HOCKEY

Same as Hand Hockey, except that dribbling is permitted. A player may dribble as in Basketball and he may also roll the ball along the floor, striking it repeatedly as he does so.

3. FLOORBALL

Same as Hand Polo, except that it is played with a medicine ball. The ball must be kept on the floor and rolled along, but a man may hit it an unlimited number of times in succession.

4. BASKET HAND-HOCKEY

This game is played with a tennis ball and follows the same rules as Hand Polo, except that it is played with basketball goals. In order to score, a player must bat the ball so that it goes through the basketball goal. As in Hand Polo, the ball may be advanced with a basketball dribble.

5. BALLOON HOCKEY
Balloon Basketball. Balloon Pushball.

This game is similar to Hand Hockey, but a toy balloon, preferably a large one, is used for a ball. The ball may be played only by batting it and it must not be allowed to touch the floor. When a player permits the ball to touch the floor it goes to the opponents out of bounds. It is permissible for a man to play the ball any number of times in succession provided he clearly bats it and does not push or carry it.

6. VOLLEY HOCKEY
Volley Sock

Same as Hand Hockey, except that the ball may be played only by batting it as in Volleyball. The goal should be a six-foot section of the end line and should, if possible, have a crossbar, about eight feet high, under which the ball must pass in order to score. When the ball goes out of bounds or touches the floor it is given out of bounds to an opponent of the man who touched it last.

7. BALLOON GOAL

This novel game is played in a closed room. There are four goals, one in each corner of the room, a goal consisting of a piece of rope stretched about six feet high across the corner. Each team attacks two goals, and the two are in *opposite corners*. The game is played with two toy balloons, one red and the other blue. The game is like Balloon Polo except that the two balloons are used, and each team has two goals. Both balloons are in play at the same time, one team trying to get the red balloon into either of the diagonally-opposite red goals, the other team trying to get the blue balloon into either of the other two goals.

8. PUNCHING-BAG GOAL (Aquatic)
Punch Bowl

This game is played by swimmers in a pool. A cable must be stretched down the middle of the pool, lengthwise. Suspended from this cable on a pulley or brass ring is an ordinary punching bag. The bag should clear the water by about one foot, and the rope connecting it with the cable should be four or five feet long.

Players are in two equal teams and each team must remain on its own side of the wire. The bag is placed in the center of the pool and at a signal all players try to advance the ball by punching it with the fist. The first team to bat the bag to its end of the pool is the winner.

Section II: Ball may be thrown

In all the games of this section, the ball may be thrown from one teammate to another, and in most of them it may also be batted with the hand, but in none of them may the ball be advanced by carrying it, by kicking it, or by using a stick or club. The section includes Basketball and the modifications of it. Accordingly, the games are divided into two parts, those that use a basketball goal, and those that use any other goal.

GROUP A: GAME USES BASKETBALL GOAL

1. BASKETBALL

Basketball was invented in 1892 by Dr. James A. Naismith, physical director of the YMCA of Springfield, Massachusetts. It was an entirely new game and not, as nearly all other major games are to a greater or lesser degree, an outgrowth or development of earlier games. It was at first played largely in YMCA's, but soon spread to schools, colleges, and recreation centers. It is now easily the leading team game of the United States both in number of players and in number of spectators. It has spread to nearly all countries of the globe and in many of them is a very important game. The style of play has changed greatly since Dr. Naismith's day but the rules, although they have changed in numerous details, are in their basic principles the same as at the beginning. In the United States, the game is nearly always played indoors and only occasionally outdoors. In some other countries it is played more frequently outdoors.

After some years of confusion resulting from varying rules formulated by different sponsoring agencies, the game has become perfectly standardized. Professional players use rules of their own, and many, but by no means all, games for women are regulated by separate rules, but for the amateur game played by boys and men there is only one rules-making body, the National Basketball Committee of the United States and Canada. This committee includes representatives of the National Collegiate Athletic Association, the Amateur Athletic Union, the YMCA, the National Federation of State High School Athletic Associations, and certain Canadian organiza-

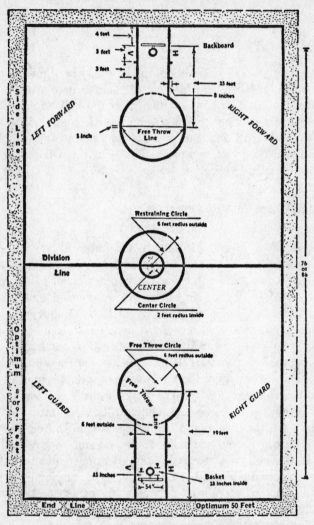

By permission of the National Basketball
Committee of the United States and Canada.

Figure 47. Basketball. The playing court.

tions. It is not perfectly accurate to say that all amateur play is governed by the same rules. There is only one rule book, but in a few cases there are alternative rules for players of different ages. The following discussion of the rules applies to those for adults. The variations for high school and younger players are listed separately.

The basketball court is a rectangle that may vary somewhat in size. The maximum legal size and the one on which most college and other senior men play is 50 by 94 feet; the minimum legal size is 42 by 74 feet. The court is divided into halves by a line across the middle parallel with the end lines. In the center of the court are two concentric circles, one with a diameter of four, the other of twelve, feet. At each end of the court, extending from the end line toward the center, and equidistant from the side lines, is a free-throw lane. Each lane is bounded in part by two parallel lines six feet apart which extend inward from the end lines, and in part by the major arc of a twelve-foot circle with its center 19 feet from the end line, the parallel lines continuing until they meet the circle. The space within the lines and the circle is all designated in the rules as the free-throw lane, but it is usual to speak of this area as consisting of two parts, a circle and a lane. Each free-throw circle has a line along the diameter that is parallel with the end line. This free-throw line is one inch wide and all other lines are two inches wide.

It is an interesting question, even if not an important one, as to which side of the lines should be taken for the specified dimensions. This question is easily answered if one considers that the lines all mark areas that some or all players must not enter, or areas that they must not leave, and that in Basketball "on the line is out." Thus the smaller center circle marks the area that center jumpers must not leave and hence is measured on the inside; the larger center circle marks the area that nonjumpers must not enter and hence is measured on the outside. Similar reasoning makes it plain that the boundary lines are measured on the inside, the free-throw lane and circle are measured on the outside, and the free-throw line is measured to the side farthest from the end line.

A certain amount of space outside the boundary lines is necessary. The rules say that this space must be three feet wide on all sides, and should be ten feet wide.

A basketball goal is a circular metal ring 18 inches in diameter inside and fixed in a horizontal position with its upper edge ten feet above the floor. Hanging from the ring is a constricted tube of netting 15 to 18 inches long that checks the ball as it passes through the ring from above. The ring is rigidly attached to a "backboard," which has a firm plane surface parallel with the end line. The horizontal distance from the backboard to the nearest point on the inside of the ring is six inches, and the plane of the inner surface of the board (the surface nearer the ring) is four feet nearer the center of the court than is the end line. Backboards vary a great deal and the rules approve two distinct types, a rectangular one 72 inches wide by 48 inches high, and a fan-shaped one 54 inches wide by 35 inches high. Backboards are made of wood, metal, or glass, and a glass one may be transparent or opaque. The latest rules state that the transparent rectangular board shall be used in college games, but prefer the fan-shaped board for other games.

The ball is a leather-covered sphere with a circumference of 29½ to 30 inches and a weight of 20 to 22 ounces. It is of the so-called "molded type" in which leather panels are cemented to fabric, and not stitched together in the traditional way. This type of ball has better balance and less pronounced seams than the stitched one. The amount of air pressure is not specified but is to be such as to give a certain rebound when the ball is dropped on a solid floor.

The game is played by two teams of five men each. A team is sometimes said to consist of a center, two forwards, and two guards, but no player is restricted to any part of the court, and the methods of play actually used make these designations of doubtful significance. To start the game an official tosses the ball upward between two opponents who stand inside the smaller center circle. All other players take any positions they wish, as long as they do not enter the larger center circle. The two men jump, each trying to bat the ball to a teammate. The object of each team is to secure the ball, advance it to the vicinity of its goal and then to score by throwing the ball so that it will pass through the ring from above. To retain possession of the ball and to advance it toward the goal the members of a team use two different methods, passing and dribbling. Perhaps the most important rule in Basketball is that a player may not run or walk while holding the ball. In passing the ball a player may throw, bounce, roll, hand, or bat it in any direction and for any distance. Passing is by far the most important element of Basketball. Rapid, accurate, and skillful passing is the chief means of getting the ball into position from which a goal can be made. Dribbling is an individual, not a team, activity. A dribbler bounces the ball repeatedly on the floor and advances as he does so. He must clearly bat the ball and not catch it, he must bat the ball with only one hand at a time, and if he stops dribbling he may not dribble again but must get rid of the ball.

The game was originally intended to be played without bodily contact, but this has been found to be impossible. Opposing players frequently come together without either being clearly at fault and nothing can well be done. However, when there is contact and an official feels that he can place the blame, he calls a foul against the offender. If a man takes hold of an opponent, or pushes him, charges against him, trips him, or otherwise makes contact with him, he has committed a foul.

Infractions of the rules are of three different kinds—violations, technical fouls, and personal fouls. A violation is considered a minor rule infraction and the penalty is that the ball is given to the opponents out of bounds. The most common violation is causing the ball to go out of bounds, and the next most frequent is running with the ball. There are several other violations, ten in all, but all are of infrequent occurrence except, perhaps, making an illegal dribble.

A technical foul does not involve personal contact. Technical fouls include delaying the game, leaving the court, making an illegal substitution, and the like, and can be charged not only against players but also against coaches or "team followers." A personal foul is any rule infringement that involves personal contact—holding, pushing, and so on. In the very rare case of an extremely serious or persistent infraction, the offender may be removed from the game, or, if he is a nonplayer, from the vicinity of the game. In all other cases the penalty is one or more free throws by the opponents. For a technical foul the free throw may be made by any player chosen by the captain of the offended team; for a personal foul the throw must be made by the man against whom the foul was committed. In certain cases two free throws are given for one foul. In the words of the rules, two free throws are awarded if:

(*a*) the foul is committed for the purpose of profiting by it or when the offending player is in an unfavorable position with little chance to reach the ball and he does not make reasonable effort to avoid contact; or

(*b*) the offended player is trying for field goal and is not successful.

With certain exceptions, a team may decline a free throw and take the ball out of bounds instead. A free throw, if successful, counts one point, a field goal, two points.

The game is played in quarters of ten minutes each, with a 15-minute intermission between halves and a one-minute intermission between the quarters of a half. Until 1951, college games, unlike high school games, were played in halves, not quarters. For several years, the rules, although specifying unbroken halves, permitted the use of quarters by agreement, but beginning with the season 1951-1952, the rules require that college games, like high school games, shall be played in quarters.

No complete basketball game can end with a tie score. If the score is tied at the expiration of the normal playing time, an extra period of five minutes is played after a two-minute intermission, and if the score is still tied as many additional periods as necessary are played until one of them ends in a score that is not tied.

2. BASKETBALL (Rules for High-School Boys)

As already explained there is no separate set of rules for high schools, but the single set of recognized rules contains in a few instances alternative provisions for colleges and high schools, or more precisely, for players of college and of high school age. The separate rules for high schools are few in number, and the important ones are as follows:

Size of court. There is no difference in the allowable dimensions of the court, but the dimensions recommended as ideal are different (50 by 84 feet for high schools, 50 by 94 feet for colleges).

Backboard. In colleges, the transparent backboard, four by six feet, is specified. For high schools, any type listed in the rules may be used, but the fan-shaped board is specified for new installations.

Size of ball. Senior high schools use the same ball as colleges, but for players below senior high school age a slightly smaller ball is specified, with a circumference of from 29 to 29½ inches, compared with 29½ to 30 inches.

Game periods. For players of high school age, a game consists of eight-minute quarters, with a ten-minute intermission between halves and two-minute intermissions between the quarters in a half. For boys aged 14 or less, the quarters are of six minutes each.

Extra periods. When a college game ends in a tie, extra periods are played until one of them ends in a nontied score, and obviously there is no limit to the possible number of such extra periods. The high school rule on extra periods is considerably different, since it is intended to eliminate the likelihood of extended overtime play. The somewhat complicated rule is as follows:

If the score is tied at the end of the fourth quarter, a two-minute intermission is declared and play is resumed without change of baskets for an extra period of three minutes. This first extra period is always played for the entire three minutes, and, if at the end of it, either team is ahead by one point or more, that team is the winner and the game is at an end. If the score is still tied at the end of the first extra period, then, after another two-minute inter-mission, a second extra period is played. The second period lasts for a maximum of three minutes but under some conditions the period and the game come to an end before three minutes. There are three possible outcomes of the second extra period: (*a*) One team scores a total of two points during the period; in this case the team that scores two points is the winner and the game ends immediately with the scoring of the second point. A team might, of course, score one point on a free throw and later two on a field goal, thus scoring a third point simultaneously with the second. It should be clear that the winning team need not be two points ahead, but must merely be the first to score two points. There is one possible exception to the general statement that the team first to score two points wins the game; if each team has one point and then a double foul is called and each team makes a free throw for a second point, there is no winner. The only logical interpretation of this situation is that the scores on the free throws were made simultaneously, so that the score has never ceased to be a tie. (*b*) During the second extra period one team scores one point and the other none. In this case the team with the one point is the winner and the game ends with the termination of the period. (*c*) The period ends with the score tied, each team having scored either no points or one point in the period. In this case a two-minute intermission is declared and then a third extra period is played.

The third period is governed by the same rules as the second with this important exception: To win by being the first team to get two points, a team need not score the two points in the third period, but must have a cumulative total of two points beginning with the second extra period. In the very unlikely event that the game is not decided even in the third overtime period, as many more periods as are necessary are played until a winner is determined. All later periods are treated precisely like the third.

3. BASKETBALL (NSWA Rules for Women)

Basketball is played to a very large extent by teams of women and girls. A majority of the games are played according to the rules for boys or with some slight modification of these rules, such modifications being local or regional in nature and not at all standardized nationally. A large and increasing number of girls' teams play according to the rules that are formulated by the National Sections on Women's Athletics, of the American Association for Health, Physical Education, and Recreation. The NSWA consists of well-trained, professional women leaders in the fields of physical education and recreation, and their rules are made on the basis of what they consider the best interests of the players, rather than of what will best exploit the girls in staging a thrilling show for the public. These rules, published annually by the NSWA in their *Official Basketball Guide,* deserve careful study by all who are interested in Basketball for girls and women.

The NSWA rules are for the most part the same as those for men, but the differences are fairly numerous and some of them are so fundamental that they make the game much different from the men's game. The following summary is intended to indicate the most important rules that are different from those for men.

The court, with its markings, and the goal, are the same, except that the line across the middle is 12 inches wide and there is only one center circle, with a diameter of six feet. Since the game is commonly played on the same court as boys' games, these two differences are often overlooked and the game is played on a court that is the same as the boys' court in all respects. There is no difference in the ball.

A team consists of six players, three forwards and three guards. The forwards are restricted to one half of the court and the guards to the other half, and no player may cross the middle line. Since a guard may not enter the forward half of the court she could hardly throw the ball at the basket, but in any case, she is specifically prohibited from doing so. Probably it is here that the women's game differs most fundamentally from the men's.

The game is played in the same periods as the high school boys' game—four quarters of eight minutes each. There are no extra periods, and when the fourth quarter ends with a tie score, the tie stands.

At the beginning of each quarter the ball is put in play at the center, but not with a center jump. A forward from one team stands alone in the center circle and is entitled to the whole area. (This is a minor exception to the rule that each player must remain in her half of the court.) The referee throws the ball to this center and she puts it into play by passing it to a teammate.

A player is permitted what is called a *limited dribble*, which means that she may dribble the ball as in the men's rules, but may bounce it only twice. She may also "juggle" the ball by throwing it into the air once and catching it again. She may not hold the ball longer than three seconds. Handing the ball to a teammate, formerly prohibited, is permitted.

In general it is not permitted for two girls to have hands on the ball at the same time. If both grasp it simultaneously it is a jump ball or "tossed ball," as in the boys' game. If a girl places her hand on the ball when another already has it, but so nearly at the same time that the official considers it unintentional, a violation is called and the player who had the ball first, or one of her teammates, takes the ball out of bounds. If the second player grasps the ball after the first has clearly had it in her possession, it is a foul against the second player.

Infractions of the rules are classed as violations, technical fouls, and personal fouls. The principal violations in addition to the ones in men's rules are: crossing the middle line, holding the ball more than three seconds, and violating any of the rules on dribbling, juggling, bouncing the ball, and so on. Technical fouls include illegally placing a hand on a ball held by an opponent, waving hands before the face of an opponent, and "boxing up." Boxing up occurs when two teammates both guard an opponent who is between them. In general, personal fouls are the same as in the men's game. Technical fouls are much more important than in the men's game; in addition to the ones listed there are a considerable number of less importance.

4. BASKETBALL (Canadian Rules for Women)

In the Canadian game for women, the court is divided into three equal zones. The six players of a team, however, are not divided among the three zones; instead each girl has the right to two zones, the guards using the rear and center, the forwards the forward and center zones. Thus all six girls can use the center zone. Except for this, the rules are the same as those of the NSWA.

5. TWO-BALL BASKETBALL
Dual Basketball

This informal game is the same as Basketball, except that two balls are used. At the start of a period, both balls are tossed at the same time between the same two men. Thereafter, the two balls are played independently, each ball being under a different official.

6. LEFT-HAND BASKETBALL

Same as Basketball except that all passing and all throwing at the basket must be done with the left hand by right-handed players, or with the right hand by left-handed ones.

7. MULTIPLE-GOAL BASKETBALL
Four-basket Ball. Four-goal Basketball.

This game requires a court with at least four basketball goals, two or more for each team. The two goals for a team are usually on the same line but the game can be played with one on the end and one on the side. Only one ball is used. Teams should be larger than the usual ones; 10 to 15 on a team is about right. The game is played as much like Basketball as its informality will permit, each side being permitted to score in any one of its baskets.

8. NINE-COURT BASKETBALL

A basketball court is divided by two longitudinal and two lateral lines into nine equal parts, the parts being numbered. Each of the two teams has nine members, one in each of the nine divisions. Each player must remain in his own division. The game is played according to Basketball rules; it is usually played by girls, and hence according to girls' rules. When a team scores, its members all rotate as in Volleyball, each one moving to the next higher number, except the one in number nine, who goes to number one.

9. PERMUTATION BASKETBALL

Mass Basketball

This game requires a floor, preferably a large one, with four basketball goals. The ideal situation is two courts side by side in the same room. The game is really six games all going on at the same time in overlapping areas. Twelve teams are paired off and each pair plays a basketball game on one of the six possible combinations of goals: teams *A* and *B* play with goals *1* and *2*, *C* and *D* with goals *1* and *3*, and so on. Each game has its own ball. There is no boundary line and no officials are used. Of course the game can be trimmed down so as to use fewer than the six possible combinations.

10. ONE-GOAL BASKETBALL

One-basket Ball

This game is a widely played and truly excellent kind of informal Basketball. Since the game uses only one goal and only one half of the court, two games can be played on a court that normally accommodates only one. But aside from its efficient use of space, the game has other advantages over the standard one, and for a pick-up game played without officials, especially when fewer than ten men are available, it is likely to be preferred by the players.

The game can be played by teams of five, but teams of four or three are better; opinion is divided as to whether three or four is the ideal number for a team. It is even played with teams of only two. At the beginning of a game, one player takes the ball beyond an imaginary line that passes through the rear of the foul circle, and throws it to a teammate. The game proceeds precisely like any standard game of Basketball, with the initial thrower and his mates being the offensive team, until the offensive team makes a goal or a member of the defensive team acquires undisputed possession of the ball. At this point play ceases and the ball is dead. It is then taken by a member of the team that has just secured it and put into play as at the beginning of the game. Players call their own out-of-bounds, held balls, violations, and fouls, but as the game is usually played, the ball is taken out of bounds when a foul is called.

Variation. The ball is not dead when it is taken by the defenders, but they must play it until they have it beyond the free-throw circle.

11. INDIVIDUAL BASKETBALL
One O' Gang

There are no teams in this game and each man plays for himself. Four or five players have a basketball with which they try to score as in One-goal Basketball, with only one man as guard against them. If the guard gets the ball, if the ball goes out of bounds, or if a man tries for a goal and misses, the ball is dead. Then the guard trades places with the one who last touched the ball, and the game is repeated. Each goal counts one point, but each missed attempt takes one point off; each player keeps his own score and the first to score ten is the winner.

Group B: Game Uses Goal Other Than Basketball Goal

1. BOUNCE BASKETBALL
Dribbleball

This game is played like Girls' Basketball (NSWA Rules) with these exceptions: (*a*) Every pass must be a bounce pass, and it is a violation for a player to catch a direct pass; (*b*) Each goal is a three-foot circle on the floor with its center four feet from the end line, and a goal is made by bouncing the ball on the floor inside this circle.

2. PIN BASKETBALL
Indian-club Ball. Pinball. Pin Guard.

Each of the two goals is an Indian club standing on the floor in the center of a ten-foot circle, the circle having its center ten feet from the end line. One player of each team may be within the circle that his team is defending, but it is a foul for any other player to touch the circle. The game is played like Basketball, girls' or boys' rules, except for scoring. A field goal is made whenever a player knocks down the club with the ball. It is a goal for the opponents if a guard knocks the club down. A free throw is a throw at the club from a distance of 40 feet.

Variation. The circles are five feet in diameter and no player is permitted within the circle.

3. BUCKET BASKETBALL

The goal is a bucket, tub, or other receptacle standing in the center of a five-foot circle, and a goal is made when the ball lands and remains in the bucket. No player may touch the circle. Otherwise the game is played like Basketball.

4. FORWARD-PASS BALL
Forward-pass Football. Passball.

This game is played óutdoors with a football. The field has goal lines and end zones, but no goal posts. A regular football field can be used, but a shorter one, say 80 yards long, is better. The two teams can be of any size, but six or seven to a team is best. The team that wins the toss puts the ball in play in the center of the field from a regular football formation. Only one play is possible, and that is a forward pass. When a man catches a pass he may not run with it; the ball is down at the spot of the catch. If a team completes a pass it puts the ball in play again from the spot of the catch, but if the pass is intercepted or incomplete it goes to the opponents and is put in play by them at the same spot as the last play. Play continues until one team completes a pass in the end zone and thus scores a touchdown.

5. FIELDBALL [11]

Fieldball is an outdoor game that closely resembles Soccer Football except that the ball is thrown and not kicked. The rules that govern handling of the ball and guarding of opponents are those of Basketball, but the field and the methods of scoring are those of Soccer. The game is played to a considerable extent by girls of high school age and for this reason the basketball and soccer rules on which it is based are usually those for women. It is played by two teams of eleven each.

---

[11] For detailed rules see: National Section on Women's Athletics, *Official Soccer-Speedball Guide, Including Field Ball,* Washington, D. C., American Association for Health, Physical Education and Recreation, published biennially.

6. FIELD HANDBALL [12]

Field Handball was developed in Germany after the first world war and was played in the Olympic Games of 1936, held in Berlin. It is probably not played anywhere in the United States at present. It is quite similar to Fieldball, but the two games were probably developed independently.

The field and goals are almost identical with those of Soccer. The ball is 24 inches in circumference. It may be thrown or struck with any part of the body above the knees, and may be carried not more than three steps. A score is made by throwing the ball into the goal.

7. CAGEBALL

Cageball was invented during the first world war by Dr. Emmett Dunn Angell. Although the original game is probably not played anywhere today, it has led to other games that are very popular, and, most important, the ball that was devised for the original game has become a standard piece of play equipment used for a great variety of activities. In view of these facts it seems in order to describe the original game in spite of the fact that it is no longer played.

The game is played with a ball 30 inches in diameter, an inflated sphere with a canvas cover, the total weight being only five pounds. The size of the field is not critical, but 100 by 120 is suggested. The goal is a horizontal surface of rope net fixed ten feet above the ground and having a rim around all sides. The goal is 4 feet wide and 20 to 40 feet long, and is located so that the field extends 10 feet beyond it. The game is played by two teams of indefinite but very large size; a team may include any number of men from ten to a thousand, one hundred being about right. To start the game, the ball is placed on the ground at the center of the field, one man from each team stands by the ball with one or both hands resting on it, and all the other men of each team must remain at least ten feet from the ball, each in his own half of the field. The referee blows a whistle and all rush for the ball; at the same time the two men at the ball try to lift and throw it or otherwise to direct it toward their respective teams. Thereafter each team tries to advance the ball

---

[12] For complete rules see: Amateur Athletic Union, *Official Rules, Handball, etc.*, American Sports Publishing Company, 1939, pp. 29-33.

toward its own goal and to score by causing it to land on the elevated platform. In playing the ball a man may throw, bat, or punch it, but not carry it or kick it. The ball may not be played on the ground and play is stopped when it touches the ground. Then all players except two opposing men move away from the ball and these two lift the ball into the air, when it is again in play. When a man commits a foul the opponents get the ball 30 feet from the goal and the offending team must remain behind a line ten feet nearer the goal.

8. BASKET CAGEBALL
Cage Basketball.

This game is played with a cageball but on a basketball court. The rules of Basketball are followed as closely as the ball will permit, but a goal is scored by causing the ball to strike against the backboard.

9. FLICKERBALL [13]

Flickerball was devised, probably in 1949, by A. H. Seidler and H. E. Kenney of the University of Illinois. The field is 30 yards wide and 53½ yards long, the curious length probably being explained by the fact that it is approximately the width of a football field. The goal is a rectangular opening, two feet high and three feet wide, in a board that is four feet by five feet. The board is in a vertical plane, parallel with the end line, and five yards beyond the end line, or, in other words, the goal is five yards out of bounds.

The game is played with a football but resembles Basketball more than any other game. The ball may be thrown in any direction at any time, and it may also be carried, but it may not be carried forward; since the ball may not be carried toward the goal the game is included here rather than in Section III. Seven men constitute a team. An incomplete forward pass that is not broken up by the defense (one that is incomplete because of poor passing or catching) goes to the defensive team; a forward pass that is broken up, or any other loose ball, is a free ball and belongs to any man who can recover it.

A score is made by throwing the ball through the opening in the goal board. Since the goal is out of bounds, it follows that a missed

---

[13] For complete rules see: Seidler, Armond, "How We Do It—Flicker Ball," *Journal of Health and Physical Education*, 1950, Vol. 21, No. 10, p. 27.

throw for goal is out of bounds, and, like any other out-of-bounds ball, is given to the opponents.

A player who commits a personal foul is sent to a penalty bench and must remain there, his team playing meawhile with only six members, until one side or the other scores a goal. Fouls are in general the same as in Basketball.

Section III: Ball may be carried

This is the last of the three sections comprising the goal games in which the ball is played only with the hands, as contrasted with those in which it must be, or may be, played with the foot or with a stick. In the first of these three sections, the ball may be played only by batting with the hands, and may not be thrown or carried; in the second section the ball may be thrown but not carried; in the third section—the one now to be considered—the ball may be carried toward the goal. In most cases it may also be thrown or batted, but in no case may it be kicked or hit with a stick. In a few cases there may be difficulty in deciding whether the ball may be carried. For example, in Pushball one may consider it impossible for a player to carry a ball that is four to six feet in diameter, but this game and others that show a similar problem are included here on two grounds: first, carrying is not prohibited, and a player may carry the ball if he can; second, players actually do carry the ball or at least they do something that, if not literally carrying, is prohibited in a game that does not include carrying.

1. PASSBALL

This game is played with an American football and on a rectangular field, but the field need not be as large as a football field and no goal posts are used. It is played by two teams with no fixed size; the teams must be distinguishable.

The teams line up as for a Football kick-off, but the ball is put into play by a throw rather than by a kick. The receiving team takes the ball and starts with it down the field toward the opponents' goal. A man with the ball may run with it in any direction, or he may pass it in any direction. There is no limit to the number of passes. The ball is down when it touches the ground, when it is caught by a defensive player, or when a player is touched by an opponent while the ball is in his possession. When the ball is down it goes to the opponents, who put it into play by an ordinary football scrimmage after which they may run with it or pass it in any direction as before. Play continues until one side scores a touchdown and then this side "kicks off" as before.

2. PUSHBALL

A game called *Pushball* was devised in 1894 by M. G. Crane of Newton, Massachusetts. This game called for a leather-covered, inflated ball 72 inches in diameter and was played by teams of 11 men each on a field 140 yards long. The goal consisted of two upright posts with a crossbar seven feet above the ground; a ball under the crossbar scored five points while one over the bar counted eight points.

This game was played in a few places, including Harvard University, but never became established and soon died out. However, the name and the general idea of the game persisted. Today there are no recognized rules for Pushball, but the name is applied to any game in which a very large ball is used and in which two opposing teams try to advance the ball to their respective goals by continuous pushing, throwing, and batting, with no formal rules and few restrictions on the players. The game has been much used in military training camps. In such camps and elsewhere the game is usually played with extremely large teams, sometimes consisting of several hundred men. The ball most often used is the 30-inch cageball. Assuming that the game is played with a cageball, it is recommended that it be played with the rules of Cageball except that the ball may be carried, thrown, or batted; and that the cage goal be eliminated, a point being scored whenever the ball crosses the goal line inside the side lines.

3. WATER PUSHBALL
Water Cageball.

Each of two teams lines up on the rim at one end of a swimming pool, with a 30-inch cageball floating on the water in the center of the pool. At a signal all dive into the pool and try to advance the ball to the goals, by pushing, batting, or throwing it. A goal is scored when the ball is pushed by one or more men against the end of the pool; throwing the ball so as to strike the end is not sufficient.

4. WATER BALLOONBALL

Same as Water Pushball except that a toy balloon, preferably a large one, is used. However, this game becomes considerably different from Water Pushball because the balloon will "take off" into the air. A goal is scored in the same way as in Water Pushball.

5. WATER BASKETBALL

Water Basketball was at one time played under formal rules but has now been completely supplanted by Water Polo, which is a similar game. However, as an informal and improvised game, it is still played to some extent. It is suggested that the game be played in a pool with an improvised basket on the floor just beyond each end, and that a rubber sport ball be used. The rules of Basketball are followed as closely as the nature of the game permits. In the original game players were permitted to carry the ball, and this rule probably should be retained.

6. WATER POLO (American)
Soft-ball Water Polo

Some sort of goal game played in the water and known as Water Polo has been played in England since the 1870's and in the United States since the first indoor pools were built in the 1880's. Definite rules were formulated about 1900, but two different games developed, one played only in the United States, the other in England and other countries of Europe. The American game flourished more or less for some years but has now given way to the international game and is no longer recognized for formal competition. The essentials of this game are as follows: The ball is from seven to eight inches in diameter and is loosely inflated so that a player can get a firm grip on it with one hand. The goal is simply a board, 4 feet long and 18 inches high, with its face parallel to, and one foot inside, the end of the pool. The court is of course the pool, and should be from 60 to 75 feet long. A goal is scored by pressing the ball against the board. A team consists of six players and the game consists of two periods of 12 minutes each with a five-minute intermission. The ball may be played by throwing, batting, or carrying it. Personal contact, including tackling, is permitted. The rules include various restrictions on players, but the game has always been recognized as extremely rough and strenuous.

7. WATER POLO (International)
Hard-ball Water Polo

International Water Polo is the only form of the game that is now generally recognized. It is used in various forms of competition and has been on the program of the Olympic Games. The rules are well standardized and administered. The game is, in comparison with games in general, strenuous and rough, but not nearly so much so as the obsolete American game.

The ball is a leather-covered sphere with a circumference of from 27 to 28 inches, and is tightly inflated. The goal is placed one foot inside the end of the pool and consists of two uprights ten feet apart and a cross-bar three feet above the water; a goal is scored when the ball passes under the cross bar. The game is intended to be played in a pool with no shallow water, but the rules provide that a pool with one shallow end can be used. Over the shallow water the cross-bar is to be eight feet above the water. A game consists of four periods of five minutes each with a five-minute intermission between halves and a one-minute intermission between the quarters of a half. A team consists of seven players, rather than six as in the American game.

8. ICE BASKETBALL

A basketball court is marked out on the ice. Each goal is a barrel or tub in the center of a ten-foot circle. All players wear skates. A goal is scored by throwing the ball into the barrel, but it is a foul to enter the circle surrounding the barrel. Rules are, as nearly as possible, the same as in Basketball.

Variation. A player may skate with the ball in his possession but must throw it instantly when he is touched by an opponent.

Division Two: Football Games

Division Two includes the goal games in which a player is permitted to kick the ball. It is concerned with the various standardized games that are called Football, with or without a qualifying adjective, and with the informal adaptations of these games. For this reason it seems in order that a few words be said at this point about football games in general.

The early history of Football has long been the subject of considerable study and speculation, and probably of a considerable amount of loose talk and writing. The question of the origin of the modern games of Football, as well as of most games, is inherently unanswerable, because the "origin of a game" is an undefinable term. It is quite likely that at some time or other some ancient Greeks kicked a ball about, and it is certain that Englishmen did so as far back as English history goes. The word *football* seems to have been recognized in the twelfth century, but whether the game of Football was actually played at that time is questionable.

In the seventeenth and eighteenth centuries there emerged in England a game with some semblance of order to it, based on local and regional customs and not on standardized rules; in fact no really definite rules for any form of Football were known until 1863. One thing was understood about the game: It was to be played with the feet and not the hands. This was the situation until 1823 when, in a football game played at Rugby, a student named William Webb Ellis, according to the inscription on a stone located on the Rugby campus: " . . . with a fine disregard for the rules of Football, as played in his time, first took the ball in his arms and ran with it, thus originating the distinctive feature of the Rugby game." Whether the story is true or not, it is a fact that about this time the game diverged and that two kinds of Football have been played in England ever since. For a time both games were simply Football but soon the new variety came to be called Rugby Football or Rugger. The kicking game was administered, starting in 1863, by the Football Association, and came to be called Association Football, the name by which it is properly known in England today. But the word *association* does not go well with Rugger so the English somehow or other extracted from the word a new word, *soccer*. The word *soccer* is nothing but a corruption or contraction, or nickname, of the word *association*. Soccer is a popular name in England, and the preferred name in America.

In the United States there was some informal intercollegiate Football as early as 1869, but this was Soccer Football. By 1875 Rugby was being played in Canada and when Harvard and McGill played Football in that year half the game was played according to Harvard's Soccer rules and the other half according to McGill's Rugby rules. The new game took hold immediately, and by 1876 it was settled that the intercollegiate game in the United States was to be Rugby. However, in this same year a series of conferences on the rules began and from that time the American rules have been changed almost every year. The game very quickly developed features that distinguished it from the English game, and now the two can hardly be recognized as variations of the same game. The American game was for many years known as American Rugby, or merely Rugby, but it seems better now that it be called American Football.

In Australia and in Canada Rugby has had an experience similar to that in the United States, so that there are now distinctive games of Australian Football, and Canadian Football. Another distinctive game is Gaelic Football, but it appears to have been derived from the original game and not from Rugby.

Section I: Ball may not be played with the hands

1. SOCCER FOOTBALL

Association Football. Football. Soccer.

The first definite rules for Soccer were formulated in 1863, and by 1866 they had become very much as they are today. The game is played chiefly in Great Britain and Ireland, where it is intensely popular among both players and spectators. In Great Britain there are 88 professional teams operated much like our major league teams in Baseball, and games among these teams occasionally draw more than 100,000 spectators. The game is also played rather extensively in other parts of the world, notably in Europe and South America. In the United States the game is played more extensively than many might guess. In several cities there are flourishing leagues, in part made up of foreign players who have learned the game abroad. In many colleges the game is played as an intramural sport both for men and for women, and a number of colleges and universities support intercollegiate teams. There is a United States Football Association, patterned after the British organization, which promotes and administers the game.

The Soccer field is about as long as the one used for American Football and somewhat wider. Exact dimensions are not required, the rules permitting lengths of from 100 to 130 yards and widths of

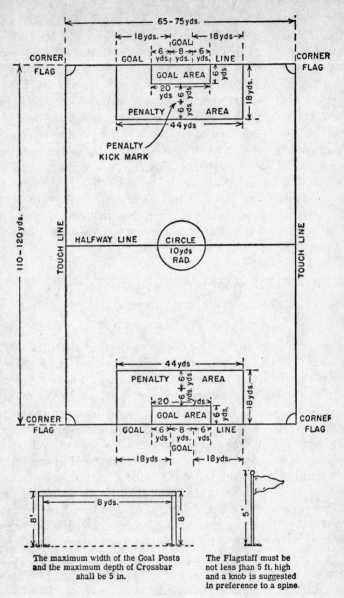

Figure 48. Soccer Football. Plan of field. N.C.A.A. rules.

from 55 to 75 yards. The lines at the ends are the goal lines and those at the sides are called *touch lines*. The field is divided into halves by a line parallel with the goal lines, and a 20-yard circle is marked in the center. At each end is a rectangle 44 by 18 yards; the center part of the goal line forms one of the long sides of this rectangle. Within the rectangle just described, and also with one long side formed by part of the goal line, is another rectangle 6 by 20 yards. The larger rectangle is the "penalty area"; the smaller, the "goal area." The goal, which is on the goal line, is a rectangular space eight feet high and eight yards wide, bounded by two up-rights and a crossbar; the goal is the area *under* the crossbar, not over it as in the American game.

The ball is a leather-covered, inflated sphere smaller than a bas-ketball, its circumference being from 27 to 28 inches and its weight from 14 to 16 ounces. The casing is made of 12 pieces of leather that form a distinctive pattern and make the ball easily recognizable. The usual costume includes a shirt or jersey with sleeves, and short pants that leave the knees bare.

A team consists of 11 players—five forwards, three halfbacks, two backs, and one goalkeeper. The forwards are known as outside left, inside left, center, inside right, and outside right; the halfbacks are left, center, and right; and the backs merely left and right.

At the beginning of each period and after each score, play is started with a kick-off. Each player must be in his own half of the field, and those of the receiving team must not enter the center circle. The ball is placed on the ground in the center of the field and kicked so that it travels forward (straight or diagonally) and at least as far as its own circumference. It is usual for the kicker to drive the ball only a short distance so that a teammate may recover it. After the kick-off the ball is in play, and each team tries to work it down to the vicinity of the opponents' goal and then to drive it into the goal. In general the ball is played by kicking, but players often butt it with the tops of their heads and in fact are permitted to play it with any part of the body except the hands or arms. Even here there is one exception, for the goalkeeper, while he is in his penalty area, is permitted to catch the ball in his hands. Players develop re-markable skill in "passing" the ball to one another and in "dribbling" it; that is, in carrying the ball along with a rapid series of gentle kicks.

A rule that is most important, and that has always caused a great deal of difficulty, is the "off-side rule." When a player kicks or otherwise plays the ball any teammate of the kicker who is in front of the ball, that is, nearer the opponents' goal than is the ball, is off-side; any teammate who is behind the ball is on-side. In general it is a foul for an off-side player to play the ball. It must be noted that the position of the player when *he* plays the ball has nothing to do with the matter; what counts is the player's position when the ball was last played by a teammate. In practice this means that a player may not kick the ball forward to a teammate who is waiting to receive it; but he can kick the ball forward, and a teammate who, at the instant of kicking, was behind the ball may run forward, overtake the ball, and then kick it. The "off-side rule" does not apply to all situations by any means but has important exceptions. It is not illegal for an off-side player to play the ball under these conditions: (*a*) if he was in his own half of the field when the ball was last kicked; (*b*) if there are two or more opponents between him and the goal line when he himself kicks the ball; (*c*) if the ball was last played by a player throwing or kicking it in from out-of-bounds.

When the ball goes out of bounds, it is kicked or thrown in by an opponent of the player who last touched it, as it is in Basketball. However, there are three different methods of play, and the one used depends on the conditions under which the ball went out: (*a*) When the ball goes across a touch line (sideline), it is played with a "throw-in"; the player making the throw-in stands out-of-bounds with both feet on the ground and throws the ball in-bounds with both hands over his head. (*b*) When the ball is driven across the goal line, but not between the goal posts, by the attacking side, the other team makes a "goal-kick," by kicking the ball into the field of play from beyond the goal line. (*c*) When the ball is driven across the goal line by a member of the defending team, the attacking team takes a "corner-kick" by kicking the ball into the field from the nearer of the two corners.

In general it is illegal for a player to touch the ball with his hands or arms, but this is not true of the goalkeeper, who has the right to use his hands so long as he is within his own penalty area. Here he may catch the ball and may take two steps with it.

The rules on bodily contact seem somewhat vague in comparison with most American rules. The general rule is as follows: "Neither tripping with the feet, legs or body, kicking, striking with the hand, elbow or knee, nor jumping at a player shall be allowed . . . . A player shall not use his hands or arms to obstruct, hold, or push an opponent. Charging is permissible, but it must not be violent or dangerous. A player shall not be charged from behind unless he is intentionally obstructing an opponent. A player may not be charged when he is in the air and has both feet off the ground in an effort to receive the ball. A player may not place his hands or arms on an opponent in an effort to reach the ball."

The penalty for a foul is a free-kick by the opponents. Fouls are divided into two classes that correspond somewhat to the violations and fouls of Basketball. For a foul in the less serious class the penalty is always a free-kick from the spot of the foul, and a goal may not be scored directly from this kick. For a foul of the more serious kind, there is a distinction between one made by a defensive player in his own penalty area, as it is very likely to be, and any other. If the foul is not committed by a player inside his own penalty area, the penalty is a free-kick as above, except that this time it is legal for the kicker to drive the ball through the goal and score. The free-kick thus far referred to is made by placing the ball on the ground at the spot of the foul, with all opponents at least ten yards from the ball until it is kicked, and then kicking it as it lies. When a foul is made by a defensive player inside his own penalty area, the penalty is a special form of free-kick called a *penalty-kick*. The ball is placed on a mark directly in front of the goal and 12 yards from it. Any member of the offended team prepares to kick the ball, the opposing goalkeeper takes his position behind the goal line, and all other members of both teams must take positions within the field of play and outside the penalty area. The goalkeeper must not cross the goal line, nor the other players enter the penalty area, until the ball is kicked. When the ball is kicked, it is in play and can then be played by any player who can get to it. However, the kicker may not play it again until some other player has played it. Thus the kicker can score immediately, or the ball may be played several times and then kicked for a goal. It should be noted that a goal from a penalty-kick counts the same as any other goal, the only possible score in Soccer being one point.

2. SOCCER FOOTBALL (Women's Rules)

The National Section on Women's Athletics, of the AAHPER formulates and publishes rules for a modified form of Soccer particularly suitable for play by women and girls, as they do for Basketball and other games.[14] The chief points on which these rules differ from the standard ones are: (*a*) The field is smaller; (*b*) the game is shorter; (*c*) a field goal counts two points, and a penalty goal one; (*d*) a player may play the ball with her arms while they are folded in front of the body.

3. SEVEN-MAN SOCCER

Like Football, Baseball, and other games, Soccer has been adapted successfully to teams smaller than the usual ones, and for Soccer seven-man teams are probably best. The rules need not be changed from the standard ones, except that a smaller field is probably desirable.

4. INDOOR SOCCER

Fug. Gymnasium Soccer.

The chief feature of this game is the ball, which must be soft and hence much less lively than the standard one. An old soccer ball or basketball not much more than half inflated is usually used, but any other ball that is soft enough will serve the purpose. A goal is made from high-jump standards or otherwise improvised, and the game is played with any desired simplification of the standard rules.

5. MEDICINE-BALL SOCCER

This is simply Indoor Soccer played with a medicine ball.

6. HOPPING SOCCER

One-leg Soccer.

In this game each player must travel only by hopping. He may change from one foot to another while he is not in a play of any kind. He may kick the ball with the hopping foot or with the free foot. He may leave the field to rest, but must not touch both feet

---

[14] National Section on Women's Athletics, *Official Soccer-Speedball Guide.* Washington, D. C.: American Association for Health, Physical Education and Recreation, published every two years.

to the floor while on the field. The game should be played on a small court, usually indoors, and according to simplified rules.

7. PIN SOCCER

Pin Football.

This is a special form of simplified Indoor Soccer. The goal is an Indian club standing in the center of a six-foot circle, and a point is scored when the club is knocked down.

8. MASS SOCCER

Mass Soccer is merely Soccer with teams considerably larger than in the standard game, say twenty-five or more players. It is necessary, of course, to eliminate the off-side rule and to make other simplifications in the rules. Most important, the game should be played with more than one ball. Two is the usual number of balls, but there is no reason why three or four balls should not be tried. It is also necessary to have more than one goal tender, and one for each ball is about right. Probably the game should be played with a goal wider than the standard one, but it is usually played with the standard goals.

9. CHASEBALL

This game is Soccer except that a player is permitted to punch the ball with his fist, as well as to play it in any of the ways permitted in the standard game. Naturally it is played with simplified rules.

10. CRAB SOCCER

Crabball

Each player assumes the "crab position" and must maintain it as long as the ball is in play. In this position a player has both hands and both feet on the floor, with his face up. If one sits on the floor with legs extended forward and hands on the floor behind him, and then raises his hips from the floor, he is in the crab position. It is permissible, however, for a player to sit on the floor at will. Players in this position play simplified Soccer with a standard ball. The standard goal should not be used, but the goal should be the entire width of the goal line.

11. LINE SOCCER
Babylonian. Soccer Drive.

Two teams play on a rectangular field, which should be considerably smaller than a soccer field and without goal posts. Each team forms in line in its own half of the field ten yards from the middle line. Each man extends his arms behind the backs of the men on either side of him and joins hands with the men second from him. A soccer ball is placed on the ground in the center of the field, and at a signal both teams rush forward to play it. They follow the rules of Soccer as closely as the situation permits, but the lines must not be broken. If a line breaks, play is stopped, the ball moved ten yards toward the offenders' goal, and the game re-started from the new position. A goal is scored when a team kicks the ball across the opponents' goal line.

12. INDIVIDUAL SOCCER
Corner-Kick Ball. Kickball. Line Football. Line Soccer. Overball.

Individual Soccer is a soccer-type game in which only two men, one from each team, are active at any one time. Two teams line up on their respective goal lines. A soccer ball is placed on the ground in the center of the field, and one man from each team comes forward and stands on a line ten yards from the ball. At a signal the two rush forward and play the ball as in Soccer, each trying to play it to and over the opponents' goal line. The other players, standing on their goal lines, may stop the ball with any part of the body including the hands, and may bat or kick it back into the field, but may not catch or throw it. After one of the first two men has scored, two others play, the original players joining their lines. When all have played, the team with the larger score wins.

Section II: Ball may be thrown but not carried

1. SPEEDBALL

Speedball was invented in 1921 by Professor Elmer D. Mitchell of the University of Michigan. It is a combination of Soccer Football and Basketball, except that the methods of scoring, of which there are five, are taken from Soccer and American Football and not from Basketball. The game is intended for players of average ability and for this reason the specifications for the field, the ball, and the size of teams are intentionally made flexible.

The official field and goal posts are the same as those for American Football except that most of the cross lines are unnecessary. The field needs goal lines, end lines, and three cross lines at the middle of the field; that is, a middle line and a line on each side of the middle line and ten yards from it. A soccer field with its goal posts is satisfactory, but the size of the field is usually reduced for informal play. The official speedball is about midway in size between a soccer ball and a basketball, but a soccer ball is often used. A team consists of eleven men but may be reduced to nine or seven players.

The rules for playing the ball are based on the distinction between a fly ball and a ground ball. A fly ball is one that has not touched the ground since it was last played; a ground ball is one that *has* touched the ground since it was last played. A ball may be high in the air from a bounce but it is still a ground ball, because in bouncing it has touched the ground. The basic rule is that a ground ball must not be touched with the hands, but played as in Soccer, while a fly ball may be caught and may not be kicked. It is possible for a player to kick a ground ball into the air (thus making a fly ball of it), and catch it himself. American boys prefer the basketball style of play and throw and catch the ball until it strikes the ground and they are forced to kick it. In general, fly balls are played according to the rules of Basketball and ground balls are played according to the rules of Soccer. One exception to this generalization is that the basketball dribble is not permitted; it is permissible, however, for a player to make one overhead dribble; that is, once during each possession of the ball he may throw it into the air and catch it himself. It is possible for a player to cover a considerable distance in this way.

The game begins with a soccer kick-off except that the opponents are restrained behind a line ten yards from the middle of the field instead of by a circle. As in Soccer the kick must travel at least the circumference of the ball and may not be played again by the kicker until it is played by another player. A held ball is defined and played as in Basketball. When the ball goes out of bounds it is played in by an opponent of the man who last touched it; if it crosses a sideline it must be played by a throw, but if it crosses the end line it may be played with a throw, a punt, or a place-kick.

There are five different methods of scoring: (*a*) A field goal counts three points and is made when the ball is kicked under the cross bar as in Soccer; (*b*) a touchdown counts two points and is made when a forward pass is caught in the end zone; (*c*) an end-kick counts one point and is made when the ball is kicked across any part of the end line, provided the kick is made from a point within the end zone; (*d*) a drop-kick counts one point and is made when the ball is drop-kicked over the cross bar from a point inside the field of play not including the end zone; (*e*) a penalty-kick counts one point and is made as explained below.

Infractions of the rules are classified as in Basketball as violations, technical fouls, and personal fouls. The following are violations: (1) carrying the ball; (2) touching a ground ball with the hand; (3) touching a fly ball with the foot or knee; (4) making more than one overhead dribble; (5) violating the rules governing kick-off, held ball, out-of-bounds ball, or free-kick; (6) violating the penalty-kick restrictions.

Technical fouls are infractions of the rules on substitutions, times out, number of men on the field, and delaying the game. Personal fouls are those involving personal contact: kicking, tripping, charging, pushing, holding, blocking, and unnecessary roughness.

In awarding penalties the distinction is made, as in Soccer, between an infraction by a player within his own penalty area, and one made by a player not in this area. The penalty area is the same as the end zone. For a violation outside the violator's penalty area the ball is given to the opponents out-of-bounds; for all other infractions the penalty is one, or two, penalty-kicks. A penalty-kick is a place-kick from a spot on the goal line and directly in front of the goal posts. One member of the defensive team stands behind the goal posts in the middle of the end line, and all other players of both teams must be in the field of play, not in the end zone. In some cases when a penalty-kick is missed the ball is still in play; in others it is dead and goes to the defensive side out-of-bounds beyond the end line.

It has already been said that for a violation outside the penalty area the ball goes to the opponents out-of-bounds. For a violation inside the penalty area, the penalty is one penalty-kick by the offended player, the ball to be in play after an unsuccessful kick, or in other words a penalty-kick with follow-up. For a technical foul outside the penalty area the opponents get one penalty-kick by any member of the team, with no follow-up; for a technical foul inside the penalty area they get the same kick but with follow-up. For a personal foul outside the penalty area the offended player takes one penalty-kick without follow-up, but for a personal foul inside the penalty area he takes two kicks, with a follow-up allowed after the second.

The game is played in quarters of ten minutes each with a ten-minute intermission between halves and a two-minute intermission between the quarters of each half. For younger boys periods of five to eight minutes are recommended.

2. SPEEDBALL (Women's Rules)

The women's rules for Speedball differ from the men's rules only in a few respects.

The field has a maximum size of 60 by 100 yards for women of college age, or 40 by 80 yards for girls of high school age. The end zone is 6 instead of 10 yards wide. The penalty mark is 12 instead of 10 yards from the goal.

The rules on guarding are the same as in women's Basketball.

A ball that crosses a sideline must be put into play by a throw, any type of throw being permitted.

For a violation not in the offender's penalty area the opponents make a free-kick from the spot of the violation.

The scoring is as follows: drop kick, three; field goal, two; touchdown, two; penalty kick, one.

3. INDOOR SPEEDBALL

Speedball may be adapted to indoor play by using a half-inflated ball as used for Indoor Soccer. Goals can be improvised and if the goal is not suitable for a drop-kick, a drop-kick may be called "good" when the ball strikes the basketball backboard.

4. SIMBALL

Simball, named for Ralph Simpson, differs from Speedball in only two respects worth noting: (*a*) a ground ball may be picked up or caught; (*b*) a player may make one basketball dribble before throw-

ing or kicking the ball. A few minor rules differ from those of
Speedball, but they do not change the nature of the game and
there seems to be no good reason for not using the Speedball rules
instead.

5. BASKET SPEEDBALL

This game is a variation of Indoor Speedball. A touchdown cannot be scored by a forward pass, but can be scored by throwing the
ball into the basketball goal. Otherwise, the rules are the same as for
Indoor Speedball.

6. PIN SPEEDBALL
Speed Pinball

In this game the goal is an Indian club standing at the center of
a circle ten feet in diameter. A goal is scored when the ball knocks
the club over. No player may enter the ten-foot circle. The game is
played like Speedball except for the scoring. When played outdoors
a larger target of some kind might be substituted for the Indian club.

Section III: Ball may be thrown or carried

This section, although it includes five or six other games of a minor
nature, is almost entirely concerned with the several games that
may be considered different varieties of Rugby Football, including
the English game of Rugby, and American Football. It is not
accurate to say that the other games are derived from Rugby, but
rather that Rugby and the others are descended from the same
source. Present-day Rugby has undergone a great deal of change
and is by no means the same game that it was when it was first
played in America.

1. RUGBY FOOTBALL

As explained in the introduction to "Football Games" in general,
Rugby may be said to have originated in 1823 when William Webb
Ellis first picked up the ball and ran with it. The fact seems to be,
however, that the exploit of Ellis did not immediately result in a
generally accepted new game, either at Rugby or elsewhere. It was
not until 1839 that any considerable amount of experimenting with
the new idea was done, and the new game was really not developed
to any degree until about 1860, when it was fairly well established
as an intramural sport in several schools. The first attempt at unified

rules was made with the formation of the Rugby Union in 1871 and the first interschool game was played in 1872. The rules have never been perfectly clear or satisfactory, and to this day there is no

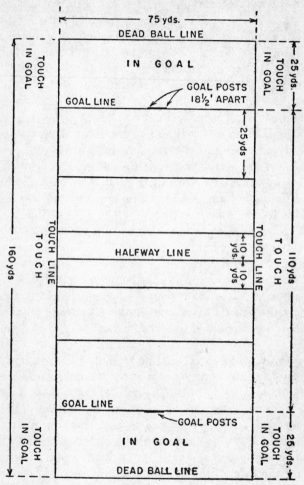

Figure 49. Rugby Football. Plan of field of maximum size.

complete uniformity of rules in England. Since the game was formally adopted as an intercollegiate sport in the United States in 1876, it has had in this country a history almost as long as it has had in England.

The rules of Rugby do not give required dimensions for the field, but rather maximum dimensions; the maximum dimensions are the actual ones for the principal fields on which the most important games are played, the situation being similar to that of basketball courts in this country. The maximum distance between the goal lines is 110 yards, but beyond each goal line is an end zone called *in goal*, which extends a maximum of 25 yards more so that the total length is 160 yards; the end line is the *dead-ball line*. The side lines are called *touch lines* and their distance apart is a maximum of 75 yards. The field is divided by a *half-way line* across the middle and each half has two lines parallel with the goal line, one 10 yards from the half-way line and the other 25 yards from the goal line. Neither of the last-mentioned lines has a very prominent place in the game. The 10-yard line is used only on a kick-off, being a line beyond which the kick must travel and behind which the receiving side is restrained. Thus it has precisely the same effect as the 10-yard line in American Football. The 25-yard line is the one from which the ball is put into play when a touchback occurs.

On each goal line is a pair of goal posts, two uprights 18 feet and 6 inches apart with a cross bar 10 feet above the ground; that is, exactly the same as the posts in the American game. The ball is a prolate spheroid much like the American football but less pointed; it is in fact the ball that was used in the American game until the pointed shape was adopted to favor forward-passing at the expense of kicking.

Play is fairly complicated, and no attempt will be made here to give a complete explanation of it, but only to point out a few of its most important characteristics. The ball may be kicked at any time, and it may always be thrown sideward or backward but never thrown forward. It may be carried in any direction by any player who can get it. There is no such thing as interference; in fact, it is illegal for any player to be ahead of a teammate who is carrying the ball or to be in front of the ball when it is kicked by a teammate. A team consists of fifteen men.

In ordinary play, after the kick-off there are no set formations, and the ball is not declared dead but remains in play as in Soccer or Basketball. This is probably the hardest point for an American to grasp, but it is not too difficult if one understands that when a ball carrier is tackled he must immediately get rid of the ball and the ball remains in play. There is in the game a play called the *scrummage*, which is historically related to our scrimmage; *scrimmage* is a corruption of *skirmish*, and *scrummage* is a variant of *scrimmage*. But as the games are played today the scrimmage and the scrummage have little in common beyond their being set formations. The scrummage is a method of putting the ball into play after certain infractions of the rules, or occasionally in other situations, and is at least roughly analogous to the jump ball in Basketball.

In scoring, the most important play is the "try," really a touchdown. After a try the scoring team attempts to kick the ball over the cross bar exactly as in the American game, and if successful scores two more points. In the early days of the game the touchdown counted no points at all and was important only because it gave the right to "try" to kick a goal and thus score. A drop-kick from the field scores four points. A successful penalty-kick, made after certain infractions by the opponents, counts three. There is also a score of three points for kicking a goal from a "mark," which is a free-kick made after a "fair catch" under certain conditions.

2. AMERICAN FOOTBALL (College Rules)
American Rugby Football. Football. Rugby Football.

The earliest date in the history of American intercollegiate Football is 1869, when Rutgers defeated Princeton by a score of six to four, but the game was Association, not Rugby, Football. Very few other intercollegiate games were played during the next few years, and then in 1875 Harvard met McGill University of Montreal in a game in which apparently one half was played under the Association rules and the other half under the Rugby rules. In the next year Harvard and Yale played under modified Rugby rules, and then in 1876 the game was really established. In this year representatives of Harvard, Yale, Princeton, and Columbia met at Springfield, Massachusetts, organized the American Intercollegiate Football Association, and decided that all games should be played under the rules of the Rugby Football Union of England. In this very first convention an important change was made in the method of scoring, and almost every year since that time the rules have been changed, sometimes fundamentally, so that the game of today is only with difficulty recognized as the direct descendant of the Rugby of 1876. It should be noted that the game had just become established in

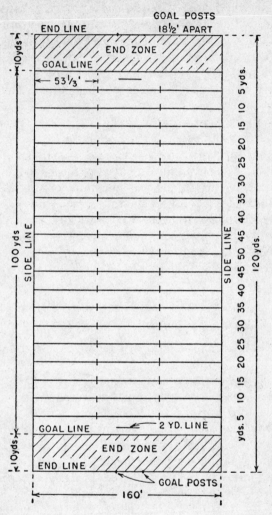

Figure 50. American Football. Field for college or high school play.

England when it was imported in America (the first interschool game in England having been played in 1872), and that in its native country it has undergone fundamental and extensive changes just as it has in America. The fact is, then, that the two countries, starting with the same game in 1876, have developed it independently and in diverse ways, so that now there are two widely different games descended from the same ancestor.

In American colleges and universities Football has become by a very wide margin the most highly developed and intensely cultivated of sports, and in some institutions has become a business enterprise of great magnitude, selling entertainment to the general public. Some stadiums accommodate spectators numbering almost 100,000, and in several schools the income from a single season exceeds $1,000,000. The regular season has been lengthened and "bowl" and other post-season games have become very numerous. The game is not confined to the playing season but extends to practice seasons in the spring and at other times of the year. Various inducements, often secret and questionable, are offered to players, and the subsidizing of players in one way or another is now an accepted practice. The situation is the cause of considerable distress on the part of many people who are interested in the welfare of the colleges.

The game is played by two teams of eleven men each. Each team tries to advance the ball toward the opponents' goal and there to score by one of several methods, and of course to prevent the opponents' doing the same thing. The rules that govern the play are very complex, requiring 48 printed pages for the formal rules and 71 pages for the rules plus official comments and interpretations.

A football field is a rectangle 160 feet wide by 120 yards long, bounded by two end lines and two side lines. Ten yards inside each end line is a goal line; the space bounded by the goal lines and the side lines is called the *field of play*, although this term is somewhat misleading since some play takes place in the *end zones*. The field of play, but not the end zones, is marked at five-yard intervals with lines parallel to the goal lines; thus it is divided into twenty zones, each five yards wide and extending across the field from one side line to the other. A few other marks of a minor nature are also on the field: A broken line is marked 53 feet and 4 inches inside each side line, and the ball is brought to this line when it is dead outside the line; a short line is marked two yards from each goal line for putting the ball into play for the "try" after a touchdown; although not required by rule, the middle of each 40-yard line is

commonly marked to indicate the spot on which the ball is placed
for a kickoff. The lines between the goal lines are numbered from
each goal line and are designated by this number and the name of
the team defending the goal. Thus if "we" are defending the north
goal, the lines, starting from this goal are "our five-yard line," "our
ten-yard line," and so on. Goals identical with those of Rugby
Football are erected in the middle of the end lines, each consisting
of two upright posts 18 feet and 6 inches apart with a horizontal
cross bar 10 feet above the ground. The game really has two different goals, one being the space above the cross bar and between
the uprights, and the other the entire end zone; that is, the space
between the side lines and between the goal and end lines.

The shape of the ball is difficult to describe, and the rules that
formerly called it a *prolate spheroid* now say only that it shall "have
the shape and dimensions shown by the diagram." In any case the
ball is elongated, and a longitudinal cross section is more or less
elliptical; it is considerably more pointed than it was in former
years and than the Rugby ball is now. It consists of an inflated
rubber bladder within a heavy leather casing. Players wear shoes
with blunt cleats of leather or rubber; they wear rather extensive
protective armor of leather, fiber, or rubber under their outer clothing.

The game is played in quarters of 15 minutes each with a 15-
minute rest period between halves and a one-minute rest period
between the quarters of each half. The actual duration of a quarter
is considerably more than 15 minutes because time is frequently
taken out for delays of various sorts. However, the time during which
the ball is actually in play amounts to considerably less than 15
minutes.

At the end of the first quarter, and again at the end of the third
quarter, the teams exchange goals and the ball is moved to the
other end of the field in its same relative position, ready to be put
into play by the team that last had possession of it. At the end of
the second quarter, on the contrary, the position of the ball is of no
consequence, since the third quarter is begun with a kickoff just
as was the first quarter. Thus each half constitutes a single and
complete playing period, except for the short intermission and the
exchange of goals.

Just before the beginning of a game the referee tosses a coin between the two captains and one of them calls "heads" or "tails." The winner of the toss may make either of two decisions: He may decide which goal his team will defend; or he may decide which team is to make the starting kickoff. In either case the other captain makes the remaining decision; for example, if the winner chooses to receive the kickoff, the loser has the choice of goals. At the beginning of the second half there is no coin-toss but the loser of the original toss makes either of the choices and the opposing captain makes the other. A kickoff is also made after a try-for-point following a touchdown or after a field goal, but in such case the team scored upon has its choice of kicking or receiving.

The game begins with a kickoff from the kicking team's 40-yard line. The kick may be a drop kick, but is nearly always a place kick, in which the ball is kicked as it rests on the ground or on a tee not more than one inch high. It may be steadied by a teammate of the kicker holding his hand on top of the ball. All members of the kicker's team must be behind the ball when it is kicked, and all members of the receiving team must be behind the 50-yard line, that is, behind a restraining line ten yards in advance of the ball. In general, a kickoff is "anybody's ball," that is, it may be recovered by any member of either team. This is true in conformity with the off-side principle as found in Soccer and retained in Rugby, and the kickoff is the only play in the American game in which this principle has survived. If a kickoff goes out of bounds between the goal lines without being touched by a receiving player, it is kicked a second time from the same spot as before; if the second kick also goes out of bounds, a rather severe penalty is imposed on the kicking team by giving the ball to the receiving team at the 50-yard line. If the kick goes over the goal line and is recovered in the end zone, the man who recovers it may touch it to the ground and thus make a *touchback*, in which case his team puts the ball into play on its own 20-yard line. In most cases, however, the kick is caught or recovered by one of the receivers and the latter runs with the ball in an attempt to carry it as far as possible toward the opponents' goal. The man with the ball may run in any direction and he may hand or throw it to a teammate at any time, except that he may not throw it forward. The teammates of the runner engage in one of the most important and most distinguishing parts of the game, known as *blocking*. They charge bodily into the men of the kicking team so as to knock them to the ground or otherwise take them out of the play and thus clear the path of the runner. The success of any team depends in very large measure on the effectiveness of its blocking. The members of the kicking team rush down the field with the purpose of eluding the blockers and tackling the runner by grasping him and throwing him to the ground. A runner is down when he touches the ground with any part of the body except hands and feet, when his forward progress is halted while he is in the grasp of an opponent, or when he goes out of bounds.

When the runner is down, play is suspended for a moment. The team that had the ball when it was declared down is now given the ball for a "series of downs." The two teams line up in scrimmage formation. The scrimmage formation is subject to a number of regulations and may vary considerably at the option of the teams, but in general it consists of a row of men on the "line of scrimmage" and other men behind them. There are two lines of scrimmage, one running through each end of the ball so that the two lines of men are separated from each other by at least the length of the ball. The team with the ball is required to have seven men on the line while the defensive team is not restricted in this respect. The men behind the line are called the *backfield* in the case of the offensive team, and the *secondary defense* in the case of the defensive team. One man, the center, bends forward with one or both hands on the ball, and at a time indicated by secret signals passes it backward between his legs and the play is on.

The offensive team tries to advance the ball and ordinarily does so either by running with it or by making a forward pass. In a running play any number of men may handle the ball and it may be handed or thrown from one to another any number of times, provided it is not thrown forward. The ball may be thrown forward from any spot behind the line of scrimmage but may be so thrown only once in any play. Only certain members of the thrower's team have the right to catch a forward pass, and if one of these does catch it, he may then run with it or make a backward pass to a teammate. A forward pass may be "intercepted," that is, caught by an opponent, or it may not be caught by any player, in which case the pass is "incomplete" and is brought back to be put into play from the same spot as before. The team that put the ball into play might lose it by having a pass intercepted or by dropping or "fumbling" it. If it does not lose the ball to the opponents, and if it does not advance it all the way to the goal, the ball is necessarily declared down, when play is again suspended and preparations are made for another scrimmage play by the same team.

The team is expected to advance the ball a total of ten yards in four tries or less and these four tries constitute the "series of downs." Progress of the ball is measured by a chain ten yards long with a vertical stick at each end, this chain being placed at the proper place on one side line. As the first scrimmage play of the game is about to begin the stick at one end of the chain is placed even with the front of the ball and the other stick, at the other end of the stretched chain, just ten yards farther down the field. It is then "first down and ten yards to go." When the first scrimmage play is terminated by the ball's being down—assuming that the same team has the ball—it is then second down, the number of yards to go depending on the success of the first play. If the team advances the ball five yards, it is second down and five yards to go; if they lose two yards, it is 12 yards to go; if they make an incomplete forward pass it is second down and ten yards to go. If the ball is advanced ten yards in less than four downs the remaining down or downs are not played at all, but the chain is moved and a new series of downs is started with "first and ten." A special case arises when the ball is less than ten yards from the goal line; in this case the point to be gained is of course the goal line itself, so that it is then possible to have first down with less than ten yards to go, usually designated simply as "first down and goal to go."

When a team tries four downs and fails to advance the ball ten yards, it loses the ball to the opponents, who begin a series of downs in the opposite direction. When a team has used up three of its four downs without gaining ten yards it will, in most situations, not try the fourth down at all, but instead will "punt" the ball, that is, kick it as far as possible down the field. The logic of the punt is that it is better to give the ball to the opponents in an unfavorable position than to run the risk of giving it to them much nearer the goal. There is a great deal more to the use of the punt than the foregoing statement may suggest, and it has been used by some of the best teams as a powerful offensive weapon.

There are four methods of scoring in American Football: a "touchdown" scores six points, a successful "try-for-point" following a touchdown scores one point, a "field goal" scores three points, and a "safety" scores two points.

A touchdown is scored when the ball is down while legally in the possession of a player behind the opponents' goal line. Nearly always this means that a player carries the ball across the line or that he catches a forward pass while he is over the line. There are, however, infrequent examples of touchdowns scored in other ways. A team might, for example, block a punt by the opponents and recover it in the end zone, or recover a fumble in the end zone, and cases are on record of a team's scoring a touchdown by recovering its own kickoff in the end zone, although the last can hardly happen against a team that knows the rules.

Whenever a team scores a touchdown it immediately makes a try-for-point. In this play the ball is placed on the two-yard line and the two teams line up as for any scrimmage play, the scoring team having the ball. If the team with the ball succeeds in any play whatever, which, according to the usual rules, would score one or more points, the try is successful and the team scores one point for the successful try. The point has been scored from time to time with a touchdown but nearly all teams have now decided that the best chance is with a field goal and the try is nearly always made with this play.

The history of the extra-point play is very interesting. When Rugby Football was established as an intercollegiate sport in the United States in 1876, a touchdown counted no points at all and the only method of scoring was by a field goal. The touchdown was important, nevertheless, because it was rewarded by a relatively easy opportunity to score a field goal; to this day the English term for a touchdown is a "try." In both England and America the rules were changed so as to count points for a touchdown, and in America the score has been changed several times, always so as to increase the relative importance of the touchdown.

A field goal is a drop kick or place kick from which the ball goes over the cross bar of the goal posts between the uprights. A drop kick is made by dropping the ball to the ground and kicking it as it begins its rebound from the ground. A place kick is made by kicking a ball as it is held in position on the ground by a teammate. The field goal, once an important and fascinating part of the game, is now tried infrequently in college games, although it is much more important in professional games. The change is attributed largely to the moving of the goal from the goal line to the end line, but this explanation is not a complete one. When a field goal is tried it is now nearly always a place kick rather than the once popular drop kick, this change probably being due to the change in the shape of the ball.

When the ball is declared dead behind a goal line while in the possession of a defending player, it may be a touchback or it may be a safety, the distinction depending on the source of the impetus that caused the ball to cross the line. If the impetus was given by an attacking player, as by a kick or pass, the play is a touchback and the ball is carried out to the 20-yard line where it is put into play by the defenders, neither team scoring on the play. On the other hand, if the impetus came from the defending team, the play is a safety and scores two points for the opponents. In general, a safety means that a team has been driven back to a point behind its own goal line. For example, a team starts a scrimmage play with the ball only a yard or two from the goal that it is defending. The ball is passed from the center to a backfield man who then has it behind his own goal line; before he can move it out, opponents break through and tackle him.

Players are subject to a great many restrictions on their positions, their motions, their playing of the ball, and especially their contact with opponents, and violations of these restrictions are punished by an elaborate system of penalties. Not counting forfeiture of the game, penalties are of three kinds: loss of a down, loss of distance, and loss of ball.

3. AMERICAN FOOTBALL (High-school Rules)

Some high school games are governed by the NCAA rules, which have been discussed above, even though these rules are made by a strictly collegiate organization and apparently claim no jurisdiction over high school play. The great majority of high school games, however, are played under rules formulated and published by the National Federation of State High School Athletic Associations. The

Federation rules are in the main identical in effect with the college rules, although their wording and organization are quite different. There are numerous minor differences, largely concerned with penalties, but only a few that have any important effect on the play. Of the latter the following are the chief ones:

1. In the case of a fumbled ball, including a backward pass that has touched the ground, the Federation rules permit any player of either team to pick up the ball and advance it, while the college rules permit only a member of the fumbling team to advance the ball, an opponent being allowed to recover the ball but not to advance it.[15]

2. In the high school rules there is no limit to the number of forward passes that may be thrown on one play *from behind the line of scrimmage.* Thus when the ball is passed from one man to another behind the line it makes no difference whether the pass is forward or backward. The college rules state that not more than one forward pass may be made on any play, and that any pass that travels forward, regardless of the place where it begins or ends, is a forward pass.

3. In the case of a kickoff (or other free kick) that goes out of bounds before crossing the goal line, there is no second kick in high school play as there is in college play. Instead, the ball is put into play by the receiving team ten yards behind (nearer its own goal) its restraining line. In college play there is always a second kickoff; if the second one is also out of bounds the ball is put into play by the receivers on their own restraining line, rather than ten yards behind it. In a normal situation, where no foul has been called, the ball is put into play by a scrimmage on the 40-yard line in high schools and the 50-yard line in colleges. In high schools this happens after the first out-of-bounds kick and in colleges only after two such kicks.

---

[15] The *backwar*d (sometimes called *lateral*) *pass* has always been legal and in the original game a fumbled backward pass could be recovered and advanced by any player. In the early 1930's a rule was adopted in both high schools and colleges for the purpose of encouraging the use of the backward pass, the rule providing that a fumbled ball could not be advanced by an opponent of the fumbler. Some people have the notion that this rule introduced the backward pass, but this is decidedly not so. Starting with the season of 1950 the high school rules reversed the action of the 1930's, thus making the rule the same as it was at the beginning of the game.

4. AMERICAN FOOTBALL (Professional Rules)

Football is played in the United States by a number of professional teams organized and administered much after the pattern set by professional baseball. Their rules show minor variations but are in general the same as the college or high school rules, being more like the latter. There is one important and conspicuous exception: In professional play, the goal posts are on the goal line and not on the end line. As a result, field goals are more easily made and hence more important in professional than in amateur games.

5. SIX-MAN FOOTBALL

Six-man Football was devised in 1934 by Stephen Epler, at the time a coach in the Chester, Nebraska, high school. It has become a well-established game and is now played as an interscholastic sport in many high schools and as an intramural sport in colleges. The game was devised to make Football available to groups too small to play the standard game, and accordingly retains as much as possible the nature of the standard game; it is in no sense intended to eliminate some of its essential features, as is Touch Football. For the most part the rules are identical with those of Football and in fact the rules as formulated and printed include only a statement of the respects in which the game is different from the standard game; the standard game may be either the college or the high school game. The essential rules of Six-man Football are as follows:

The field has a width of 40 yards, and a length of 100 yards between end lines or 80 yards between goal lines. The goal posts are 25 feet apart and the upright is nine feet above the ground.

A team consists of six men. On the offensive team, at least three must be on the line. Any man may catch a forward pass.

A kick-off is made from the 30-yard line. After a touchback or safety the ball is played from the 15-yard line.

The distance to be gained in four downs is 15 yards instead of ten.

A forward pass made from behind the line of scrimmage and which does not cross this line is not treated as a forward pass at all but as a backward pass. Thus it is legal for a team to make more than one forward pass on a play provided all but one are of the kind mentioned.

The man who first receives the ball from the center is not per-

mitted to carry it across the line of scrimmage. He is permitted to
kick it or to make a forward pass with it, but unless he does so he
must transfer the ball to a teammate and this transfer must be by a
throw in which the ball is clearly seen to travel through the air; in
other words, the ball must be clearly thrown, and not handed, to
the teammate.

The scoring is different from that in Football, the differences being
such as to encourage scoring by kicks. A field goal counts four and
a successful try for point after touchdown counts two, provided that
the ball is kicked.

A game may be terminated before completion of the four periods
under certain conditions of very unequal scores. The first half is
always completed, but if one team leads by a margin of 45 points
or more the game is terminated at the end of the half. If the second
half is started and, during this half, one team acquires a lead of 45
points or more, the game is terminated immediately.

6. TOUCH FOOTBALL

Touch Football is a development of Football in which there is no
tackling and which is therefore suited to players who are not rugged
enough for Football. It therefore does not require the elaborate protective equipment of this game. Its most distinctive characteristic
is that a ball carrier is downed merely by touching him with the
hands, the usual rule being that he must be touched with both hands
simultaneously. In spite of its being played very widely, the game
has no standardized rules. The NFSHSAA issues rules but they are
intentionally quite indefinite and incomplete. The following rules,
formulated by Professor A. J. Stankowski of the University of
Missouri have been found very successful:

Playing Rules

The variations of the rules for Touch Football from the rules for
regulation collegiate Football are outlined. In all other respects
Touch Football rules are the same as those for college ball.

1. *Field markings* Zoned into strips of 20 yards.
2. *Number of players* Nine players shall constitute a team. On
the offensive, five players must be on the line of scrimmage. A team
may not play with less than seven players.
3. *Equipment of players* Players are prohibited from wearing the

following: any cleated shoes, padded suits, or special protective devices such as shoulder pads, helmets, and so on.

4. Length of game Two periods of 20 minutes each. Ten minutes between periods. Clock stops only on scores and when time out is called by the referee. The referee shall have the right to order the timekeeper to start or stop the watch if in his opinion the offending team is trying to profit by conserving or consuming time.

5. Yards and downs When the ball is first down in a zone, the team in possession of the ball is allowed four downs in which to move it from that point into the next zone.

6. Eligible pass receivers Any member of either team.

7. Fumbles Any time the ball is muffed or fumbled and touches the ground after a lateral pass or kick, or during a run, or a pass from center; the ball is then dead and belongs to the team that muffed the ball at the spot where it touches the ground. After a blocked kick the ball goes to the team that blocked the kick, and is dead at the point of contact with the ground.

A muffed ball striking the ground always belongs to the team last in possession of the ball unless it was fourth down and the team failed to make its necessary yardage.

A ball that becomes dead behind one's goal under this rule is an automatic safety.

8. Touching or tackling A touch (tackle) occurs when an opponent touches the ball carrier with *both hands simultaneously.* The ball shall be declared dead at that point. No part of the toucher's body except his feet shall be in contact with the ground throughout the touch. Penalty for infraction—15 yards.

9. Blocking Blocking shall be permitted on the line of scrimmage as in regulation Football. In the open, no part of the blocker's body except his feet shall be in contact with the ground throughout the block. Penalty for infraction—15 yards.

10. Use of hands Defensive players are restricted in the use of their hands to the shoulders and body of the offensive player. Penalty for infraction—15 yards.

11. On the so-called *sleeper play,* the intended receiver must be 15 yards in from the side lines and on his feet when the ball is snapped.

12. In games deciding divisional, fraternity, independent, or

school championship, two ten-minute extra periods will be played
in case of tie games. If the score is still tied at the end of the extra
periods, the team with deepest penetration other than a score wins.
(Two extra time-outs for each team in extra period).

13. *Penalty* For unnecessary roughness in *touching* or *blocking* a
player—15 yards.

14. *Penalty* For *diving* or *leaving feet* in attempt to recover a
fumbled or muffed ball—15 yards.

Division Three: Stick-and-Ball Games

The stick-and-ball games are, of course, goal games in which a ball
is advanced by the use of a stick or club. This division includes
four major games—Field Hockey, Ice Hockey, Polo, and Lacrosse—
and a few minor ones that are similar to them. Lacrosse uses a
stick with a net in which the ball may be caught and then thrown
or carried, but all other games of the division require that the ball
be struck or pushed with the stick. Ice Hockey is played with a
disk-shaped puck, which can hardly be called a ball, but it is no
different in principle from the other games. The games are in two
sections: those in which the players travel on foot, and those in which
they travel on a horse or a vehicle.

Section I: Player travels on foot

1. LACROSSE

The word *lacrosse* was, of course, the French *la crosse* in which *la*
is the definite article. The word *crosse* has nothing to do with the
English word *cross*, for which the French is *la croix*, but refers
rather to a crosier (or crozier), the ornamental staff that is the
ensign of office of a bishop, and which is shaped not at all like a
cross but more like a shepherd's crook. The modern game is derived
from one played for centuries by Iroquois Indians known as *bagat-
away* or *baggataway*, in what is now upper New York and lower
Ontario. About 1840, the game was adopted by French Canadians
and named by them *lacrosse* on account of the resemblance of the
curved and netted stick with which it was played to a bishop's
crosier. It is now a major summer game in Canada and is played
intensively in parts of northestern United States, but has never be-

come widespread in this country. A number of colleges and universities engage in intercollegiate competition in the sport. It is played to some extent in a number of other countries and has had a place in the Olympic Games.

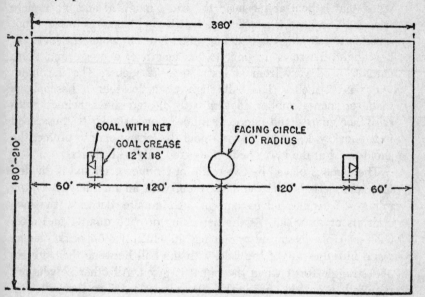

Figure 51. Lacrosse. Plan of field. N.C.A.A. rules.

The field is from 60 to 70 yards wide and 110 yards long, but the goals are 15 yards inside the end lines and thus only 80 yards apart. Each goal is six feet square and formed by two uprights and a cross bar which is six feet above the ground. The goal is fitted with a netting attached to the entire length of the uprights and cross bar that extends backward to a single point seven feet to the rear, thus forming a horizontal pyramid. It is in the center of a rectangle marked on the ground, called the *goal crease*, the dimensions of which are 18 feet from side to side and 12 feet from end to end of the field. Since the goal is six feet wide and of negligible depth, it is six feet from the crease in every direction. A line parallel with the end lines divides the field in halves, and a 20-yard circle is marked in the center of the field. Each player has a "crosse," which may possibly suggest a racket but which is an entirely different kind of implement. The framework of the crosse is made of a single piece of wood that is bent at the head to form a modified and incomplete triangle. The head is loosely laced with rawhide so as to form, not a racket for striking the ball, but rather a net in which the ball may be caught. There is no limit to the length of a crosse and those actually used vary from at least 30 to 72 inches. The maximum width is 12 inches. The ball, slightly smaller than a baseball, is made of sponge rubber. Players wear cleated shoes, helmets with wire face guards, and padded gauntlet gloves similar to those used in ice hockey. Light pads worn under the jersey serve to protect the shoulders, but the lower body is covered only with shorts.

The game is played by two teams of ten men each and is divided into four periods of 15 minutes each, with an intermission of ten minutes between halves and of one minute between the two quarters of each half. At the beginning of each quarter and after each goal, play is started by "facing," in which two opposing players stand in the center of the field with the ball between their crosses and struggle for it when the signal is given. All other players are required to remain outside the 20-yard circle. When the ball is in play as a result of the facing, any player may catch it in his crosse and then run with it at will or throw it to a teammate. An opponent may charge a player who has the ball or who is about to catch it, but may not interfere with other players. Also, an opponent may attempt to dislodge the ball by striking with his own the crosse that holds the ball. The ball may be kicked at any time, although kicking is not an important part of the game, but it may never be touched with the hands except by the goalkeeper. An attacking player is not allowed inside the goal crease, and, accordingly, all goals must be made by throws from outside the crease.

Each team is required at all times to have at least four men in the defensive half of the field and at least three in the offensive half, not always the same men. The remaining three may be in either half.

Infractions of the rules are classed as technical and personal fouls, and the penalty may be a free throw by the opponents, or suspension of the offender from the game. The suspension system is essentially the same as the one used in Ice Hockey; under it a player may be kept out of the game for a period of from one to three minutes and his team required to play without him for this period.

In the case of a tie game, play is continued for ten minutes with an exchange of goals after five minutes. If the score is still tied after the ten-minute overtime, it remains a tie and no more is played.

Modified rules for play by women are published by the National Section on Women's Athletics. These rules vary somewhat from the standard ones with respect to restrictions on players, but the only fundamental difference is that 12 players instead of ten constitute a team under the women's rules.

2. FIELD HOCKEY

The word *hockey* is probably derived from the Old French word *hoquet*, a shepherd's crook, and is related to the work *hook*. Originally, and to some extent still, the word referred to the stick with which the game is played.

Some form of game in which a ball is struck with a stick was undoubtedly played in ancient times in various places, but it was about 1875, in England, that a game that can be identified with modern Field Hockey was first played. The game developed rapidly, and in 1876 the English Hockey Association was founded and definite rules formulated. The game has become very popular in Great Britain, where it is widely played by men and women. It is played in a number of other countries, and the statement has been made that it is played more extensively in India than in any other country including England. In the United States it is a major game for women, but for some reason is almost never played by men. Play in the United States is governed by rules formulated by the National Section on Women's Athletics, of the AAHPER. These rules are the basis of the following description.

The field is 100 yards long and from 55 to 60 yards wide. In the middle of each end line is a goal four yards wide and seven feet high with a box-like netting behind it. Three lines are marked parallel with the goal lines, one in the middle of the field and one twenty-five yards from each goal line. A restraining line is marked parallel with each side line and five yards inside it. At each goal a so-called *striking circle* is formed thus: two quarter-circles are marked on the field, each with the base of one goal post as the center, and the two quarter-circles are joined by a straight line that is necessarily four yards long. Each player has a stick with a straight handle and a curved head. The head is round on the right side and flat on the

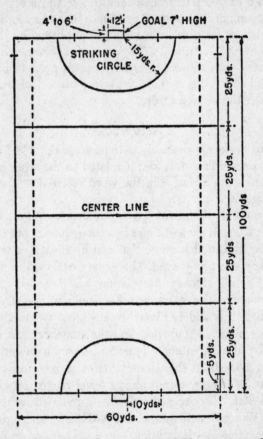

Figure 52. Field Hockey. Layout of field. N.S.W.A. rules.

left and the ball must be struck with the flat side, so that left-hand clubs or left-hand play is prohibited. The ball is much like a base-ball, having a circumference a quarter-inch smaller and a weight a half-ounce greater.

The game is played by two teams of 11 each. Players are designated as five forwards, three halfbacks, two fullbacks and one goal-keeper, but they are not restricted to any particular part of the field. A game consists of two periods of 30 minutes each and there is no overtime play in case of a tied score.

The game is started by two opponents' "bullying" the ball in the center of the field. The ball is placed on the ground and the two players stand with the ball between them, each in position to drive the ball toward the other's goal. Then in unison the two strike the ground with their sticks, strike the two sticks together, strike the ground again, and so on until they have struck the ground and the sticks three times. After the third striking of the sticks they struggle for the ball and it is in play. The object of play is, of course, to drive the ball down the field and into the opponents' goal. This is done chiefly by striking or pushing the ball with the stick, but it is legal for a player to catch the ball or stop it with any part of his body provided he drops it immediately and does not throw it. One player, designated as the goalkeeper, is permitted to kick the ball while he is within his own striking circle. It is illegal to strike, hook, lift, hold, or interfere with an opponent's stick. A very important rule is that a goal cannot be made by a shot from outside the striking circle, or more precisely, that a goal does not count unless the ball is touched by an attacking player inside the circle.

The off-side rules is almost identical with that of Soccer; that is, a player is off-side if, when the ball was last played by a teammate, the player was in front of the ball, and an off-side player may not play the ball unless he is in his own half of the field or unless there are three or more opponents (two in Soccer) between him and the goal line. It is a foul for a player to raise his stick above the shoulders in playing the ball. There are various other fouls for violating rules on playing the ball or on contact with opponents.

When the ball crosses a side line it is rolled in by an opponent of the one who last touched it; all other players are restrained by the five-yard line. When the ball crosses the goal line without going into the goal there are two possibilities: (*a*) If it was driven out by an attacking player, or by a defensive player from beyond the 25-yard line, it is taken straight in to the 25-yard line and there bullied. (*b*) If it was driven out by a defensive player inside the 25-yard line, one of the opponents puts it into play with a "corner hit." (This assumes that the ball was driven out unintentionally; if it was intentionally it is treated as a foul.) To make a corner hit the player hits the ball from a point within five yards of the nearest corner. Of the defending team six players must be behind the goal line and the others beyond the nearer twenty-five yard line.

The penalties for fouls distinguish between one made by a defender within the striking circle and one made elsewhere, being more severe for the former. If a foul is committed outside the striking circle, the penalty is a free hit at the spot of the foul with all opponents at least five yards from the ball. If a foul is committed by an attacking player within the striking circle, the penalty is substantially, but not exactly, the same: a free hit from any desired spot within the striking circle with all opponents outside the circle. If a foul is committed by a defender within the striking circle the penalty is a "penalty corner," a term that is somewhat misleading since the play is not made from the corner at all. To make a penalty corner, any player of the offended team takes a free hit from any desired spot on the goal line, except that the spot must be not less than ten yards from the nearest goal post; all teammates of the hitter must be on the field of play outside the striking circle, and the defenders are restricted as for a corner hit. After the ball is hit it cannot be played again by the original hitter until it is played by some other player, and a goal cannot be scored directly from a penalty corner. A special case is made of a wilful violation of the rules or one that probably prevents a goal from being scored. In this case, the punishment is a "penalty bully." The offending player and any one selected from the opposing team bully the ball as at the beginning of the game, the bully taking place five yards from the goal. All other players of both teams must remain on the field of play beyond the 25-yard line until the bully is completed. If the bully results in the ball's going over the goal line without scoring, off the stick of the offender, the bully is played again.

3. SIX-MAN FIELD-HOCKEY
Six Hockey. Six-player Field-Hockey.

Field Hockey, like several other major games, has recently been adapted for play by teams smaller than the standard ones. Only a few changes need be made from the standard rules, and these are fairly obvious. The game, although not well standardized, has been studied and tried out to a considerable extent.[15]

4. SHINNY
Shinney

Shinny is simply informal Field Hockey, played with any available crooked sticks and with a battered tin can, a block of wood, or other improvised substitute for a ball. There is no off-side rule, but each player must "shinny on his own side," that is he must always play with his left side toward the goal that he is attacking, as right-handed players usually do. Shinny is not by any means a recent simplification of Field Hockey, but on the contrary the game and the name are both quite ancient.

5. BROOM FIELD-HOCKEY
Broom Hockey

This game is improvised Field Hockey played with an inflated rubber ball five or six inches in diameter, and with ordinary house brooms. A codeball, which is six inches in diameter, is quite satisfactory, but any other ball of similar size will do as well. Old brooms should be used and the handles should be sawed off to make the entire broom about 30 inches long.

6. RING HOCKEY
Deck Hockey

Each player has an ordinary gymnasium wand or similar stick. Instead of a ball a Deck Tennis quoit or rope ring is used. The game is played indoors on a smooth wooden floor with Field Hockey rules, simplified to meet the conditions present.

7. BAR-BELL HOCKEY
Bar-bell Polo. Stick Polo.

This game is played with a basketball and with wooden gymnastic bar bells; if bar bells are not available other sticks will do, but bar

---

[15] Taylor, Maurie, "Six-Hockey for the Small School," *Journal of Health and Physical Education*, October, 1940, Vol XI, page 484; Rahl, Katherine M., "Recent Developments in Six-Player Field Hockey," *Journal of Health and Physical Education*, October, 1941, Vol. XII, page 474.

bells are best. The game is played according to field-hockey rules, simplified as much as desired or necessary.

Section II: Player travels on a horse or vehicle

This small section includes the major games of Polo and Ice Hockey and also a very few minor games based on these two. The word *vehicle* is used so as to include ice and roller skates, wheelbarrows, and even canoes. The idea of these games could easily be adapted to other vehicles not mentioned here.

1. POLO

The word *polo* is of Asiatic origin, probably derived from the Tibetan *pulu*, a ball. Great antiquity is often claimed for the game but without very much in the way of evidence and, as with so many other games, without any definition of terms. Certainly the game as now known is the modern form of one played by British army officers in India in the 1860's and carried by them to England in 1869. The game was undoubtedly suggested by activities of Tibetan horsemen, but that these activities constituted the game of Polo is at least doubtful. The game was played under uncertain and confused rules until 1874 when the Hurlingham Club drew up a set of rules that were generally accepted. The Hurlingham rules as changed from time to time are still accepted as official everywhere except in the United States where the United States Polo Association is the governing body. At present the two sets of rules are almost identical except for a difference in the playing periods.

Polo is played by two teams of four men each, who ride horses and strike a wooden ball with a long-handled mallet in an attempt to drive it into a goal. The horses used in the best play are especially bred for the purpose and are very expensive. A player does not use the same horse throughout a match but requires about four. It is obvious, then, that the game is one for wealthy men and is in no sense a game of the people.

A polo field is extremely large—300 yards long by 160 yards wide. It is surrounded by a low board fence 11 inches high. The goal line (or end line) is marked by two uprights 24 feet apart and 10 feet high, the goal being the space between the uprights and of indefinite height. The ball is made of wood, usually willow, and painted white. It has a diameter of 3 1/4 inches and a weight of from 4¼ to 4¾ ounces. The mallet has a bamboo shaft about 50 inches long and a wooden head set at an angle. The ball is struck with the side of the mallet, not with the face as in Croquet. Each man wears a helmet for protection.

There is no restriction on the size of the horses used in the game. Formerly only relatively small horses were permitted and hence were commonly called *polo ponies*. In 1919 all restrictions were removed.

The principles of play are very simple: Each team tries to drive the ball into the opponents' goal by striking it with the mallets. However, there is the inevitable set of restrictions on the activity of players, and a complicated and highly subjective set of penalties for infractions of the rules. The most important rule of play is that a player who has just hit the ball has the right of way in following it, and an opponent who cuts in ahead of him is guilty of a foul. Penalties are graded and include the awarding of an automatic goal, disqualification of a player, and free hits from various distances.

The game is played in periods called *chukkers*. In England there are seven chukkers of eight minutes each, but in the United States eight chukkers of seven and one-half minutes each.

Most Polo games, except those in international competition, are played with a system of handicapping. Each player has a handicap rating in terms of goals, ranging from one goal to ten. When two teams meet, the handicaps of the players of each team are added to make a team total, and the team with the lower handicap is given the difference as a score with which to start the game.

Polo is sometimes played indoors and necessarily, of course, on a court smaller than the outdoor field. Rules for indoor play are modified in various ways, but usually provide for teams of three and for play with an inflated rubber ball.

2. ICE HOCKEY

Ice Hockey was originated in Canada during the 1870's and is now the national winter sport in that country. It is a major game in certain parts of the United States where it is well developed as an intercollegiate sport, enthusiastically patronized when played by professionals, and played informally by innumerable teams and groups. It is a goal game played on ice by skaters, who propel a disk-shaped object (puck) with flat-bladed curved sticks. In details of play the game apparently has borrowed elements from Field Hockey, Lacrosse, and Soccer or Rugby Football. In the United States there are two recognized sets of rules, professional and intercollegiate, but the two differ only slightly. The following discussion

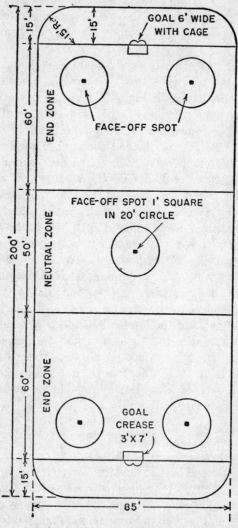

Figure 53. Ice Hockey Rink of recommended size. N.C.A.A. rules.

is based on the college rules, formulated by the National Collegiate Athletic Association.

The ice surface on which the game is played is called a *rink*. The rink may be outdoors but usually an indoor rink with artificial ice is used. The recommended dimensions are 200 by 85 feet but many rinks are smaller, and a few larger, than this. The corners are not square, but are quarter-circles with a radius of 15 feet. The rink is completely surrounded by a solid board wall or fence, which must be at least three feet high and is usually somewhat higher. The puck is played as it rebounds from this wall and, accordingly, is never out-of-bounds except when it goes over the top of the wall. The goal is a vertical rectangle six feet wide and four feet high, with a net or cage behind it. The goal is not located on the end line but at least ten, and preferably 15, feet inside this line. Two lines parallel with the end lines divide the rink into three zones, a neutral zone in the middle, and two end zones, each end zone being the defensive zone for one team and the attacking zone for the other. Each of the two lines that mark the zones is 60 feet from the nearer goal line, so that the end zones, when measured to the goal lines are always of the same size; however, the neutral zone is variable, its width depending on the size of the rink. Five *face-off* marks are located on the rink, each being a one-foot square surrounded by a 20-foot circle. In front of each goal is a *goal crease,* seven by three feet, the crease being only one foot wider than the goal and extending three feet inward from the goal line.

The *puck* is a disk of vulcanized rubber one inch thick and three inches in diameter. Each player carries a curved wooden stick with a flat blade, the maximum length of the stick being 55 inches, and the maximum width of the blade three inches; the goalkeeper's stick may be a half-inch wider. All players wear heavy gloves and headguards. The goalkeeper wears extra protective equipment, including leg pads, which may be ten inches wide; his equipment is not entirely for protection but serves also as a means of blocking the puck.

The game is played by two teams of six men each; the players are known as goalkeeper, right defense, left defense, center, right wing, and left wing. It is played in three periods of twenty minutes each, with ten-minute intermissions, thus showing an interesting deviation from the almost universal two-period or four-period system

used in other games that are played by time. If the score is tied at the
end of the third period, play is resumed after a ten-minute intermission and continued for a maximum of ten minutes. If either team
scores during the overtime period, that team is the winner and the
game is terminated at once; this is the so-called *sudden-death* system.
If neither team scores during the overtime period, the game ends
with a tied score. Each goal scores one point.

At the beginning of each of the three periods and after each score,
play is begun with a *face-off*, a play very similar to the center-jump
of basketball. Two opposing players stand about a club's length
apart at the center of the rink, each with body and feet squarely
facing the opponents' goal and with the blade of his stick resting
on the ice. Every other player must remain, until the puck is in
play, at least ten feet from the puck and in his defensive half of the
rink. An official holds the puck at knee height and drops (not
throws) it to the ice between the two players at the center. The
players must allow the puck to strike the ice before touching it and
then they fight for it and the game is on. The face-off is used on
numerous occasions throughout the game, since it is the method by
which play is resumed after it has been stopped for any reason. The
play is frequently, but by no means always, made from one of the
five face-off spots, or special spots.

For the most part the puck is played with the stick, and the usual
method is by sliding it along the ice in a dribble or a pass to a
teammate. However, the puck may be lifted with the stick and
thrown; in fact nearly all goals are scored in this way. Also, the
puck may be played with the stick while it is traveling through the
air, provided it is not higher than two feet above the ice. It is a foul
to play it at a greater height, and it is also a foul to hold the stick
at a height greater than four feet even without playing the puck.
The use of the so-called *kick-shot* is prohibited and penalized very
severely; in this shot the puck is driven by kicking the shaft or blade
of the stick. The puck may be played with a skate, and it may be
stopped, either on or off the ice, with the hand or any other part of
the body, but it may not be thus held or carried. The goalkeeper, so
long as he is within a certain area surrounding the goal, has special
privileges in playing the puck. He may play it with feet or stick
without restriction; he may "trap" it to prevent a score; and he may
catch and throw it provided he does not throw it forward,

When a player shoots the puck from his own defensive zone so that it travels across the other two zones and over the goal line, he is said to have *iced the puck*. This play is legal when, as a result of a penalty, the player's team has fewer men on the ice than the opponents, and it is legal if any player of either team has a reasonable chance to play the puck; otherwise the play is assumed to have been made for the purpose of stalling and is a foul.

Ice Hockey has three different rules that restrict the positions in which men may play, and that, accordingly, correspond more or less to the off-side rules of Soccer Football and some other games. These three are the *anti-defense* rule, the *goal-crease* rule, and the *zone-play* rule. The anti-defense rule states that, with certain special exceptions, not more than three teammates may be in their own defensive zone unless the puck is also in that zone. If the puck is in the zone and leaves it, no foul is committed provided all but three defensive players leave the zone immediately. The goal-crease rule is intended to prevent the crowding of attacking men at the goal. This rule states that no member of the attacking team may be in the goal-crease (the three by seven foot area immediately in front of the goal) while the puck is outside the crease, and also that he may not be in the crease while a goal is scored by a teammate from outside the crease. Any attacking player may enter the crease only when the puck is already there or while the puck is in his possession. This rule is effective only when the defensive goal-keeper is in the crease and does not apply at all when the goalkeeper is outside the crease. The zone-play rule is probably an adaptation of the off-side rule of Soccer and is the same in principle although quite different in detail. Under this rule any player is always free to play the puck when it was last played by an opponent or when he is in his own defensive zone or the neutral zone; in his attacking zone he may play the puck only under certain conditions. Unless it was last played by an opponent he may play the puck in his attacking zone only if: (a) he himself took the puck into the attacking zone, or (b) the puck preceded him into the attacking zone.

The regulations that govern contact with opponents are quite complicated and can only be hinted at here. A considerable amount of body contact is legal, but the amount varies with the situation; generally the player in possession of the puck may be treated more roughly than another player. It is never legal to block out an op-

ponent in order to help a teammate, that is, to give interference
in the American-Football sense. Various kinds of rough play are
specifically prohibited, and "cross-checking," or holding the stick
against an opponent, is illegal.

The system of penalties is quite different from that of most well-
known American games. Not counting forfeiture of the match and
disqualification of a player, there are three different types of penalty: *face-off*, *penalty shot*, and *time penalty*. For violation of the
icing rule or the anti-defense rule, or for defensive stalling or intentional off-side, the penalty is merely a face-off at one of the special
spots. The penalty shot, which might be expected to be the usual
penalty, is in fact used for only a few offenses and in nearly all cases
is in addition to, rather than in place of, a time penalty. In a penalty
shot only two players, the shooter and the opposing goalkeeper, are
involved. The shooter starts at the zone line with the goalkeeper in
the crease; he must take the puck and skate with it continuously
toward the goal, where he makes one attempt to score against the
opposition of the goalkeeper. A goal made in this way counts one
point, the same as any other goal. Two complications should be
noted here: first, if a foul that calls for a penalty shot is made in an
attempt to prevent a score but the score is made in spite of the foul,
the penalty shot is not taken; second, when a foul calls for both a
penalty shot and a minor time penalty, and the penalty shot is
successful, the time penalty is canceled.

The distinctive and most common penalty in Ice Hockey is the
time penalty. When such a penalty is imposed the offending player,
or in certain cases any player selected by his captain, must leave
the game and sit on the *penalty bench* for a designated period of
time, his team playing meanwhile with a reduced number of players. Time penalties are of three classes: minor, major, and misconduct, and are imposed for two, five, and ten minutes respectively.
The misconduct penalty is imposed for use of the kick-shot, interference with a penalty shot, and directing abuse or disrespect at an
official. The major time penalty is imposed chiefly for a foul against
the goalkeeper while he is in his crease, or for flagrant or injurious
roughness. A special and interesting case of the time penalty is one
imposed upon a team for not being ready to play at the beginning
of any period. The team at fault is required to play without one of
its members for a time equal to that by which it was late.

Ice Hockey uses the system of the *delayed whistle*. Under this system, when a foul is committed by a member of the team not in possession of the puck, the official raises his arm above his head but does not stop the play "until it is apparent that the stopping of the playing will not be a disadvantage to the attacking team."

3. BROOM ICE-HOCKEY

This game is informal Ice Hockey played by skaters who use brooms instead of hockey sticks. A tin can is sometimes used in place of the puck but a fairly large ball is better, even one as large as a soccer ball. The rules are of course simplified as desired.

4. ROLLER-SKATE HOCKEY
Roller Polo. Roller Shinny.

Using simplified Ice-Hockey rules, players on roller skates play with real or improvised hockey sticks and an ice-hockey puck or block of wood.

5. WHEELBARROW POLO

This very informal game requires several wheelbarrows, at least three for each team. Each wheelbarrow has a rider with a stick, and a pusher. Any type of stick may be used, and the puck should be a ball of about the same size as a soccer ball.

6. CANOE HOCKEY
Canoe Polo.

Each team has one or more canoes; one will work but several are better. Each canoe holds one or more paddlers and one or more men each carrying a ten-foot pole. A large ball, preferably a 30-inch cageball, floats on the water and each team tries to push this ball with the poles to the opponents' goal.

Advancing Statues (*See* Silent Statues, 180; Statues, 180)

Aerial Dart (*See* Paddle Badminton, 266)

Aerial Tennis-Dart (*See* Paddle Badminton, 266)

Affinity Tag (*See* Foot-to-Foot Tag, 19)

All Across, 40

All Change, 95

All-fours Jump-the-Shot, 165

All Run, 127 (*See also* Spud, 128)

All Throw, 235

Alphabet, 173

American Football—College Rules, 387

American Football—High-school Rules, 395

American Football—Professional Rules, 397

American Rugby Football (*See* American Football, 387)

Animal Cage, 30

Animal Chase, 45

Ankle Tag, 19

Ante-Over, 130 (*See also* Curtain Newcomb, 251)

Antony-Over (*See* Ante-Over, 130)

Archery Golf, 202

Arithmetical Catch-the-Cane, 163

Around-the-World, 224

Association Football (*See* Soccer Football, 373)

Attention (*See* Elimination Drill, 175)

Austin Boston (*See* Trades, 59)

Automobile Tag (*See* Hoop Tag, 134)

Babylonian (*See* Line Soccer, 380)

Back-to-Back, 97

Back-to-Back Tag, 19

Badminton, 262

Ball Chase (*See* Cap Tag, 79)

Ball-in-Cap (*See* Cap Tag, 79)

Balloon Basketball (*See* Balloon Hockey, 352)

Balloon Battle, 142

Balloon Battle—Team Form, 142

Balloon Battle-Royal (*See* Balloon Battle, 142)

Balloon Goal, 352

Balloon Hockey, 352

Balloon Keepball, 238

Balloon Pushball (*See* Balloon Hockey, 352)

Balloon Volleyball, 259

Ball Puss, 126

Ball Puss-in-the-Corner (*See* Off-the-Spot, 126)

Ball Snatch, 57

Ball Stand (*See* Spud, 128)

Ball Tag, 133 (*See also* Circle Touchball, 236)

Bar-bell Hockey, 407

Bar-bell Polo (*See* Bar-bell Hockey, 407)

Barley Break, 71

Barnyard Battle-Royal (*See* Duck Fight, 144)

Baseball, 298

Baseball on Skates (*See* Skating Baseball, 323)

Baseball Overtake (*See* Beatball, 320)

Baseball Twenty-One (*See* Twenty-One Baseball, 320)

Base-line Push, 153

Base-line Tug, 153

Base-line Tug—Variation, 153

Base-to-Base Ball (*See* Beatball, 320)

Basketball, 353

Basketball—Canadian Rules for Women, 362

Basketball—NSWA Rules for Women, 360

Basketball—Rules for High-school Boys, 358

Basketball Golf, 222

Basketball Twenty-One (*See* Twenty-One, 224)

Basket Cageball, 367

Basket Captainball, 243

Basket Hand-Hockey, 351

Basket Speedball, 384

Basket Three-Deep (*See* Animal Cage, 30)

Baste-the-Bear, 72

Batball, 327 (*See also* Hand Batball, 328; Volley Batball, 329)

Battering Ram (*See* Break-the-Ring—Partner Form, 138)

Batting Drive, 248

Battleball, 119 (*See also* Medicine Catchball, 235)

Battleboard Tennis, 295

Battle of Legs (*See* Leg Fight—Team Form, 144)

Battle Royal, 151

Beanbag Scramble, 245

Beanbags-Over-the-Head (*See* Beanbag Scramble, 245)

Bear and Keeper (*See* Baste-the-Bear, 72)

Bear Battle (*See* Rooster Fight, 143)

Bear Hunt, 107

Bear-in-the-Pit, 139

Bears and Bulls, 63

Bears and Cattle (*See* Chain Pom-Pom-Pullaway, 42)

Beatball, 320

Beater Goes Round (*See* Swat to Right, 103)

Beat-the-Beater (*See* Swat to Right, 103)

Beat-the-Beetle (*See* Swat to Right, 103)

Belled Cat, The (*See* Blind Bell, 83)

Bell-the-Cat (*See* Blind Bell, 83)

Big Black Bear (*See* Shepherd and Wolf, 53)

Index

Birds Fly, 178

Black and Blue, 64

Black and Red (See Black and White, 61)

Black and White, 61 (See also Stooping Heads-and-Tails, 85)

Black Man, 41 (See also Who's Afraid of the Black Man?,49)

Black Tom, 44

Blind Bell, 83

Blind Hop-Tag, 80

Blind Line-Tag, 81

Blindman's Buff, 82

Blindman's Number-Change (See Blind Numbers-Change, 84)

Blindman's Ten-Steps (See Blind Ten-Steps, 82)

Blind Medicine-ball Newcomb, 251

Blind Medicine-ball Tennis (See Blind Medicine-ball Newcomb, 251)

Blind Numbers-Change, 84

Blind Partner-Tag, 81

Blind Ten-Steps, 82

Block Horseshoes, 207

Blue and White (See Black and White, 61; Stooping Heads-and-Tails, 85)

Boat Whale—Aquatic, 148

Bob (See Tip-Cat, 326)

Bodyguard (See Bodyguard Tag, 23)

Bodyguard Tag, 23

Bogey Man, 41

Boiler Burst, The, 52 (See also The Car Was Wrecked, 97)

Boloball (See Hand Hockey, 351)

Bombardment, 338 (See also Battleball, 119)

Booting the Circle (See Kick Circle, 348)

Boot-the-Pin (See Kick Pin-Guard—Team Form, 346)

Boston, 84 (See also Change Right or Left, 96)

Bounceball, 260

Bounce Basketball, 364

Bounce Dodgeball (See One-man Dodgeball, 115)

Bounce Volleyball, 260

Bouncing Line-Guard, 341

Boundary Tag, 9

Bound Hands (See Chain Pom-Pom-Pullaway, 42)

Bowl Beatball (See Beatball, 320)

Bowl Clubball (See Pin Batball, 329)

Bowling, 184

Bowling in the Gymnasium (See Improvised Duckpins, 190)

Bowling on the Green (See Lawn Bowling, 207)

Bowls (See Lawn Bowling, 207)

Break-the-Ring, 138

Break-the-Ring—Partner Form, 138

Break-the-Ring—Team Form, 138

Broncho (See Broncho Three-Deep, 30)

Broncho Busting, 147

Broncho Four-Deep, 31

Broncho Tag, 21 (See also Broncho Three-Deep, 30; Tandem Tag, 22)

Broncho Three-Deep, 30

Broncho Three-Deep on Skates, 31

Broom Field-Hockey, 407

Broom Hockey (See Broom Field-Hockey, 407; Broom Ice-Hockey, 415)

Broom Ice-Hockey, 415

Brothers, 108

Buccaneer—Aquatic, 154

Buck, 182

Bucketball, 326

Bucket Basketball, 365

Bucket Cricket (See Bucketball, 326)

Bucking Broncho (See Bronchoo Busting, 147)

Bull-in-the-Ring, 138

Bull-in-the-Ring—Partner Form, 139

By the Numbers Change (See Numbers Change, 98)

Cabinetball (See Medicine-ball Newcomb, 251)

Cageball, 366

Cageball Circle-Touch, 237

Cageball Pursuit-Relay, 33

Cage Basketball (See Basket Cageball, 367)

Callball, 233

Call Dodgeball, 114

Can Cricket, 336

Candlepins, 188

Canoe Hockey, 415

Canoe Polo (See Canoe Hockey, 415)

Canoe Tag—Aquatic, 134

Cap Chase (See Cap Tag, 79)

Cap-roll Ball (See Roly Poly, 131)

Cap Rush (See Object Rush, 92)

Cap Scramble, 108

Cap Tag, 79 (See also Giveaway Tag, 23)

Captainball, 240 (See also Centerball, 242)

Captain Basketball (See Basket Captainball, 243)

Carpet Bowls (See Improvised Lawn-Bowling, 213)

Carry to Base (See Base-line Tug, 153)

Car Was Wrecked, The, 97

Cat and Mice, 50

Cat and Mouse (See Cat and Rat, 68)

Cat and Rat, 68

Catball, 337

Catch-a-Fish (See Fish Net, 46)

Catch-and-Pull Tug-of-War (See Ditch Tug, 152)

Catch-and-Run Ball (See Spud, 128)

Catch-and-Throw (*See* Tackling Pom-Pom-Pullaway, 42)

Catchball, 250 (*See also* Callball, 233; Number Scrambleball, 245)

Catching Spud (*See* Spud, 128)

Catch Numberball (*See* Callball, 233)

Catch-of-Fish (*See* Fish Net, 46)

Catch-the-Balloon, 164

Catch-the-Balloon—Team Form, 164

Catch-the-Caboose, 21 (*See also* Broncho Tag, 21)

Catch-the-Cane, 162

Catch-the-Cane—Team Form, 163

Catch-the-Snake 20

Catch-the-Staff (*See* Catch-the-Cane, 162)

Catch-the-Stick (*See* Catch-the-Cane, 162)

Cat Tail (*See* Wheel Pursuit Race, 33)

Cavaliers' Combat (*See* Knights' Combat, 145)

Centerball, 242

Center Base, 78

Center Catchball (*See* Circle Touchball, 236)

Center Dodgeball (*See* One-man Dodgeball, 115)

Center Strideball (*See* Circle Strideball, 343)

Center Touchball (*See* Circle Touchball, 236)

Centipede, 104

Centipede Overtake-Race (*See* Centipede Pursuit-Race, 32)

Centipede Pursuit-Race, 32

Chain Break, 141

Chain Dodgeball, 118 (*See also* Train Dodgeball, 116)

Chain Pom-Pom-Pullaway, 42

Chain Tag, 36

Chair Scramble, 100

Chair Tag, 27

Change All (*See* All Change, 95)

Change Places (*See* Blind-Numbers-Change, 84)

Change Right or Left, 96

Channelball (*See* Channel Touchball, 237)

Channel Tag (*See* Channel Touchball, 237)

Channel Touchball, 237

Charley-Over-the-Water, 87

Chaseball, 379

Chase-the-Chaser Tag, 25

Chicken Hops (*See* Hop-the-Blocks, 169)

Chinese Chicken (*See* Hop-the-Blocks, 169)

Chinese Wall, 41

Chips (*See* Stealing Sticks, 73)

Circleball (*See* Circle Touchball, 236)

Circle Ball-Bounce (*See* Circle Bounceball, 261)

Circle Blind-Chase, 81

Circle Blind-Guess (*See* Circle Blind-Chase, 81)

Circle Blindman's-Buff (*See* Blindman's Buff, 82)

Circle Blindman's Swat-Tag (*See* Circle Blind Swat-Tag, 81)

Circle Blindman's-Tag (*See* Circle Blind-Chase, 81)

Circle Blind-Swat (*See* Circle Blind Swat-Tag, 81)

Circle Blind Swat-Tag, 81

Circle Bootball (*See* Kick Strideball, 344)

Circle Bounceball, 261

Circle Broncho-Tag (*See* Broncho Three-Deep, 30)

Circle Channel-Tag (*See* Channel Touchball, 237)

Circle Chase (*See* Circle Pursuit-Elimination, 34)

Circle Chaseball (*See* Circle Touchball, 236)

Circle-Chase Tag, 65

Circle Club-Bowl, 347

Circle Club-Bowl—Team Form, 347

Circle Dodgeball (*See* Dodgeball, 117)

Circle Duck-on-the-Rock, 78

Circle Hockey-Dribbling Race (*See* Hockey-Dribble Fill-the-Gap, 101)

Circle Jump (*See* Jump-the-Shot, 164; Jump-the-Stick, 165)

Circle Kickball, 347 (*See also* Circle Kickball—Team Form, 348)

Circle Kickball—Team Form, 348

Circle Lock-Tag (*See* Hook-arm Tag, 29)

Circle Missball, 232

Circle Passball, 234

Circle Poleball, 348

Circle Pursuit-Elimination, 34

Circle Pursuit-Race, 31

Circle Race (*See* Circle Pursuit-Race, 31; Reverse Pursuit-Race, 32)

Circle Rush, 89

Circle Shuffleboard, 219

Circle Soccer (*See* Circle Kickball—Team Form, 348)

Circle Squat, 175

Circle Squat-Tag, 50

Circle Strideball, 343

Circle Strideball—Partner Form, 343

Circle Strideball—Team Form, 344

Circle Tag, 86

Circle Tagball (*See* Circle Touchball, 236)

Circle Touchball, 236

Circle Touch-Race (*See* Pursuit Elimination—Team Form, 34)

Circle Tug (*See* Poison, 156)

Circle Weave-Tag, 66

Circle Zigzag (*See* Zigzag Fill-the-Gap, 102)

Clear-the-Fort, 150

Climb-a-Man Tag, 19

Clock Golf, 197 (*See also* One-hole Clock Golf, 198)

Index

Club Chase (*See* Elimination Object-Rush, 93)

Club Kickball (*See* Kick Bombardment, 341)

Club Rush (*See* Object Rush, 92)

Club Snatch (*See* Pin Snatch, 56)

Cocked Hat, 187

Cocked Hat and Feather, 188

Cock Stride, 104

Codeball-in-the-Court, 288

Codeball-on-the-Green, 201

Column Dodgeball, 114

Come Across, 44

Come Along (*See* Come With Me, 91)

Come, Blackey, 40

Come With Me, 91 (*See also* Huntsman, 108; Swing Around, 102)

Command Drill, 175

Contrary Children, 176

Cops and Robbers, 154

Corkball, 325

Cork Retrieve (*See* Cork Scramble—Aquatic, 109)

Cork Scramble—Aquatic, 109

Cornerball, 243

Corner Keepball (*See* Cornerball, 243)

Corner-kick Ball (*See* Individual Soccer, 380)

Corner Mat-Rush, 149

Count-and-Throw, 127

Couple Fill-the-Gap, 101

Couple Hill-Dill, 41

Couple Tag, 22

Court Tag (*See* Two-court Pom-Pom-Pullaway, 42)

Court Tennis, 282

Cowboy Tag (*See* Pickaback Tag, 22)

Crabball (*See* Crab Soccer, 379)

Crab Soccer, 379

Crackabout, 135

Crawl-the-Dragon (*See* Mount-the-Broncho, 146)

Cricket, 332

Crocodile Chase (*See* Snake Chase, 32)

Croquet, 199

Croquet Golf, 198

Crossball (*See* Cross Volleyball, 260)

Cross-country Bowling, 228

Crossing No-Man's-Land, 41 (*See also* No-Man's-Land, 46)

Crossing-the-Lake (*See* Poison Carpet, 182)

Cross-Out (*See* Cross-Out Baseball, 318)

Cross-Out Baseball, 318

Cross Tag, 24

Cross-the-Pool—Aquatic, 43

Cross Volleyball, 260

Crown-the-Dragon (*See* Mount-the-Broncho—Team Form, 146)

Crown-the-King, 112

Crows and Cranes, 179 (*See also* Black and Blue, 64; Black and White, 61; Heads and Tails, 63)

Crows, Cranes, and Crabs, (*See* Black and Blue, 64)

Cumulative Dodgeball, 116

Curling, 213

Curtainball (*See* Curtain Newcomb, 251)

Curtain Newcomb, 251

Cushion Dance (*See* Poison, 156)

Dare Base, 42

Dart Baseball, 221

Dart Games, other, 221

Day and Night (*See* Black and White, 61; Stooping Heads-and-Tails, 85)

Day or Night (*See* Black and White, 61)

Days of the Week (*See* Spud, 128)

Deck Hockey (*See* Ring Hockey, 407)

Deck Tennis, 252

Deck Tennis—NSWA Rules, 253

Deer Stalking, 84

Den (*See* Every Man In His Own Den, 75)

Den-Tag Elimination (*See* Every Man In His Own Den, 75)

Dethroning-the-King, 149

Disco, 216

Ditch Pull (*See* Ditch Tug, 152)

Ditch Tug, 152

Dizzy-Izzy (*See* Dizzy Tag, 10)

Dizzy Tag, 10

Dodgeball, 117 (*See also* One man Dodgeball, 115; Throwing Pom-Pom-Pullaway, 123)

Dodge Baseball, 318

Dodge Batball (*See* Volley Batball, 329; Volley Long Base, 330)

Dog and Deer 36

Dog and Rabbit (*See* Hound and Rabbit, 25; Lame Fox and Chickens, 50; Three-Deep Chase-the-Chaser, 30)

Dog-in-the-Manger (*See* Master-of-the-Ring, 151)

Dog Tag, 71

Do This, Do That 177

Double-chaser Tag, 20

Double-circle Fill-the Gap, 102

Double-column Channelball (*See* Channel Touchball, 237)

Double Foot-and-a Half, 171

Double Fox-and-Geese (*See* Fox and Geese, 16)

Double Leader-and-Footer 171

Double-pass Schoolball, 234

Double-rim Fox and Geese (*See* Fox and Geese, 16)

Double Spud, 135

Double-up Baseball, 321

Drag Tag, 10

Dribbleball (*See* Bounce Basketball, 364)

Dribble Hand-Hockey, 351

Dribble Keepaway (*See* Dripple Keepball, 239)

Dribble Keepball, 239

Dribble Spud, 128

Drill Elimination (*See* Elimination Drill, 175)

Driveball (*See* Batting Drive, 248; Punt Drive, 246)

Driving Contest (*See* Driving Game, 173)

Driving Game, 173

Drop-kick Drive, 247

Drop the Handkerchief, 66

Drop the Handkerchief—Variation, 101

Dual Basketball (*See* Two-ball Basketball, 362)

Duck Fight, 144

Duck Fight—Team Form, 144

Duck-on-a-Rock (*See* Duck-on-the-Rock, 76)

Duck-on-Rock Object-Rush, 94

Duck-on-the-Rock, 76

Duckpins, 187 (*See also* Rubber-band Duckpins, 187).

Ducks Fly, 179

Dumbbell Tag (*See* Giveaway Tag, 23)

Eliminationball, 135

Elimination Bombardment, 340

Elimination Drill, 175

Elimination Object-Rush, 93

Elimination Swat-Tag, 35

Endball, 244

Every Man In His Own Den, 75

Exchange (*See* Blind Numbers-Change, 84; Exchange Tag, 48)

Exchange Tag, 48

Falling Stick (*See* Catch-the-Cane, 162)

Feeling Blindman's-Buff (*See* Blindman's Buff, 82)

Feet-out Tag—Aquatic, 19

Fence and Bars (*See* Maze Tag, 68)

Fenceball (*See* Fence Newcomb, 250)

Fence Newcomb, 250

Fence Tag, 18

Fieldball, 365

Field Dodgeball, 123

Field Handball, 366

Field Hockey, 403 (*See also* Six-man Field-Hockey, 406)

Fifth Column, 252

Filling-the-Gap (*See* Swing Around, 102)

Fill-the-Gap, 101

Finding-a-House, 99

Find-the-Coin—Aquatic, 110

Find-the-Swatter, 103

Fire-on-the-Mountain, 94

First of May, The (*See* Finding-a-House, 99)

Fish and Net (*See* Fish Net, 46)

Fisherman (*See* Water Fish-Net, 43)

Fishing (*See* Fish Net, 46)

Fish Net, 46

Fistball (*See* Fist Volleyball, 260)

Fist Volleyball, 260

Fives 288

Flag Raid (*See* Stealing Sticks, 73)

Flag Tag (*See* Giveaway Tag, 23)

Flashball, 329

Flickerball, 367

Floorball, 351 (*See also* Hand Hockey, 351)

Floor Tag, 17 (*See also* Stoop Tag, 86)

Flowers and the Wind, 60

Flowers and the Wind—Variation, 54

Flying Dutchman (*See* Fill-the-Gap, 101)

Follow Chase (*See* Circle Weave-Tag, 66)

Follow-my-Leader (*See* Follow-the-Leader, 174)

Follow-the-Leader, 174

Follow-the-Miss, 226

Foot-and-a Half, 169

Football (*See* American Football, 387; Rugby Football, 384; Six-man Foot ball, 397; Soccer Football, 373; Touch Football, 398)

Football Newcomb, 250

Football Tag (*See* Kick Ball-Tag, 133)

Foot Tagball (*See* Kick Circle-Touchball, 236)

Foot-to-Foot Tag, 19

Forcing-the-City-Gates (*See* Hitting-the-Line, 137)

Forward-pass Ball, 365

Forward-pass Drive (*See* Throwing Drive, 247)

Forward-pass Football (*See* Forward-pass Ball, 365)

Forward-pass Newcomb (*See* Football Newcomb, 250)

Foul-line Twenty-One, 227

Four-basket Ball (*See* Multiple-goal Basket-ball, 362)

Four-court Dodgeball, 120

Four-goal Basketball (*See* Multiple-goal Basketball, 362)

Four-man Circle Chase (*See* Circle Pursuit Elimination, 34)

Four-mat Tug-of-War (*See* Corner Mat-Rush, 149)

Four-wall Handball, 283

Fox (*See* Fill-the-Gap, 101; Lame Fox and Chickens, 50)

Fox and Ball (*See* Ante-Over, 130)

Index

Fox and Chickens (*See* Catch-the-Caboose, 21)

Fox and Farmer (*See* Circle Weave-Tag, 66)

Fox and Gander (*See* Catch-the-Caboose, 21)

Fox and Gardener (*See* Circle Weave-Tag, 66)

Fox and Geese, 16 (*See also* Catch-the-Caboose, 21; Run, Geese, Run, 40)

Fox-and-Geese Dodgeball (*See* Train Dodgeball—Team Form, 117)

Fox-and-Geese Tag, 11

Fox and Goose (*See* Three Deep, 27)

Fox and Hound (*See* Maze Tag, 68)

Fox and Squirrel (*See* Hound and Rabbit, 25)

Fox Chase (*See* Line Weave-Tag, 67)

Fox-in-the-Hole (*See* Lame Fox and Chickens, 50)

Fox's Tail (*See* Catch-the-Caboose, 21)

Fox Trail (*See* Fox and Geese, 16; Fox-and-Geese Tag, 11)

Free-ball Tag, 134

Free-for-all Cock Fight (*See* Rooster Fight, 143)

Free Shot, 229

Free-throw Twenty-One, 227

Freeze-Out (*See* Third Man, 29)

Freeze-out Around-the-World, 224

French and English (*See* Ditch Tug, 152)

French Blindman's Buff (*See* Blind Numbers-Change, 84)

French Bowls (*See* Cross-country Bowling, 228)

French Tag (*See* Boundary Tag, 9)

Frog-in-the-Middle (*See* Frog-in-the-Sea, 87)

Frog-in-the-Sea, 87

Fruit Basket, 99

Fug (*See* Indoor Soccer, 378)

Fungo, 323

Fungo Baseball, 316

Garden Scamp, 67 (*See also* Circle Weave-Tag, 66)

Gateball, 55

German Batball (*See* Batball, 327; Volley Batball, 329)

Get-the-Cap, 237

Giant Volleyball, 259

Giveaway Tag, 23

Goal Duck-on-the-Rock (*See* Duck-on-Rock Object-Rush, 94)

Goal-post Newcomb, 251

Goal Tag (*See* All Change, 95; Exchange Tag, 48)

Going-to-Jerusalem (*See* Musical Chairs, 90)

Golf, 191

Good Morning, 102

Goofy Golf, 198

Gopher Golf, 198

Go Stop (*See* Statue Hide-and-Seek, 106)

Go To It (*See* Line Tug-of-War, 148)

Grab-a-Pin, 73

Grab Ball (*See* Object Rush—Team Form, 93)

Grab-the-Bone, 58

Green Wolf (*See* Throw-the-Stick, 105)

Groundball (*See* Catchball, 250)

Grounders Burn Out, 341

Groups, 95

Guarding the Pins, 348

Guessball, 229

Guessball—Team Form, 229

Gymnasium Soccer (*See* Indoor Soccer, 378)

Haley-Over (*See* Ante-Over, 130)

Ham, Chicken, Bacon (*See* Ham, Ham, Chicken, Ham, Bacon—Variation, 40)

Ham, Ham, Chicken, Ham, Bacon, 44

Ham, Ham, Chicken, Ham, Bacon—Variation, 40

Handball (*See* Four-wall Handball, 283; One-wall Handball, 286; Two-wall and Three-wall Handball, 287)

Hand Baseball, 317

Hand Batball, 328 (*See also* Volley Drive, 248)

Hand Beatball (*See* Beatball, 320)

Handgrasp Tag, 28

Hand Hockey, 351

Hand-slapping Tag (*See* Hands Up, 142)

Hand-slap Tag (*See* Hands Up, 142)

Hands Up, 142

Hand Tag (*See* Hands Up, 142)

Hand Tennis, 261

Hang Tag, 17

Hard-ball Water Polo (*See* Water Polo-International, 371)

Hare and Hound (*See* Maze Tag, 68)

Hatball (*See* Roly Poly, 131)

Hat Fight, 142

Hat Fight—Team Form 142

Have You Seen My Sheep?, 66

Heads and Tails, 63 (*See also* Black and White, 61; Stooping Heads-and-Tails, 85)

Heads or Tails (*See* Black and White, 61)

Helper Tag (*See* Island Tag, 21)

Help Tag (*See* Hip, 36)

Hen and Chickens, 118

Here I Buy, Here I Bake, 139

Herr Slap Jack (*See* Fill-the-Gap, 101)

Hide-and-Find (*See* Shepherd and Wolf, 53)

Hide-and-Go-Seek (*See* Hide-and-Seek, 105)

Hide-and-Seek, 105

High Windows, 66

Hill-Dill, 40

Hinder Tag, 45

Hindoo Tag (*See* Hindu Tag, 17)

Hindu Tag, 17

Hip, 36

Hitball (*See* Speed Baseball, 319)

Hit-or-Out, 324

Hit-pin Baseball, 319 (*See also* Hit-pin Beatball, 321)

Hit-pin Beatball, 321

Hit-the-Spot Tag (*See* Sore-spot Tag, 10)

Hitting-the-Line, 136 (*See also* Over-the-Top, 140)

Hoax Hot-Hand, 181

Hockey (*See* Field Hockey, 403; Ice Hockey, 409)

Hockey Ball-Snatch, 58

Hockey-Dribble Fill-the-Gap, 101

Hockey Golf, 198

Hockey Keepball, 239

Hockey Ten-passes (*See* Hockey Keepball, 239)

Hog Tying, 145

Hold Fast and Let Go, 176

Holding-the-Line (*See* Over-the-Top, 140)

Holeball (*See* Roly Poly, 131)

Homeball, 318

Hook-arm Tag, 29

Hoop Tag, 134

Hop Across, 141

Hopaway (*See* Fill-the-Gap, 101)

Hopping Circle (*See* Jump-the-Shot, 164)

Hopping Numbers-Change, 98

Hopping Pom-Pom-Pullaway, 42

Hopping Soccer, 378

Hopping Toads (*See* Jump-the-Shot, 164)

Hopscotch, 166

Hopscotch Golf, 203

Hop Tag (*See* Lame Fox and Chickens, 50)

Hop-the-Blocks, 169

Hop-the-Hats, 168

Hop-to-the-Gap (*See* Zigzag Fill-the-Gap, 102)

Horns, 179

Horse-and-rider Circle-Jump (*See* Pickaback Jump-the-Shot, 165)

Horse-and-rider Spud (*See* Pickaback Spud, 129)

Horse-and-rider Tag (*See* Pickaback Tag, 22)

Horseshoe Pitching, 203

Horseshoes (*See* Horseshoe Pitching, 203)

Horse Tag (*See* Climb-a-Man Tag, 19)

Hotball, 120

Hot Butter and Blue Beans (*See* Find-the-Swatter, 103)

Hot Hand, 181 (*See also* Paired Hot-Hand, 181)

Hot Rice, 113

Hound and Rabbit, 25

House-Hiring (*See* Finding-a-House, 99)

Hunt, The (*See* Animal Chase, 45)

Hunter, The (*See* Circle Rush, 89; Huntsman, 108)

Huntsman, 108 (*See also* Circle Rush, 89)

Hunt-the-Fox (*See* Line Weave-Tag, 67)

Hunt-the-Slipper, 85

Ice Basketball, 371

Ice Hockey, 409

Imitation Tag, 10

Improvised Bowling, 190

Improvised Duckpins, 190

Improvised Lawn-Bowling, 213

In-and-Out-the-Window (*See* Circle Weave-Tag, 66)

Indianball, 324

Indian-club Ball (*See* Pin Basketball, 364)

Indian-club Baseball (*See* Pin Batball, 329)

Indian-club Circle Pull (*See* Poison Snake, 155)

Indian-club Guard (*See* Pin Guard, 345)

Indian-club Wrestle (*See* Poison Snake, 155)

Individual Basketball, 364

Individual Dodgeball (*See* One-man Dodgeball, 115)

Individual Soccer, 380

Indoor Bowls (*See* Improvised Lawn-Bowling, 213)

Indoor Cricket, 336

Indoor Soccer, 378

Indoor Speedball, 383

Informal Bowling (*See* Improvised Bowling, 190)

Informal Duckpins (*See* Improvised Duckpins, 190)

Informal Horseshoe-Pitching, 206

Into the Ring (*See* Poison Snake—Team Form, 155)

Iron Tag, 14

I Say, 176

I Say Stoop, 176

Island Tag, 21

I Spy (*See* Hide-and-Seek, 105)

Jack and Jill, 83

Jack Be Quick (*See* Circle Rush, 89)

Jacks (*See* Jackstones, 162)

Jackstones, 162

Jacob and Jacobine (*See* Jack and Jill, 83)

Index

Jacob and Rachel (*See* Jack and Jill, 83)
Jai Alai, 296
Jail Delivery (*See* Chain Break, 141)
Japanese Tag (*See* Sore-spot Tag, 10)
Jumping Circle (*See* Jump-the-Shot, 164; Jump-the-Shot—Team Form, 165)
Jumping Jack (*See* Jump-the-Shot, 164)
Jumping-the-Shot (*See* Jump-the-Shot, 164)
Jump-the-Cane, 165
Jump-the-Shot, 164
Jump-the-Shot—Team Form, 165
Jump-the-Stick, 165

Keepaway (*See* Keepball, 238; Variety Keepball, 239)
Keepball, 238 (*See also* Variety Keepball, 239)
Keeping Away (*See* Keepball, 238)
Keep-the-Ball (*See* Keepball, 238; Number Keepball, 238)
Kelly Says (*See* Simon Says, 177)
Kentucky Fox-and-Geese (*See* Run, Geese, Run, 40)
Kettle Drive, 131
Kick-and-Hide (*See* Kick-the-Can, 106)
Kick-and-Pass Drive (*See* Kick-or-Throw Drive, 247)
Kick-and-Throw Pin-Guard, 346
Kickball (*See* Individual Soccer, 380; Kick Batball, 329; Kick Beatball, 321)
Kick Ball-Tag, 133
Kick Baseball, 317
Kick Batball, 329
Kick Beatball, 321
Kick Bombardment, 341
Kick Bowling, 190
Kick Centerball (*See* Kick Strideball, 344)
Kick Circle, 348
Kick Circleball (*See* Kick Circle-Touchball, 236)
Kick Circle-Strideball (*See* Kick Strideball, 344)
Kick Circle-Touchball, 236
Kick Dodgeball, 117 (*See also* Kick Batball, 329)
Kick Drive, 247
Kick Hide-and-Seek (*See* Kick-the-Can, 106)
Kickit (*See* Kick-over Ball, 341)
Kickoff Ball (*See* Kickoff Tag, 47)
Kickoff Tag, 47
Kick-or-Throw Drive, 247
Kickover (*See* Kick-over Ball, 341)
Kick-over Ball, 341
Kick Pin-Guard, 346
Kick Pin-Guard—Team Form, 346
Kick Strideball, 344

Kick-the-Block, 25
Kick-the-Can, 106
Kidnaper's Tag (*See* Giveaway Tag, 23)
Kingdom Tag (*See* Throne Tag, 71)
King-of-the-Mountain, 151 (*See also* Battle Royal, 151)
King's Bodyguard (*See* Bodyguard Tag, 23)
King's Land, 52 (*See also* Puss-in-the-Circle, 70)
Kitty-Ki-Over (*See* Curtain Newcomb, 251)
Knave-in-the-Garden (*See* Garden Scamp, 67)
Knights (*See* Knights' Combat, 145)
Knights' Combat, 145
Knights' Combat—Team Form, 145
Knock-'em-Down (*See* Poison Snake, 155)
Knocking Down, 240
Knock-Out, 324

Lacrosse, 400
Lame Fox and Chickens, 50
Lame Goose (*See* Lame Fox and Chickens, 50)
Lariat Tag (*See* Rope Tag, 13)
Last-Couple-Out, 56
Last-Man-Across (*See* Last-Man-Over, 107)
Last-Man-It (*See* Three-Deep Chase-the-Chaser, 30)
Last-Man-Over, 107
Last-One-Out (*See* Musical Chairs, 90)
Lawn Bowling, 207
Lawn Bowling—The Crown-green Game, 212
Lawn Bowls (*See* Lawn Bowling, 207)
Lawn Tennis (*See* Tennis, 270)
Leader and Footer, 170 (*See also* Double Leader-and-Footer, 171)
Leapfrog Pursuit-Relay, 33
Leapfrog Tag (*See* Leapfrog Two-Deep, 26)
Leapfrog Two-Deep, 26
Leeball (*See* Volleyball Badminton, 268)
Left-hand Basketball, 362
Leg-dive Tag (*See* Underneath Two-Deep, 26)
Leg Fight, 144
Leg Fight—Team Form, 144
Liberty Batball (*See* Volley Batball, 329)
Lineball (*See* Line Bat, 342)
Line Bat, 342
Line Dodgeball, 113
Line Football (*See* Individual Soccer, 380)
Line Guard, 340
Line Interference 69
Line Shuffleboard, 216
Line Soccer, 380 (*See also* Individual Soccer, 380)
Line Tag, 11 (*See also* Chain Tag, 36)
Line Tug (*See* Ditch Tug, 152)

Line Tug-of-War, 148
Line Weave-Tag, 67
Line Wrestling (*See* Ditch Tug, 152)
Lingball, 331
Link Chase (*See* Chain Tag, 36)
Link Pursuit-Race (*See* Centipede Pursuit-Race, 32)
Link Tag (*See* Centipede Pursuit-Race, 32)
Lock-arm Tag (*See* Hook-arm Tag, 29)
Lock Tag (*See* Hook-arm Tag, 29)
Locomotive Dodgeball (*See* Train Dodge-ball, 116)
Log—Aquatic, 51
London, 220
Lone Bandit, 136
Longball, 330
Long Base, 330 (*See also* Kick Batball, 329; Longball, 330)
Long-shot Basketball Golf, 223

Machine-gun Fire, 120
Magic Carpet (*See* Poison Carpet, 182)
Mailman, 99
Marble Golf, 203
Marching Attack (*See* Marching Signal-Chase, 60)
Marching Chase, 52
Marching Command-Drill, 175
Marching Object-Rush, 93
Marching Rush (*See* Black and Blue, 64)
Marching Signal-Chase, 60
Marching Tag (*See* Marching Signal-Chase, 60)
Marching-to-Jerusalem (*See* Musical Chairs, 90)
Mass Basketball (*See* Permutation Basket-ball, 363)
Mass Block-Horseshoes, 207
Mass Soccer, 379
Master-of-the-Ring, 151
Master-of-the-Ring—Team Form, 152
Mathematical Catch-the-Cane (*See* Arith-metical Catch-the-Cane, 163)
Mat Tag, 123
Maze Tag, 68
Medicine-ball Newcomb, 251
Medicine-ball Soccer, 378
Medicine Catchball, 235
Merry-Go-Round, 95
Midget Golf (*See* Putting Golf, 197)
Midnight, 51
Miniature Golf (*See* Putting Golf, 197)
Modified Badminton (*See* Paddle Bad-minton, 266)
Modified Volleyball, 258
Mohammedan Tag (*See* Hindu Tag, 17)
Monkey Tag (*See* Dog Tag, 71)

Mother Carey's Chickens (*See* Train Dodgeball—Team Form, 117)
Mother Goose (*See* Hen and Chickens, 118)
Mountball (*See* Pickaback Passball, 235; Pickaback Spud, 129)
Mounted Bear-Hunt, 107
Mounted Hide-and-Seek (*See* Mounted Bear-Hunt, 107)
Mounted Immunity-object Tag, 16
Mounted Musical-Chairs, 91
Mounted Pom-Pom-Pullaway, 43
Mounted Spud (*See* Pickaback Spud, 129)
Mounted Tag, 12
Mount Tag (*See* Climb-a-Man Tag, 19)
Mount-the-Broncho, 146
Mount-the Broncho—Team Form, 146
Multiple-goal Basketball, 362
Mumble-the-Peg, 172
Mumble-the-Peg Baseball, 172
Mumblety-Peg (*See* Mumble-the-Peg, 172)
Mumblety-Peg Baseball (*See* Mumble-the-Peg Baseball, 172)
Musical Chairs, 90
Musical Marbles, 92
Music Rush (*See* Circle Rush, 89; Musical Chairs, 90)

Nest Tag (*See* Animal Cage, 30)
Netball (*See* Newcomb, 250)
Newcomb, 250 (*See also* Catchball, 250)
Newcomb Over-the-Goal-Posts (*See* Goal-post Newcomb, 251)
Newcomb Over-the-Tent (*See* Over-the-House, 251)
New Orleans (*See* Trades, 59)
New York (*See* Trades, 59)
Nine-court Basketball, 362
Nine-court Keepball, 240
Nine-court Ten-Catches (*See* Nine-court Keepball, 240)
No-Man's-Land, 46
Nose-and-Ankle Tag (*See* Nose-and-Toe Tag, 17)
Nose-and-Toe Tag, 17
Numberball (*See* Spud, 128)
Number Catchball (*See* Number Scramble-ball, 245)
Number Keepaway (*See* Number Keepball, 238)
Number Keepball, 238
Numbers Change, 98 (*See also* Exchange Tag, 48; Throwing Numbers-Change, 126)
Number Scrambleball, 245
Number Tag (*See* Spud, 128)
Object Rush, 92
Object Rush—Team Form, 93
Object Scramble, 109

Index

Object Tag (*See* Circle Touchball, 236)

Odd Bag (*See* Object Rush—Team Form, 93)

Odd-Man-Out (*See* Marching Object-Rush, 93)

Odd Man's Cap (*See* Get-the-Cap, 237)

Off-the-Spot, 126

O'Grady in the Water (*See* Water Simon-Says, 178)

O'Grady Says (*See* Simon Says, 177)

Old Grady (*See* Simon Says, 177)

Old-Man Tag (*See* Sitting Tag, 18)

Old Woman from the Woods (*See* Trades, 59)

O'Leary, 158

One-basket Ball (*See* One-goal Basketball, 363)

One-Foot-Off, 44

One-foot Statues, 180

One-goal Basketball, 363

One-hole Clock-Golf, 198

One-leg Soccer (*See* Hopping Soccer, 378)

One-man Dodgeball, 115

One-man Tag, 45

One O' Cat (*See* One Old Cat, 314)

One O' Gang (*See* Individual Basketball, 364)

One Old Cat, 314

One-Over (*See* Last-Man-Over, 107)

One-Step-Off, 40

One-wall Handball, 286

One-wall Squash, 294

Opposites (*See* Hold Fast and Let Go, 176)

Ordinary Tag (*See* Simple Tag, 9)

Ostrich Tag, 17

Out-Hopping Game (*See* Shoulder Shove, 144)

Out-of-the-Ring, 152

Outside Tagball (*See* Outside Touchball, 237)

Outside Touchball, 237

Overball (*See* Individual Soccer, 380)

Overtake Relay (*See* Pursuit Relay, 33)

Over-the-Bridge, 41

Over-the-House, 251

Over-the-Shed (*See* Over-the-House, 251)

Over-the-Top, 140

Oyster Shell (*See* Black and White, 61; Slap-and-Run, 54)

Oyster Supper (*See* Slap-and-Run, 54)

Paddle Badminton, 266

Paddleball (*See* Paddle Squash, 295)

Paddle Bounceball, 270

Paddle Squash, 295

Paddle Tennis, 278 (*See also* Platform Paddle-Tennis, 280)

Paired Hot-Hand, 181

Paper, Stone, and Scissors, 183

Par (*See* Foot-and-a-Half, 169)

Par and Leader (*See* Foot-and-a-Half, 169)

Parcel Post (*See* Fruit Basket, 99; Mailman, 99)

Partner-Change Tag, 48

Partner Circle-Strideball (*See* Circle Strideball—Partner Form, 343)

Partner Skipaway (*See* Couple Fill-the-Gap, 101)

Partner Spud, 129

Partner Tag, 36 (*See also* Chair Tag, 27; Hook-arm Tag, 29)

Pass-and-Change, 126

Passball, 368 (*See also* Forward-pass Ball, 365; Six-court Keepball, 240; Whistleball, 182)

Pass Newcomb (*See* Football Newcomb, 250)

Pavementball, 160

Pebble Chase, 79

Peg Driving (*See* Pig-in-the-Hole, 344)

Pegging First, 322

Pelota (*See* Jai Alai, 296)

Permutation Basketball, 363

Philadelphia Batball (*See* Volley Baseball, 317)

Pickaback Jump-the-Shot, 165

Pickaback Passball, 235

Pickaback Spud, 129

Pickaback Tag, 22

Pig-in-a-Hole (*See* Pig-in-the-Hole, 344)

Pig-in-the-Hole, 344

Pinball (*See* Pin Basketball, 364)

Pin Basketball, 364

Pin Batball, 329

Pinch-O, 53

Pin Duck-on-the-Rock, 78

Pin Football (*See* Pin Soccer, 379)

Ping-pong (*See* Table Tennis, 280)

Pin Guard, 345 (*See also* Pin Basketball, 364)

Pin Guard—Team Form, 346

Pin Pickup, 125

Pin Rush (*See* Object Rush, 92)

Pin Snatch, 56

Pin Soccer, 379

Pin Speedball, 384

Pin Strideball, 344

Pit Bowling, 213

Place-kick Baseball, 317

Platform Paddle-Tennis, 280

Playground Kickball (*See* Kick Baseball 317)

Plus-and-Minus Club-Snatch (*See* Plus-and-Minus Pin-Snatch, 58)

Plus-and-Minus Pin-Snatch, 58

Poison, 156 (*See also* Poison Snake, 155; Poison Tag, 52)

Poison Areas (*See* Poison Carpet, 182)
Poison Carpet, 182
Poison Circle (*See* Poison, 156; Poison Spud, 129)
Poison Seat (*See* Poison Spot, 97)
Poison Snake, 155
Poison Snake—Team Form, 155
Poison Spot, 97 (*See also* Poison, 156)
Poison Spud, 129
Poison Stake (*See* Poison Snake, 155)
Poison Sticks (*See* Poison Snake, 155)
Poison Tag, 52
Polo 408
Pom-Pom-Pullaway, 39
Porpoise and Fishes (*See* Circle Rush, 89)
Posse Tag, 20
Postball, 243
Post Golf, 198
Posture Tag, 24
Pots 159
Potsy, 168
Prisoner's Base, 73 (*See also* Simplified Prisoner's Base, 72)
Progressive Captainball, 243
Progressive Dodgeball, 118 (*See also* Three-court Dodgeball, 120)
Pull Across Line (*See* Ditch Tug, 152)
Pullaway (*See* Pom-Pom-Pullaway, 39)
Pulling-in-Circle (*See* Poison, 156)
Pull-Into-Circle (*See* Poison, 156)
Punch Bowl (*See* Punching-bag Goal— Aquatic, 352)
Punching-bag Goal—Aquatic, 352
Punkin Baseball, 316
Punt Back (*See* Punt Drive, 246)
Punt Baseball, 317
Punt Drive, 246
Pursuit Elimination, 34
Pursuit Elimination—Team Form, 34
Pursuit Race (*See* Pursuit Elimination, 34)
Pursuit Relay, 33
Pursuit Vault-Race (*See* Leapfrog Pursuit-Relay, 33)
Push Across the Line (*See* Base-line Push, 153)
Pushball, 369
Puss-in-a-Corner (*See* Puss-in-the-Corner, 100)
Puss-in-Corner Tag, 48
Puss-in-the-Circle, 70
Puss-in-the-Corner, 100 (*See also* Finding-a-House, 99)
Pussy Wants a Corner (*See* Puss-in-the-Corner, 100)
Putting Golf, 197

Quadrant Dodgeball, 122
Quick Commands (*See* Command Drill, 175)

Quoitennis (*See* Deck Tennis, 252)
Quoits, 206

Rabbit and Hound (*See* Line Weave-Tag, 67)
Rabbit-in-the-Circle (*See* Puss-in-the-Circle, 70)
Rabbit's Nest (*See* Hound and Rabbit, 25)
Rackets (*See* Racquets, 288)
Racquets, 288
Raft Baseball—Aquatic, 322
Random Pursuit-Race, 35
Range Practice (*See* Target Practice, 228)
Rattlesnake 83
Red Light (*See* Statues, 180)
Red Lion, 52
Red Rover, 41
Relay Basket-Shoot, 223
Reverse Chase (*See* Reverse Pursuit-Race, 32)
Reverse Circle-Passball, 234
Reverse Pursuit-Race, 32
Riderball (*See* Pickaback Spud, 129)
Riding-the-Broncho (*See* Mount-the-Broncho, 146)
Riding-the-Snail (*See* Black and White, 61)
Ring Callball (*See* Callball, 233)
Ring Hockey, 407
Ring-on-the-String, 85
Robbers and Soldiers (*See* Cops and Robbers, 154)
Rob-o-Ling, 190
Roller Polo (*See* Roller-skate Hockey, 415)
Roller Shinny (*See* Roller-skate Hockey, 415)
Roller-skate Hockey, 415
Roll Tag, 18
Roly Poly, 131 (*See also* Pavementball, 160)
Rooster Fight, 143
Rooster Fight—Team Form, 143
Rooster Rumpus (*See* Duck Fight, 144)
Rope Pull (*See* Rope Rush, 147)
Rope Push, 148
Rope Rush, 147
Rope Skip (*See* Jump-the-Shot, 164)
Rope Tag, 13
Roque, 201
Rotation (*See* One Old Cat, 314; Rotation Baseball, 316; Three Old Cat, 316; Two Old Cat, 315)
Rotation Baseball, 316
Rough-and-Tumble (*See* Clear-the-Fort, 150; Ditch Tug, 152)
Rough-Ride Roughhouse (*See* Knights' Combat, 145)
Roundball (*See* Rotation Baseball, 316; Three Old Cat, 316)

Index

Royal Tennis (*See* Court Tennis, 282)
Rubber-band Duckpins, 187
Rugby Football, 384 (*See also* American Football, 387)
Run For Your Supper, 102
Run, Geese, Run, 40
Run, Rabbit, Run, 51
Run, Sheep, Run, 106
Rushing-the-Spots (*See* Circle Rush, 89)
Rush-the-Pole, 150
Rush-the-Stick (*See* Rush-the-Pole, 150)
Rush Tug-of-War (*See* Rope Rush, 147)
Ruth and Jacob (*See* Jack and Jill, 83)

Sack Chase (*See* Sack Pursuit-Race, 32)
Sack Pursuit-Race, 32
Sack Rush, 149
Saddle-the-Nag (*See* Mount-the-Broncho— Team Form, 146)
Safety-zone Tag, 14
Same-side Tag (*See* Fence Tag, 18)
Scat, 51
Schlagball (*See* Kick Batball, 329; Volley Batball, 329)
Schoolball, 233
Scouts and Indians, 154
Scrambleball, 245
Scrambleball—Team Form, 245
Scramble Twenty-One, 227
Scrimmageball (*See* Hand Hockey, 351)
Sculptor (*See* Statues, 180)
Setback, 189
Seven-man Soccer, 378
Shadow Tag, 13
Sharp Shooting, 229
Sheepfold (*See* Cat and Rat, 68)
Shepherd and Wolf, 53
Shepherdess and Wolf (*See* Catch-the-Caboose, 21)
Shinney (*See* Shinny, 407)
Shinny, 407
Shooting Gallery (*See* Target Practice, 228)
Shoulder Push (*See* Shoulder Shove, 144)
Shoulder Shove, 144
Shove Struggle (*See* Base-line Push, 153)
Shuffleboard, 217 (*See also* Line Shuffleboard, 216)
Shyball, 342
Side-toss Baseball, 317
Sidewalk Tennis, 261
Signal Chase (*See* Marching Signal-Chase, 60)
Silent Statues, 180
Simball, 383
Simon Says, 177 (*See also* Simon Says Thumbs Up, 178)
Simon Says Stoop, 178
Simon Says Thumbs Up, 178

Simple Dodgeball (*See* One-man Dodgeball, 115)
Simple Tag, 9
Simple Water-Tag (*See* Water Tag, 12)
Simplified Prisoner's Base, 72
Single-rim Fox and Geese (*See* Fox-and-Geese Tag, 11)
Singles or Doubles Volleyball, 259
Sitting Circle-Passball, 234
Sitting Circle-Rush, 90
Sitting-circle Tag (*See* Straddle-Jump Two-Deep, 26)
Sitting Tag, 18
Sitting Two-Deep, 26
Six-court Keepball, 240
Six Hockey (*See* Six-man Field Hockey, 406)
Six-man Baseball, 313
Six-man Field-Hockey, 406
Six-man Football, 397
Six-player Field-Hockey (*See* Six-man Field Hockey, 406)
Skating Baseball, 323
Skiddles, 189
Skipaway (*See* Fill-the-Gap, 101; Swing Around, 102)
Skipping Circle-Chase, 65
Skipping Tag, 10
Skip Tag (*See* Skipping Circle-Chase, 65)
Skittle Rounders, 319
Skittles, 189
Skunk Tag (*See* Nose-and-Toe Tag, 17; Ostrich Tag, 17)
Slap-and-Run, 54
Slap Catch (*See* Hands Up, 142)
Slap Jack (*See* Circle-Chase Tag, 65; Fill-the-Gap, 101)
Sling-the-Monkey, 87
Snake and Bird (*See* Fish Net, 46)
Snake Catch (*See* Catch-the-Snake, 20)
Snake Chase, 32
Snake Tag (*See* Catch-the-Caboose, 21)
Snatch-a-Club (*See* Snatch-a-Pin, 92)
Snatch-a-Pin, 92
Snatchball (*See* Ball Snatch, 57)
Snatch-the-Beanbag, 57
Snatch-the-Bone (*See* Grab-the-Bone, 58)
Snatch-the-Handkerchief, 57
Snatch-the-Hat, 57
Snowball Bombardment, 340
Snowball Bowling, 190
Snowball Duck-on-the-Rock, 78
Snowball Pom-Pom-Pullaway, 123
Snowball Tag, 133
Snowball Tenpins (*See* Snowball Bowling, 190)
Soak About (*See* Spud, 128)
Soccer (*See* Soccer Football, 373)
Soccer Ball-Snatch, 57

Soccer Baseball (*See* Kick Batball, 329)

Soccer Batball, 329

Soccer Centerball (*See* Kick Circle-Touch-ball, 236)

Soccer Circle-Strideball (*See* Kick Stride-ball, 344)

Soccer Dodgeball (*See* Kick Dodgeball, 117)

Soccer Drive (*See* Line Soccer, 380)

Soccer Football, 373 (*See also* Seven-man Soccer, 378)

Soccer Football—Women's Rules, 378

Soccer Keepball, 239

Soccer Tag (*See* Kick Ball-Tag, 133)

Soccer Ten-kicks (*See* Soccer Keepball, 239)

Softball, 311

Soft-ball Water Polo (*See* Water Polo—American, 370)

Sole-mate Tag (*See* Foot-to-Foot Tag, 19)

Somersault Tag (*See* Roll Tag, 18)

Sore-spot Tag, 10 (*See also* Touch-the-Spot Tag, 13)

Spanish Fly, 171

Spat 'Em (*See* Slap-and-Run, 54)

Speedball, 380 (*See also* Speed Baseball, 319)

Speedball—Women's Rules, 383

Speed Baseball, 319

Speed Pinball (*See* Pin Speedball, 384)

Spider and Flies, 50

Spider and Fly (*See* Spider and Flies, 50)

Spin-the-Plate, 163

Spin-the-Plate—Team Form, 164

Spin-the-Platter (*See* Spin-the-Plate, 163)

Sponge Badminton, 268

Spotball (*See* Circle Bounceball, 261)

Spot Duck-on-the Rock (*See* Duck-on-Rock Object-Rush, 94)

Spot-point Basket Shoot, 222

Spot Tag, 24

Sprintball, 331

Spud, 128

Square Dodgeball (*See* Battleball, 119)

Squash (*See* Squash Racquets, 291; Squash Tennis, 293)

Squash Rackets (*See* Squash Racquets, 291)

Squash Racquets, 291

Squash Tennis, 293

Squat Tag, 16

Squirrel and Trees (*See* Squirrels in Trees, 96)

Squirrel in the Trees (*See* Squirrels in Trees, 96)

Squirrel in Tree (*See* Squirrels in Trees, 96)

Squirrel in Trees (*See* Squirrels in Trees, 96)

Squirrels in the Trees (*See* Squirrels in Trees, 96)

Squirrels in Trees, 96 (*See also* Tree Rush, 91)

Stagecoach, 98

Standball (*See* Spud, 128)

Statue Hide-and-Seek, 106

Statues, 180 (*See also* Silent Statues, 180)

Statues—Team Form, 180

Statue Tag, 17

Stealing Ammunition (*See* Stealing Sticks, 73)

Stealing Sticks, 73

Steal-the-Flag, 57

Steeplechase, 55

Step (*See* Statues, 180)

Step-by-Step, 232

Steps (*See* Silent Statues, 180; Statues, 180)

Stick Polo (*See* Bar-bell Hockey, 407)

Stiff-knee Tag, 10

Still Pond (*See* Still Pond, No More Moving, 82)

Still Pond, No More Moving, 82

Still Water, Stop (*See* Still Pond, No More Moving, 82)

Stone Tag, 14

Stoolball, 346

Stooping Heads-and-Tails, 85

Stoop Tag, 86 (*See also* Squat Tag, 16)

Stop Thief, 125

Stork Tag, 16

Storming-the-Fort, 140 (*See also* Storming the-Heights, 150)

Storming-the-Heights, 150

Story of the Crows and Cranes, 64

Straddleball (*See* Circle Strideball, 343)

Straddle-Jump Two-Deep, 26

Straddle Tag, 15

Straddle-the-Pole (*See* Straddle Tag, 15)

Streets and Alleys (*See* Maze Tag, 68)

Strideball Tag (*See* Kick-the-Block, 25)

Strike-and-Chase (*See* Slap-and-Run, 54)

Stroke Tag—Aquatic, 12

Stump-the-Leader, 174

Stunt Ball-Catch, 159

Stunt-Catch Elimination, 157

Stunt Elimination (*See* Stump-the-Leader, 174)

Stunt Leapfrog (*See* Spanish Fly, 171)

Sunken Treasure (*See* Treasure Scramble—Aquatic, 110)

Swat Down (*See* Elimination Swat-Tag, 35)

Swat Tag, 12 (*See also* Swat to Right, 103)

Swatter Snatch, 58

Swat-the-Bear (*See* Swat to Right, 103)

Swat-the-Fly, 86

Swat to Right, 103

Swat-Your-Neighbor (*See* Swat to Right, 103)

Index

Swimming-pool Baseball, 323
Swing Around, 102
Sword Tennis, 254

Table Tennis, 280
Tackling Pom-Pom-Pullaway, 42
Tag (*See* Simple Tag, 9)
Tag-a-Third (*See* Slap-and-Run, 54)
Tagball, (*See* Circle Touchball, 236)
Tail Fight, 143
Tail Fight-Team Form, 143
Tail Snatching (*See* Tail Fight, 143)
Tail Tag (*See* Drag Tag, 10)
Taking-the-Trench (*See* Over-the-Top, 140)
Tale of the Crows and Cranes (*See* Story of the Crows and Cranes, 64)
Tandem Tag, 22
Tap-the-Bucket, 80
Target Practice, 228
Teacher and Class, 232
Team Cap-Scramble (*See* Cap Scramble, 108)
Team Circle-Strideball (*See* Circle Strideball—Team Form, 343)
Team Club-Guard (*See* Kick Pin-Guard—Team Form, 346)
Team Poison-stake (*See* Poison Snake—Team Form, 155)
Team Spin-the-Platter (*See* Spin-the-Plate—Team Form, 164)
Team Spud, 136
Team Tag (*See* Chain Tag, 36)
Ten Catches, 238
Tenikoit (*See* Deck Tennis, 252)
Tennis, 270 (*See also* Court Tennis, 282)
Tennis Golf (*See* Goofy Golf, 198)
Tenpins (*See* Bowling, 184)
Ten-second Chain-Break (*See* Chain Break, 141)
Ten-shot Twenty-One, 226
Ten Steps (*See* Blind Ten-Steps, 82; Statue Hide-and Seek, 106)
Ten Volleys (*See* Volley Keepball, 239)
Tetherball, 268
Tether Tennis (*See* Tetherball, 268)
Third Man, 29
Third Slap (*See* Slap-and-Run, 54)
Three Broad, 28 (*See also* Handgrasp Tag, 28; Hook-arm Tag, 29)
Three-court Dodgeball, 120
Three-court Keepball, 239
Three Deep, 27
Three-Deep Chase-the-Chaser, 30
Three-Deep Tag (*See* Three Deep, 27)
Three High, 28
Three O'Cat (*See* Three Old Cat, 316)
Three Old Cat, 316
Three-shot Twenty-One, 226

Three-team Dodgeball (*See* Progressive Dodgeball, 118)
Three, Two, and One, 226
Three Wide (*See* Hook-arm Tag, 29)
Throne Tag, 71
Through-the-Circle, 79
Throw Centerball (*See* Circle Strideball, 343)
Throwing Baseball, 317
Throwing Drive, 247
Throwing Numbers-Change, 126
Throwing Pom-Pom-Pullaway, 123
Throw-the-Stick, 105
Tip-cat, 326
Tire Bowling, 190
Tomball, 319
Tommy Tiddler's Ground, 70
Tommy Tiddler's Land (*See* Tommy Tiddler's Ground, 70)
Tom-Thumb Golf (*See* Putting Golf, 197)
Tony Says (*See* Simon Says, 177)
Toss-up (*See* Scrambleball, 245)
Touch-and-Run (*See* Slap-and-Run, 54)
Touchball (*See* Ball Snatch, 57; Circle Touchball, 236; Outside Touchball, 237)
Touch Baseball, 318
Touch Football, 398
Touch-the-Spot Tag, 13
Touch Wood-and-Whistle (*See* Wood-and-Whistle Tag, 18)
Towel Tag (*See* Swat to Right, 103)
Towerball (*See* Pin Guard, 345)
Trades, 59
Train Dodgeball, 116
Train Dodgeball—Team Form, 117
Treasure Scramble—Aquatic, 110
Tree Rush, 91
Tree Toad (*See* Hang Tag, 17)
Tree-Toad Tag, 17
Triple Change, 98
Triple Dodgeball (*See* Three-court Dodgeball, 120)
Tumbleball (*See* Tumble Baseball, 322)
Tumble Baseball, 322
Tumble Shuffleboard, 217
Turkish Tag (*See* Hindu Tag, 17)
Turtle Tag, 17
Twelve O'clock at Night (*See* Midnight, 51)
Twelve O'clock Midnight (*See* Midnight, 51)
Twenty-One, 224 (*See also* Twenty-One Baseball, 320)
Twenty-One—Partner Form, 225
Twenty-One—Team Form, 225
Twenty-One Baseball, 320
Twenty-One for Speed, 226
Twenty-One Touchball, 237
Twice Around, 65

Two-ball Basketball, 362
Two Broad, 27
Two-chaser Tag, 20
Two-court Pom-Pom-Pullaway, 42
Two Deep, 25
Two-Deep Leapfrog (See Leapfrog Two-Deep, 26)
Two-man Change Tag, 45
Two O'Cat (See Two Old Cat, 315)
Two Old Cat, 315
Twos and Threes (See Three Deep, 27)
Two Times Around (See Twice Around, 65)
Two-wall and Three-wall Handball, 287

Underneath Three-Deep, 29
Underneath Two-Deep, 26
Under the Water—Aquatic, 43

Variety Circle-Passball, 234
Variety Keepaway (See Variety Keepball, 239)
Variety Keepball, 239
Variety-kick Drive, 247
Vis-à-Vis, 97
Volleyball, 254
Volleyball—Women's Rules, 258
Volleyball Badminton, 268
Volley Baseball, 317
Volley Batball, 329
Volley Drive, 248
Volley Hockey, 352
Volley Keepaway (See Volley Keepball, 239)
Volley Keepball, 239
Volley Long-Base, 330
Volley Newcomb (See Newcomb, 250)
Volley Sock (See Volley Hockey, 352)

Walk, Moon, Walk (See Cock Stride, 104)
Wall Ball-Drill (See Wall Stunt-Catch, 158)
Wall Scrambleball, 245
Wall Spud, 114 (See also Spud, 128)
Wall Stunt-Catch, 158
Wall Tennis, 295
Wand-Balance Elmination, 172
Water Balloonball, 370
Water Baseball, 322 (See also Raft Baseball—Aquatic, 322)
Water Baseball in Pools (See Swimming-pool Baseball, 323)
Water Basketball, 370
Water Battle-Royal, 151
Water Black-and-White, 64
Water Cageball (See Water Pushball, 369)
Water Circleball (See Water Circle-Touch-ball, 236)

Water Circle-Touchball, 236
Water Crows-and-Cranes (See Water Black-and-White, 64)
Water Dodgeball, 117
Water Endball, 244
Water Exchange-Tag, 48
Water Fish-Net, 43
Water Follow-the-Leader, 174
Water Foot-Tag, 13
Water Immunity-object Tdg, 16
Water Keepball, 238
Water Knights (See Water Knights'-Combat, 145)
Water Knights'-Combat, 145
Watermelon Scramble—Aquatic, 111
Water Mine (See Treasure Scramble—Aquatic, 110)
Water Numbers-Change (See Water Exchange-Tag, 48)
Water Poison, 156
Water Polo—American, 370
Water Polo—International, 371
Water Pushball, 369
Water Safety-position Tags, other, 19
Water Simon-Says, 178
Water Spud, 128
Water Tag, 12
Water Ten-Catches (See Water Keepball, 238)
Water Volleyball, 259
Weight Retrieve (See Weight Scramble—Aquatic, 110)
Weight Scramble—Aquatic, 110
Whale—Aquatic, 148
Wheel Away, 44
Wheelbarrow Polo, 415
Wheel Pursuit-Race, 33
Whip Tag (See Swat Tag, 12; Swat to Right, 103)
Whistleball, 182
Who's Afraid of the Black Man?, 49 (See also Black Man, 41)
Wicket, 336
Wink, 88
Wolf (See Shepherd and Wolf, 53)
Wolf and Rabbit (See Fox and Geese, 16)
Wolf and Sheepfold (See Cat and Rat, 68)
Wood-and-Whistle Tag, 18
Wood Tag, 14
Wood Tag Variations, 14
Work-up (See Three Old Cat, 316)
Wrestle Royal, 146
Wrestle Royal—Team Form, 146

Yards Off (See Throw-the-Stick, 105)

Zigzag Fill-the-Gap, 102